The Makers of American Wine

The Makers of American Wine

A RECORD OF TWO HUNDRED YEARS

Thomas Pinney

UNIVERSITY OF CALIFORNIA PRESS

BERKELEY LOS ANGELES LONDON

University of California Press, one of the most distinguished university presses in the United States, enriches lives around the world by advancing scholarship in the humanities, social sciences, and natural sciences. Its activities are supported by the UC Press Foundation and by philanthropic contributions from individuals and institutions. For more information, visit www.ucpress.edu.

University of California Press
Berkeley and Los Angeles, California

University of California Press, Ltd.
London, England

Library of Congress Cataloging-in-Publication Data

Pinney, Thomas.
The makers of American wine : a record of two hundred years / Thomas Pinney.
  p. cm.
  Includes bibliographical references and index.
  ISBN 978-0-520-26953-8 (cloth : alk. paper)
  1. Viticulturists—United States—Biography. 2. Vintners—United States—Biography. 3. Viticulture—United States—History. 4. Wine and wine making—United States—History. I. Title.
  SB387.68.P56 2012
  381'.456632—dc23   2011035922

Manufactured in the United States of America

20 19 18 17 16 15 14 13 12 11
10 9 8 7 6 5 4 3 2 1

To Gail Unzelman
eminent collector, distinguished editor,
generous friend

CONTENTS

ILLUSTRATIONS

ACKNOWLEDGMENTS

The splendid collections of Gail Unzelman, whose generosity is acknowledged in the dedication to this book, were invaluable to me throughout, but particularly for the information they provided for the chapters on Husmann and Morgan. I have leaned heavily on the books of Charles Sullivan, the unrivaled master of American wine history, and have profited from his review of the manuscript. The librarians, without whose willing help no book of this kind can be written, that I would like to thank include in particular Axel Borg, in charge of the Amerine Room, and John Skarstad, in Special Collections, both at the Shields Library, University of California, Davis. Robert Zerkowitz was my guide to the rich archives of the Wine Institute, San Francisco. John Barden, great-grandson of Paul Garrett, and his wife, Polly, generously opened their impressive collection of Garrett memorabilia to me and enabled my account of Garrett by giving me a copy of Garrett's unpublished memoir. To all, and to the many unnamed others, my best thanks.

INTRODUCTION

The Makers of American Wine

A RECORD OF TWO HUNDRED YEARS

THIS BOOK TELLS THE STORY of American wine through the lives of thirteen people—twelve men and one woman—who made a difference in that history, or who represent a significant change in the direction of things, or both. The more recent names are probably familiar to all who take an interest in wine—Mondavi and Gallo certainly are—but other names will be unknown. To give them their deserved recognition is one of my aims in writing this book. I start with Jean Jacques (or John James) Dufour, a Swiss, who did not make the first commercial wine in this country but who made it possible for others to do so. Nicholas Longworth, a man of wealth, used his fortune to produce the first popular American wine; the German immigrant George Husmann became the Johnny Appleseed of the grape, urging every American to plant the vine and make wine. Charles Kohler brought the wine of California to the country at large, and through Andrea Sbarboro the Italians entered into California wine-making, an activity they have seemed to dominate ever since. The era of big business is represented by Percy T. Morgan of the California Wine Association; Paul Garrett showed how wine-growing in the South, the East, and the West could be profitably combined. The others in my select company had equivalent roles to play, as each chapter undertakes to show. In the rest of this introduction I give a summary account of the fortunes of wine in this country to place my subjects in a general scheme.

• • •

"NONE HAD THE LEAST IDEA
OF WHAT A NEW COUNTRY IS"

It has been about two hundred years since the first commercial wine was produced in what is now the United States. The exact date is not known, and even if it were, this is an anniversary not likely to be much observed, if it is at all, for our historians write very little about such things. But the fact is that one of the interesting and not insignificant themes of American history is the quest for wine. North America first appears to European awareness as "Vinland"—the land of wine. Every one of the early explorers reported that vines abounded in the new country, and every early settlement had wine making as a part of its purpose. The Pilgrims might have had religious freedom as a main motive for their emigration, while the gentlemen of the Virginia Company were simply looking to make money. But both agreed that making wine was one of the first items on their different agendas. The idea was reasonable. North America, as those first explorers saw at once, abounds in wild grapes—more species of grape are found here than in any other region of the world, and it was not just in certain parts of what is now the United States that these grapes were to be found. They were everywhere, north and south, east and west.

Wine-making trials began immediately. And all of them immediately failed. The first trials were naturally made with the native grapes that flourished around every new settlement. But, as was quickly discovered, they were utterly unfit for wine. The European species of grape, named *Vitis vinifera*—the wine-bearing vine—by the great Linnaeus himself, has grown for millennia in association with human settlement and, by a long process of selection, has been brought to yield a juice fitted for wine making. The many American species of grapes had grown unrestrainedly in their own wild way. No Native American community made any alcoholic drink from fruit, and wine was as unknown as the horse on this continent. None of the many native American grapes would yield a decent wine: the fruit was too low in sugar, too high in acid, too loaded with strange and unpleasant flavors; typically, the berries were small, with large seeds and meager flesh.

So the early colonists, having at once discovered the defects of the native vines, immediately began to import cuttings of the European grape. This was done over and over again, all up and down the coast of the country, by every sort of settler—Puritan, Pilgrim, Dutchman, Swede, German, Greek, Frenchman, Englishman; by syndicates, by religious communities, by exiled soldiers, by uncounted numbers of scattered individuals. Vinifera cuttings by the tens of thousands were planted on islands, along the riverbanks, among woods, in pastures, and on the slopes of hills, from Maine to Florida. Every single one of these plantings failed, though the effort was renewed again and again. The vines would grow for a time; then they sickened and died. Sometimes they endured long enough to yield a tiny harvest of grapes, but no wine in anything close to commercial quantity was made in this country for two centuries following the beginnings of sustained settlement.

North America presented a paradox, for it was just *because* native vines abounded that the European vine would not grow. In South Africa, in South America, in Australia, when these regions were colonized the European grape flourished at once, for there were no indigenous grapes there. In North America, however, native pests and diseases had grown up with the native grapes, and, over the long periods of undisturbed cohabitation, the surviving native vines had come to terms with the pests and diseases. Chief among these were fungal diseases known as powdery mildew *(Uncinula necator)*, downy mildew *(Plasmopara viticola)*, and black rot *(Guignardia bidwelli)*; a bacterial infection known as Pierce's disease *(Xylella fastidiosa)*; and an insect pest called phylloxera *(Daktulosphaira vitifoliae* Fitch). Add to this the severe winters of much of the continent, and the high humidity in most of the eastern United States, and you had a recipe for disaster for *Vitis vinifera*.

Why, in these conditions, was the same dismal story tediously repeated over and over again? Why did it take so long to give up on the European vine and turn to something else? Part of the answer, of course, lies in frontier conditions: there was no organized means of collecting and disseminating information about what had been done and was being done, so each new hopeful could proceed in ignorance of what had gone before. There are stories of fresh trials of vinifera being made and fresh disappointments produced as late as the mid-nineteenth century, 250 years after the first failures at Jamestown.

Another, and important, part of the answer lies in the fact that finding the reasons for the failure necessarily took a long time. The early settlers knew nothing about many of the conditions they were working in, and the scientific understanding of plant pathology hardly existed in the first two centuries and more of settlement. So there was no limit to speculation about the causes of the failure and to the invention of fanciful and futile solutions. Only gradually, and only after the development of a genuinely scientific understanding of the forces at work, did effective measures appear. Until then, repeated failure followed repeated failure, for, as one of the pioneers put it, "none had the least idea of what a new country is."[1]

How was success at last achieved? First, by the discovery of chance hybrids between the European vine and one or more of the American natives. If a vinifera vine survived for a few seasons, it might very well cross-pollinate with a wild American vine, and the seedlings produced from such a combination would exhibit some of the qualities of each parent. The fruit quality might be improved and the power of resistance increased. Chance hybrids of this sort were discovered in the eighteenth century, though they were not then recognized for what they are. Once that recognition was made, and the possibilities of hybrid combinations realized, people began the work of deliberate, artificial hybridizing, beginning in the 1840s.

Before the nineteenth century was over, hundreds of new varieties had been created and hopefully introduced, most of them by enthusiastic amateurs. Only a handful have had any staying power, and of that handful most have been chance hybrids rather than the product of art: Catawba, Isabella, Delaware, Dutchess, Lenoir, Norton. The native hybrids—some of them at any rate—possessed a resistance to phylloxera that no pure vinifera vine had, and so were able to survive that devastating pest. But the fungal diseases—particularly mildew and black rot—remained a potent threat, as the destruction of the Catawba vineyards around Cincinnati in the middle of the nineteenth century made clear.

The answer came from Europe. The American diseases had been exported to Europe, with disastrous effect; Europe had a large and important wine-growing establishment, as the United States did not, and so the Europeans had a much more urgent reason to do something than did the Americans. Phylloxera was checked by grafting vinifera scions to rootstocks of resistant American species. Sulfur, the Europeans found, would deal with powdery mildew; Bordeaux mixture, a compound of copper sulfate and unslaked lime, controlled black rot and downy mildew. A program of careful spraying with these fungicides made it possible for wine growing, based on a selection of native hybrid grapes, to survive and develop in the eastern United States in the latter half of the nineteenth century. Eastern wine growing continued on the same basis down to Prohibition and after, when the introduction of French hybrid vines opened a new chapter in that history. The early successes with native hybrids were in Ohio and Missouri, but New York has long been the leader in wine production among the eastern states. More or less substantial quantities of wine have also been made at various times in New Jersey, Virginia, the Carolinas, Michigan, and Arkansas.

For most of the frustrating history of wine growing in America, the official attitude had been one of encouragement and practical support. Wine growing was a main object in the settlement of Virginia, and many official acts were passed to try to bring it about. Lord Baltimore hoped to grow wine in Maryland; so did the gentlemen who founded the Carolinas. When General James Edward Oglethorpe planned the establishment of Georgia, wine growing was to be a basic part of its economy. These are but a few of many examples that might be cited. After the United States had been formed, Congress supported a number of wine-growing enterprises, including those of Dufour in Indiana and exiled French officers in Alabama. When the Department of Agriculture was created in 1862, it at once undertook research in support of wine making, as its predecessor agency, the Patent Office, had already been doing. Almost all of the founding fathers were would-be winegrowers: Jefferson's interest is well known, but Franklin, Washington, Madison, and Monroe were almost as eager as he was to see wine growing succeed in this country. Perhaps in the future we will have a wine-growing president who will have succeeded in what so many of our earlier leaders hoped to achieve.

This tradition of official support was extinguished by national Prohibition (1920–33). After repeal it was not restored; the prohibitionist power, though defeated, was still formidable enough to frighten the politicians. Instead, wine was subjected to burdensome regulations and restrictions. Only in very recent years have signs of a renewed disposition to be helpful in the cause of wine appeared in the behavior of state and federal authorities.

The story of wine on the West Coast of America is very different from that east of the Rockies. The Spanish who began the colonization of California toward the end of the eighteenth century found that the European grape grew readily there, as it already had in some areas of Mexico and in parts of South America; vineyards were established at most of the Franciscan missions of Alta California and, from there, began to spread to the small towns and dispersed ranches of the province. After the annexation of California in 1848 and the great influx of population produced by the gold rush, the wine industry quickly developed; by the end of the century California was producing 30 million gallons of wine, all of it vinifera. The most important obstacles to the flourishing of the industry have come not from nature, as in the East, but from artificial impediments, of which the fourteen years of Prohibition and their complex aftermath are the most important.

I had hoped to include a chapter in this book about some of the leaders of the Prohibition movement, since they certainly made a big difference to the history of wine in this country; but it was felt that their presence would be seen as incongruous. Perhaps so; in any case, Bishop Cannon, Wayne Wheeler, and Pussyfoot Johnson have been left out of the story.

The recovery from the disruptions of Prohibition was slow and was complicated first by the Great Depression and then by the Second World War. From the 1960s on, however, wine growing in America has expanded remarkably and has generated an interest among the American people such as it never had before. By all measures, American wine is flourishing: there are now more acres of vines planted, more wineries in more states, and more wine produced than the most optimistic booster could have imagined possible in the generation following the repeal of Prohibition.[2]

In this book I have attempted a version of this story through the lives of some of its key figures. From the many, many possible candidates for inclusion, I have aimed to select those whose lives illustrate the various things that needed to be done as the story unfolded; the problems were of more than one sort, and they demanded more than one sort of solution. At one time, it was a matter of learning to use the native vine; at another, the great object was to persuade the American public that an American wine could be any good; at yet another, the question was how to organize the trade in order to survive hard times. And so it went.

In beginning with John James Dufour at the end of the eighteenth century, I neglect the many who had tried wine growing in the two centuries preceding. The only reason for my skipping so much history is that it is largely undocumented. We know many names—Louis de St. Pierre, William Stephens, Robert Bolling, Edward Antill—but do not have enough detail to fill out a history. But the reader should keep in mind the fact of the many early trials in which individuals persisted throughout the seventeenth and eighteenth centuries despite uniform failure.

Since this is an American story, one of the things that appears at once is the variety of origins and callings that figures in it: among my exemplary instances are a Swiss vinedresser, an Ohio lawyer, a German musician, an Italian banker, a Russian viticulturist, and an English businessman. I hope that by telling their stories, and those of my other subjects, I can suggest something of the richness of America's wine history.

ONE

John James Dufour,
or the Uses of Failure

A MAN WITH A MISSION

THE BRIG *SALLY,* CAPTAIN MITCHELL COMMANDING, arrived at the
port of Philadelphia on August 12, 1796, after an uneventful voyage of sixty
days from Le Havre. Among its passengers was a Swiss named Jean Jacques
Dufour (John James in his American years), no longer in his first youth—he
was then thirty-three years old—and remarkable at first glance only for having a left arm that ended at the elbow, probably a congenital defect.[1] Whether
he had any English before he left home is uncertain, but no doubt he had
learned some on the voyage to add to his native French.

Among the stream of emigrants seeking their fortunes in postrevolution-
ary America, Dufour had nothing to distinguish him, except for the accident
of his arm. But he came to the new republic possessed by a single purpose: to
make wine for a wineless country. And the extraordinary fact is that he succeeded. That success was limited, it was of brief duration, and it was largely
carried out by others. But without Dufour's determination and his willingness to take advantage of what the country offered, it would not have come
about as it did.

Dufour was the eldest son of a family of vinedressers, as the term was then,
living in the commune of Chatelard, near Vevey, on the terraced northern
slopes of the Lake of Geneva between Lausanne and Montreux. This region,
called La Côte in Switzerland, is ancient wine-growing country, the largest single concentration of vines in the country and the source of some of
Switzerland's most distinguished white wines. Vevey is also the home of the
venerable Fête des Vignerons, a celebration whose recorded history goes back
to 1651 but which is probably even older than that.

Dufour would thus have grown up in an atmosphere saturated in wine.
But why, one wonders, should he have left a secure and established wine

1

FIGURE 1. A scene from the procession Fête des Vignerons, Vevey, Switzerland, as it looked in 1791. In that year Jean-Jacques Dufour may well have been a part of this winegrowers' festival in his native town, where it has been produced from the seventeenth century down to the present day. From Sabine Carruzzo-Frey and Patricia Ferran-Dupont, *Du Labeur aux Honneurs. Quatre Siècles d'Histoire de la Confrérie des Vignerons de Vevey,* 2nd ed. (Montreux: Imprimerie Corbaz S.A./Confrerie des Vignerons de Vevey, 1998).

region for the infant United States, where wine growing was effectively unknown? That very fact seems to have been a part of Dufour's reason for making the venture: it had not been done, and he was romantic enough to think that he might be the one to do it (more prosaically, the family historian, Perret Dufour, says simply that the elder Dufour determined that his children should go to America for the sake of opportunity).

John James Dufour himself said that he had been fascinated by the idea of making wine in America from the time he was fourteen years old and read in the papers some reports from French soldiers serving with the American armies in the Revolution complaining about the lack of wine "in the midst of the greatest abundance of everything else."[2] There were all-too-good reasons for the absence of native wine in America, as explained in the introduction. Those reasons, however, remained essentially unknown in Europe, just as they were largely unrecognized still in America itself.

When he consulted a map of the country to which he had determined someday to go, Dufour found that parts of America lay in the latitude of "the best wine countries in the world—like Spain, South of France, Italy, and Greece," and this seemed to him to be a promise of sure success.[3] It is a fact that the northern limit of wine growing in Europe is roughly the fiftieth parallel, and that in America all of the contiguous states lie south of that. New York City and Rome are both on the forty-second parallel; Richmond, Virginia, and Athens are both on the thirty-eighth parallel. These coincidences seduced many an early entrepreneur into believing that wine might be grown as readily in New York or Richmond as in Latium or Attica. But the belief was a delusion; the differences in climate are so extreme as to make the argument from latitude utterly unreliable. Dufour, however, did not yet know that.

When, at the end of his life, Dufour set down his account of his experience in the new world in his *American Vine-Dresser's Guide* (1826), he took an almost sacramental view of his purpose. By successfully producing wine, he wrote in his loose and difficult sentence style, he would "engage and enable the people of this vast continent to procure for themselves and their children, the blessing intended by the Almighty; that they should enjoy, and not by trade from foreign countries, but by the produce of their own labor, out of the very ground they tread, from a corner of each one's farm, wine thus obtained, first handed from the grand Giver of all good, pure, genuine, and unmixed by avarice, that it may have the effect on his heart and family intended by the Creator."[4] Not only that, native wine would turn Americans away from their habitual use of ardent spirits—whiskey especially—and contribute to making the country temperate and sober. These arguments for the high social value of wine growing were heard from the very beginning of American settlement and form a kind of chorus behind almost every one of the countless attempts to establish it. Dufour was one of a long line in this matter too.

Of course Dufour hoped to make money as well as to confer solid public benefits. He never did get rich, but something of his high expectations may still be heard in his language at the end of his life: "Millions," he wrote, "will accrue to the country at large" from the work he had done.[5] And that, too, is one of the constant themes in the pioneer history of wine growing in this country: temperance, good cheer, and unbounded wealth are all mingled in the vision of America as a wine land. It is still an attractive vision.

His preparation lasted much longer than one would expect. For twenty years or more, after he had formed his resolve to go to America, he was still in Vevey, where he had a wife and a son—hardly evidence of a restless spirit. About the wife nothing is known, except that she would never go to America; the son was an only child, named Daniel Vincent. Dufour was surrounded in Vevey by a large family: his father, also Jean Jacques, was still living, as were seven other children of the father's two marriages. What determined the moment at which John James Dufour finally set out for America can only be guessed, but the anxieties created by the French Revolution and by the Napoleonic Wars that followed are likely to have been among the main reasons. Following the outbreak of the French Revolution in 1789, there were severe political disturbances in Geneva felt all along the lake. When Dufour at last left Switzerland for America in 1796, Napoleon had not yet invaded the country, but he would do so two years later. Maimed as he was, it is not likely that Dufour would have been drafted as a soldier into the French armies, but the uncertainty of the times made the possibility of finding a new security in America attractive as it had never been before. Probably the idea of having the whole family emigrate to America had already been discussed, for Dufour was making inquiries about the possibility within a few months of his arrival in the United States.[6]

In any event, John James Dufour at last set out, alone, on his journey to America in March 1796, traveling by way of Paris to the port of Le Havre. While in Paris he bought fifty-nine silver and gold watches. These were to be used as a form of negotiable wealth after he arrived in America. When he needed to pay for something there, he could sell a watch. I suppose he feared that he would suffer considerable loss if he exchanged his Swiss money in America; the watches would have been less vulnerable to the vagaries of exchange rates.

IN SEARCH OF WINE

Once Dufour had landed in Philadelphia, he lost no time in scouting out the land. His disappointment was immediate and disturbing, for wherever he went he found only evidence of failure or of struggling and unprosperous survival in all attempts to grow wine grapes. At first, of course, he toured the settled East. We do not have a detailed record of his movements, but we know that he went to Baltimore, where he visited the small vineyard maintained by Charles Carroll of Carrollton; he went up the Susquehanna River to Middletown, Pennsylvania, where a German had kept a then-decayed vineyard that had, allegedly, produced some wine. He saw some vines growing successfully in gardens in New York City and in Philadelphia, but these did not offer much encouragement to a commercial grower. Outside Philadelphia he visited the vineyard at Spring Mill where Pierre Legaux carried on the most ambitious and most promising of all the early efforts to produce an American wine.

Legaux (1748–1827), originally from Metz, had bought the Spring Mill property in 1786 and began planting vines—all French—in 1787. He seems to have been a difficult and unlikable man, but he had a knack for publicity. His vineyard excited wide interest, and when, in 1793, he proposed to incorporate as the Pennsylvania Vine Company the idea was well received in Philadelphia. In that same year he announced that "the first vintage ever held in America" would be held at Spring Mill; it wasn't that, of course, but there was no way to contradict such statements. Legaux did not explain why his first vintage waited until six years after his vines had been planted, but one may guess: most of the original vines had probably died, and those that survived gave only a meager yield. Still, he did manage some sort of vintage (no figures for it are known), as few had managed to do in the many years since American settlement began.

When Dufour visited Spring Mill in 1796, he found a desolate scene. The shares of the Pennsylvania Vine Company had not been fully subscribed and would not be for another six years; Legaux was in desperate financial circumstances, and his vineyard was not prospering. Dufour found that only "about a dozen" of Legaux's vines appeared to be worth the trouble of cultivating— and this after some thousands of vines had been planted.[7] Yet no one else was doing any better than, or even as well as, the struggling Legaux. When the time came for Dufour to buy vines, he would get them from Legaux, who maintained a nursery in connection with his vineyard.

Since the coastal settlements offered Dufour almost nothing hopeful, he would see what the frontier West might offer. At the end of September 1796, about six weeks after he had landed in Philadelphia, Dufour set out for Pittsburgh, three hundred miles away, probably on foot. From Pittsburgh he went down the Ohio River as far as Marietta, Ohio, but the winter was now closing in. Dufour retreated to Pittsburgh, where he dug in for the winter.

In the spring of 1797 Dufour was on the move again. He had heard, while in Philadelphia, that the Jesuits of the Kaskaskia mission in Illinois, founded in 1703 on the banks of the Mississippi River, had had a flourishing vineyard. Since the Jesuit order had been suppressed in 1762 in France's American possessions, including Kaskaskia, the chances that anything useful still survived after thirty-five years of neglect were obviously poor indeed. Yet Dufour decided to make the long and difficult trip despite the odds; since he had not yet found anything at all promising in this country, why not? When he reached Kaskaskia he did in fact find the Jesuits' asparagus bed there, but no vines: "A thick forest was covering that spot, with a luxuriant undergrowth."[8] Dufour doubted that they had ever had any luck with vines in that place, despite the stories he had heard.

Dufour did not venture farther up the Mississippi than Saint Louis, where, after a stay of some weeks, he bought what seems to us a strange commodity for a traveler, nearly six and a half tons of lead pigs (the upper Mississippi region, in what is now Missouri, Iowa, Illinois, and Wisconsin, has abundant lead). These he would sell on his return journey. The lead was not conveniently portable, as his supply of Parisian watches was; to move it he had to hire a barge and six oarsmen, who engaged to transport the pigs as far as Cincinnati. It seems to have been a successful venture; the last of the lead was sold in Lexington early in 1799 after much labor and expense in moving it up river and over land.[9]

THE KENTUCKY VINEYARD SOCIETY

Before the last lead had been sold, however, Dufour had taken a new direction. In October 1797, he reached Cincinnati, then a frontier town in the Northwest Territory. There he sold a quantity of his lead, put the rest in storage, and headed south for the boomtown of Lexington, Kentucky, across the river and eighty miles south of Cincinnati. Kentucky had been made a state in 1792—the first of the trans-Alleghany states—and Lexington was its most thriving town. Dufour spent some days in and around Lexington and liked what he saw of the men and the countryside there. By this point he had decided to quit the fruitless search for a successful viticulture; it was now time to begin for himself. He had Pierre Legaux's Pennsylvania Vine Society as a model for his scheme, which he no doubt discussed with the leading citizens of Lexington during his stay in the town. By January of 1798 he had sufficiently matured a plan to offer it to the public.

The January 17, 1798, issue of the *Kentucky Gazette,* the weekly published in Lexington, contained a letter from Dufour addressed "To the Citizens of Kentucky" and proposing the formation of a Kentucky Vineyard Society to

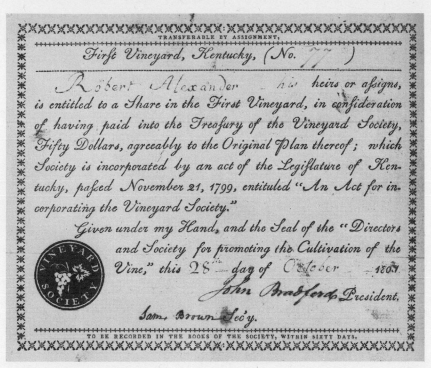

FIGURE 2. Share certificate in Dufour's "First Vineyard," Kentucky Vineyard Society, 1799. The shares were never fully subscribed and the vineyard was abandoned in 1809. From Edward Hyams, *Dionysus: A Social History of the Wine Vine* (London: Thames and Hudson, 1965).

carry out grape growing and wine making in Kentucky: "Now, ye citizens of Kentucky," he said, "is the time to begin to plant the vine." Dufour explained that he was an expert in the matter, or, as he put it, "my predominant inclination since my infancy is the culture of the grape vine." The company was to issue two hundred shares at fifty dollars each; with the money thus raised it would buy land—Dufour had already seen that "convenient situations" abounded in Kentucky. The company would need to buy horses, tools, and ten negroes to work the land. Dufour himself would travel to Europe to buy about forty thousand vines with which to start the enterprise. He promised that an acre of Kentucky vineyard would produce at least five hundred gallons of wine, and, at a dollar a gallon, the costs of establishing even a small vineyard of six acres would be quickly paid off; after that, it would be all profit.

In August 1798 he returned to Lexington and began the work of the company in earnest. The first thing to be done was to obtain land for the vineyard. Dufour found what he wanted on the banks of the great bend of the Kentucky River some miles south of Lexington, where he arranged for the purchase of 630 acres. By November of 1798, preparation of the land began.

Dufour's contract with the Kentucky Vineyard Society called for him to supply vines of all kinds, "indigenous as exotic," but the "greater part . . . brought from Europe"; the expectation was that he would travel to Europe to secure these, and he was given two years in which to make the trip.[10] Accordingly, he set out at the beginning of 1799 on a winter journey overland for the East; characteristically, he detoured to inspect Thomas Jefferson's vineyard at Monticello—he found that it had been abandoned, like most of the other projects he had gone to see in America. At some point in the course of this journey to the eastern ports, Dufour decided not to go to Europe after all but to buy his stock of vines from sources in this country. The voyage to Europe was too dangerous; it would take too much time; and the vines would be at risk over such a long journey. He would remain in the United States and get his vines here. He thus failed to live up to the terms of his engagement with the Vineyard Society; but as it happened, this failure is ultimately what saved Dufour's whole enterprise.

He bought a few vines in Baltimore from a German nurseryman, went on to New York, where he bought a few more vines, and then went to Pierre Legaux at Spring Mill, Pennsylvania, who sold him ten thousand cuttings of thirty-five different varieties. That, at any rate, is what Legaux must have told Dufour, though it is highly unlikely that all the varieties were as named, or that the number of varieties was exact. We know for certain that at least two of the vines Dufour bought from Legaux were native hybrids, though no one knew it at the time.

But the important thing at this point is that Dufour and the Kentucky Vineyard Society seemed to be set on precisely the same path toward certain failure that all earlier ventures had taken. The idea was still to plant vinifera, or vines "brought from Europe," even if one did not actually get them in Europe. Dufour had now spent more than two years traveling the length and breadth of this country without finding a single successful planting of European vines; he had, on the contrary, found overwhelming evidence that all vinifera plantings had failed. So why would he now plant vinifera? Had he learned anything from all his observations? The answer was, at this point, No. So far as Dufour—and everyone else—was concerned, there really was no alternative. Dufour's contract stipulated that he was to plant "all kinds of grapes," but effectively only one kind was in question. The native hybrids were not recognized for what they were, so the only thing to do was to plant vinifera in new regions and hope, against all hope, for the best.

Thus Dufour returned to Kentucky with a wagonload of what he supposed were cuttings of European vines, as no doubt most of them were. Planting began in the spring of 1799 at "First Vineyard," as Dufour styled the site: in that first season twenty-two thousand vines went in. By the next year, twelve thousand of them had died, but Dufour attributed this heavy loss to the lack of labor he suffered. Had they been planted early enough in the season they would, he thought, have survived. And the remaining vines were remarkable for their vigor—Dufour had never seen such rapid growth as his Kentucky vines showed.[11]

He now wrote home to Switzerland to advise his relatives and friends that the time had come to join him in America, where his affairs appeared to prosper. Instead, at the beginning of 1801 a small group—seventeen people—of Dufour's family and neighbors left Switzerland for Kentucky; they were all, Dufour said, "poor people who have . . . only the means to make the trip."[12] They arrived in America at the end of April, and by July they had safely reached Kentucky, where they entered into partnership with their brother and patron, John James Dufour, to cultivate First Vineyard. Most of the men among the newly arrived Dufours were, confusingly enough, named John: John Daniel, John David, and John Francis, all of them sons of John James Rudolf Dufour of Vevey and brothers of John James Dufour of First Vineyard, Kentucky: there was thus a generous provision for the conservation of Johns. With them were the sisters Antoinette, Suzanne, Marguerite, and Jeanne Marie Dufour, all under the age of twenty. The Dufours were accompanied by three other families, named Bettens, Boralley, and Siebenthal. A single gentleman, Jean Daniel Morerod, was also of the group; he was in love with Antoinette Dufour and had followed her to Kentucky. Notably absent, to us, was Mrs. John James Dufour, who remained in Switzerland with her child. Did she object to America? To Dufour? To both? We don't know.

Dufour had already begun to make arrangements for the independent settlement of the newcomers, since the Kentucky vineyard could hardly sustain them all. The idea from the outset was that the Swiss would devote themselves to wine growing. The opening of the Northwest Territory for settlement just at this time provided a welcome place to begin. Land along the Ohio River in what is now Indiana was made available for sale, beginning in April 1801, at a price of two dollars an acre. Dufour had already managed to buy nearly eight hundred acres in this region. Now, early in 1802, he petitioned Congress for a grant, on credit, of some two thousand acres along the Ohio River, to be paid for over a ten-year period. The inducement he held out in asking for these special terms was the great promise of successful wine making: on their new lands, the Swiss would undertake, at a minimum, to plant ten acres of vines within two years of their settlement and to add to them thereafter; they would also give vine cuttings and instruction to people who asked for them, so as to "render the Cultivation of the Vine familiar to the people of the United States."[13]

TO THE BANKS OF THE OHIO

Congress, following the long tradition of official encouragement of wine growing established in this country since the earliest colonial days, granted the petition in order "to promote the culture of the vine within the territory of the United States." Instead of the ten years Dufour had asked for as the period for payment, Congress allowed him a generous twelve.[14] In the summer of 1802, the Bettenses and Morerods (Jean Daniel Morerod having married Antoinette Dufour early in 1802), accompanied by John James Dufour, left the Kentucky vineyard, traveled by boat down the Kentucky River to the Ohio, and up the Ohio to their new lands on the right bank of the river. John James, according to the family story, stepped ashore from the boat, announced that he would "cut down the first tree on our lands," and proceeded to do so, operating with a hatchet on a sapling. The Bettenses and Morerods then began the formidable struggle to clear the land of the powerful forest growth that covered it, while Dufour returned to First Vineyard and the rest of his family. Cutting a sapling was a nice symbolic gesture, but the site abounded in walnut, oak, and tulip trees of "enormous" size, and it would be the work of years to clear the ground.[15] The land was shared with wild life: bears, deer, wolves, and wild turkeys roamed the woods and competed with the settlers for the crops they planted after the labor of clearing had been done.[16] There were Indians about, and there was much anxiety about the threat they posed; luckily, the Swiss never had to fight any Indians on their new property.

In the course of the next few years, most of the Swiss would migrate from Kentucky to the new settlement, called "New Switzerland," where they were joined by some other Swiss immigrants who bought land from Dufour. The little colony was under way, but the frontier conditions were anything but easy. Steam had not yet come to the rivers of America; if the people at New Switzerland wanted salt, or iron, or groceries, or dry goods, they had to work their way up the Ohio to Cincinnati in "canoes, skiffs and pirogues" to buy what they needed. And there was always the forest to be dealt with.[17]

FAILURE AT FIRST VINEYARD

Meanwhile, back at First Vineyard, what were the prospects? The first year's planting had, as we have seen, suffered devastating losses, but enough survived to provide cuttings for new plantings, and the survivors looked vigorous in the second season, 1800, and again in the third, 1801. Dufour's problems were not only with the vineyard but also with his Kentucky investors, who had not fully paid up their subscriptions to the stock of the Kentucky Vineyard Society; without funds, Dufour could not pay to develop the vineyard as he had originally planned. Together with his family at First Vineyard, he could only conduct a holding operation, on property that had not even been paid for and probably never would be. And if the vineyard could not be made to prosper, the chances that the delinquent shareholders would wish to pay up steadily diminished.

Still, the fame of Dufour's work had gone abroad. The possibility that wine might be made to flow from the Kentucky wilderness was intriguing to the popular imagination and even, in some quarters, a cause for anxiety. The distinguished French botanist François André Michaux, on a mission of scientific inquiry in the United States for Napoleon's government in 1802, hearing of the prosperous new vineyards in Kentucky, determined to visit them to see if they might actually pose a threat to the French wine trade. Dufour received him politely and invited Michaux to spend the night and the next day with him. Michaux at once saw that Dufour's vineyard was anything but promising. The vines, he found, were unhealthy, the fruit "thin and poor," the chances of a successful vintage slim, for the fruit always rotted before it ripened. Only about six acres had been planted. The stockholders, he wrote, "concerned themselves but very little" with the vineyard and its fortunes, evidently having already concluded that the business was a failure. The accounts of the "pretended flourishing" of the vineyard that had appeared in the press were contradicted by a very different reality. France, Michaux correctly thought, had nothing to fear from this quarter.[18]

Dufour was compelled to agree; in this fourth season of the vineyard,

1802, the vines that had seemed so vigorous were all afflicted with a sickness and produced no useable fruit. Michaux had observed that "the grape generally decays before it is ripe," which suggests that the dominant affliction was black rot, though no doubt other diseases were at work too. Black rot, which would later exterminate the vineyards of Cincinnati, would be a sufficient cause of failure by itself. Black rot first appears as small irregular spots on the young leaves of the vine in the spring. It then passes to the fruit, where its effects are not at first evident. When the grapes are well grown, they color prematurely, begin to shrivel and darken, and exhibit ugly black dots on their surface. In a few days they become completely dried and shriveled and are unfit for any use—"hard black mummies," as one authority describes them.[19] The infection may be limited to a few vines only or may devastate an entire crop. Once it is established, it cannot be checked. It grows in humid conditions, and summer rainfall helps to spread it. The disease, once unknown in Europe, was imported there with American vines. By a happy chance, a compound called Bordeaux mixture (copper sulfate and unslaked lime) was later found to control black rot, so it may now be dealt with, though at a heavy cost for labor and materials. In Dufour's day—and in the days of all those unsuccessful would-be colonial vine-growers before him in the eastern regions—nothing could be done against the disease.

In this crisis there was one hopeful sign. Amid the general wreckage of his vineyard Dufour noted that two sorts of vine survived and fruited: one was called the Cape grape, the other, Madeira. Dufour had these names from Legaux, who had sold him the vines. The Cape grape, Legaux had said, came from South Africa and was the source of the great wines of Constantia. Madeira was of course supposed to have come from the wine island, though which of the several varieties grown on Madeira it might be was not said.[20] Both of these surviving vines were not what they were supposed to be—they would not have survived had they been. They were instead native hybrids, accidental crossings between some European vine that had managed to survive long enough to flower and a native vine. A seed from the resulting fruit would, if it managed to grow, produce a hybrid vine. If Dufour had gone to Europe to buy his grapes, he would never have found these hybrids and so would never have had the limited success they provided. Whether Legaux deliberately misrepresented his Cape grape, or genuinely believed it to be a true vinifera, does not now matter: in either case he unwittingly helped to bring about the first commercial wine in America.

The variety that Legaux called the Cape grape was the first of the acciden-

FIGURE 3. The Alexander grape. A chance hybrid of the native grape with a European grape, the Alexander was the source of the nation's first commercial wine. It acquired various names at various times and places, one of them being "Schuylkill," as in this painting. Painting by C. L. Fleischman, 1867, courtesy Special Collections, National Agricultural Library.

tal hybrids to have been brought into cultivation. It had been found originally near the place where William Penn had planted European vines along the banks of the Schuylkill River outside of Philadelphia in the seventeenth century. The discovery was made in 1740 by James Alexander, the gardener of Thomas Penn, William Penn's son, and so the grape, which has had many names since, was first called the Alexander. Despite its critical importance for the beginning of American wine making, the Alexander has virtually disappeared from cultivation.[21]

Dufour never doubted that the Alexander was a vinifera variety, as Legaux had assured him it was. His reason for thinking so was that the Alexander was perfect-flowered; that is, its flower contained both male and female parts and so was self-fertile. Native American grapes are mostly imperfect-flowered (*diœcious* is the botanical term for this condition), and Dufour therefore had what seemed to him an irrefutable proof of European identity. Others, noting the foxy character of the fruit, the vine's proven ability to survive, and its presence in the American woods, concluded that the Alexander/Cape was a native vine. Both sides were partly right, since, as a hybrid, the Alexander was a bit of both. The fact that hybrids of the American and European grape are generally perfect-flowered was simply not known then.

Whether the Cape and Madeira vines were native or foreign hardly mattered to Dufour in 1802. What he needed was a grape that would grow, and these alone had showed that they could do that. Dufour now determined to replant his vineyard entirely to Cape and Madeira vines and to discard all the rest. When he carried out the replanting, we don't know for sure, but presumably he began as early as 1802. The work could not have been done rapidly because he had only a few vines of each variety to supply cuttings for the replanting. More important for the future, Dufour's decision meant that the vineyards in New Switzerland, too, would be exclusively planted to the Cape and Madeira, and so the same old mistake that had baffled all attempts at wine growing in this country would be avoided. Dufour did not know the meaning of what he had done, for he thought that he was still planting vinifera. But he was not, and that made all the difference.

First Vineyard produced a little wine from the Cape and Madeira grapes in 1802, and this, Dufour tells us, was drunk by some of the Vineyard Society's shareholders early the next year.[22] There was another vintage in 1803, and Dufour thought well enough of this to send some of it to President Jefferson. Henry Clay, prominent in Lexington society though not yet in national politics, and a shareholder in the Kentucky Vineyard Society, collected money to help pay for getting the wine to Washington. The trip was made by Dufour's younger brother Francis, who led a horse carrying two five-gallon kegs of wine through the winter wilderness to Washington in January–February 1804. The wine was duly presented to Jefferson for his opinion; he diplomatically replied that the wine was too young for an opinion to be given. Always more than eager to find and encourage any evidence, however slender, of promising American wine making, Jefferson could only say in this case that Dufour's Cape and Madeira wines had "a body capable of becoming good."[23] He then presented the wine to a committee of Congress. Dufour had to be disappointed.

In the next year, Dufour determined to return to Switzerland to collect his family and settle his affairs there. Leaving the First Vineyard in the care of his brothers Francis and David, Dufour set out for the East Coast early in 1806, just short of ten years from the date of his arrival in the United States. In New York he booked passage (in steerage) on a brig named *Edward Young,* which sailed for Bordeaux in April 1806. When the ship was approaching Bordeaux early in May, it was captured by an English ship, one of many such incidents at the time, when England was seeking to deny supplies to Napoleon by intercepting neutral ships—the practice that was a main cause of the War of 1812. Dufour and the other passengers were taken to Plymouth and kept there for a month before being released. Dufour then went to London, took passage to Rotterdam, and arrived in Vevey on August 14, 1806.

And now follows an episode—perhaps one ought to call it a long, long chapter instead—vividly showing the difference between the pace of life then and now. Dufour had returned to Switzerland in order to close out his affairs there, intending to go back to America afterward. With whatever he might realize from the sale of the property belonging to him and to others of the Swiss colony, he hoped to pay off the debt on the Ohio lands.[24] One supposes that a few months, at most, would be sufficient for the purpose, and that a few months more would see him back at First Vineyard. As it happened, Dufour spent the next ten *years* in Vevey! Why? Doing what? We don't know that there were any special difficulties in his affairs. Europe was still at war, but that had not barred his return to Switzerland. He had a wife and son in Vevey, but he had already managed to endure a ten-year separation from them (and would again leave them behind him when at last he returned to the United States). And while he remained in Switzerland, the people in New Switzerland would get nothing of the financial assistance that had been the reason for the trip in the first place. Whatever the reasons may have been, the fact is that Dufour did not return to America until 1816.

Back in New Switzerland, the Swiss could not generate enough profit from their farms and vineyards to pay the debt and had to petition Congress for an extension; Congress obliged by a special act in 1813, allowing another five years for payment.

Up until his return to Europe in 1806, Dufour, though living at First Vineyard in Kentucky, had kept in touch with the fledgling Swiss colony in New Switzerland. We learn that he delivered a Fourth of July oration there in 1805, and he must have been the source of vines for the vineyards there when they were first planted.[25] During his ten years' absence back in Switzerland, he corresponded with his American family and kept himself informed of their activities as well as the slow communications across the wartime seas would allow. But the establishment of New Switzerland, and the achievement of a regular commercial production of wine for the first time in the United States, were not his work. Without him this production would not have been possible, but the actual work was done by other people, and it was done in Dufour's absence.

Having cleared away some of the forest, and having reached some sort of accommodation with the local wildlife, the settlers in New Switzerland managed to produce a small quantity of wine in 1806 or 1807—the date is not certain.[26] The very earliest time at which vines might have been planted in New Switzerland was 1803, in the first spring after the settlement began. Once the vineyards were started, their growth was gradual but steady, though of course never sufficient to support the community. They lived as general farmers, growing much of their own food, producing grain and grinding it for flour, planting orchards, and raising hogs and cattle, just as the rest of rural America did. Wine making was an essential activity, but not a primary one. A boost to the settlement came in 1809, when Francis and David Dufour at last abandoned First Vineyard and, with their families, came to settle in New Switzerland. The Kentucky venture, after ten years of struggle, was ended; all of the Dufours—except for the absent John James—were now united on the banks of the Ohio.[27]

Official statistics don't exist, but from scattered and imperfect sources one may construct some notion of the scale of wine production in New Switzerland. In 1810, there were 2,400 gallons from about eight acres of vineyard; that would mean roughly two tons an acre (using 150 gallons to the ton as a conventional measure), a small but not unusual yield. It was promising enough to inspire a prophecy from Francis Dufour, who wrote in this year that "there is no doubt but in the course of a certain number of years the United States will be able to do without importing wine."[28] That was a very spacious conclusion to reach on the basis of a 2,400-gallon vintage; it certainly shows confidence. In 1811 the production was 2,700 gallons from twenty acres of vineyard—much of it presumably newly planted and so not yet producing. In 1812, from the same acreage, New Switzerland produced 3,200 gallons of wine. This vintage so excited the local schoolmaster that he was moved to produce a Latin ode, "The Empire of Bacchus," the opening of which has been translated thus:

> Columbia rejoice! smiling Bacchus has heard
> Your prayers of so fervent a tone
> And crown'd with the grape, has kindly appear'd
> In your land to establish his throne.[29]

The image of a smiling Bacchus on the unkempt banks of the Ohio is comic enough, but the excitement and pleasure behind the extravagance of the poem seem genuine.

The development of wine-growing at Vevay (as the town laid out in 1813 had been named, the spelling changed to guide American pronunciation) probably reached its peak around 1820, when 12,000 gallons of wine was produced from forty to forty-five acres of vineyard. These are hardly overwhelming figures, but in such matters all is relative. Relative to the long history of failure, the 12,000 gallons of Vevay wine was a sensational success; and if that kind of success could be achieved in what was still frontier country, what might the more settled places accomplish?

What was the wine like, really? The American experience of wine at the beginning of the nineteenth century was not very sophisticated, to put it mildly, and it is doubtful that many experts ever drank any Vevay wine. Moreover, it is always difficult to express judgments about such subjective matters as taste in a clear and persuasive way. Besides, people obviously *wanted* Vevay wine, the first American wine ever produced in any volume, to be good, and were willing, as patriots or well-wishers, to stretch the truth a bit in reporting on it. The Cape grape, the child of a native labrusca vine and an unknown vinifera, certainly had the notorious "foxy" taste and aroma of labrusca grapes. Dufour spoke of it as having "the taste of the strawberry, which gives a fine perfume to the wine."[30] A dark blue grape, the Cape grape was fermented on its skins to make a red wine.

One of the earliest to report on Vevay wine, a woman writing in 1809, said that it was made from "Clarret Grapes" and was "excellent." Two years later, a gentleman reported cautiously that the wine "is found to be of good quality" but did not explain who found it so. Another reported in more detail: "The Claret was rich in quality, but too acid. It was, however, a very palatable and pleasant beverage when diluted with water."[31] Ten years later the wine of Vevay was given a most enthusiastic endorsement by a traveler named William Hall: "The wine is like Claret and very fine. We bought some at a dollar per gallon: and I never desire to taste better."[32] On the other hand, Timothy Flint, the much-traveled writer, editor, and missionary, found that the wine of the Cape grape was "not pleasant," and the German traveler Karl Postel was even harsher: Vevay wine, he thought, was "an indifferent beverage, resembling any thing but claret, as it has been represented."[33] Most emphatic of all was Dr. John Godman, a distinguished anatomist and naturalist who had lived in Cincinnati and so would have had ample opportunity to try what the Swiss were making. "Vevay wine," he wrote, "is a perfect nondescript; in colour it slightly approaches thin claret; its taste is altogether peculiar ; something like it might be made by sweetening vin de grave with brown sugar. Nothing but a strong effort of courtesy, however, can induce any one seriously to call it *wine,* unless the fact of its being made from grapes be sufficient to secure it this title."[34]

The list of such conflicting opinions might be greatly extended without helping much to settle the question. But it is more than probable that Vevay wines would not please us today. The American hybrids don't make good red wines, and only when nothing else is available would one choose to drink them. Nicholas Longworth, who did know something about wines, thought the Swiss had made a mistake by making a red wine from the Alexander; it was, he said, "a hard rough red wine... only calculated to make a fine wine sangaree."[35] A white wine, such as Longworth made from the Catawba, might have been a better bet.

Whatever the truth might be about the quality of Vevay wine, the Swiss had no trouble in selling it. The vintage of 1810 was sold at $1.40 a gallon, and it was reported that the markets for the wine then stretched from Cincinnati to Saint Louis. It was advertised in Cincinnati in 1813 at $2 a gallon, and when Vevay's first tavern opened in 1814, the price of the local wine was officially set at $1 a quart for local "Madeira" and $0.75 a quart for Vevay red wine. ("Madeira" was always fortified with brandy, which made it more expensive; it was also produced in much smaller quantities than the red wine from the Cape grape.)[36]

While John James Dufour was still absent in Switzerland, Indiana wine making received an unexpected boost when the religious community founded by George Rapp at Harmony, Pennsylvania, migrated in 1814 from the stony hills of western Pennsylvania to the rich flatlands along the Wabash River in southwestern Indiana. George ("Father") Rapp (1757–1847)) had been a vine-dresser at Iptingen in his native Württemberg before receiving the religious revelation that made him a prophet to his own community and a heretic and rebel to the functionaries of the Duchy of Württemberg. Rapp preached, among other things, that baptism and communion were of the devil, and that schools were evil; within the community of believers that grew up around him, communism and celibacy were the rule. Holding to such beliefs obviously set the Harmonists apart wherever they might go, and though they were not officially persecuted in America as they had been in Germany, they never fit easily into the life around them—nor did they wish to. They lived in the certainty of the Last Days, when Rapp would present his congregation to Christ and superintend their transfer to Heaven.

Though firmly otherworldly, the Harmonists were nevertheless a thrifty and efficient people; within a few years they created a prosperous community in Pennsylvania, and they duplicated the feat after the move to Indiana, where they again called their settlement Harmony.[37] They had had a vineyard in Pennsylvania and had made wine there, not very successfully, from the Cape and Madeira grapes, as the Swiss were doing in Indiana. A major reason for their leaving Pennsylvania for Indiana was the hope that the new territory would be better suited to viticulture. It was and it wasn't. The climate was warmer, but the native diseases were just as lethal along the banks of the Wabash as they had been along the banks of the Connoquenessing. And the Harmonists, though they made Indiana wine from the Cape and the Madeira, could never accept, as Dufour had unknowingly taught the Swiss at Vevay to accept, that they must learn to do without vinifera. They imported large quantities of all the standard German varieties in 1816, and again in 1823, though the vines of course inevitably failed.

By that time, they were ready to move on, or rather, back, to Pennsylvania. In 1825 Rapp managed to sell Harmony, lock, stock, and barrel, to the wealthy Welsh philanthropist Robert Owen, who meant to convert what had been the site of a religious community into that of a secular community with Utopian aspirations. The vineyards of Harmony at the time of Owen's purchase had an extent of some fifteen acres, but they had no future: Owen proclaimed that New Harmony, as he now called it, would be teetotal. The communal experiment under Owen's direction soon foundered, although the Owen family remained as proprietors in New Harmony. No more is heard about Wabaschwein, as George Rapp had called the produce of his Harmony vineyards. He had led his community back to Pennsylvania, where they founded their last settlement, called Economy, on the banks of the Ohio below Pittsburgh. There they made only a little wine but prospered greatly in other ways before declining into extinction, as is the habit of celibate institutions.[38]

For the ten years that Harmony and Vevay had both made wine—from 1815 to 1825—Indiana was the unchallenged leader in the first era of commercial wine production in this country. The wine wasn't very good, and there wasn't much of it, but it made a beginning, and it renewed the idea that this might, after all the earlier disappointments, become a wine-growing country.

John James Dufour at last returned to this scene in 1816, when the wars that had convulsed Europe were ended. Again, his wife did not accompany him. His position in the family had, inevitably, been greatly changed in his long absence. A whole community had grown up when he was away, and he was not among its leaders. As though to signify this change, Dufour, on his return, settled on the property he had bought in 1801 some miles up the river from the main property around Vevay.

He built a house, described as a modest one-story structure of brick, on his farm, which he now named "Dufouria." There he planted vines and fruit trees, maintained a nursery from which he supplied cuttings and young trees to the neighbors, and perhaps made a little wine: we aren't sure.

In the first years following Dufour's return from Switzerland, the wine business at Vevay was doing well, but in the decade of the 1820s the signs of decay began to appear. The agricultural depression following the banking panic of 1819 lowered prices and slowed the markets, so the attractions of wine growing declined while its difficulties increased. Improved transportation made imported wine more readily available and gave Vevay wine a competition it could not long withstand—to say nothing of the cheap whiskey that was everywhere available, on the frontier as well as in the settled regions. The first generation of Vevay's settlers were all bred to wine making and had come to America with the express purpose of continuing in that trade; their children had no such commitment and were drawn to the many other opportunities before them in a developing country. Finally, and probably most important, the obstacles of disease and climate were at last too much to struggle against. By the 1830s, the wine business at Vevay was over. The condition of the decaying town is described by a visitor in 1828: "The town is on the decline; it has a court-house, and two stores very ill-supplied. The condition of these, and the absence of lawyers, are sure indications of the poverty of the inhabitants, if broken windows, and doors falling from their hinges, should leave any doubt on the subject."[39]

Dufour must have seen all this coming. There is even some reason to think that he intended to leave Vevay and return to Switzerland to live. His wife died in 1823; by law, half of her estate went to her son, who had followed his father to Vevay. The son then transferred his inheritance to his father in exchange for Dufour's property in and around Vevay, a move that seems to show the father's intent to abandon Indiana for Switzerland.[40] But if that was the plan, it did not come to pass.

In 1825 Dufour began what would be his last work, a book about wine making for Americans. In preparation for it, a circular bearing the name of his brother Francis was sent out asking for any experience in grape growing and wine making to be reported.[41] How much information Dufour may have received from this inquiry we don't know, but the book, though padded by long extracts from various authorities, is in part written out of Dufour's own experience. He had learned for himself what he had to say.

The American Vine-Dresser's Guide, Being a Treatise on the Cultivation of the Vine, and the Process of Wine Making, Adapted to the Soil and Climate of the United States, was published in Cincinnati in 1826. It is, in many ways, a clumsy effort at bookmaking, ill organized, padded, often obscure. But one is grateful to have it for the history of Dufour's stubborn and determined effort to make wine in America. It makes clear Dufour's conviction that the would-be winemaker in America has no choice but to accept what the country allows—in Dufour's case that was the Cape grape—and to forget what one knew in Europe. He also urged those who had time and money to continue searching for new varieties and to assist nature in their creation—that is, to take up hybridizing.[42]

Dufour was unlucky with his book, as he had been unlucky in so many other ways. It was on a trip he made to Kentucky to sell the book that he fell ill; he died back at his farm on February 27, 1827. Some two hundred copies of his book were in his house at the time of his death, a substantial part of the entire printing of five hundred. The book could not have been widely disseminated and is now rare.[43]

The American wine making career of John James Dufour was in many ways unimpressive: it was slow to start, it was much interrupted, and it was of brief duration. Nor did it culminate in any obvious or substantial achievement. First came the nearly twenty years of preparation in Switzerland; then eight years of frustrated labor in Kentucky; and then ten years of inactivity in Switzerland while others carried to success in Indiana the work that he had begun. The last eleven years of his life he spent working apparently in self-imposed solitude. It seems somehow characteristic that even his grave site in not now certainly known.[44] Had he not written *The American Vine-Dresser's Guide,* Dufour would by now have been wholly forgotten. As it is, he has a secure niche in the early history of American wine growing. Despite the failure of the Kentucky Vineyard Society, and despite Dufour's failure to recognize the true nature of the Cape grape, it was with the grape that he selected and at the place he selected that commercial viticulture and wine making began in the United States.[45] Dufour deserves at least a modest monument.

TWO

Nicholas Longworth

THE NECESSARY ENTREPRENEUR

GROWING RICH IN CINCINNATI

Dufour had an heir, in effect if not in law. This was Nicholas Longworth of Cincinnati, about fifty miles up the Ohio River from Vevay. He knew about Dufour's work, was much interested in it, determined to carry it on, and did so with far greater success than Dufour could have imagined. For Longworth had two great advantages over Dufour: he was wealthy, and he had a better grape to use.

Take the matter of wealth first. Longworth (1782–1863) was born in Newark, New Jersey. His grandfather and father were both Loyalists during the Revolution and, as the price of their politics, had had their considerable property confiscated. His inheritance gone, young Longworth had his own fortune to make (it is sometimes said that he was put to the trade of shoe-making). He went south first, to work in an elder brother's store in South Carolina; he also spent some time in Savannah, Georgia. But the South did not agree with his health, and, it may be, he had no liking for slavery. There was also an unhappy love affair. He returned to New Jersey and there began the study of law. In 1804, at the age of twenty-two, he determined to go west and chose Cincinnati, then a small village of log huts on hilly ground along the Ohio River. Like Dufour's property downriver in Indiana, Cincinnati was in the newly opened Northwest Territory, the very frontier of the country at the turn of the nineteenth century and a free rather than a slave region. When Longworth got there, by flatboat drifting down the Ohio, it had only about eight hundred inhabitants, but it had the prospect of unlimited expansion.

Longworth completed his legal studies at Cincinnati by reading in the office of a local judge and was then admitted to the bar, where he practiced until 1819. But from a very early point in his Cincinnati career, he made the acquisition of real estate rather than the courts his main business. Raw as it was, Cincinnati was prospering as an agricultural, industrial, and transportation center, and its rapid growth sent land values up and up. Longworth's first deal, in which he bartered a couple of whiskey stills for thirty-three acres of undeveloped land, was worth $2 million to him by the middle of the century.[1] And that deal was only the beginning. Even after he had sold more lands and lots than any other man in Cincinnati, he was still, in 1850, the "largest landholder in the city."[2]

By 1828 Longworth concluded that he was rich enough to retire from active business and devote himself to his other interests: these were, especially, horticulture and the patronage of the arts. That he was prepared to do something else besides make money shows that his interests were genuine. By this time Longworth was perhaps the First Citizen of Cincinnati. In 1807 he had married a widow named Susan Howell Conner, by whom he had four children; he owned a splendid house, called Belmont, on Pike Street in the city's Mount Adams district (the house is now the Taft Museum; Longworth's vineyards on Mount Adams are now the city's Eden Park). He had supported and encouraged several young artists, the most notable of whom was Hiram Powers, the sculptor, and had formed an important art collection of his own. Longworth was, in short, the very model of prosperity, possessed of a large fortune, a thriving family, and a patron's prestige.

He did not, however, behave like the ordinary rich man. On the contrary, he cultivated eccentricity and seemed to despise his own wealth. A short, dark man with a wide, thin-lipped mouth and snapping black eyes, he dressed in slovenly fashion and was much gratified when people visiting his splendid estate mistook him for a gardener and tipped him after he had given them a tour. This, he said, was the only honest money he ever made, having been a lawyer by profession. His speech was often brusque, sarcastic, and obscure, no more polite than his habits of dress. He would pin slips of paper to his sleeve containing instructions for errands and go about town to fulfill them, tearing off a slip when its business had been done. He kept a drawer in his desk that he filled with coins each day so that his grandchildren could take what they wanted without troubling him about it. He made a point of refusing to take part in conventional charity, since, as he said, there were plenty of others to do that. "I shall," he declared, "assist none but the idle, drunken, worthless vagabonds that nobody else will help."[3] He would send anonymous contri-

FIGURE 4. Nicholas Longworth, the "Western Millionaire," an obituary portrait from
1863. From *Harper's Weekly* (March 7, 1863).

butions of money to local ministers with the notation: "To the relief of the
depraved."

Yet he was an active supporter of all civic causes, a man who could be
counted on as a quiet participant: he had no wish to hold office or to head
committees. Longworth seems to have had no respect for the respectable,
knowing from his own practice in moneymaking how fraudulent much of
respectable life was. "Old Nick," he was inevitably called. But if Longworth
sometimes resembled a cynic philosopher, neither he nor his community ever
for a moment forgot that he was also a rich man: that made all the difference.

THE CATAWBA

Dufour had as his sole dependence in wine making the grape he knew as the
Cape grape and that we identify as the Alexander. No one, given a choice,
would prefer the wine of the Alexander to that of any decent vinifera, but the
American pioneers had no choice: the Alexander was the only grape known

in this country that would both grow and yield an at least drinkable wine. In the early years of the nineteenth century, that situation began to change as more and more chance hybrids were discovered and brought into cultivation—Lenoir, Herbemont, Isabella, and a great number of others whose names have now been forgotten. Chief among these newcomers was the grape called Catawba, whose introduction begins the second chapter in the history of American wine growing.

The fame of the grape was owing in the first place to the efforts of John Adlum (1759–1836), who, after some military service (he was always known as Major Adlum), made a career as a surveyor and land speculator in the expansive days of the frontier after the Revolution. Adlum always had his eye on the possibilities of wine making in America—as a surveyor he had known at first hand the abundant wild grapes growing in all the woods and fields of eastern America—and after his retirement he had planted grapes and made wine, first at Havre de Grace, at the top of Chesapeake Bay, and then at Georgetown, in the new District of Columbia, where he called his farm "The Vineyard."

Like every other would-be American winegrower, Adlum was always on the lookout for new varieties to try. He found one in 1819 growing on the farm of the widow Scholl, in Clarksburgh, Maryland. The late Mr. Scholl had called it the Catawba, and that was all that was known about it. Its exact origins are still unknown, but the likeliest story is that it was originally found growing near the Catawba River in the vicinity of Asheville, North Carolina. The fruit of the Catawba is a lovely reddish-purple—"lilac," some call it—with a clear white juice high in acid. It has the foxy character of its labrusca parent, but not to an offensive degree, and it yields a white wine that Philip Wagner describes as "dry to the point of austerity" and having "a very clean flavor and a curious, special, spicy aroma."[4]

Adlum propagated vines from the cuttings he took from Mrs. Scholl's vine, made wine from them, and most important, began to promote the Catawba to the country at large. Adlum wrote about it with unrestrained enthusiasm in the agricultural press and did all he could to promote it among the influential citizens of the young Republic. It was not long before Nicholas Longworth heard about the Catawba and Major Adlum's bold claims for it. "In introducing this grape to public notice," Adlum wrote to Longworth, "I have done my country a greater service than I should have done, had I paid the national debt."[5] The national debt was a much less terrifying sum then than it is now, but the claim is sufficiently grand. In Longworth's hands, and for a time in the hands of others who tended the vineyards in and around Cincinnati, the Catawba seemed to fulfill at last the long-held hope that America might have a wine of its own.

This is, however, to get ahead of our story. Longworth was busily engaged in making money for the first twenty-five years of his residence in Cincinnati, but not so busy that he did not find time to indulge in his horticultural hobbies. He collected and planted fruits and other plants of all kinds from an early point in his Cincinnati years and, like many other patriotic Americans in the early days of the Republic, was active in distributing plants, in corresponding with other enthusiasts, and in encouraging trials of new things to advance the cause of horticulture. Chief among his many interests was always the grape, and he is known to have experimented with different sorts as early as 1813, though he did not yet have anything that might be called a vineyard. The very modest success in wine growing that the Vevay Swiss achieved after 1810 was of course known to Longworth, and though he had no high opinion of Vevay wine, he planted Dufour's Cape grape—that is, the Alexander—and made wine from it for many years.

Like every other hopeful viticulturist, Longworth tried to grow vinifera and, despite uniform failure, persisted in the effort over many years. Longworth tells us that at one time he imported six thousand European vines from Madeira; at another, seven thousand from the Jura region. Such vines from the limit of European wine growing would, he hoped, be able to succeed in America. As late as 1830 he had "upwards of one hundred and fifty varieties of foreign grapes" in his nursery.[6] It took a long time, but at last, after more than forty years of trial, Longworth conceded that we had nothing to hope for from vinifera in this country and had better see what we could do with the natives instead.[7]

While he allowed himself to be lured by the fascination of vinifera, Longworth did not neglect the native vine. In the early decades of the nineteenth century, there was much eager experimentation with grapes in all the settled parts of the country: William Prince of the Prince Nursery on Long Island, John Adlum in the District of Columbia, Nicholas Herbemont in South Carolina, and Thomas McCall in Georgia were only the most prominent among many hundreds of enthusiasts whose trials of the grape made a staple subject for discussion and argument in the nation's agricultural press. Longworth was in touch with them all and never ceased to appeal for information about any new and promising variety of grape that might appear: Alexander, Isabella, Herbemont, Lenoir, Orwigsburgh, Clinton,

Union Village—he had tried them all, and found them all wanting. But the American woods were, he knew, still full of yet-untried native grapes;[8] he also urged that new types be raised from seed or created by crossing the natives with the European grape. That is what he would do, he often said, if he were granted another life.

MAKING WINE IN CINCINNATI

Cincinnati, young as it was, did not wait for Longworth's appearance before undertaking trials with grapes. At the end of the eighteenth century, at the very beginning of the city's history, a Frenchman named Menissier had planted a small vineyard in what is now the heart of downtown Cincinnati. Another pioneer, Martin Baum, Cincinnati's leading merchant, manufacturer, and banker, built a handsome mansion on Pike Street, where he maintained a collection of native and foreign vines. This was the house and property that Longworth himself acquired in 1829; the purchase added Baum's vines to Longworth's own collection.

Longworth made the move from purely domestic viticulture to a commercial operation in 1823. In that year he planted a four-acre property on Baldface Creek, downriver from Cincinnati, in Delhi Township, using the Alexander grape from Vevay. He had the idea that, unlike the Vevay Swiss, who made a red wine from the Alexander, he would make a white wine. And so he did; but he found that he had to add sugar to the juice before fermentation in order to raise the alcohol level, and brandy to keep the wine from turning to vinegar. This treatment, Longworth said, made a "tolerable Madeira," but that was not what he wanted.

Longworth was no farmer himself; I do not know that he ever got his hands dirty in a vineyard. He was, rather, a promoter and a patron: he would put up the money to start things, and he would have distinct ideas about what to do and how to do it; others, however, would do the work needed to produce a result. For his wine-making enterprise, he had a convenient resource in the large community of Germans who had come to Cincinnati. His chosen method was to install a German as a tenant at each vineyard and to share the harvest with him. The Germans, Longworth thought, were a distinct advantage for Cincinnati wine growing. Besides a favorable climate in the region, he wrote, "we have also the right kind of people among us. Emigrants from the wine countries of Germany. Poor, but industrious and frugal. Bred from their infancy to the cultivation of the vine, and anxious to engage in the same business. All they know, is hard labour and coarse diet, having in Germany supported themselves from a vineyard, often not exceeding an acre in extent."[9] It was, Longworth said, the German women who, more often than not, did the main work in the vineyards. The supply of Germans in Cincinnati never failed: by the middle of the nineteenth century there were 30,000 German-born residents of the city in a total population of 115,000.[10]

Longworth has been accused of exploiting his German tenants, but there is some reason to think that the relation between tenant and owner was one of mutual respect and dependence. In the early years of Cincinnati wine production it was Longworth's practice to sell back his half of the wine produced to his tenant at a low price so that the tenant could then resell that half at a good profit. This does not sound like grinding the faces of the poor.

By means of the tenant method, Longworth's vineyards grew steadily; he had nine vineyards in 1833, thirteen in 1842; ultimately he had forty vineyards in and around Cincinnati, adding up to 130 acres. After 1825, when he received his first cuttings of the Catawba grape from Major Adlum, these vineyards were mostly devoted to the Catawba. Longworth found that he could produce something like what he had in mind from this grape as he could not from the Alexander—that is, a pure, dry table wine. The American taste, he thought, had been sadly corrupted by imported wines that were always fortified with brandy to keep them sound under the difficult conditions that an exported wine was bound to suffer. According to Longworth, the wine drunk in this country usually contained about 25 percent alcohol, "and," he added, "I have seen it contain forty percent."[11]

He could now offer them something else—an unfortified white table wine. Unfortunately the Americans were not yet ready to like such a wine: it was too acid, too thin for the native taste. So Longworth's wine, in the early years of Catawba production, was not only grown by the Germans, it was drunk by them too: "All the wine made at my vineyards," Longworth wrote, "has been sold at our German coffee-houses, and drank in our city."[12] As one of Longworth's fellow growers put it, Catawba was "a little too hard and sour to be loved at first tasting," but local pride and persistent promotion began to have an effect: "People set themselves to learn to admire it."[13] By the time Longworth was ready to distribute his Catawba wine nationally, he had taught the people of Cincinnati to take pride in their local wine.

Here it must be admitted that there is evidence that Longworth did make

FIGURE 5. The Catawba grape, like the Alexander, is a chance hybrid between a native and European vine, but, unlike the Alexander, is still flourishing in eastern vineyards today, providing both still and sparkling wines, though in diminishing quantities. Nicholas Longworth was its great promoter. Painting by C. L. Fleischman, 1867, courtesy Special Collections, National Agricultural Library.

some concessions to the American taste for something less austere than pure, dry Catawba. He is reported to have bought large quantities of Scuppernong juice from North Carolina to boost the flavor of his Catawba wine. The Scuppernong (properly, the muscadine), the native grape of the South, has a strong musky flavor that all Americans liked, or so Longworth thought (he must have encountered the Scuppernong when he worked briefly in the South). So he gave it to them, in the official words of the report, "to impart flavor and a bouquet not otherwise obtainable to his celebrated Cincinnati wines."[14] Barring this perhaps pardonable adulteration, Longworth's wine-making methods were irreproachable: the grapes in Cincinnati's vineyards were picked at full maturity and then sorted over to remove defective berries. The clusters were destemmed and crushed before being fermented in cool conditions under water seal. No sugar was added to the must. After fermentation the wine was racked into clean casks to undergo the clarifying and aging process. It would be hard to improve on these basic procedures today.[15]

As well as cultivating in his fellow citizens a taste for Catawba, Longworth had also to overcome a strong prejudice in favor of European wines even among those who might like Catawba but saw it as necessarily inferior because a domestic product. "Some of our best judges of Hock," he wrote, "have not been able to drink our still Catawba, but when old Hock labels have been put on the bottles, have not only been able to relish it, but led to pronounce it the best Hock wine they ever drank." Longworth had counterfeit German labels prepared with such mock designations as "Ganz Vorzüglicher" (wholly superior) and "Versichert" (guaranteed). He did not sell the bottles so labeled, but he no doubt made sure they were seen by his prejudiced friends.[16] The scheme is, at any rate, evidence of Longworth's cynical sense of humor. It also makes clear his understanding that a strong prejudice had to be dealt with, and that a determined propaganda campaign would be required. Seeing the need, he was tireless in his efforts to promote a pure native product, the Catawba of Ohio.

SPREADING THE WORD

Quite by accident, Longworth produced a sparkling Catawba in 1842 and found it so good that he determined to make it his means of opening up the markets beyond Cincinnati. First, however, he had to learn how to make it. After trying unsuccessfully to duplicate his accidental wine, he sent for a French expert. The run of bad luck continued, however: the poor Frenchman drowned in the Ohio River before he could apply his art to Ohio wine. Another French expert followed, and, though he managed to produce a sparkling wine, the losses from bursting bottles were appallingly high: forty-two thousand of fifty thousand bottles in one season. No wonder Longworth sometimes doubted whether it was worth continuing the struggle.[17]

A third Frenchman, named Fournier, came in 1852, and with him the production of sparkling wine became more secure. The workers in Longworth's sparkling-wine house were all said to be recruited from the great Champagne region around Épernay. Despite the French element, Longworth insisted that his sparkling wine was strictly American. "I shall not," he said, "attempt to imitate any of the sparkling wines in Europe"; he would, instead, produce a "pure article, having the peculiar flavor of our native grape."[18] Nor did he ever call his sparkling wine "champagne." It always went to market as "Sparkling Catawba."

Longworth's main role, besides paying for these developments, was to publicize them. He was an assiduous writer of letters to the editor that appeared in a variety of papers and journals to explain his work and to promote the virtues of Catawba wine. Longworth never wrote anything of any length; his most extended effort appears to have been a pamphlet of nineteen pages called *On the Cultivation of the Grape and the Manufacture of Wine* published in Cincinnati in 1846; this got a wider circulation by being reprinted by the New York Agricultural Society and by the U.S. Patent Office (the predecessor of the Department of Agriculture) in its annual report for 1847—evidence of the growing interest that Longworth's wine making was beginning to create. He also sent samples of his wine to any likely individual or agency—to the National Convention of Farmers, Gardeners, and Silk Culturists held in New York in 1846, for example, and to several of the official horticultural societies established in the various states.

A sample that he sent to the poet Longfellow made a lucky hit. Longfellow scribbled some doggerel lines in praise of Longworth's Sparkling Catawba; these were imprudently published in 1854 and have been embarrassing Longfellow's reputation ever since. A few lines will be enough to show their character:

> Very good in its way
> Is the Verzenay
> Or the Sillery soft and creamy;
> But Catawba wine
> Has a taste more divine,
> More dulcet, delicious, and dreamy.

Whatever this effusion may have done to Longfellow's poetic status, it certainly helped to boost Longworth's wine among patriotic Americans.

The nineteenth century was the great era of the fair and the exhibition as means for encouraging manufactures and for disseminating information. Longworth participated in them to good effect. As early as 1833 he won the premium at the local Hamilton County Fair with his Catawba in competition against some German wines. But his finest triumph in this line came at the Great Exhibition of London in 1851—the *fons et origo* of all the international exhibitions that adorned the latter half of the nineteenth century. There, the Catawba wines of Longworth and other Cincinnati producers secured the respectful attention of the English judges. As the catalogue of the Exhibition put it, "In all essential particulars, [Catawba] wine resembles the German hock or Rhenish wine; is slightly acid in taste, holding in solution a small portion of tartaric acid, which in process of time is deposited, when the wine becomes more mild and smooth; it is very light and delicate in flavor."[19] This is surely among the earliest notices of a native American wine in Europe, and it is remarkable for its friendliness.

By 1854 Longworth had an agency in New York for the sale of his wines, and through this and his own establishment in Cincinnati, Catawba wine was made available in most of the cities of the country. In Cincinnati, bottles of still Catawba sold for $6 a dozen, sparkling Catawba for $12; in New York, the prices were $7 and $13. For comparison, one may note that Longworth's New York agent was selling Burgundy at from $14 to $24 per dozen, Rhine and Moselle wines at from $7 to $30. Ohio wine evidently had some advantage in price, but not so much as might have been expected. It if sold—as it seems to have done—it could do so only because people liked it, or were moved by patriotic impulse, or perhaps both. I do not suppose that patriotism alone would have sold many bottles.

Cincinnati—"the Queen City of the West"—attracted many travelers and curious visitors, so there is a good deal of testimony recorded as to the qualities of its wine. One of the earliest and most formidable to go on record was Frances Trollope, the mother of the novelist, who, in an effort to rescue the fortunes of her feckless husband, opened a bazaar in Cincinnati in 1829. This was a combination exhibition hall, theater, coffeehouse, social center, and fancy-goods store—a harebrained scheme doomed to quick extinction. The episode had a lasting result, however, in Mrs. Trollope's *Domestic Manners of the Americans* (1832), a book long notorious in the American consciousness for its unsparing representation of the democratic way of life. "During my residence in America," she wrote, "I repeatedly tasted native wine from vineyards carefully cultivated, and on the fabrication of which a considerable degree of imported science had been bestowed; but the very best of it was miserable stuff. It should seem that Nature herself requires some centuries of schooling before she becomes perfectly accomplished in ministering to the luxuries of man, and, perhaps as there is no lack of sunshine, the champagne and Bordeaux of the Union may appear simultaneously with a Shakspeare, a Raphael, and a Mozart."[20] She does not name him, but she certainly has Longworth in mind: no one in else in Cincinnati could have provided native wine in 1829. Later travelers, coming to Cincinnati after Ohio Catawba had

FIGURE 6. A view of Longworth's vineyards on the Ohio in 1866, a view very much *en beau*. By 1866 the vineyards around Cincinnati were in terminal decline, but the wish to display a flourishing American viticulture no doubt prompted this fanciful image. From *Frank Leslie's Illustrated Newspaper,* March 31, 1866.

grown famous in the land, left conflicting reports about the wine, according to their varying moods and characters.

Isabella Trotter and her husband, for example, English tourists in America, visited Cincinnati in 1858 and were distinctly unimpressed by the wine they found there. They were entertained by Longworth himself, who gave them a dinner of quails and oysters. Later in the evening, "a table was laid out in the drawing-room with their Catawba champagne, which was handed round in tumblers, followed by piles of Vanilla ice a foot and a half high." Mrs. Trotter does not say what she thought about the wine on this occasion, but the next night she and her husband were entertained by one of Longworth's daughters, who gave them "most copious supplies of their beloved Catawba champagne, which we do not love, for it tastes, to our uninitiated palates, little better than cider. It was served in a large red punch-bowl of Bohemian glass in the form of a Catawba cobbler, which I thought improved it."[21] The fact that Mr. Trotter was hung over all the next day could not have raised their opinion of the wine.

But another British traveler, visiting Cincinnati in the same year as Mrs. Trotter did, was unrestrained in his enthusiasm for Catawba. Charles Mackay, writing in the *Illustrated London News,* pronounced still Catawba to be "a finer wine of the hock species and flavour than any hock that comes from the Rhine"; sparkling Catawba was "far superior to any sparkling wine which Europe can boast, whether they came from the Rhine or Moselle, or from the champagne districts of France." Mackay's enthusiasm ran so high that it burst out into verse:

> Ohio's green hilltops
>   Glow bright in the sun,
> And yield us more treasure
>   Than Rhine or Garonne;
> They give us Catawba,
>   The pure and the true,
> As radiant as sunlight,
>   As soft as the dew,
> And fragrant as gardens
>   When summer is new:
> Catawba that sparkles—
>   Catawba at rest—
> Catawba the nectar
>   And balm of the West.[22]

What can such extravagance mean? Perhaps only that the wine was better than might have been expected, or perhaps only that Mackay knew nothing about wine.

SPLENDORS AND MISERIES

Longworth's slow development of wine growing in Cincinnati did not, for many years, seem to have much effect. The business was seen as just another of Longworth's eccentric interests, one that he, as a rich man, could indulge with the help of his German tenants, who grew the grapes and then drank the wine. At last, by the 1840s, Longworth's growing success began to attract others so that, in a very few years' time, one could speak of a wine-growing industry in Cincinnati, now newly identified as the "Rhineland of America."

The booming character of the Cincinnati trade in wine is shown by the jump in vineyard acreage from 250 in 1846 to 900 in 1850. In the next year, the somewhat grandiosely named American Wine Growers Association was formed in Cincinnati. The model for the Cincinnati people was, as in so many other things, German, in this case the institution of the Weinbau Verbesserungs Gesellschaft, established to promote and improve grape culture and wine making. Among other things, the Cincinnati Horticultural Society, beginning in 1847, sponsored a "Longworth Cup," a trophy awarded annually to the producer of the best native wine of the year. By 1853 there was enough production—some 320,000 gallons—to make the competition for the cup a significant contest. By 1859 the Cincinnati *vignoble* had reached two thousand acres, from which 568,000 gallons of wine were produced. Ohio, which largely meant Cincinnati, led the nation in the production of wine in that year, though serious competition was beginning to develop from the vineyards of the Finger Lakes in New York, from the Germans in Missouri, and from remote California.

An important development accompanying the expansion of vineyards and wine making was the establishment of large "wine houses," as they were called.[23] Here too Longworth took the lead: by 1853 he had two such operations and an interest in a third. The Cincinnati vineyards were small—usually only a few acres—and were divided among many hundreds of proprietors and tenants. Wine making on a small scale and carried out by many different producers was an inefficient and unreliable proceeding; few knew what to do, and even fewer had the proper means to do it, since the small scale of production would not support the expense of good equipment and good methods. In this situation, the wine house supplied an effective means to consolidate and regularize production. The wine houses, with their large-scale means, made it possible to obtain a secure and uniform method of production and a storage capacity adequate to supply the national demand.[24] Robert Buchanan estimated that the Cincinnati wine houses in 1853 had put up 245,000 bottles of sparkling wine and 205,000 of still wine.[25] This was no longer a cottage industry.

All things considered, the prospect for wine growing in the "Rhineland of America" seemed to open out into a boundless prosperity: the thing could not fail. The received view was nicely expressed in 1851 by Charles Cist, the local newspaper editor and a friend of Nicholas Longworth. The example of Cincinnati, Cist thought, would soon spread throughout the United States. "It is therefore evident, that in a country like ours, of vast extent, of great diversity of soil and climate, abounding in native grapes, and settled by an intelligent and enterprising population, the making of our own wines is no longer problematical, but will soon be established on a sure and permanent basis, as one of the great branches of home production."[26] But far from being "no longer problematical," wine growing in America was still thoroughly problematical, a fact that reasserted itself even at the moment Cist was making his assured prophecy.

The Catawba vine, in the first years of its flourishing around Cincinnati, did not appear to suffer particularly from diseases, but that condition did not last long. As the acreage grew and so offered an expanding, homogeneous plant population to work on, the attacks of the main diseases—powdery mildew, downy mildew, and black rot—became more and more frequent. Black rot has already been described (see chapter 1). Powdery mildew (*Uncinula necator*) was another affliction native to North America; it, too, was exported to Europe in the nineteenth century, with disastrous effects. Known there as oidium, it was rampant in the vineyards of France, Italy, Spain, and Portugal.

The ravages of powdery mildew in Cincinnati did not cause such distress as in Europe, but they were bad enough. A third fungal disease, downy mildew (*Plasmopara viticola),* also native to North America, was also at work. Powdery mildew attaches itself to the green parts of the vine—the leaves, shoots, and fruit—and covers them with a grayish powder, especially the leaves. The leaves drop off, the shoots are weakened, the fruit breaks open. The mildew has a moldy odor that comes through if wine is made from the affected fruit. Downy mildew flourishes in humidity, unlike powdery mildew, which likes hot dry conditions. It forms downy white patches on the underside of the vine's leaves and leads to the defoliation of the vine and the withering of the fruit, so that it is useless for wine. Powdery mildew may be controlled by dusting with sulfur, but the growers around Cincinnati did not yet know that.[27] Downy mildew and black rot are controlled by Bordeaux mixture, but that weapon had not yet been devised.

The effects of these diseases were already apparent by the 1840s, when sharp variations in the annual harvests were created according to whether the diseases did or did not flourish in a given year. By the 1850s the effects of disease were such that the whole enterprise began to seem doubtful. In that decade there were only three good years—1853, 1858, and 1859; all the others were so afflicted by disease that the crop was cut down to uneconomic levels. In the good year 1853, for example, Cincinnati produced 320,000 gallons of wine; but in 1854, a disease-smitten year, only about 70,000 gallons. There were desperate searches for new and resistant varieties. Longworth himself was tireless in seeking out and trying new varieties; in 1851 he wrote that he was then "trenching and benching twenty acres on which to plant new varieties, and raise seedlings from our best native grapes." He appealed to the public to send him cuttings of promising finds. "If the wild hills of California be as rich in grapes as of gold dust," he wrote, "Jerseyman though I am, I shall be more gratified to receive a grape cutting, than the largest lump of gold that region has ever produced."[28] In 1858 he wrote to the American Wine Growers Association that he had wines from thirty new varieties of grape to be tried by the group, and this was presumably a more or less regular practice.[29]

At his suggestion he and the Horticultural Society offered a standing prize of five hundred dollars for a better grape than the Catawba. The prize was claimed for a grape of local origin called the Ives Seedling, but it soon showed more defects than virtues. No one knew what to do: there was no clear recognition of what different diseases were in question, and in a climate of general ignorance fantastic explanations and fantastic remedies abounded.

Some said that the problem was a matter of pruning; if the vine were pruned long rather than short it would resist disease. Some said that no such methods could possibly help, since the problem was "bad weather and atmospheric changes," about which one could do nothing. Others said that the trouble lay in "excess roots" in the vine, or in "excess moisture" in the vineyard, or in too much plowing. But all agreed that, for whatever reason, the Catawba was dangerously liable to mildew and rot. Many growers gave it up; they might plant some other variety, or more likely, they turned to some other crop.

As bad year succeeded bad year, people began to talk about certain failure as they had, not many years before, talked about the certain success of Ohio wine growing. In 1857 the Cincinnati Horticultural Society appointed a committee to inquire into the prospects of "grape growing as a remunerative crop," hoping by this means to confound the naysayers. As one hopeful member of the Society put it, they meant to "put to rest the nonsensical statements now current in some parts of the country to the effect that the Grape-Culture and Vine-Growing in this country is unremunerative and therefore impracticable."[30] The committee reported in December 1857, bravely affirming that vine growing was undoubtedly remunerative "in the right places." and that even in bad years most vineyards were profitable. But they had nothing to say about the diseases that afflicted them, since no one had a remedy.[31]

One solution to the trouble in Cincinnati was emigration. There had long been some small vineyards on the shores of Lake Erie, two hundred miles to the north of Cincinnati; and as the fame of the Cincinnati Catawba grew, the grape was tried out in the Lake Erie vineyards. The results were excellent: the limestone soil of the region, the lake effect that delayed the spring and protracted the autumn, and the lakeshore breezes providing good air ventilation, all suited the Catawba, which enjoyed far better health on the flatlands of the Lake Erie shore and islands than it ever had on the hills along the Ohio River. From that point on, viticulture and wine making continued to grow in the Lake Erie region in proportion as the Cincinnati region declined. By the end of the century there were more than thirty thousand acres of vines in Ohio, almost all of them around Lake Erie, not on the slopes of the Ohio River Valley.

The Civil War contributed to the decline of Cincinnati wine growing. The war sent prices up, but new planting slowed and the shortage of labor meant that the vineyards could not be properly maintained. Meantime, the ravages of disease went on unaffected by war: in 1862 the average yield of wine was a bare sixty gallons per acre, scarcely a third of what one might reasonably expect. Longworth died in the next year, and though the wine business in Cincinnati persisted for a few years after that, his death, combined with all the other hostile circumstances of the time, seemed to mark the end of an enterprise that had been identified with Longworth for more than forty years. By 1870 Longworth's wine house had been converted to an oil refinery, and the forty vineyards that he planted were being pulled out. Longworth had seen the end coming, but, so his son-in-law W.J. Flagg reported, "he refused to despair," always hoping to find that magic variety that would resist the mildew and the rot.[32]

The failure of Cincinnati wine growing was so complete that even after controls had been found for the diseases that had destroyed Longworth's vines, no one ventured to plant anew. Today there is still only a modest number of vines in the Ohio Valley, though grape growing and wine making are flourishing in all sorts of sites in the eastern United States unthought-of in Longworth's day. But Longworth certainly contributed to that flourishing. As a man both wealthy and enthusiastically committed, he performed several vital services. He experimented with many, many varieties under many different conditions of cultivation; he could afford good methods of production with good equipment under the direction of skilled winemakers; and he increased the production of Cincinnati wine to a large volume and made it a significant part of the local economy rather than a backyard hobby. Most important, he promoted the idea of an American wine, produced from a native grape and sold under its own name, to the country at large. All of this took both time and money: fortunately, Longworth had both and was prepared to use them in the cause of American wine. We owe him much.

THREE

George Husmann

A PURE AND LOFTY FAITH

MISSOURI GERMANS

Saint Louis and the region around it have long been associated with wine. The Jesuits of Saint Stanislaus Seminary at Florissant, just north of the city, began making wine in 1823 and continued down to 1960; the American Wine Company, founded in 1859 by a Chicago politician, produced a well-known sparkling wine, called "Cook's Imperial," in cellars dug beneath the streets of Saint Louis (they are still there, but are disused and inaccessible). It was the Germans, however, who really put the region on the wine-making map. Lured by the seductive account of his life in frontier Missouri published by Gottfried Duden in 1829, many Germans, as individuals or in groups, came to settle in the Saint Louis region. They were pulled by Duden's idyllic descriptions, and, at the same time, pushed by genuine economic distress and by political repression in the post-Napoleonic German states.[1]

They were not necessarily from the German wine regions (as George Rapp was, for example), but Duden had stressed the potential of the Missouri country for wine growing, and, like all of the other early settlers, the Germans could hardly help being struck by the wild grapes that abounded all around them in the new country. So it was natural that many of them went in for growing grapes and making wine, with results both like and unlike those of the many settlers who had preceded them in this country and had tried their hands at wine making. In German fashion, they also took up the scientific study and classification of vines and entered into the demanding work of hybridizing new ones. Dr. George Engelmann of Saint Louis, a passionate amateur scientist, became the leading authority on the classification of native American vines; the Bushberg Nursery, near Saint Louis, developed by the Austrian Isidor Bush, specialized in native vines. A few miles up the Missouri River from Saint Louis at Washington, Missouri, the Lutheran minister Friedrich Muench tended his vines and urged the civilizing virtue of wine-growing upon Americans: "With the growth of the grape," he wrote, "every nation elevates itself to a higher degree of civilization—brutality must vanish, and human nature progresses."[2] Off to the southwest of the state, the German-speaking Swiss Herman Jaeger was indefatigable in searching out and testing native varieties of grape and in developing seedlings and hybrids in his nursery at Neosho.

Among the many German-flavored regions of Missouri, the most German of all was the town of Hermann on the south bank of the Missouri River some fifty miles upstream from Saint Louis. The town had been created by a group of Germans in Philadelphia who aimed at making a new-world community that should be thoroughly German in all its parts. They formed a company called the Deutsche Ansiedlungs-Gesellschaft (German Settlement Society) in 1836 and sold shares to pay for the purchase of land and the building of a community: one share of twenty-five dollars entitled the purchaser to one city lot in the new town. The Society decided to make Missouri the scene of its "new German Fatherland" and sent out an agent to inspect the territory and buy land. What he came up with were eleven thousand acres of hilly, forested, not very fertile land in an angle formed where the Gasconade, coming up from the south, flows into the Missouri River. The first settlers ventured into this difficult territory in December 1837 and began to build the town of Hermann, named for the Germanic hero called Arminius by the Romans, whom he defeated in battle in the Teutoburger Wald in 9 C.E.

THE HUSMANNS OF HERMANN

Among the early settlers in Hermann was the family of Husmann, from Meyenburg, in what was then the kingdom of Hanover. The father, Martin, had been a schoolmaster in Germany and brought up his children to a high standard of education and conduct. The youngest of the family was George Husmann (1827–1902), the only child of a second marriage. He was not yet ten when the family left Germany on its way to the wilds of Missouri, where they arrived in 1838 and at once joined in the work of building the town of Hermann.

George was a delicate child—"sickly and puny," he said[3]—and though

FIGURE 7. George Husmann, c. 1875, in his late 1840s, after the failure of his work at Hermann and before its renewal at the University of Missouri. Courtesy Gail Unzelman Collection.

he grew to live a strenuous and hardworking life, he remained a small man (5' 5"). He had no formal education beyond what he had received in German schools, but he lived in the family atmosphere of respect for education and active self-improvement; moreover, his older brother Fritz was an effective tutor. Young George developed a love of reading and showed that he could carry on his own education. He also showed a spirit of indomitable optimism and resilience. The losses, the disappointments, the family bereavements that he suffered in the course of his life were heaped up in overflowing measure. His mother died of "brain fever" in 1840, not long after the family's arrival in Missouri; his older sister, in Philadelphia, died in the same year; in 1845 his admired brother Fritz died of typhoid, and two years later his father died in ghastly fashion, crushed to death in the machinery of the mill that he operated in Hermann. In 1851 his brother-in-law died in Hermann, leaving two small children to the care of Husmann; three years later their mother, Husmann's sister, died of cholera. His partner in the Hermann nursery was killed by bushwhackers during the brutal conflicts that tormented Missouri during the Civil War. Husmann himself had ten children, four of whom died before adulthood, one of them, eight-year-old Charlie, was shot and killed by an older boy playing with a pistol. The wine business that he started with high hopes after the Civil War failed, as did the magazine that he founded; the nursery he operated never thrived; one of his homes was struck by lightning and burned; and his animating vision of wine grown on every American farm never came remotely close to realization.

Yet despite these manifold afflictions and disappointments, he never lost an eager hopefulness that refused to despair. The last word in the last book he published breathes the same spirit with which he began his work as grape grower and winemaker forty years before: "What should hinder us from becoming the greatest grape growing nation on earth?... I hope that the sun of 1900 may rise on the most prosperous wineland the world ever saw, on the most prosperous, happy and sober commonwealth on the shores of the Pacific, the Golden State of California, richer in her golden wine and fruits than its mines ever made it."[4] After all those vicissitude-filled years, how could Husmann continue to write in this way? And what had he done to bring about the end so ardently desired? I don't think there is an answer to the first question: why are enthusiasts enthusiasts? Does anyone know? But the second question can be answered in some detail.

WINE AT HERMANN

Wine growing was seen as one of the possibilities for Hermann from a very early time in the history of the town, particularly since Longworth's work with the Catawba at Cincinnati had caught the attention of the Missouri Germans.[5] What Longworth was doing on the banks of the Ohio might well be done on the banks of the Missouri too. The town offered lots on a credit basis to be devoted to grape growing; six hundred such lots—a total of one hundred acres—were subscribed for, and so the basis for commercial production was laid, with vines largely obtained from Longworth.[6] A first small harvest was gathered in 1845. And then the whole community of Missouri Germans seems to have joined in boosting the work. A prize was offered for the best Missouri wine, to be judged in Saint Louis in 1847; the winner was a Catawba from Hermann, and the town celebrated the event with a party at the vineyard of the victor, Herr Riefenstahl. In the next year, 1847, Michael Poeschel built a winery at Hermann, and in the next year, 1848, the town celebrated its first wine festival, assisted by boatloads of ladies and gentlemen who had come up from Saint Louis to enjoy the fun. By this time the vintage had grown to ten thousand gallons.

There were problems amid the rising prosperity. The wine making, mostly carried on by small proprietors without experience and without the means to provide good equipment, was of a highly uneven quality. The Cincinnati people, who could sell more wine than they could grow, visited Hermann in 1852 with an eye to buying wine but did not like what they found; instead, they bought fresh juice from the Hermann growers, to be shipped to Cincinnati, where they would make it into wine themselves.[7] And, like the Cincinnati Germans, the Germans of Hermann found that the Catawba grape was a dangerous reliance: disease began to show up almost at once in the newly planted Hermann vineyards, and production varied wildly from year to year according to whether the ravages of black rot and other diseases were greater or less.

As Longworth was doing in Cincinnati, the Hermannites too made trial of many different native varieties. The Hermannites found what they wanted in a variety that, curiously enough, Longworth had rejected. This was the blue grape called the Norton or Norton's Seedling, an aestivalis-vinifera hybrid propagated by Dr. D. N. Norton of Richmond, Virginia.[8] It yielded a dark, astringent wine, only moderately foxy, and it did not have the same susceptibility to disease that plagued the Catawba. For some reason, Nicholas Longworth, who had tried it, had found it wanting.[9] The growers at Hermann, though intimidated by Longworth's judgment, nevertheless gave the Norton a fair trial and gratefully noted its freedom from disease. It had been planted in Hermann as early as 1843 by the strangely named Hans Widersprecher (Jack Contradictor) but had not been especially attended to.[10] But after the weakness of the Catawba was revealed, the Norton quickly became, and remained, the signature grape of Hermann. Jacob Rommel is credited with the first Norton wine at Hermann in 1848. Husmann wrote that the Norton was especially adapted to Missouri and, in diplomatic deference to Longworth's judgment, suggested that it was perhaps not suited to Ohio, where it did not do so well. "And why should it?" he could not help adding, in Husmannesque fashion: "They drove it from them and discarded it in its youth: we fostered it, and do you not think, dear reader, there sometimes is gratitude in plants as well as in men?"[11]

The Norton was by no means the only grape for Hermann; the Concord arrived in 1856, only two years after its introduction in Massachusetts by Ephraim Bull, and soon became an important part of the Hermann vineyards ("hundreds of acres," according to Husmann).[12] The Hermannites also grew such old-line varieties as the Isabella and Lenoir, as well as Dufour's Cape grape; nor did the Catawba wholly disappear. By the time of the Civil War, there were some thirty-five different varieties growing around Hermann.[13]

The first winery in Hermann was built by Michael Poeschel, and so was the first large-scale winery, which went up in 1861; this, as the Stone Hill

Winery, grew to be the largest of Missouri wineries and operated successfully down to Prohibition. So did a number of other, smaller wineries, solidly identifying Hermann with wine growing throughout the nineteenth century and after: Rommel, Langendoerfer, Grein, Heinze, Sohns, Voigt, Loehnig—such were the names in the trade. The high point was reached in the first years following the Civil War; after that, competition, especially from California, had a discouraging effect, and the trade was much diminished. Still, it persisted.

GEORGE HUSMANN'S ROLE

George Husmann joined the infant Hermann wine industry in 1847, when he planted on the family farm some cuttings of Catawba and Isabella vines obtained from Cincinnati. This was an inconclusive beginning, however, for later in the year, after the death of his father, he left the farm and took up residence with his brother-in-law Charles Teubner, who had begun a nursery specializing in fruit trees and vines (also from Cincinnati) on the river just east (downriver) of Hermann. Teubner had a vineyard of three acres already planted there. And there Husmann, as an apprentice to his brother-in-law, developed that special interest in grapes that marked him for life, or, to use his own terms, here he "imbibed the love for all choice fruits, but especially for the noble grape, the finest of all, which has clung to me during good and bad fortune all my life."[14] Teubner built a wine cellar on his property in 1848, and that is probably where Husmann began his apprenticeship in actual wine making.

His love of the noble grape did not, however, keep him from joining the California gold rush in 1850. Husmann was then only twenty-three, and unmarried; he had lost both parents and had nothing in particular to hold him in Hermann when such exciting things were happening on the remote West Coast. It was perhaps as much for the adventure of the thing as for any hopes of striking a bonanza that Husmann went west. In any case, like most other gold seekers, he found little gold, though perhaps he found adventure enough. When his brother-in-law Teubner died in September 1851, George was summoned back to Hermann by his widowed sister to manage her husband's nursery and to take on the wardship of her two small children. Probably he was not sorry to return, having had his adventure.[15]

In the course of the decade of the 1850s, the nursery at Hermann grew and prospered under Husmann's management. He also continued to apply himself to the study of "the noble grape," and he began what would be a long career of publication devoted to propagandizing for the vine. His first essay appeared in 1857, in German (one must remember that Husmann's first language was also the daily language of Hermann, as it was the language of its schools, its theater, and its weekly newspaper): "Weinbau in Amerika. Im Speziellen: Die Cultur [sic] der Rebe in Missouri" (Winegrowing in America, especially the Culture of the Vine in Missouri) published in Allentown, Pennsylvania, in 1857.[16] This little treatise is mostly about grape growing, with special reference to the varieties recommended for planting: Catawba, Lenoir, Norton, Missouri Bird's Eye, North Carolina. It is also clear from this essay that he had already been making wine on his own, though probably only on a modest scale.

As his nursery flourished, Husmann was able to buy property to the east of Hermann on a high bluff overlooking the Missouri River, where he planned to develop a substantial vineyard and winery. He had begun planting there before the Civil War put a temporary stop to the work. Husmann volunteered for military duty along with many other patriotic Hermannites in October 1861—the town, as was true of the German-American communities generally, had always been fiercely antislavery in its political principles. Husmann did not have an exciting military career but was merely one of the thousands who served obscurely. He was made quartermaster of the Fourth Regiment of Missouri Volunteers, a unit that spent its entire period of service guarding the bridges across the Missouri against Confederate attacks that did not materialize. This was dull enough, but it was necessary to do it.

Husmann returned to civilian life in February 1863 and resumed work on his vineyard property, which he had left in the care of a tenant, August Loehnig. A house, winery, and cellar were built and wine was produced with Loehnig as the tenant farmer, an arrangement whose success no doubt encouraged Husmann in his next, and most ambitious, scheme, the formation of the Bluffton Wine Company, to be discussed in a moment.

"Weinbau in Amerika," in 1857, had been followed in the same year by Husmann's first publication in English, "On the Cultivation of the Grape in Missouri," a prize essay that appeared in a Saint Louis journal called the *Valley Farmer*. Husmann continued to work this field in his first (very short) book in English, *An Essay on the Culture of the Grape in the Great West,* published in Hermann in 1863 by Husmann's brother-in-law C. W. Kielmann (Husmann had married Louisa Kielmann in 1854). More ambitious was *The Cultivation of the Native Grape and the Manufacture of American Wines,* published in New York in 1866. This, Husmann's first substantial book and the first to have a metropolitan rather than a provincial publisher, is written in a kind of euphoric excitement that combines the spirit of victory in the Civil War with a vision of wine growing spread all over the nation. Every one who plants a vine, he wrote in Whitmanesque exaltation, is a "laborer in the great work to cover this glorious land of the free with smiling vineyards, and to make its barren spots flow with noble grape juice, one of the best gifts from an all-bountiful Creator. All hail to you, I greet you from *Free* Missouri."[17] Husmann reports that 2 million vines had been sold from Hermann in 1865, and that everywhere in the country "vineyards spring up as if by magic, even on the prairies." This was the era of the grape boom in America, or, as Husmann put it, "the nation is affected with grape fever." Husmann thought that the country now had 2 million acres of vines planted—a fantastic exaggeration, but clear evidence of the excitement he felt.

The democratic spirit of the book appears in Husmann's wish to show that grape growing and wine making are things that poor men may do; accordingly he is at pains in the instruction that he gives to avoid costly measures. And after the excitement of the book's opening statements, Husmann settles down to the task of writing a careful how-to book: on propagating, on vine training, on the choice of variety, and so on.

His treatment of wine making is marked by his enthusiasm for the methods of Dr. Ludwig Gall, of Trier, Germany, who taught winemakers in the northern districts of the world that they could overcome the deficiencies of unripe grapes by adding water to reduce acidity and sugar to raise the potential alcohol. Since both water and sugar are natural components of the grape, these additions are in no way adulterations but only enhancements of otherwise deficient material, or so Gall's defenders argued. Husmann enthusiastically agreed. What would you rather have, he asked: a "natural" wine that was simply undrinkable, or an "artificial" wine that was at least tolerable? As for himself, he had no doubts in the matter and cheerfully "gallized" when the harvest conditions called for the process. "Gallizing" differs from the method called chaptalization (a legal practice in some places). Chaptalization is the addition of sugar to the must to raise the potential alcohol content; gallizing, by adding large quantities of water as well as of sugar, greatly increases the yield of a given quantity of grapes. It is therefore inevitably seen as cheating—unless one thinks as Husmann did. He boasted that he was getting by this method twenty-five hundred gallons of wine from an acre of Concord grapes![18] That would be the yield, according to conventional measures, of

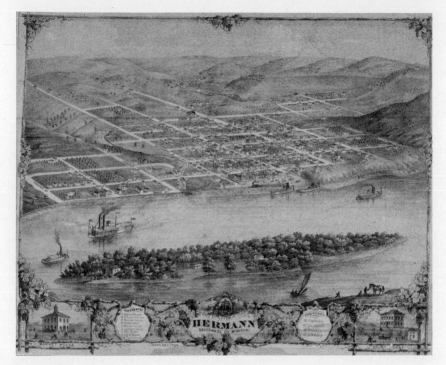

FIGURE 8. A view of Hermann, Missouri, in 1869, the year in which Husmann's Bluffton enterprise opened for business. It lay on the left bank of the river, shown at the bottom of the print, across from the town of Hermann. Courtesy Gail Unzelman Collection.

about sixteen and a half tons of grapes—from one acre! In a Midwestern vineyard!

Another of Husmann's favorite themes was the formation of "grape colonies," by which he meant a cooperative arrangement through which poor men might combine to provide the means of wine making in common. By joining together, they could assist each other in the work of cultivation and could build a wine-making facility that, separately, none could afford. Husmann had seen the small-scale wine making that went on in and around Hermann and thus knew the defects that went with it.

But when he undertook a large-scale wine-making scheme of his own in the same year that saw the publication of *The Cultivation of the Native Grape*, he did not follow the "grape colony" idea. Instead he seems to have found his model in Nicholas Longworth's combination of tenant farming with a big, efficient wine house where the contributions of many small growers could be converted into wine by good methods and good equipment directed by trained experts. The Bluffton Wine Company was formed in 1866, at the height of the grape boom, largely through the efforts of Husmann, who was the president of the company. The company proposed to settle tenants on a large tract of land—sixteen hundred acres—that it bought on the Missouri River on the bank opposite Hermann, and where it laid out the town of Bluffton. In order to get properly started, the company built propagating houses capable of turning out three hundred thousand vines a year.[19] The tenants, who had ten-year leases on houses and property, would grow grapes, and the grapes would be sold to the Bluffton Wine Company to be made into wine. Samuel Miller, a well-known horticulturist and grape breeder from Pennsylvania, was brought in to manage the vineyards, and when, in 1869, the company cellars were completed and ready for production, George Husmann moved across the river, from Hermann to Bluffton. The party held to inaugurate the cellars attracted a large crowd, and the exuberant officers of the company were able to announce that they had received an order for forty cases of their Missouri wine from President Grant himself.

INTERREGNUM

Within two years of that festive moment, the Bluffton Wine Company was bankrupt. Disease had smitten the vineyards; a collapse of prices had ruined the wine trade, and, though this was never said, the wines were not much good. Husmann himself offered the rather obscure explanation that his cellar master had sent out wines too young to southern markets; they became cloudy, were returned to the shipper, and ruined the trade.[20] What was all too clear was the fact that, after all the expansiveness, and all the rhetoric about the certain success of wine growing, the sober truth was that wine was *not* an economic possibility for most of the country. The certainty of disease, and the uncertainty of the market, made a lethal combination.

Husmann, who had lost heavily in the wreck,[21] withdrew from Hermann to Sedalia, in west-central Missouri, where he set up a nursery in combination with a florist and grocery shop. But before we follow him there, a word must be said about one of Husmann's most interesting undertakings, the journal called the *Grape Culturist*. This was a monthly magazine entirely devoted to the subjects dearest to Husmann's heart, the cultivation of the native vine and the production of native wines. Husmann, who took much the most active part in the work, originally shared the editorship with Dr.

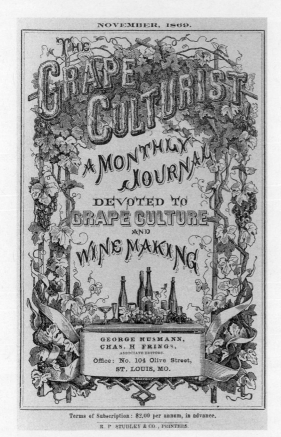

FIGURE 9. The cover of George Husmann's *Grape Culturist,* the first journal devoted to viticulture and wine making in this country. The editors' enthusiasm could not overcome the fact that it was ahead of its time. Courtesy Gail Unzelman Collection.

C. W. Spalding, the Saint Louis physician associated with him in the Bluffton Wine Company; the publisher was Conrad Witter of Saint Louis, a firm that kept a stock of books on grapes and wines, and which published Friedrich Muench's *School for American Grape Culture* in 1865.

A single issue of the *Grape Culturist* from 1871 gives an idea of the character and content of the magazine. There is an article on the use of the saccharometer in wine making, and another (reprinted from a German-language paper in New York) on the wines of California. Husmann could not resist adding a jealous note of regional pride to the article's praise of California's wines: they are not, he says, as healthful as the high-acid wines of the Mississippi Valley. There are reports on the prospects of the vintage from various places, and correspondence from Georgia, Missouri, Indiana, Illinois, Kansas, Iowa, Texas, and New York. And there are advertisements from several nurseries offering vines and from wine-making supply houses.

All of this suggests how widespread and lively the national interest in grapes and wines was, but the *Grape Culturist,* like so many first ventures, was premature. The magazine expired before its third volume was complete, and files of it are now rare.[22] Husmann had no doubt overestimated the extent and intensity of interest, measuring things by his own invincible enthusiasm rather than by a sober view of the actual market among the farmers of the upper Mississippi.

In his Sedalia nursery Husmann did not concentrate on vines but spread himself as widely as possible, offering every sort of ornamental plant and fruit tree and advertising his services as a landscape gardener. But luck was against him here too. The six years in Sedalia were, he wrote, "nothing but a series of struggles against adverse circumstances."[23] His daughter Louise fell gravely ill; Husmann himself came down with typhoid and was put out of action for months; hail destroyed his greenhouses; and then his house burned down.

Vines turned out to be the one prosperous part of the business. This was the period of greatest devastation to European vineyards by phylloxera, the plant louse native to North America that had been set loose in Europe in the 1860s and was now wreaking havoc in the vineyards of France, Germany, Spain, and Italy. The European vine was utterly unable to resist the fatal root damage inflicted by the insect, and by the 1870s the future of wine growing there seemed to be in serious doubt. The French government offered a large prize for a successful remedy, dozens and scores of which were fruitlessly applied: some were plausible, some were fantastic, but all of them were ineffective. Finally, the observation that certain native American vines were resistant to phylloxera suggested the remedy: grafting the tender European vine to a tough American rootstock. But which rootstocks? And where would one find the millions upon millions needed for the vast work of replanting a continent's vineyards?

Here Missouri stood out as a most hopeful resource. It had both an abundance of vines, and, in the Germans who had taken up viticulture, it had a set of experts. Husmann, after all his misfortunes, now stood to profit from the misfortune of others. Through the intermediation of C. V. Riley, the state entomologist of Missouri who was in touch with the French researchers, Husmann in Sedalia, Herman Jaeger in Neosho, and Isidor Bush at Bushberg received orders for large quantities of native American rootstocks.[24]

Husmann had always been active in professional and public affairs. He helped to found the Horticultural Society of Missouri; he was a founding member of the Missouri State Board of Agriculture; he was a delegate to the

Missouri State Constitutional Convention in 1865 and in that capacity drew up the provision abolishing slavery in Missouri; and he served as one of the governors of the state university. When the agricultural college of the university created a new professorship of pomology and forestry in 1878, it was offered to Husmann, who, though in one view merely an obscure nurseryman without formal education, was also a man of considerable distinction who had established himself as an expert in his chosen field. Husmann modestly declined the offer at first, on the grounds of his lack of qualifications. But the authorities wanted, they said, a practical man, and so Husmann accepted the offer, sold his nursery, and transferred his activity to the university in Columbia. Here he produced his second substantial book, *American Grape Growing and Wine Making,* in 1880. This has had the longest life of all his books. It reached a fourth edition in 1896 and was kept in print down to 1928.

The book makes an interesting contrast with the unchecked enthusiasm of the earlier *Cultivation of the Native Grape.* Husmann's tone is now tempered and subdued. The prospect in 1866 had been boundless; but after the setbacks of the 1870s—the collapse of prices and the onslaught of diseases—it was difficult to maintain confidence. Husmann admits that, for a time, "it seemed almost as if grape growing had become a failure." He could still, however, offer a diminished promise: "If our hopes are no longer so sanguine as before, we think we see our way clear to a sure, if moderate, success." His book, he says, in a soberly chastened mood, will instruct the reader in "what I have learned by bitter experience." And then the old vision suddenly surges up again: "America," he declares, "is yet to be the Vineland of the future." The destruction of the European vineyards by phylloxera might mean that the native vine of America would be the future of the world's wine: "The day may not be so far distant, when the despised grape of North America will become the only hope of the failing grape-growers of all nations."[25] Husmann could not maintain his chastened mood for very long; there was too much to be done, the promise was too alluring, to allow for moping about. Toward the end of the book he has worked himself up to the conviction not merely that native American vines are worthy but also that wine from the Norton, the Neosho, and other aestivalis varieties will excel *all* the world's wines, so "the sooner we turn our attention to them the better."[26] He was wrong, of course, but he did not know that then, and the idea clearly delighted him.

As for his wine-making instructions, Husmann is unrepentant about his liking for Dr. Gall's method, though, as he says, he had been "severely censured" for it.[27] It is interesting to find Husmann in 1880 still taking a doubtful view of California. He thinks that the wine of California is too low in acid and bouquet—and besides, phylloxera, which had become a serious problem in the state from the early 1870s, will, he says, probably annihilate the vineyards if the Californians, who have been reluctant to admit that they are in difficulties, do not take radical action, and soon.

CALIFORNIA

Despite this prophecy—or perhaps because of it—Husmann himself went to California in the next year. He paid a visit to the state in the summer of 1881, where he was already well known. Among his customers for resistant root-stock were a number of the leading wine men of the state, including H. W. Crabb of the To Kalon Vineyard; Charles Kohler, of the firm of wine merchants and growers Kohler and Frohling; Julius Dresel of Sonoma; and Jacob Schram, of the Schramsberg Winery on the slopes of Diamond Mountain. Was he planning a move to California then? It seems possible. The phylloxera invasion was now recognized as a genuine crisis: California's Board of State Viticultural Commissioners and a viticulture department at the university had just been created by act of the state legislature to cope with the problem, but that work had only begun. It was a time for experts in California, and Husmann had an unrivalled knowledge of native American vines.

Husmann became as enthusiastic a Californian as he had been a Midwesterner before. Starting in Los Angeles, he was soon in Napa County. There he met James Simonton, a newspaper proprietor and the manager of the Associated Press, who had just bought a large property in the Carneros, the far southern reaches of Napa and Sonoma counties along the shores of San Pablo Bay. This was just at the beginning of the planting boom that swept California in response to the phylloxera plague in Europe, and Simonton wanted to plant vines at his new place, which he called the Talcoa Ranch. He was thus in want of an expert to supervise the work, and who better than Husmann? So, in September of 1881, Husmann said farewell to the native-vine wine making that he had encouraged in season and out for all of his working life; he would now be part of the vinifera world of California. But of course it was his knowledge of the native vine that took him to California, so that the move was not so much an abandonment as it was a merger of interests.

Husmann had charge of both the wine making and the grape growing at Talcoa. The Napa region had an extensive and sophisticated experience in wine making by the time Husmann arrived there, but this in no way intimidated a man who had had no experience in making wine from vinifera but who knew the elements of wine making and—more important— knew his own mind in perfect confidence. A year and a half after his arrival, he was bold enough to write an essay for the *Transactions* of the California State Agricultural Society, "Wine Making in Napa Valley." As he modestly allowed, he had been in Napa for only a short time and had made only two vintages: but they were very successful vintages, and, since they "brought the highest price in the market, perhaps it may be interesting to the public to hear how I make wine."[28] And how did he make wine? There was, of course, no need for gallizing now; one always had ripe grapes in California. He had no secrets, but followed proven procedures. Husmann had no interest in fortified wines: light wines—"hocks, sauternes, and clarets"—were what the soil and climate of Napa and Sonoma were fitted for.

The great question in California in Husmann's time was the choice of resistant rootstock. Growers had gradually been persuaded by painful experience and by the arguments of the experts that grafting vinifera to native rootstocks was the only salvation of their vineyards, that all other remedies against the phylloxera were futile. But grafting to what? Dean Eugene Hilgard of the university was certain that the species of choice was the native *V. californica,* and Husmann concurred—Husmann was a loyal supporter of Hilgard in this and in other matters, perhaps influenced by the fact that Hilgard, like Husmann himself, came from one of the settlements of Lateinische Bauern around Saint Louis. Hilgard, who argued that a native species must naturally be resistant to phylloxera, turned out to be wrong: he grafted his own vineyard at Mission San Jose to *V. californica* and had the mortification of seeing the vines die.

But all that took time, and in the meantime there was ample scope for argument and counterargument repeated and compounded. Husmann himself was a persistent and cranky opponent of the view taken by Arthur Hayne of the University of California, that the French experience with resistant rootstocks should be a guide for California. That experience pointed to the rootstock called rupestris Saint George; Husmann, on the other hand, championed riparia stocks and insisted that local experience was far better than anything imported from France. Husmann put forth his ideas rudely and loudly in the agricultural press; beginning in 1895, as Charles Sullivan has written, "the old Professor now set out on a three-year letter-writing campaign, denigrating Haynes's ideas and rejecting the French approach."[29] In the end, however, after all his stubborn resistance, Husmann sided with the majority opinion in favor of the rupestris Saint George as the rootstock best suited to California conditions.[30] It is still one of the available choices.

Husmann carried on work with varietal testing at the Talcoa Ranch, regularly wrote for the press about the choice of varieties, and propagated resistant vines for sale to California growers.[31] It was not long before he set up as a winegrower on his own. In 1884 he bought the Peterson Ranch in the Chiles Valley, over the front range of hills to the east of the main Napa Valley. There was already a small vineyard on the property, and here, working with his sons George and Fred, he began the construction of a winery called Oak Glen. Husmann remained at Talcoa until 1886, when his contract expired (Simonton himself had died in 1882), after which he moved to the city of Napa. How much he had to do with the daily operation of Oak Glen Winery is not clear, but most of the work seems to have been done by his sons. The winery was in fact sometimes known as "Husmann Brothers." It was never more than a small operation: the winery, finished in 1890, had a capacity of only twenty-four thousand gallons.

Though Husmann was now in semiretirement, he remained busy, as he had always done. He had written in 1880 that "mine has been an incessantly busy life, and the time for these scribblings [his *American Grape Growing and Wine Making*] has been stolen mostly from the 'small, still hours.' I know of no holidays, and have often had to force exhausted nature to the task."[32] Things were not much different now. He was appointed state statistical agent for the USDA in 1886. He acted for the department in gathering California wines for display at the Paris Exposition of 1889, a thankless job: "I was treated more like a beggar asking alms," he complained, "than the agent of a Department."[33]

He continued to write busily: for a number of years he wrote regular columns for the *California Fruit Grower, American Wine Press,* and *Pacific Wine and Spirit Review,* and his letters to the editor on all the issues of the wine trade peppered the newspapers of the state. In these he often took on dissidents, those who rejected his emphatic views, in a distinctly pugnacious style: Husmann was a good fighter as well as a congenital optimist. He had to be, given the journalistic style that then prevailed. The editor of the *San Francisco Merchant,* for example, reviewing Husmann's *American Grape Growing and Wine Making,* found that Husmann was "the same inaccurate, spiteful, half-educated writer on these subjects which he was three years ago. His is a bad case of blighted development or congenital narrow-mindedness."[34] No tender-skinned spirit would survive long against invective like that.

Husmann also had to take on many doubters about the resistance of native vines, and he and Charles Wetmore, the combative head of the Board of State Viticultural Commissioners, sometimes clashed, largely owing to their common impetuosity. Husmann's main theme, through all the troubles of the industry, was the need for quality, first, last, and always. California, he thought, disgraced itself by sending "milk-sour trash" to the market when it might be making excellent wines. There would be no difficulty in selling wine at a fair price if it were good wine. "Our motto should be 'Excelsior,' and we can reach it, if we earnestly try."[35]

In 1888, only six years after he had arrived in the state, he published his book on the California scene. *Grape Culture and Wine-Making in California,* Husmann's final book, has all the qualities of his earlier books in full measure. The late 1880s were desperately bad times for the California wine trade. Overproduction, slovenly wine making, cutthroat competition—to say nothing of the phylloxera devastation—had brought commercial disaster. In 1886, wine was selling at six to eight cents a gallon, and hundreds of wineries closed; grapes did not pay the cost of their picking, and so hogs were turned into the vineyards to eat the crop. Such depressed conditions continued into the decade of the 1890s and were particularly hard on the small winemaker, who did not have the resources to ride out a period of low prices. Yet it was just the small, struggling winemaker that Husmann hoped to encourage and instruct by his book. In the midst of this gloomy situation, he addressed his fellow winemakers in this fashion: "Nature has designed this to be *the* great Vineland, the France of the new Continent, where every one can 'sit under his own vine and fig tree.' Be ours the happy task to work out this problem and prove worthy of it, profiting by the errors of the past, with hopes that never flag, of its happy ultimate accomplishment."[36]

By the end of Husmann's life, in 1902, the California wine trade had recovered, and no one yet imagined the possibility of national prohibition, which would shut it down in 1920. Husmann could thus take comfort in thinking that his work had contributed to an ongoing enterprise, and that his vision of America as the greatest wine-growing country of the world, if far from fulfillment, was nevertheless perfectly possible.

Not much remains in a material way of Husmann's various undertakings, though his books are still looked at by historians of the subject. The Bluffton winery has disappeared, as has the Oak Glen Winery. But there has been a renewal of interest in Husmann and in what he stood for. Wine making in Missouri dwindled almost to the vanishing point after Prohibition, and with it the memory of such pioneers as Husmann; but it has now made a vigorous comeback, and the current generation is very much aware of Husmann and his work. And, he would be pleased to know, the Norton is still the signature grape of Missouri wine making.

FOUR

Charles Kohler

PUTTING CALIFORNIA WINES ON THE MAP

THE FATHER OF THE CALIFORNIA WINE INDUSTRY

The old town of Sonoma is dominated by its spacious plaza, laid out when the town was founded in 1835 and now a state historical monument. In the northwest section of the plaza, on June 15, 1946, Joseph Knowland, the publisher of the *Oakland Tribune,* and the officers of the Sonoma County Wine Growers' Association met to dedicate a bronze plaque to a pioneer wine grower of Sonoma County, the Hungarian Agoston Haraszthy (1812–1869). Variously styled Count or Colonel (though he was neither) Haraszthy, the man was, the plaque declared, the "Father of California Viticulture"; the plaque, sponsored by the California State Chamber of Commerce, and participating in the dignity of the plaza, is still there, and its bronze assertion has become a received truth.

The claim is false, but such things by mere force of repetition can take on a weight that makes them hard to dislodge. There is, of course, no single "father" of the California wine industry (which "viticulture" would include), any more than there is a unique "father" of the automobile or the airplane or the computer. There are, rather, miscellaneous lots of pioneers, all of whom made their separate, essential contributions, without which no creation would have taken place. Many of these humble builders of California's wine industry long antedated Haraszthy: the priests of the Spanish missions, for example, who established wine growing in most of their settlements thirty years before Haraszthy was born; or the various Mexican, French, and Yankee settlers in early Los Angeles who made that town a city of vines and wine thirty years before Haraszthy ventured into the Golden State; or the nurserymen of the Santa Clara Valley district who were selling many varieties of the European vine before Haraszthy bought property in the Bay Area. If one wants to establish the mere fact of priority, then that distinction belongs to Don José Camacho, commander of the ship *San Antonio,* which, it has been plausibly argued, must have brought the first vinifera vines to California in 1778. Camacho may thus claim to have been the true Bacchus of California, though he remains unknown.[1]

But who first put California wine on the map? And did so in a lasting way? To those who have studied the question, the answer seems to be a German immigrant named Charles Kohler, whose life story is characterized by many of the elements that mark the history of wine in America. In the first place, he was a German, and Germans have had more to do with bringing about the culture of wine in this country than any other nationality. In the second place, he did not come from a wine-growing region; neither did the Germans who founded wine growing in Missouri, nor did such German pioneers of California wine as Charles Krug, Jacob Gundlach, and Isador Landsberger. And in the third place, he knew nothing about wine when he decided to become a winemaker and a wine merchant; the same might be said of many of the American wine pioneers.

MUSICIAN TO WINEMAKER

Charles Kohler (1830–87) was a musician—a violinist—by training. He was born in the town of Grabow, in what was then Mecklenburg, in the flatlands of northern Germany, far from any of the German vineyards. In 1848 he immigrated to the United States, settling first in New York, where he played in the orchestra of the Italian Opera Company and with Dodworth's Brass Band (he must have had skill on some instrument besides the violin).[2] After a couple of years there, he moved on to San Francisco, where he was soon prominent among the German musicians of the city, who were then, against heavy odds, attempting to charm the miners and merchants of the city into an appreciation of classical music. San Francisco had a precocious musical life. The first opera there—Bellini's *La sonnambula*—was performed as early as 1851. The pianist Henri Herz arrived even earlier, in 1850, as did Rudolph Herold, who founded the Germania Musical Society. It may well have been the activity of such German musicians in San Francisco that lured Kohler to that city, to say nothing of the high wages being paid in gold rush days.

There was plenty for Kohler to do. He began by helping to form the

Verandah Concert Society in 1853, a group that grew (in 1855) into the more impressive Germania Concert Society, whose stated aim was "to educate the people, to soften their manners and wean their minds from low sensual pleasures"[3]—a noble aim in that raw, bawdy place. Kohler was not only a performer in this group's weekly concerts but also its leader, and so he was instrumental in bringing Haydn, Mozart, and Beethoven to the Pacific Coast. But his activity was not confined to the Germania or to the violin. He also founded and directed the Union Brass Band, and in 1856 he was the leader of the Amateur Musical Club. We also hear of Kohler as a member of the notorious San Francisco Vigilance Committee, a self-appointed body formed to put down the violent crime that troubled the young city.[4] Whether Kohler participated in the acts of summary justice carried out by the committee we don't know. Later he would show his public spirit in a more decent and lawful fashion. He was, among many other things, a founder of the German Savings Bank, a trustee of the public library, and a member of the board of education. By the end of his not very long life he stood high among the solid and respectable citizens of San Francisco; and when his obituary came to be written, he was described in tones of the highest respect and admiration for his personal qualities as well as for his business achievements.

Even before the Germania Society was founded, Kohler's life had taken a turn that would lead it entirely away from music. Among Kohler's colleagues and friends in the community of German musicians were John Fröhling, a flutist, and John Beutler, a tenor. These three were in the habit, so the story goes, of amusing themselves by walking to the cliffs above the Pacific where later the Cliff House was built, to enjoy the fresh air, the antics of the seals at Seal Rocks, and an alfresco lunch. On one of these days, in September 1853, Kohler produced a bunch of fresh grapes brought that morning by a steamer just come up the coast from Los Angeles. Seeing them, Beutler, who came from the wine-growing town of Baden, was moved to eloquent speech: "My native country," he said, "famed the world over for its vine-growing, never produced such a fine large cluster as that, where every grape is perfectly ripe, and none are rotten or blighted. The country which produces such fine grapes as those must eventually become a great wine-growing region. And I have an idea, boys. We will start a vineyard. We will build an altar to the God Bacchus, and make wine for the weary multitude. We will introduce wine making to this coast."[5] Beutler spoke half in jest, and was badly informed as well, since wine making had long been established in California, though the fact was evidently not well known in San Francisco. Beutler had, nevertheless, planted an idea that grew.

LOS ANGELES BEGINNINGS

By May 1854 they had matured their plans. Beutler was no longer with them, having left California owing to the illness of his wife. But he had perhaps told the other two, neither of whom had ever yet seen a vineyard, something of the routines of vineyard and winery as he had known them in Baden. The first step was to secure a base in Los Angeles. But why Los Angeles? readers may ask in some surprise. Why the land now known for freeways, smog, and showbiz but hardly for grapes and wine? It was all very different then. The California wine trade descends directly from the Franciscan missions established in a chain from San Diego in the south to Sonoma in the north between 1769 and 1823. All of the missions experimented with grapes and wine: some (San Francisco, for example) gave it up as unsuccessful, for the marine air defeated all attempts; others (San Miguel) persisted in a small way; and some developed a fairly substantial production. These latter tended to be in the southern part of the state and were led by Mission San Gabriel, a few miles northeast of the small pueblo of Los Angeles.

From the Mission San Gabriel's vineyards it was an easy step to Los Angeles; and well before the 1820s, small vineyards were scattered over the town to serve a small and not yet commercial wine-making effort. Gradually the scale of things grew; by the time of the American takeover in 1847 it was possible to speak of a wine-growing industry in and around Los Angeles. The contemporary idea about what California's best wine region was is neatly summed up in the *Alta California,* a San Francisco paper, for November 8, 1857: "Nearly all the wine and brandy made in California comes from Los Angeles county, which is no doubt better fitted, in soil and climate, for the culture of the vine than any other part of the state." When the gold rush drew thousands of newcomers to California, there was already a supply of grapes and wine in the south of the state ready to be shipped north. In 1854, then, when Kohler, Fröhling, and Beutler determined to become winegrowers, they naturally looked to the south, where the prospects had already been proven. It is true that there was already some pioneering wine growing in Northern California, especially in the foothills of the gold country and in Santa Clara County, south of the bay. But Napa had not yet been heard from, and Sonoma was only a little bit ahead of Napa. Los Angeles was the place.

John Fröhling accordingly traveled to Los Angeles to begin their venture. The town that he found was a dusty, unprepossessing straggle of low adobe buildings. There were at most around four thousand people there, a motley population of Mexicans, Indians, Yankees, Hawaiians, and adventurers from all over the world. The local amusements were cockfighting and horse racing, varied by the occasional lynching. There was, on average, a murder a day. The wine making, or some of it at least, was comparably primitive. In the established practice, one first drove four posts into the ground to form a square, and over these posts one fastened a raw cow-hide, hair-side down, the middle of the hide bagging down in the center of the square: "This bag is nearly filled with grapes; an Indian gets in, mashes the grapes with his feet by tramping about; the juice is then dipped out, poured into a barrel, left a few weeks to ferment and the wine is ready for use."[6]

Whatever Los Angeles lacked in amenities, it was abundantly supplied with vineyards. Fröhling needed only a little time to find one for sale and soon sent a short message to Kohler in San Francisco: "I have bought a vineyard. Send me down four thousand dollars."[7] The property in question was a twenty-acre tract belonging to one Cristobal Aguilar, of which 12 acres were planted in vines, located at what is now the intersection of Central Avenue and Seventh Street. Whether there was a winery on the property as well is not said, but Fröhling must have soon acquired the necessary equipment, for wine making began in the fall of 1854.[8] The business plan they now followed divided the work of Kohler and Fröhling into two parts: the care of the vineyards and the wine making were in the hands of Fröhling, who remained in Los Angeles; Kohler, in San Francisco, was responsible for selling what they made. This arrangement lasted until Fröhling's early death, in 1862.

Fröhling was born in 1827 in Arnsberg, Westphalia, a northern region just as wineless as Kohler's native Mecklenburg. Fröhling left Germany for America at the age of sixteen; in New York he worked in a dry goods store, learned English, and continued to practice the flute that he had been playing from an early age. He then moved westward, to Saint Louis, where he performed in a "small orchestra."[9] He arrived in San Francisco in 1853, in the same year that Kohler did, and the two men would have become acquainted at once though their common employment, first in the Verandah Concert Society and then in the Germania Concert Society. And in the same year, as we have seen, came the plan to become winemakers. Before his death Fröhling became one of the leading citizens of Los Angeles, as Kohler did of San Francisco. Fröhling married Amalie Hammes in 1859, and their residence at the winery property in Los Angeles became one of the attractions of the town, rhapsodically described by a visiting journalist from San Francisco as "a beautiful home" where one received "the genial, old fashioned hospitality of Los Angeles" and "the inimitable cuisine of our generous hosts."[10]

The vineyard that was to provide wine for the firm of Kohler and Frohling at its beginning was planted exclusively in vines of the grape variety known in California as the Mission.[11] So was every other Los Angeles vineyard, and, for some time, so was nearly every other vineyard anywhere in California. The Mission grape was for years a viticultural mystery. It is without question a true vinifera grape, that is, a variety belonging to the European grape species from which the world's wines, with few exceptions, are made.[12] But no one, until quite recently, found a grape growing in Europe to match the Mission. So where did it come from? In 2007 a team of scientists in Spain and Chile published the results of a genotypic analysis of many varieties cultivated in the New World, including the Mission. This showed that the Mission is in fact an ancient Spanish variety known as Listán Prieto, no longer cultivated in Spain but surviving on the Canary Islands.[13] The many stories invented to account for the origins of the Mission may now be disregarded.

The Mission was grown so widely in California that it ceased to be recognized as a European variety; it was called the "native" or the "California" grape, in distinction from "foreign" grapes that were recognized as coming from Europe, though all were equally foreign and equally vinifera. The qualities of the Mission as a wine grape are clear enough. It is easily grown and is an abundant bearer, virtues that assured its spread in California. But it makes a poor dry wine, weak in color and low in acid. The sweet wines from the Mission are better and can, in fact, be quite good.

For this reason, the wines that one hears of most often in early California wine making were apparently sweet and fortified with brandy, wines in the style of Port. Another favorite wine was the compound known as Angelica, a *mistelle* made from fresh, unfermented juice to which brandy is added.[14] But without sweetness, and without fortification, wine from the Mission is flat and dull. The defects of the Mission were well known by the time Kohler and Fröhling came on the scene, and it is said that they began at once to plant other, superior varieties.[15] Perhaps so, though no details are given; and they would have had to wait several years before such vines would yield any wine.

Wherever he learned them, Fröhling's wine making procedures were unexceptionable. No sweating Indians or raw cowhides here. In a lengthy description of Fröhling's wine-making crew at work in 1859, published in the local *Los Angeles Star,* we learn that the grapes were first destemmed and then fed through a mechanical crusher before being disinfected with sulfur and then (if they were making white wine) pressed. Perfect cleanliness was the rule at all stages of handling: "Every night all the presses and appliances used about [the grapes] are all washed thoroughly to prevent acidity. Everything that comes in contact with the grape juice from the time the grape is bruised till it reaches the cask is kept as pure as abundance of water and hard scrubbing can make it."[16]

WINE BY DAY, MUSIC BY NIGHT

Back in San Francisco, Charles Kohler began his work by renting premises at 102 Merchant Street, where he stored his original stock of five hundred gallons of wine. Where he found that wine, and where it might have been produced, are questions to which there is no answer. It could have come from Los Angeles, but it could not yet have been of Kohler and Frohling's manufacture. There was at the time in San Francisco no specialized wine house, nor any one dealing specifically in so-called native wines; they were of course available, but no one had yet thought to make them an exclusive stock in trade. By the time of Kohler's death, there were many large and prosperous houses in San Francisco dealing extensively in California wines, but they all followed in the wake of Kohler and Frohling's original success.

The first customers were largely found among the newly arrived Europeans in the city, particularly the French and the Germans, who knew wine and wanted it. At first Kohler might sell only a few bottles a day and be happy to deliver them, on foot, in a wicker basket. Soon his reputation for fair dealing and, presumably, the reliable character of the wine led to a steadily growing business. This was matched by the growing volume of wine coming from Fröhling's work in Los Angeles: the firm produced fifteen thousand gallons in 1856, sixty thousand in 1857, and one hundred thousand in 1858. By 1860 Fröhling had five hundred thousand gallons in storage in Los Angeles and had had to seek storage space wherever he could find it, including the basement of city hall.[17] Of course not all of this large production could come from their original twenty-acre property; Fröhling bought grapes from many vineyards in and around Los Angeles, but the wine making, whether carried out on Kohler and Frohling's own premises or at other wineries in the region, was always under the direct supervision of Fröhling himself. The firm also bought wine in bulk from other producers.[18] By 1859, in a development prophetic of the future, Kohler and Frohling was buying grapes and juice from vineyards in "Sonoma and other counties in the northern part of the State," as well as from those of the Los Angeles region.[19]

In an era when the fair and the industrial exposition were standard institutions for education, entertainment, and commercial promotion, Kohler and Frohling was notably successful in garnering prizes for their wares. In 1856, only two years after their beginning, they won a diploma for port from the United States Agricultural Society meeting in Philadelphia, and in the same year theirs was "the best wine from grapes grown in this State" at the California State Agricultural Fair. The next year they were awarded a diploma at the fair for "superior native wine," and, the year after, their port took a gold medal at the fair.[20] The list might be considerably extended; such distinctions are good evidence that, by the standards of the time, Kohler and Frohling was making a superior wine. They also show that the firm was eager to grasp every chance to distinguish its wines as quality products. It was necessary to show what they could do in California before they attempted to show back East what California could do.

Despite the accumulating signs of success, Charles Kohler still depended on his career as a musician to support himself in the early years of the company. He sold wine by day, but by night he was a violinist with the Germania, or the director of the Union Band, or the leader of the Amateur Musical Club of San Francisco. Not until 1858 did he give up work as a professional musician. Fröhling, too, continued to practice his art, though the opportunities in Los Angeles were hardly as rich as those in San Francisco. There is record of his performing publicly in San Francisco on his frequent business trips there.[21] Kohler and Fröhling together put on a "musical soiree" in Los Angeles in 1855 to benefit the local brass band.[22] And perhaps Fröhling played at the Harvest Home celebration that he put on for friends and fellow citizens of Los Angeles at the end of the vintage of 1860; this was held in the winery building, now called the Pioneer Winery, which was richly decorated for the feast and for the music and dancing that followed. Long after Fröhling's death, the decorations, dried out, dust-covered, and decaying, remained in place like the decorations for Miss Havisham's wedding feast in *Great Expectations*. Charles Kohler, faithful to the memory of his dead partner, refused to have them removed, just as he refused to alter the name of the firm, which always remained Kohler and Frohling.[23]

What were the kinds of wine Kohler and Frohling made in Los Angeles? And how good were they? The first question is the easier to answer. Given the absolute dominance of the Mission grape, there was no need to specify varieties: wine was Mission, whether red, white, or fortified. As has already been noted, Kohler and Frohling was said to have imported other varieties, but there is no evidence to identify any of them or any of the wines they might have contributed to. By 1858 Kohler and Frohling was offering a red and a white wine (presumably dry), port, Angelica, brandy, and something strangely called, without explanation, "Home Made."[24] In 1860 a "golden wine" and a "Constantia" were added to the list; one suspects that they were products of the Mission too, though there is some reason to think that Kohler and Frohling may have had varieties from Spain and Portugal by this time.[25] An advertisement by the firm in 1863 adds Hock and Muscat to the list. Dry red and white table wines are not conspicuous in the early days: port, Angelica, and brandy are more prominent, a state of affairs no doubt owing to the defects of the Mission grape and to the difficulty of keeping unfortified wines in sound condition in an era without refrigeration. The judges at the state fair in 1858 had encouraging words for the state's dry red wines, in which they noted "an improvement," and they gave the red wine of Kohler and Frohling a second place after General Vallejo's Sonoma red. But, significantly, at the same time, they emphasized the need for new and better varieties.[26]

Intelligible remarks on the quality and character of the wines are not easy to find. A reporter for the *Alta California,* San Francisco's daily paper, visited Kohler and Frohling's premises at 102 Montgomery Street in 1856. After sampling the wines, he was loud in praise of their "purity" but somewhat restrained in his assessment of their quality; "a few more years," he thought, would be required to improve them.[27] Kohler had, by the way, already set up a bar at 102 Montgomery Street to demonstrate the character of his wines: there, for the price of one bit—twelve and a half cents—one could have a glass of any wine in the company's cellar and so decide the question of quality for oneself. Another, indistinct, report about Kohler and Frohling's wines comes from New York in 1862. There, the Farmers' Club of the American Institute held a tasting of six wines produced in Los Angeles by Sainsevain Brothers and by Kohler and Frohling: this was felt to be a distinctly exotic occasion, California wines being a largely unknown quantity to the assembled tasters. They liked the Sainsevains' sparkling wine, and disliked the Angelica—"A bottle full of it contains I don't know how many headaches," one taster said. The maker of the port is not identified, but it was probably Kohler and Frohling. This wine was highly approved as "better than nine tenths of the imported ones" and "a real acquisition."[28]

HOME ON THE SANTA ANA

When their business had barely begun, Kohler and Fröhling had a bold idea that showed a remarkable confidence in their future. They were certain that they would soon require more wine to sell than they could produce themselves. So why not organize a wine-growing colony to help supply their needs? This idea, which was first discussed in 1855, was the foundation of the settlement that became Anaheim, now known as the home of Disneyland but originally a community of German immigrants wholly devoted to wine growing. San Francisco by then had a large German community, and the idea was circulated among these Germans as prospective investors and settlers in the planned community. Early in 1857 the plan was acted on. A Los Angeles Vineyard Society was organized,[29] with Kohler prominent in it; an agent was hired to purchase land and to supervise the layout of the new community. When finding a suitable property turned out to be difficult, Kohler went down to Los Angeles to help settle the choice; and when that choice was made, John Fröhling put up the money (to be repaid later) to secure a quick purchase of the land.[30] The property was a tract of some 1,165 acres of bare land lying near the Santa Ana River, from which irrigation water could be diverted. All this was accomplished by the end of 1857. Early in 1858 the members of the Vineyard Society, meeting in San Francisco, voted to name the new town "Annaheim," meaning "home on the Santa Ana River."[31]

The scheme of the Vineyard Society was simple and effective. There were fifty shares issued at fourteen hundred dollars each. Each shareholder would receive a twenty-acre tract, each tract containing eight acres of vineyard. While the land was being prepared and the vineyards planted, the shareholders could continue their work in San Francisco and so have the means to pay for their shares by installments. Not until everything was in readiness would they move down south to their new property.

The work was carried out in two years by a crew of Indians and Mexicans, who dug the irrigation channels, cleared the land, fenced it about with willow, alder, and sycamore (very necessary to keep out the wandering livestock and wild animals still abounding in Los Angeles County), and planted the vineyards with cuttings of Mission vines. The first shareholders arrived in September 1859, and the Anaheim venture was under way. Production leaped from a token two thousand gallons in 1859, the first year that any wine was made on the new property (and probably the grapes came from other sources around Los Angeles), to three hundred thousand gallons in 1864. Kohler and Frohling, as had been the plan from the outset, took much of the production, and the wine soon began to acquire a reputation.

The death from consumption of John Fröhling in 1862 put an end to the special relation between Anaheim and Kohler and Frohling, which, despite the good name of Anaheim wines, was probably finding other sources for its wines. The counties around San Francisco Bay were producing substantial quantities of grapes and wines by 1862 and enjoyed an obvious advantage over Los Angeles as suppliers to the San Francisco wine trade.[32] The winegrowers of Anaheim entered into competition with Kohler and Frohling in 1863 when they set up a depot in San Francisco for the Anaheim Wine Growers' Association. This was managed by Benjamin Dreyfus, who had a winery of his own in Anaheim and later opened an agency in New York for the sale of Anaheim wines. There was, so far as I know, no hostility between the Anaheim winemakers and Kohler and Frohling. Anaheim, to shorten a long story, enjoyed growing success for a generation after its founding; in 1884, the high point of its wine-making history, Anaheim produced 1,250,000 gallons of wine and 100,000 gallons of brandy, most of it still made by the original German settlers or by their heirs. Then disaster struck. The vines were observed to be diseased in an unidentifiable way: they were late in starting growth; the shoots, when they grew, grew irregularly and slowly; the leaves were discolored; the fruit withered. No one knew what it was; no one knew what to do. The Board of State Viticultural Commissioners sent experts, who were baffled; so were the men from the U.S. Department of Agriculture. By 1891 there were a mere fourteen acres of vines around Anaheim, and its wine making days were over. Growers turned to oranges and walnuts, and some of the German winemakers became brewers instead.

What was the "Anaheim disease"? We know now that it was Pierce's disease, named after the plant pathologist who studied it only after it had worked its devastation in Anaheim. The disease is thought to be native to the southeastern United States, where the native muscadine grape is the only species that appears to have any resistance to it.

Long thought to be caused by a virus, Pierce's disease is instead a bacterial infection, spread by a variety of vectors but especially by the insects known as sharpshooters. The infection blocks the water supply of the vine and so causes death. There is no known cure, and the only practical response is to pull the infected vines and, keeping one's fingers crossed, start over.

GOOD WINE FROM CALIFORNIA

In 1860 the U.S. Census reported that the American wine trade was still firmly centered upon Cincinnati and its satellite regions in Kentucky and Indiana. New York was just beginning to be heard from, and Missouri was making substantial quantities of wine at Hermann and a few other places along the Missouri River. But Ohio was then thought to lead all the states, with 568,000 gallons of wine.[33] California did not, according to official (and inaccurate) figures, make half that quantity. More to the point, its wines were effectively though not wholly unknown on the Atlantic Coast. California was still isolated from the rest of the country, separated from the settled regions by vast stretches of the Great American Desert and the Rockies, and connected only by the slow and difficult traffic of ships sailing round the Horn or by transshipment of goods and passengers across the Isthmus of Panama.

Despite the difficulties of shipment, the rapid growth of California's wine production from regions in both the north and south of the state made it clear to the winemakers that they would soon have to export or drown in their own wine.[34] There are reports from early times of shipments to all sorts of places. Kohler himself claimed to have shipped wine to New York, England, France, Germany, the Sandwich Islands, Australia, and China by 1856, but such shipments can only have been small, intermittent, and insignificant.[35] Any of the many ships leaving the port of San Francisco for points all over the globe might have carried a barrel or two of California wine, but this was not the basis of a regular trade. The first substantial shipment we know of was made by Kohler and Frohling and the Sainsevain Brothers jointly in 1860, when the *Alta California* for October 17, 1860, reported that the clipper ship *E. T. Willets* with a "number of pipes" of wine on board would soon sail from San Francisco bound for New York. More important, this was to be the beginning of regular shipment to New York; henceforth there would be a constant supply of California wine in the chief market of the United States. Don Pedro Sainsevain (as Pierre Sainsevain was known in California) was reported to be in New York seeking an agency for his wines; Kohler and Frohling already had one. This was the firm of Messrs. Perkins and Stern, of 180 Broadway, New York, who were in business to deal exclusively in California wines.[36] Richard Perkins and Charles Stern were licensed to open subagencies in all states as trade might dictate, and they held the rights to Europe as well, though Europe was hardly aware of that fact as yet.

Inevitably, there was skepticism about the wines from California when they reached the East Coast. One New York paper reported that the wine was invoiced at seventy-five cents a gallon and could not therefore be much good. When this remark reached California, it provoked an indignant reply from Charles Kohler. He had shipped fifty pipes of the 1857 vintage, which he knew to be pure and sound wine, for the wine of California was steadily increasing in quantity and quality: "The shipment of these wines [he wrote] is the commencement of a great wine-trade to be carried on between the Pacific and the Atlantic States, and those who have embarked in the enterprise are content to wait the issue. They believe that the wines of California will ere long supplant the imported wines, and find an extensive and remunerating market." And he closed this defiance with the assured statement that in this year his firm would produce "150,000 gallons of the finest wines in the world."[37] This was said in the same supremely confident style that Kohler had used as early as 1857, when he predicted that, despite all difficulties, "on the long run we will beat Europe anyhow."[38]

The cost of the wine shipped round the Horn from San Francisco was only ten cents a gallon more than its price on the Pacific Coast, and it was claimed (and perhaps believed) that the long voyage greatly improved the wine. "The brandies improve very much by a sea voyage, especially those *via* Cape Horn to New York—crossing the line twice.... The wines also improve very much—all of 50 percent.—from the effect of a sea voyage."[39] The difficulties of transport remained formidable: the transcontinental railway did not open until 1869; and the Civil War years, 1861–65, doubtless created even more difficulties. Yet by 1862 Kohler could boast that he had already shipped wines valued at seventy thousand dollars, and that he expected to ship another fifty thousand dollars' worth in that year; four years later, in 1866, the figure was one hundred thousand dollars.[40] Two years from that date the firm opened an agency in Chicago; it already had agencies for its wines in Asia and South America: "at Shanghai and Hongkong, China; at Hakodadi, Japan; and the Amoor River, Russia; at various ports in the East Indies, and at Lima and others of the principal cities in South America."[41]

In 1876, little more than twenty years after the firm began operations, Kohler and Frohling could claim that its wines were available in every American city of middle size or more. From the red, white, Angelica, and port that were its first offerings, the wines produced by the firm were "white wine or Hock, Riesling, Muscat, Tokay, Gutedel, Claret, Zinfandell, Malvosie, Burgundy, Sherry, Port and Angelica."[42]

ACHIEVEMENT AND DECLINE

Putting California wine into the cities and towns of America was Charles Kohler's great contribution; he showed that good wine was made in California, and he undertook to supply it to the country at large. He won a large reward, for the growth of his business continued without a check through his entire career. The death of John Fröhling in 1862 might have been a serious crisis, but it seems to have been taken in stride. In that year the San Francisco business moved to new and bigger quarters in the Montgomery Block, where a reporter for the *Alta California* was mightily impressed by the scale and efficiency of the operation. Kohler himself conducted the reporter on a tour of inspection. There were ten men at work in the cellars, racking wine, cleaning barrels, washing bottles, bottling wine, and packing bottles; carpenters were making boxes for the finished wine: and coopers were assembling new barrels and repairing old ones. "We passed pipes upon pipes of wines and brandies, arranged in tiers, which appeared interminable."[43]

A special testimony to the quality of Kohler and Frohling's wines was given in this same year, 1862, when it was announced that the U.S. government had contracted with Kohler and Frohling to provide wines to be used in the army and navy hospitals.[44] Kohler, like most Germans in America, was a strong and determined Unionist, but presumably his politics had less to do with this development than did the reliable character of his wines.

Another notable event in 1862 was the founding of the Pacific Glass Works in San Francisco, a venture in which Kohler and Frohling had a one-sixth interest and which promised to solve the problem of obtaining an adequate supply of bottles on the West Coast. The reporter who toured the Montgomery Block cellars that year noted that the firm was then using 120,000 bottles annually, and that they were mostly obtained secondhand from the city's junkmen: cleaning these so as to render them fit to receive wine was one of the main jobs in the cellar. But bottled wine, though a significant part of the business, would have accounted for only a small part of annual sales; the greater part went out in barrels of varying sizes, as California wine mainly continued to do down to Prohibition.

Charles Kohler's standing in the wine trade was such by 1862 that, when a state wine convention met in San Francisco that year, it was Kohler who called it to order. The convention had assembled in order to ask for a higher tariff on foreign wines and for lower taxes on domestic wines—American wine had borne no tax in this country until the Civil War, when Congress, needing money for the war, passed an Internal Revenue Act that laid a five-cents-a-gallon tax on wine. This of course produced loud groans from the wine men, who succeeded in having it lifted after the war. The convention also organized a California Wine-Growers' Association to act as a permanent body, and of this Kohler was elected treasurer.[45]

The opening of the transcontinental railway in 1869 was essential to the spread of Kohler and Frohling's wines through the country, though shipment by water always continued to be important. And as the railroad took wines to the East, Kohler and Frohling's California operations began to move north. The ability of the North Coast counties to produce a better dry table wine than Los Angeles could had become increasingly clear. Los Angeles in 1870 still made more wine than the Bay Area wineries did, but not much more, and it would not be long before the Bay Area took and kept the lead. Kohler and Frohling is said to have "discovered" the Zinfandel grape around 1870 and to have appreciated its virtues as a source of a good dry table wine when grown in the north.[46] Probably every observant Sonoma winemaker

FIGURE 11. The cellar at Kohler and Frohling's Tokay Vineyard, Glen Ellen, Sonoma County, in 1887, the year of Charles Kohler's death. This Sonoma property was regarded as among the finest of all California wine-making establishments. From *Frank Leslie's Illustrated Newspaper*, December 24, 1887.

had made the same discovery by 1870. But Kohler did not just make the discovery: he acted on it. In 1874 Kohler acquired an 800-acre property in the Sonoma Valley near Glen Ellen, a property including a 35-acre vineyard planted by Judge Jackson Temple known as the Tokay Vineyard.[47] Under Kohler's management, the vineyard was over the years extended to 350 acres planted to such varieties as Riesling, Traminer, Cabernet Sauvignon, and Zinfandel.[48] From these vines the better table wines of Kohler and Frohling were made. They put up a new winery building at the Tokay Vineyard with a capacity of 250,000 gallons and added a sherry house and a distillery.[49] The Tokay Vineyard establishment was regarded in the trade and by the public as a model of cleanliness, order, and efficiency.

In 1887, the year of his sudden death, Kohler could survey his consider-

FIGURE 12. The flamboyant headquarters of Kohler and Frohling, the "finest in San Francisco," built by Charles Kohler's sons in 1890. For the fate of the building, see figure 17. Courtesy Gail Unzelman Collection.

able and prosperous enterprise with a pardonable pride. The firm now occupied ten cellars in San Francisco's Montgomery Block; in Los Angeles there was a new winery of two stories, as well as a distillery and a cooperage, where 200,000 gallons or more of wine was produced annually; in New York, a new building for Kohler and Frohling's headquarters there (the company had long since absorbed Perkins and Stern) sat over vaults holding 250,000 gallons of wine and brandy.[50] Kohler had also expanded into the Central Valley, newly developed as a source of sweet, fortified wines, where he had a one-third interest in the huge Sierra Vista Vineyard in Madera County—1,000 acres of vineyard and a million gallons of winery capacity. Through his operations in Los Angeles, Madera County, and Sonoma, Kohler covered all of California's main wine-growing regions. Besides his own production, he also contracted for large quantities of wine from the Hagen Winery of the city of Napa and the Dowdell Winery in St. Helena. By this time Kohler shared his eminence with a number of other pioneer California winemakers: George West of Stockton, Isaac De Turk of Santa Rosa, Charles Krug of St. Helena, and Hamilton W. Crabb of Oakville, to name a few. But among these peers he was clearly recognized as first, the "pioneer and founder of the present wine trade in California," as one of his eulogists, the veteran Charles Wetmore, put it.[51]

This splendid achievement did not long survive Kohler's death. His two sons, Hans and Charles Jr. (there were also five daughters), carried on the expansion of the firm, acquiring the Hoen Winery at Windsor, Sonoma County, and building the Scandinavian Colony Winery in Fresno; they also had an interest in the Natoma Winery, near Folsom, and held stock in the Italian Swiss Colony Winery, in Asti. In 1890, to crown their prosperity, the brothers put up a magnificent new headquarters building at the corner of Folsom and Second streets in San Francisco. The offices were, so the local paper declared, "without doubt the finest in San Francisco"; the cellars beneath the building held 3 million gallons of wine.[52] This was not, however, a good moment for expansion. The idea that California might supply wine to a Europe suffering under the attack of phylloxera had led to a great boom in planting and production in the decade of the 1880s. California made 10 million gallons of wine in 1880; six years later the figure had soared to 18 million. And the hoped-for new markets had not developed. The inevitable result was a severe slump in prices and a consequent free-for-all of price cutting and dumping. By 1892, Zinfandel grapes were selling for less than it cost to pick them; wine at wholesale fetched ten cents a gallon or less.[53]

The firm of Kohler and Frohling was already carrying too much debt when the financial panic of 1893 struck the country. In these conditions, the firm was glad to join in the founding of the California Wine Association, the cartel formed in 1894 to rescue the California wine trade from the deep depression in which it wallowed. Charles Jr. died in that year, and in the next the Kohler family lost their stock in the cartel to the firm's old creditors, and so the tale came to its sad end.[54] Charles Kohler's work, however, has had a lasting effect, for, as the anonymous writer of Kohler's story in the Bancroft papers put it, "the wine manufacture of California today [c. 1887] is a monument to the wisdom, the enterprise, and the industry of Charles Kohler."[55]

FIVE

Andrea Sbarboro

THE ITALIANS ARE COMING

MOST AMERICANS, IF THEY THINK ABOUT IT ALL, are likely to think that wine making in this country has always been an Italian affair. That is understandable enough, for the dominant names in American wine since the repeal of Prohibition *have* been largely Italian: Gallo, Cella, Foppiano, Petri, Bisceglia, Martini, Mondavi—the list is long and impressive. But this large Italian presence in the foreground of things distorts our perspective: the fact is that there were few Italians to be found on the American wine-making scene until the end of the nineteenth century. Before that, the odds were that any man growing grapes and making wine was French, or Mexican, or English, or most likely of all, German. And that is understandable too, since Italian immigration into the United States did not amount to much until the nineteenth century was well along. There had been a few Italians among the early pioneers: Philip Mazzei in eighteenth-century Virginia, and the anonymous Italians who took part in the failed wine-growing colony of New Smyrna, Florida, also in the eighteenth century. But of course they did not succeed in producing any wine.

A change began in the decade of the 1880s, when there *were* substantial numbers of Italians in this country; California had some seven thousand, and of those it was estimated that five thousand were living in the San Francisco Bay Area. A good many of these went into wine growing through the offices of Andrea Sbarboro, grocer and banker of San Francisco.

HORATIO ALGER, TAKE NOTE

When, toward the end of 1910, Andrea Sbarboro sat down to write his life story, he had a perfectly clear notion of what that story meant: it was the classic American success story, a model for all ambitious youth to emulate. He had begun his life as a simple peasant immigrant, without education, without advantages, without prospects. But "by self-reliance, prudence and perseverance," he wrote with a pardonable complacency, "I succeeded year by year in overcoming all kinds of obstacles and reaching every goal for which I aimed." And, he modestly added, "there is no reason why other ambitious boys cannot win even greater success."[1]

Sbarboro (1839–1923) was born in the village of Acero, north of Genoa, the seventh child of peasant parents.[2] The father emigrated to New York in 1841 and sent for his family in 1844. After a time the father, perhaps weary of the struggle in America, returned to Italy, but the children remained in New York with their mother (she later rejoined her husband in Italy). Andrea at first received no formal schooling, for his mother distrusted the secular schools; instead, he went to work selling toys on the streets and on the ferry boats to help the family. He was determined to teach himself, however: he studied the posters outside theaters, wondering whether he could ever learn to read the mysterious signs; later he was a student in an Italian American school where the teacher made a pet of him and gave him private instruction in both English and Italian.[3]

What might have become of him had he remained in New York, who can say? No doubt he would have prospered. But as it happened, the gold rush gave him his opportunity. An older brother, Bartolomeo, was already set up in business in San Francisco when, in 1852, Andrea Sbarboro, aged thirteen, determined to go to California. He traveled in the company of a friend of the family, by way of the Isthmus of Panama. In San Francisco his brother put him to work as a bookkeeper. Sbarboro's account of this development is typical: "I knew very little of book-keeping at the time [how many thirteen-year-olds do?], but I was determined to fill the bill, so I bought a book on book-keeping and soon became familiar with the work."[4] "I was determined" seems to be all the explanation required for this achievement, at least in Sbarboro's mind. Were there any special difficulties? Did he get any help? Was the book adequate? How long did it take? Such questions did not occur to him. Perhaps the way was always made smooth to him, for there is no question that he had special gifts.

Bartolomeo at that time was acting as a commission agent for Italian miners in the gold country, but in 1855 he opened a grocery store in San Francisco, where Andrea Sbarboro worked for the next twenty years, eventually becoming sole owner of the enterprise. Applying the formula of "self-reliance, prudence, and perseverance," he was soon in secure circumstances, and in 1860, on attaining his majority (and his American citizenship), he made a trip to Italy. In the next year, as his business enjoyed what he called "excellent progress," he made a trip to New York, where he met and married his first wife.[5]

Sbarboro was soon a leader in San Francisco's community of Italian immigrants, who must have admired his fluent English, his business intelligence, his powers of application, his cultivated tastes. ("Why," he asked his card-playing friends, "do you not spend your evening in the company of some notable historical personage, or read the book of some standard author" as he did?)[6] He also seems to have genuinely wanted to be helpful. When several Italians asked him for English lessons, he agreed to give them; and when parents, hearing of this, began to send their children to him for instruction in both English and Italian, he soon had a flourishing school to engage his evening hours. That he made money from this work in no way detracts from his generosity in doing it.

In 1871, ten years after his first return to Italy, he went there again, this time for an entire year, long enough for him to travel up and down the length of the country and to meet and marry his second wife, Romilda Botto. There were five children of this marriage.[7]

On his return from Italy with his new wife, Sbarboro bought out his brother's interest in the store, built a vulgarly pretentious house on Washington Street, and began to invest in San Francisco real estate. In 1875, a year of economic depression, Sbarboro was invited to hear a lecture on the virtues of the building and loan society plan. "I did not know then what a building and loan society was," he wrote, but he went to the meeting and was at once converted. "The mutual building and loan association," he later declared, "is the best financial institution ever invented for wage earners by man."[8] Sbarboro at once joined the society that the meeting had been called to organize, was elected secretary, persuaded all his friends to join, and never looked back. Between 1875 and 1890 he founded four other building and loan societies and served as secretary—in effect, manager—of all of them.[9]

The plan of such associations, was, as Sbarboro explained it, "a sort of family co-operative banking institution": "Two or three hundred persons, generally neighbors, would subscribe to stock and pay into the funds every month not less than five dollars nor more than $50 each. At the end of the month they would have on hand from $5,000 to $10,000, according to the number of members, and this money was loaned out, only to the members, and only for the purpose of building a home for their families."[10]

Sbarboro at this point ceased to be a grocer and became exclusively a manager of investments, his own and those of others. He tells us that in thirty years his various associations accumulated $6.5 million, and that this was the means for building twenty-five hundred homes in and around San Francisco. Sbarboro moved to a new level of financial dignity in 1889, when, thinking that the Italian community had a sufficient commercial importance, he organized and was made president of the Italian American Bank, an institution that prospered from its beginning until, after Sbarboro's death, it was absorbed by the Bank of America.

Sbarboro was now recognized as the model of immigrant success, both in San Francisco and in Italy. No civic occasion was complete without him to represent the Italian community. And as for the Italian authorities, they showed their appreciation for his example of what an Italian could do with American opportunities by making him a Knight of La Croce della Corona D'Italia—he was, thereafter, the Cavaliere Andrea Sbarboro.

THE ITALIAN-SWISS AGRICULTURAL COLONY

All this is sufficiently edifying, but our interest in Sbarboro concerns not these things but a work of philanthropic intention that turned into a highly successful investment. Sbarboro, early in 1881, happened to read one of the reports of the new Board of State Viticultural Commissioners, which gave so bright a picture of the prospects of grape growing that, he said, "I began giving the subject considerable thought." It was true that California grape growing was prosperous at that time. The continued devastations of the phylloxera pest in European vineyards, particularly those of France, naturally suggested to people that the misfortunes of the Europeans offered a splendid opportunity for the Californians. As wine growing in Europe declined, so it would expand in California to make up the difference. An acre of California vineyard might produce five tons of grapes at $30 a ton, and since the cost of production was only $20 an acre, every acre of grapes would produce a annual profit of $130. This was a calculation that Sbarboro and many others found irresistible. The result was, from the beginning of the 1880s, a wild boom in the planting of new vineyards. What Sbarboro failed to pick up from the report was that phylloxera now threatened California too: indeed, the Board of State Viticultural Commissioners had been created in the preceding year, 1880, largely in response to that threat. Nor did the report caution that increased planting might, as in fact it did, lead to a serious problem of overproduction.

Sbarboro's discovery of the profits of grape growing came at a time when he was concerned about the problems of an increasing Italian immigration. Much of it was composed of *contadini,* who, without English and without any of the skills particularly wanted in San Francisco, sank to the bottom of the labor pool. They would come to his office hoping for his help. Now he thought he had found a way: since many of them did know something about growing grapes, why not take advantage of that fact? "I thought that some of the money of one of my building and loan associations, which we had on hand and could not place advantageously, might be properly invested in buying a tract of land for the association with a view of putting these Italian vineyardists at work."[11]

A consultation with his lawyer at once put an end to that idea: the money in the building and loan associations could be used only for building homes for members. But, the lawyer added, there was nothing to prevent Sbarboro from creating a new association whose bylaws would meet the new purpose. Sbarboro set to work at once to organize such an association, largely relying on the support of the prosperous members of the city's Italian community.

The articles of incorporation of the Italian-Swiss Agricultural Society were signed on March 10, 1881. The shareholders of the Society, who were required to hold no fewer than five shares and not more than fifty, were almost all San Francisco Italians: for their shares they agreed to pay $1 per month for a period of five years.[12] Sbarboro, after his usual practice, was secretary to the Society. The bylaws stated that preference in employment "shall be given to Italians and Swiss" who were "citizens of the United States or had made a legal declaration of intention for citizenship."[13] The inclusion of "Swiss" was an acknowledgment of the presence of immigrants from the Italian-speaking Swiss canton of Ticino, but it is doubtful that they were ever a very important element in the Italian-Swiss Agricultural Colony. According to Sbarboro, 2,250 shares were subscribed, producing an income of $2,250 a month, and as soon as $10,000 was in the treasury the directors set out to buy land for the colony. Sbarboro and two other directors scoured the state and soon settled on a large property in northern Sonoma County, a fifteen-hundred-acre tract of low rolling hills on the Russian River that had so far been given over to pasturing sheep. For this splendid tract they paid $25,000, $10,000 down and the rest over fifteen months. Sbarboro christened the local whistle-stop on the Northwestern Pacific Railroad "Asti," after the celebrated wine-making town of the Italian Piedmont, and as a sign of what the place might hope to become. There was already a "Medoc" in North Carolina, and a "Rheims" in the Finger Lakes of New York, where they made sparkling wine; why not an "Asti" in California?[14]

It was now time to set to work to convert pasture into vineyard. But first Sbarboro called together his workers to explain the Society's plans for them. Each worker would be required to subscribe for at least five shares of the Society's stock and would have five dollars a month from his thirty- or forty-dollar monthly salary deducted to pay for them. To his chagrin, Sbarboro found that the men wanted no part of this scheme: "They thought cash for their work was better than any part in stock."[15] Sbarboro pleaded with them, "pleaded with them until he was hoarse," as one of his directors put it, but in vain.[16] In the end, Sbarboro had to accept that the cooperative savings provision in the bylaws was a dead letter; the workers were workers only, without being shareholders. The Italian-Swiss Agricultural Colony was a stock company like any other. The work of clearing, plowing, and planting went on swiftly and efficiently through 1881. In the spring of the next year, planting began. At the end of 1884 the vineyards covered a very substantial six hundred acres.

About 1885—the year is not clearly established—an important addition was made to the vineyards when cuttings of several choice Italian varieties were received through the agency of Dr. Giuseppe Ollino, then residing in Italy and later a vice president of the colony. In this way Barbera, Nebbiolo, Grignolino, and Sangiovese vines were added to the colony's vineyards and provided a source for what was to become the company's flagship wine, called "Tipo Chianti." The name, of course, flagrantly exploits the reputation earned by Chianti among the world's wines, but such theft was the universal practice in California then, and the qualifier *Tipo* made a more modest claim than many other such appropriations did; ultimately, the word *Chianti* was dropped from the label and the wine called simply "Tipo."[17] The success of Tipo Chianti was immense. Bottled in Chianti fiaschi wrapped in raffia coverings imported from Italy, and labeled in the colors of the House of Savoy—green, white, and red—Tipo Chianti became, in the words of Charles Sullivan, "the single most important brand name product of the California wine industry," being almost "synonymous with Italian Swiss Colony and sound California wine. No other brand did so much to promote the idea that the American consumer could depend on brand names for quality and dependability."[18]

FIGURE 13. Tipo, the flagship wine of Italian Swiss Colony, based on the company's plantings of Sangiovese and other Italian varieties of grapes. Courtesy Gail Unzelman Collection.

The harvest of 1886, the first substantial one from the vineyards of Italian Swiss Colony, would put to the proof Sbarboro's glowing expectations of profits from California grapes. Instead of profits, he found, as he put it, "ruin staring us in the face."[19] The overplanting that had been going on since Sbarboro decided to become a grape grower had destroyed the market; instead of thirty dollars a ton, the San Francisco merchant houses, his sole reliance, offered a derisory eight dollars, from which four dollars would be subtracted for freight![20] The colony had been founded simply to grow grapes, but Sbarboro now saw that he would have to become a winemaker if he were to stay in business. He called together his directors, described the situation, recommended that they build a winery so that they would not be at the mercy of the annual grape market, and proposed an assessment of ten dollars a share to pay for the cost of the new winery.[21] The directors approved the plan, and by the time of the vintage of 1887 the winery was ready to receive the crop. It was built with a capacity of three hundred thousand gallons; some of the directors thought this was too large, little imagining that the cellars at Asti would, twenty years later, reach a capacity of 4 million gallons.

The teething troubles of the colony were not yet over. The first commercial vintage, that of 1887, was made in a very difficult year. Hot weather at harvest time sent the sugar content of the grapes soaring, so that the fer-

P. C. ROSSI   A. SBARBORO

FIGURE 14. Pietro Rossi and Andrea Sbarboro, the two men who combined the technical abilities of the one and the entrepreneurial energy of the other to make Italian Swiss Colony a leader among California wineries. Courtesy Gail Unzelman Collection.

mentation of the sugar-loaded grapes could not be controlled. There were no temperature-controlling means in those days, apart from dumping ice into the vats, and the combination of heat and high sugar overwhelmed the yeasts and produced "stuck" fermentations—fermentations that did not go through to the end but petered out, leaving an unstable, partially fermented wine whose fate would be to turn milk-sour or decline into vinegar. That was a general affliction throughout California that year, and that is what happened at the Italian Swiss Colony.

Sbarboro now determined to find someone with "the highest scientific knowledge of the growing of grapes and the making of wine."[22] Luckily, he knew where to look. Pietro Rossi, a graduate of the University of Turin with a degree in agricultural chemistry and the descendant of a long line of wine-growers, had come to San Francisco in 1875 and established a drugstore. He married a daughter of Sbarboro's friend Justinian Caire; but even without that connection he would have been known to Sbarboro, who knew every-one of any standing in the Italian community. Sbarboro was able to persuade Rossi to join Italian Swiss Colony as general manager; and with that, the fortunes of the colony took a new turn.

The crop of 1886 had had no market; the crop of 1887 was partly lost through bad fermentations; in 1888, under Rossi's direction, a large crop was success-fully fermented into good wine, 130,000 gallons of it. But, once again, Ital-ian Swiss Colony ran into the barrier of the San Francisco merchants: they offered a mere seven cents a gallon for the colony's wines. So another crucial management decision was taken: as they had determined to go into the mak-ing of wine, they now determined to go into the selling of wine as well. The first, tentative move was a success: the company, in Sbarboro's words, sent "a few carloads East, some to New York, Chicago, Philadelphia, and New Orleans to be sold on commission for our account. To our delight, the wine was so much liked that it brought in returns of from 35 to 40¢ per gallon with requests that we send more. 'But be sure,' wrote one agent, 'that you send me the same quality of wine that you forwarded before.'"[23]

So began the Rossi era (he added the title of president to that of general manager in 1892), under which Italian Swiss Colony underwent steady, not to say spectacular, growth through the decade of the 1890s. By 1900 Italian Swiss Colony boasted a winery with a capacity of more than a million gallons at the original Asti site; it had a cellar and a bottling plant in San Francisco; and it had built a winery at Madera, in the Central Valley, for the produc-tion of sweet (i.e., fortified) wines, allowing Asti to concentrate on dry table wines.[24] There was a new headquarters building in San Francisco, which held a million gallons of wine in its cellars. A new winery had been built at Fresno with a capacity of 300,000 gallons, soon expanded to more than 2 million. And it had added, by purchase, the Fulton Winery near Healdsburg to its list of properties.

The good reputation of Italian Swiss Colony wines was as important as the material expansion. That reputation was, after all, what had generated the material expansion. It was the result of good varieties, including those Italian varieties that yielded Tipo; of good wine making under Rossi's direc-tion; and of good management practices. Key among these was the practice of establishing brand identity. Most—in fact nearly all—of the wine that left California did so in bulk shipments by rail or by water to bottlers and distrib-utors all over the country. These put their own labels on what they bottled, and since laws governing wine labeling could hardly be said to exist, those labels could be whatever the proprietor fancied. But they would not, in any case, identify the California producer or the varietal source of the wine in the bottle. The Italian Swiss Colony policy, in opposition to the general practice, was to have its wines bottled under its own name, even when the bottling was done by an independent wholesaler. It thus developed a brand identity that no other widely distributed California wine enjoyed.[25]

Sbarboro's original idea of enabling his workers to a share in the company may have foundered at once, but a strong paternalistic atmosphere nevertheless prevailed at Asti. By the end of the century a comprehensive, nearly self-sufficient little community had been created. There were cottages for the married people, a dormitory for the single men, a "Colony House" for visitors, a dining hall, a bakery, a blacksmith shop, a horse barn, a dairy, a post office, a school, and a church.

A few years later Sbarboro built a summer house for himself at Asti, a copy of the Casa dei Vettii in Pompeii; Rossi, too, built a house nearby, called Buen Retiro. The grounds of these houses were converted into lush gardens. Here Sbarboro loved to play the expansive host to a stream of visitors from San Francisco and elsewhere. No dignitary visiting the Bay Area could complete his tour without a visit to Sbarboro at his Asti villa; or as Sbarboro more modestly put it: "Nearly every Californian of prominence has made the journey to Asti."[26] There Sbarboro was just in his element. A short, dapper man, plump, energetic, and enthusiastic, always sporting a boutonniere, he reveled in company and delighted in showing off the splendors of Asti.

A NEW DEAL

After years of self-denial while the company went through its early struggles, the shareholders in the Italian-Swiss Agricultural Colony at last, in 1897, began to receive dividends. Indeed, their patience was more than well rewarded. The investment of the original shareholders had amounted only to $125,000, plus the $22,500 specially assessed in 1886 in order to build a winery at Asti. By 1897 the value of their original investment had multiplied many times over, and it would continue to grow. But the directors of the colony appear to have been shaken by a conflict with the giant California Wine Association, which sought to dominate the wine trade. That conflict took up the years from 1896 to 1898. Sbarboro himself disliked conflict and was eager for harmony with his competitors. The result was that in 1900 the Italian-Swiss Agricultural Colony was reorganized. The word *Agricultural* was dropped, and the new company, now officially Italian Swiss Colony, was owned half by its original stockholders and half by the California Wine Association. This arrangement was not publicized: the CWA did not wish to stir up the already-great hostility to it on the part of those who resented its size and its power. As with the other elements that made up the CWA, Italian Swiss Colony, to all outward appearances, preserved its independence. But its policies would henceforth be those of the CWA.

Now the money power of the CWA enabled an even greater expansion of Italian Swiss Colony than the one that had been accomplished in the 1890s. In 1901 the latter acquired the Cloverdale Wine Company and then the Sebastapol Winery. In the next year Italian Swiss Colony erected a big new storage facility in San Francisco, giving the firm three locations in the city.[27] Next was a new winery at Kingsburg, in Fresno County, and then another at Lemoore, Kings County, where they also developed large vineyards. They began as well to promote vineyard planting in Mendocino County, just over the border from Asti, at the northern edge of Sonoma County. The demands of the colony's many wineries always exceeded the capacity of its vineyards to supply them, so it made sense to invite others to join in the game. And the company continued to buy vineyards in many different sections of the state, both in the Central Valley and in the coastal counties. At the end of 1911, the tally of Italian Swiss Colony's producing facilities stood thus:

Place	Capacity (gallons)
Asti	4,000,000
Cloverdale winery	500,000
Fulton winery	500,000
Sebastopol winery	500,000
Mount Diablo winery	400,000
Madera winery	3,000,000
Lemoore winery	1,000,000
Kingsburg winery	1,000,000
Selma winery	750,000
TOTAL	11,650,000

In addition, there were cellars in San Francisco with 2 million gallons of storage capacity, and a New York property, called La Cantina, that held about a million gallons.[28]

This was the high point of Italian Swiss Colony's fortunes. In that year Pietro Rossi was killed in a carriage accident at Asti, an unhappy event that at once diminished the energy of the enterprise. In 1913 Andrea Sbarboro sold out his interest, and Italian Swiss Colony was entirely absorbed by the California Wine Association.[29] Then came national Prohibition (1920) and the general destruction of the California wine trade. Italian Swiss Colony survived the dry years, under the care of Rossi's twin sons, Edward and Robert, and flourished again after repeal for a time. It now, after a variety of vicissitudes, survives merely as a label. The vineyards are still there, however, as are the old plant and the nearby homes that Sbarboro and Rossi had built: the Casa dei Vettii and Buen Retiro.

THE FIGHT FOR TRUE TEMPERANCE

After all his services to the Italians of San Francisco, Sbarboro attempted an even greater service to his countrymen at large. This was to fight against the ever-increasing menace, as he saw of it, of the so-called temperance movement, which, when interpreted, is not about temperance at all but is a demand for the intemperate condition of legislated dryness—no alcoholic drink of any kind permitted. Popular movements directed toward "temperance" were an old story in American history; but the general failure of the efforts to create voluntary abstinence led some citizens to take up a different method. This was to give up talk about temperance and to seek the prohibition of alcoholic drink by legal means. The first step in the campaign was to secure prohibition by installments: first by city, then by county, then by state. The final goal was to secure national prohibition through a constitutional amendment. The main force in the campaign was called the Anti-Saloon League, founded in Ohio in 1893. It generated a tremendous public relations campaign, flooding the country with pamphlets and tracts, supplying the newspapers with useful information, sending out lecturers to instruct the public (by 1916 there were twenty thousand of them in the field),[30] and forming branches in every state. The goals of the Anti-Saloon League were set forth from thousands of Protestant pulpits every Sunday. Even more important, the league played politics, supporting any candidate who would accept the dry cause and opposing all who declined, never mind what other issues and principles might be involved. The league, as one of its high officers put it, was "intensely practical" in the pursuit of its "ideal."[31] Even before the passage of the Eighteenth

Amendment, it controlled, on the question of prohibition, a majority of the state legislatures.

The effect of the league began to be unmistakably clear. Georgia went dry in 1907; the next year Mississippi and North Carolina went dry; Tennessee went dry in 1909; West Virginia in 1912; and Virginia in 1914. Paul Garrett, the leading winemaker on the East Coast, was forced to retreat from his North Carolina and Virginia properties and take refuge in New York. Things were not yet so bad in California, though there had long been dry cities in the state (e.g., Hollywood, Pasadena, Long Beach) and the dry sentiment was very powerful in the rural areas of a state that was still mainly rural.

Andrea Sbarboro was one of the first of the relatively few California wine men who saw what was happening and tried to do something about it. Most of the others preferred simply to deny that anything so preposterous could actually come about, and then did nothing. Unfortunately, when Sbarboro went into action he chose an utterly useless method: he tried to reason with the enemy. Indeed, it seems clear that he never had the slightest understanding of the mentality of the people who were working against him. Sbarboro, good Italian that he was, took the view that wine was a food, a pleasant and healthful adjunct to meals, and that the moderate consumption of wine was the most effective basis of a "true" temperance. The saloon might be a social evil, cheap whiskey and widespread drunkenness certainly were: but wine had nothing to do with these things. "No nation is drunken where wine is cheap"—Thomas Jefferson's well-known assertion—was Sbarboro's watchword. It followed that wine, instead of being a prohibited drink, ought to be on every domestic table: "If you good ladies," he advised America's mothers, would "give your children in early years a little wine and water at their meals, they would grow up with the habit of using wine only at table[;] and I assure you that none of those boys or girls would ever become drunkards."[32]

He was, of course, preaching to the deaf. For the ardent prohibitionist, all alcoholic drink was equally identified with the sole enemy, the monstrous Demon Rum, which threatened to debauch the youth of the country, destroy the family, and bring down the Republic.[33] It was, to such people, merely paltering with the truth to try to make distinctions: alcohol was alcohol, and alcohol was absolutely evil.[34] Poor Sbarboro could not even imagine such a mentality; he found it baffling, as a dairyman in Wisconsin might find it baffling if there were suddenly to be a campaign against drinking milk. And that being so, Sbarboro was severely handicapped in his valiant effort to defend wine from its attackers. His first move was to publish a pamphlet called

THE FIGHT FOR
TRUE TEMPERANCE
By
CAV. ANDREA SBARBORO

FIGURE 15. Published in 1908, *The Fight for True Temperance* was one in a series of Andrea Sbarboro's vain attempts to counter the forces of prohibition. The polemical combination of "true temperance" with a bunch of wine grapes would have outraged his opponents. Courtesy Gail Unzelman Collection.

Wine as a Remedy for the Evil of Intemperance in 1906: the argument of this, plainly announced in the title, no doubt seemed self-evident to Sbarboro, while to the people of the Anti-Saloon League it must have seemed a grotesque oxymoron.

In 1908 Sbarboro called a general meeting of grape growers in San Francisco to form a protective association. This was called the Grape Growers of California; Sbarboro, inevitably, was its president, elected "by unanimous vote."[35] Sbarboro was his usual indefatigable self. For the public relations campaign in California, he produced a motion picture about the California wine industry, showing that "it was made of ordinary folks and was not a tool of the liquor interests.[36] He attended congressional hearings in Washington to present the case for wine, and he delivered addresses to public meetings up and down the state and beyond: the *Pacific Wine and Spirit Review* reported that, on his trip to New York to address the state's grape growers in 1908, Sbarboro "was welcomed at every stoppage of his train by representatives of the press who listened to his arguments and secured a copy of his book. So we have every reason to believe the press of the entire country will now take up the good fight."[37]

If only it were so easy. Sbarboro continued his pamphlet warfare, publishing *The Fight for True Temperance*" in 1908 and *Temperance versus Prohibition* in 1909. The latter title collected testimony from American consuls in all the wine-drinking parts of Europe to the effect that they saw no drunkenness where they lived. Sbarboro sent copies to President Roosevelt, Secretary of War Taft, the cabinet officers, all the members of Congress, and to a long list of other notables.[38] One has the feeling that Sbarboro's efforts to make his reasonable voice heard in the tempest raised by the Anti-Saloon League was like playing a pennywhistle in competition with the Marine Band. But at least he tried.

National Prohibition was achieved in January of 1919, when the Eighteenth Amendment to the Constitution of the United States had been ratified by the necessary number of states. The Volstead Act, spelling out the conditions under which the amendment would be enforced, went into effect a year later. California, despite determined efforts to secure prohibition in the state, had not gone dry by the time of the amendment; but the legislature ratified the amendment and added a state law to enforce the Volstead Act. The fight, so far as Sbarboro was concerned, was over. He lived on until 1923, when the dark night of Prohibition seemed to have settled permanently over the country. It is a pity he could not have lived to see the dawn that came at the end of 1933, with the passage of repeal. As noted at the beginning of this chapter, it was the Italians who then came forth to dominate the stage—Gallo, Rossi, Cella, Foppiano, Seghesio, Martini, Pedroncelli, Guasti, Cribari, Vai. Sbarboro would be proud to know how prominent they are in the resurrected industry, no longer embarrassed *contadini* unable to speak English and in dire need of a helping hand, but, like him, leaders in a respected community.

SIX

Percy T. Morgan and the CWA

WINE AS BIG BUSINESS

A BUSINESS CRISIS

By the 1890s the modest beginnings of a California wine trade nurtured by Charles Kohler had burgeoned into a business large enough to support a number of substantial wine merchants, or wine houses, as they were called. Kohler and Frohling was still chief among them, but others had grown big too: Lachman and Jacobi, C. Carpy and Company, S. Lachman and Company, Kohler and Van Bergen.[1] The traditional three-part structure of the wine business—vineyard, winery, and merchant house—was confusingly mixed in the activities of these firms: they owned or controlled vineyards; they owned or controlled wine-making and storage facilities; and they were merchants of wine. It was the latter function that set them apart. There were many independent growers; there were many independent wineries; but the business of selling and distributing California wine was almost exclusively in the hands of the San Francisco merchants. Since practically all wine that went out of California had to pass through their hands, they had an advantage over grower and winemaker, and there were always complaints about how the merchants took most of the profits of the trade for themselves. Probably they did. Their practice was to buy wine from all quarters of the state, to store it in San Francisco cellars, where it could be blended to standard, and to hold it for a favorable market, if possible.

At the beginning of the 1890s an accumulation of troubles in the wine business had reached the point at which men began to despair of keeping it alive: overproduction; incompetent wine making; insects and diseases, including phylloxera and Pierce's disease; a surplus of wine; and, in 1893, a national financial panic; all combined to devastating effect. Prices were cut, and cut again; wine was dumped on the market, and profits disappeared.

In the midst of these troubles there were plenty of notions about what might be done for the wine trade but precious little action. One suggested remedy was to distill a third of the year's wine production in order to create a shortage; a variant of this idea was the proposal to use only two-thirds of any grower's crop, or to dry a portion of the crop as raisins. More positive was the proposal to establish cafés "to dispose of California wines in three or four of the great Eastern cities."[2] Everyone agreed that what was really needed was cooperation among all segments of the trade or, rather, as Pietro Rossi put it, "a strong syndicate of the wine makers with one central and crystallized authority."[3] That would control the supply and so would control prices. But how did one get such a thing?

At this point Percy Tredegar Morgan enters the story. He had nothing to do with wine making or with selling wine,[4] but he understood business organization and commercial finance, and so he became, in one point of view, the savior of the trade or, in another, the creator of a monstrous monopoly.

Morgan was an Englishman, born in London in 1862. From school he joined an accounting firm in London, which sent him out as accountant and bookkeeper to a Nevada gold mine. He then migrated to Colorado, where he opened an office with another, older Englishman, William Hanson, to serve the mining industry as accountants, auditors, and general agents. Hanson and Morgan were never parted thereafter, but moved together through their many business ventures. In 1886 they moved on to San Francisco, where they launched a variety of businesses. By 1889 Morgan was a substantial figure in the San Francisco business world and remained so, serving on the boards of the Pacific Telephone and Telegraph Company, the Union Trust Company, and the Wells Fargo Bank, and as a trustee of Stanford University. By the time he was thirty he was one of the city's most eligible bachelors. Two years later, he married an heiress, Fanny Ainsworth, daughter of an Oakland banker.

Morgan does not seem to have been a vivid or striking type. He was tall, he was English, and of course, given all that precocious success, he had a reputation as "a man of great energy, always ready to take on extra labours."[5] In business affairs he maintained the style of the reasonable man, patient, conciliatory, and fair, but as a reasonable man he could see and deplore the unreason, the inefficiency and self-destructiveness, of business competition. An overpowering desire to put a stop to the ignorant strugglings of competing interests and to create instead harmonious cooperation is, in my opinion, what drove him in his work for the wine trade: he could not stand the spectacle of wasteful, unregulated competition when a strong hand might make everything harmonious and smooth. At any rate, that is what he set out to achieve. His watchwords were "concentration of capital," "cooperation," and "unanimity in management," all backed by "the strong hand."[6]

THE CALIFORNIA WINE ASSOCIATION

Who managed the preliminaries, and how, we do not now know, but Morgan was certainly involved in the talks that lay behind that moment on August 9, 1894, when the articles of incorporation of the California Wine Association (CWA) were filed with the California secretary of state. According to Charles Sullivan, Morgan's firm had been handling the accounts for S. Lachman and Company, one of the original members of the CWA, and had evidently concluded from that experience that "consolidation was the only logical way" for the wine business to follow; the CWA was Morgan's "brainchild."[7] In its original form, the CWA was a combination of seven of the leading wine houses in San Francisco, namely, C. Carpy and Company, Benjamin Dreyfus and Company, Arpad Haraszthy and Company, Kohler and Frohling, Kohler and Van Bergen, S. Lachman and Company, and the Napa Valley Wine Company. How many compromises, how many concessions may have been necessary to bring about this combination of competing companies, who can say? The reason for it was clear enough. As a brochure put out by the company to celebrate its first year of operation explained, the founders, "all men of long and practical experience in the making and handling of wine, were confronted in 1894 with the serious question of saving the industry from almost total wreck, of conserving their capital, and of placing the wine-producing interests on a basis satisfactory to all."[8]

In other words, they had been facing ruin. The idea of combination was of course familiar enough; it would occur to any observer of the marketplace. But bringing it about was quite another thing; the catalytic element appears to have been Morgan, whose persuasive arguments for the virtues of cooperation, aided by the desperate circumstances of the time, carried the necessary weight.

To form the CWA, the participating firms turned over their assets to the new company; in return they received stock in the CWA. The directors were

FIGURE 16. The trademark of the California Wine Association: young Bacchus, with the California bear, sails forth, bringing California wine to the world. Courtesy Gail Unzelman Collection.

all well-known members of the wine trade with the single exception of Percy Morgan, whose anomalous presence is presumptive evidence of his importance in bringing about the long-desired "combination of interests" embodied in the CWA. Morgan, despite being one of the major stockholders in the association, did not have a position in its hierarchy at the beginning, though he was appointed to several committees. His practical importance, however, was quickly recognized. By 1895 he was general manager of the CWA, and when Charles Carpy, the original president of the CWA, resigned in 1896, it was Percy Morgan who succeeded him, becoming president as well as general manager, in virtue of his "executive ability, broad and liberal ideas, keen intelligence and extraordinary push and enterprise."[9]

So far as the public was concerned, the member firms went on unchanged: they continued to operate as though they were independent businesses, keeping their own premises and doing business with their own labels, trademarks, and sales arrangements. According to their agreement, "the individuality of the various houses and the brands they have established will be maintained."[10] But the CWA would also sell wine under its own trademark. This, which became one of the best-known emblems of the American wine trade before Prohibition, was an elaborate sort of Victorian composition showing a youthful Bacchus, accompanied by the California bear, holding up a wine glass as he stands at the prow of a sailing ship being oared out through San Francisco's Golden Gate. The sail of the ship bears the seal of the state of California (in unorthodox form) as well as some bunches of grapes, and inscribed on an arch behind the ship is the name "California Wine Association." This trademark, the CWA declared, would be "the synonym for purity, soundness and quality."[11]

The plan of the CWA was simple: control enough of California's wine production to allow the organization to control prices at either end—the price of grapes at the producing end, and the price of wine at the selling end. The size of the different firms brought together in the combine made a good start toward domination. C. Carpy and Company, though it had only a modest San Francisco property, was the owner of the big Uncle Sam Winery in the city of Napa, as well as the even bigger Greystone Winery north of St. Helena and the smaller but still substantial Pacific Winery in San Jose. All of the other firms that entered into the original CWA had large cellars in the city of San Francisco. Kohler and Van Bergen had cellars of 2 million gallons' capacity; Benjamin Dreyfus's Eagle Wine Vaults held a million gallons; Kohler and Frohling, 3 million; S. Lachman, 2 million; the Napa Valley Wine Company, a half million, and Arpad Haraszthy and Company an unreported but certainly substantial quantity.[12]

But more than this was needed. As soon as the CWA had been formed, it sent out canvassers to sign up producers all over the state: the goal was to secure, by firm contracts, the handling of "at least 80 percent of the wine product of the State," and it was reported that there would be no difficulty in obtaining that number.[13] Whether in fact it did or not, we don't know, though it seems unlikely. It did, however, corral enough of the total to put it in position to dominate the California wine business, as it continued to do for the next quarter century, until Prohibition put an end to all wine business.

How did the CWA avoid an antitrust action against it?[14] It was quite clearly an organization dedicated to the restraint of trade in order to secure an advantage to itself, but so far as I know, it escaped attention from the Department of Justice. The lawyer who drew up the scheme of the company wrote, "I desired to found this Organization in such way and manner as to steer clear of the rocks upon which so many organizations have been wrecked."[15] And evidently he did. One loophole was the fact that wine was not regarded as a staple commodity, so that the law did not concern itself with its free marketing. The CWA could fly under the radar, which was aimed at much bigger bodies. Another was the practice of maintaining the ostensible independence of the constituent firms: Kohler and Frohling, for example, continued to operate as Kohler and Frohling; to all outward appearances they were still in competition with the other houses.

Another was Morgan's conciliatory style of operation, so that the independent winemakers did not bring legal complaints, even though they were no doubt anxious about what the CWA might do to them. Most important, probably, was Percy Morgan's steady principle of maintaining moderate prices; his CWA might enjoy near-monopoly power, but Morgan saw that in the long run the real profits would come from expanding the market by making wine affordable to all. And if the CWA did not seek to gouge the public, then the public defenders had nothing to charge against it. That, in order to maintain modest prices, it might be necessary to gouge the grape grower and the winemaker, was of no apparent concern.

THE WINE WAR

The appearance of the CWA was greeted in the press with approval. It would usher in a "new era" for California wine, one in which better prices would prevail for all concerned, and so the industry would be saved from ruin. That was one view; there was, however, quite a different one. The winemakers outside the ring created by the CWA saw that they would be utterly at the mercy of the new company unless they could unite against it. Accordingly, in November of 1894, an organization called the California Wine-Makers' Corporation (CWC) was formed to combine the interests of as many independents as could be persuaded to join. The movement was led by Andrea Sbarboro and Pietro Rossi, of Italian Swiss Colony, the largest of the firms not included in the CWA. Another major player was one of the biggest and most powerful of the San Francisco wine merchants, Lachman and Jacobi. The manager of the CWC was John H. Wheeler, a vineyardist in the Napa Valley who had been secretary to the Board of State Viticultural Commissioners and who was thus prominent in the industry. The corporation, capitalized, like the CWA, at $10 million, would undertake to handle wines from all producers, big and small, hold them for a reasonable market, and divide the proceeds on a cooperative basis.

Percy Morgan's conduct of the relations between the two hostile camps, the CWA and CWC, is a model instance of his style. He was nothing if not accommodating. The CWA, early in 1895, signed a huge contract with the CWC on the latter's terms. The deal was for a total of 19 million gallons of wine from the CWC, 4 million to be delivered in 1895, the remaining 15 million over the next three years. The price for the wine of 1895 was twelve and a half cents a gallon, five cents better than the current depressed market was offering. Prices for later years were to be negotiated. In a remarkable concession, Morgan agreed to withdraw from the business of making wine: the CWA's wineries were leased to the CWC for a term of five years. As the *Pacific Wine and Spirit Review* put it, "Merchants will go out of business as dry wine makers, and attend strictly to the business of wine selling."[16] When this contract was signed, Pietro Rossi was triumphant: "We have won our fight," he crowed, "and the backbone of the opposition is now broken." This happy outcome, he said with an eye on those who had not yet come into the fold, shows that "it pays to organize."[17]

The deal did not last long. In the next year, the CWC asked to get out from its leases of the CWA's wineries. There had been a severe frost that spring, and the prospect was for a short crop; the CWC felt that the agreed-on prices for wine should be negotiated upward.[18] "Trouble," the *Pacific Wine and Spirit Review* reported, "has been brewing for months over the price to be paid for ordinary red dry wines of the vintage of 1896."[19] If there was going to be a fight, it "would be better for the California Wine Association to handle its own properties." Percy Morgan took this turn of things with perfect calmness: taking back the leases, he said, was a move made "in the interests of the Wine Makers' Corporation, the relations between that body and the California Wine Association being of the most cordial nature."[20] But that smoothly tactful comment masked the fact that a storm threatened. In his annual report for 1896 Morgan told his directors that the CWC people had acted in bad faith and had demanded an "exorbitant and prohibitory price" for their wines. Luckily, the CWA had already laid in large stocks of wine at low cost, so that it need not be troubled by a short crop. The CWC would thus have no way of squeezing the CWA.[21]

Open war was declared early in 1897, when the CWC sued the CWA for nonpayment for wine delivered in 1896; Wheeler, the CWC's manager, complained that "we have never been treated by any of our customers as the Wine Association has treated us."[22] Percy Morgan and the CWA responded at once with a countersuit for nondelivery of wine contracted for in 1896. Morgan was now talking in a different style: no more Mr. Nice Guy. If the CWC would not cooperate with the CWA in its sweetly reasonable pursuit of order and profit, it would simply be crushed. "The war has begun," he declared, "and will be carried out to the bitter end. . . . There will be no compromise."

And there wasn't. In the court case that followed, it was allowed that the CWA had held back payment to the CWC, but that was only because the CWC had in fact failed to deliver the quantity it had contracted for, since it was hoping for a higher price than the CWA would give. Judgment was given for the CWA, along with damages in the amount of $130,000.

Before the trial had been settled, the year 1897 saw a huge vintage in California of 30 million gallons. The CWC was awash in wine, but the CWA, having prudently laid in large stocks at low prices, would buy no wine; it was in no mood to assist an enemy but was, instead, happy to see it go to the wall. The CWC's answer was to go into sales on its own. But to do this against the competition of the CWA meant that it would have to cut prices, and so it did. The CWA followed suit. Percy Morgan, whose policies were the cause of it all, maintained a pose of injured virtue: the CWA, he said, did not cut prices, but only lowered them when compelled to do so by the misconduct of others.[23]

What Morgan really thought and felt about this mutually destructive conflict he allowed to escape in a rare moment of frankness some years later. In a speech he made in 1902, Morgan looked back at the time when the huge vintage of 1897 had overwhelmed the trade. In those desperate days, he recalled, "Each vied with the other in a frantic endeavor to realize on the wines. Vineyardists, wine makers and merchants were rushing like a herd of stampeded animals toward a precipice of ruin; many went over never to rise again; many were injured; and a few only, shying at the edge, pulled up in time to save themselves. . . . Consumers viewed with amazement and ridicule this spectacle of insane business procedure."[24] The melodramatic language culminates in what must for Morgan have been the most telling phrase of all: "insane business procedure." However coolly he may have expressed himself at the time, as a reasonable man he saw his competitors as "stampeded animals," their behavior simply and hopelessly "insane." Only a CWA could restore order and sanity to the deplorable scene.

Fortunately, the CWC was now beaten, and Morgan could resume his smooth and conciliatory style. At the end of 1898 an arrangement was worked out between the CWA and the CWC to buy the latter's wines at a decent price; at the same time the CWA agreed to adjust the damages it had been awarded from $130,000 to about $8,000, with a promise from the CWC that the case would go no further.[25] The CWC was not formally dissolved until 1900, but it was no longer a factor in California wine. The two main holdouts against the CWA, the Italian Swiss Colony Winery and the merchant house of Lachman and Jacobi, also saw the handwriting on the wall and hastened to join up with the CWA. So did another of the recalcitrant San Francisco merchants, the firm of C. Schilling and Company. In exchange for stock in the California Wine Association, these rivals were now part of what they had opposed in vain.

Percy Morgan did not allow himself to vaunt over the bodies of a defeated enemy but remained discreetly polite. The relations between the CWA and Lachman and Jacobi, he said, for example, "have always been pleasant . . . and the so-called war which is said to have existed between us has simply been competition."[26] Now there would be no more competition; instead, there would only be enlightened cooperation achieved through what Morgan liked to call "unanimity in management."

THE FAT YEARS

The way was now clear for the CWA to operate as it had been intended to do from the first. The prices that had been cut in the latter days of the wine war were gradually restored. And the CWA swept up properties all over the state. As soon as its rivals had been absorbed, the company, in 1900, went on a buying spree, for it saw that, unless it produced as much of its own wine as possible, it would always have to face demands for prices that it did not want to pay. It purchased the distinguished Brun and Chaix Winery in the Napa Valley, and it acquired "interests" in the Los Gatos Cooperative Winery, the Los Gatos–Saratoga Wine Company, the Alexander Valley Winery, the Sebastapol Winery, the Cloverdale Winery, the Fresno Vineyard Company, and the Reedley Winery, and it planned to get more still. It also entered into a contract with the big Natoma Vineyard near Sacramento and leased the Yolo, Mount Diablo, and Chateau Chevalier wineries. As Morgan told his directors in his report that year, the company was on so solid a basis that the big financial powers of California were now looking at the CWA with a new interest, for the CWA had earned their confidence.[27]

The CWA soon not only owned or controlled dozens of wineries, but it also owned thousands of acres of vineyard, though never enough to satisfy its own wine-making needs. It is interesting to note that Morgan thought the small farmer rather than the big corporation would make the best grape grower, not because Morgan had any Jeffersonian ideas about sturdily independent yeoman farmers but because the small proprietor, he believed, could produce a bigger yield and bigger profits! "It is from the small vineyardist, cultivating from ten to fifty acres; cultivating and looking after his lands individually, and thereby obtaining from 30 to 50 per cent more tonnage to the acre than is possible from great vineyard tracts, that the very remunerative results will accrue."[28]

When Morgan said that the financial interests of the West Coast now had "confidence" in the CWA, he meant simply that the moneyed men were now prepared to invest in the company. And so they did. Three San Francisco bankers, Isaias W. Hellman, Antoine Borel, and Daniel Meyer, together put a million dollars into the CWA; they were soon joined by Henry E. Huntington, the leading developer of transport and real estate in Los Angeles County. Huntington and Isaias Hellman Jr. were added to the CWA's board of directors, in recognition of the power now held by the new investors. They do not seem to have made any change in Morgan's policies. Nor would Morgan have been suspicious of that power, for he regarded "capital" with an almost religious awe. "Concentration of capital" was for him a guiding principle, and he sometimes spoke of capital as though it were a living presence, as in these remarks at the Annual Fruit Growers' Convention in December 1902: "Would you return to the old conditions . . . or are you satisfied to let well enough alone and co-operate reasonably and heartily and loyally with capital, which while benefiting itself to a limited degree, is earnestly striving to put and keep the wine industry of California on a permanent and prosperous basis?"[29] The image is striking: "Capital," taking only a modest recompense for itself, strives "earnestly" in the service of others. Hellman and Huntington and the rest must have taken great comfort in the thought that their servant, "Capital," was employed in such self-sacrificing philanthropy.

There does not seem to be much record of the practices followed by the CWA in its dealings with growers, winemakers, and other merchants. The authors who know most about it have only a single summary remark on the subject. "We must concede," Ernest Peninou and Gail Unzelman write, that the CWA was "a monopoly" and was "sometimes ruthless."[30] The CWA surveyed the grape crop every year, balanced that figure against the wine that it already had on hand, and then set the price for grapes. The growers were bound by these "ruling figures," for there was no one to challenge the CWA by offering a higher price.[31] No doubt the growers often felt oppressed by CWA's rigidity.

The years from 1900 through 1915 were halcyon years for the CWA. There were ups and downs, of course: years of large harvest in 1902 and 1903, a short harvest in 1904, and, from time to time, efforts by competitors to cut prices and undersell the CWA. Phylloxera continued to be a problem; there were threats of new taxes, safely averted.[32] But every year was profitable, every year the CWA paid dividends, and every year it grew a little larger. In 1902, Morgan reported that the CWA had made two-thirds of all the wine produced in California that year.[33] By 1906 Morgan was able to assure his directors that the company was now so large that there was no reason to fear any hostile combination.[34] At one time or another in its brief history, the CWA owned or controlled eighty-one wineries in the state, from Sonoma and Napa counties to Los Angeles and Orange counties and at all points in between.[35] All this was owing to the policies of the CWA. In Percy Morgan's words to his directors at the end of 1901: "The relations of your Association with leading factors in the industry continue very harmonious, and by a policy of fair dealing with all, coupled with a strong hand against those who attempt to destroy or jeopardize the existing prosperity, it is hoped that the ties of mutual interest may be closer cemented as time goes on."[36] In short, the "concentration of capital," the "unanimity in management," and the "community of interests" that Morgan was so fond of invoking were operating nicely.[37]

EARTHQUAKE, FIRE, AND AFTER

The great earthquake of April 18, 1906, followed by the catastrophic fire that consumed large parts of the city of San Francisco, had erratic effects: parts of the city escaped relatively unscathed, others were thoroughly destroyed. The wine trade of the city, concentrated as it was in the old commercial district, was hard hit. And since most of the big properties were CWA properties, it was the CWA that suffered most. Of all its many cellars in the city, only that of the Italian Swiss Colony at Greenwich and Battery Streets, and the Calwa cellar at Third and Bryant, survived.[38]

Perhaps the most painful loss was that of a large stock of bottled wines that the CWA had been maturing under a program begun in 1904. Morgan had very much at heart a plan to produce and to market a superior line of California wines, to be bottled at the winery. He saw that an exclusive reliance on bulk sales would never give American wine drinkers any idea of what California could do. The bulk wines shipped from California were only standard wines to begin with, blends from many sources created to provide a uniform product. And bottlers might do anything to them once they left

FIGURE 17. The headquarters of the California Wine Association after the San Francisco earthquake and fire of 1906, formerly the headquarters of Kohler and Frohling. The building as it looked originally may be seen in figure 12. The tall figure on the left is Percy Morgan. Courtesy Gail Unzelman Collection.

California; adulteration and mislabeling were, the Californians were convinced, practiced wholesale all over the country to the great detriment of the reputation of California's wine.[39] Even if the bottler were honest, he might not have the right means of storage, the right equipment, or adequate knowledge to do the job properly. The solution, or at least a useful countermove, was to select, mature, and bottle wines at the CWA's own facilities. According to Morgan, writing in 1904, bulk shipments from California might reach 18 million gallons, but bottled wines, from all sources, "rarely reach in any year fifty thousand cases."[40] That was hardly enough to have an effect nationally. No single winery or small wine house could supply a market for superior wines, but the CWA could. As Morgan put it,

> Only a very large house ... with almost unlimited capital and the selection from millions of gallons of wine, on the lines of the great Bordeaux houses, can hope successfully and permanently to create a market under a brand which will command the confidence of wine drinkers, whether in Maine or in Florida or in New York or California.... The fine wines must be bottled in the cellars in which they have matured and immense vaults must be established for the proper ripening of wines in bottles.... These wines must be marketed in the original package, so that the consumer can be assured of a standard of excellence under labels which have everything to lose by any variation in quality or purity.[41]

He was already acting on his own advice. A building to provide those necessary "immense vaults" was built in 1905. The new brand of bottled wines was to go to market under the Calwa brand, and so the new building was named the Casa Calwa.[42] The building survived the earthquake and fire, but the bottled wines that it was meant to receive mostly did not; out of 250,000 bottles in the CWA building on Third Street, only some 35,000 were saved. The loss, Morgan sadly wrote, was the CWA's most serious, for such "old matured stocks . . . are impossible of replacement."[43] Morgan did not give up his plan but doggedly resumed it after the fire: the CWA, it was reported, "will at once begin the accumulation of new stocks for the purpose of carrying out their original plan."[44]

The wines of the Calwa brand were introduced to the market around 1910. Aged and bottled at the winery, long before this became a standard practice in California, they also bore proprietary and varietal names rather than the borrowed names of European wines. Vine Cliff was a pure Riesling, named for the Vine Cliff Vineyard in Napa Valley but bottled at the CWA's Greystone Winery outside St. Helena; Hillcrest was a Cabernet franc bottled at Winehaven but named after the wines of A. L. Tubbs, an original stockholder in the CWA, from his Napa Valley estate. Other wines introduced under the Calwa label, all named for CWA properties, included Winehaven, Greystone, and Wahtoke.[45]

The earthquake and fire were disasters, to be sure, but the CWA came through them with remarkable speed and energy; if anything, it emerged stronger than ever. Because it had large stocks of wine lying in its many wineries and cellars outside of San Francisco, it had wine ready for shipment, by rail and by sea, to its customers only two weeks after the fire: this, the *Pacific Wine and Spirit Review* declared, was proof that the CWA had "proper brains at the head of it."[46] The CWA was also reported to have made wine from its reserves available to its competitors.

The fire gave Morgan the opportunity to realize what he had long desired—that is, it allowed him to consolidate the operations of the CWA in the East Bay, where there was direct access to rail and water transport. The CWA's finances were still in good order. Morgan had published as early as May 1906, only a month after the quake and fire, a statement saying that the CWA would continue to pay "the modest dividends which the stockholders have lately been receiving."[47] Now he announced that the CWA would not rebuild any of its properties in San Francisco: it would instead move all of the San Francisco operations to a forty-seven-acre property on the shore

FIGURE 18. Winehaven, on Point Molate, San Francisco Bay, the final work of Percy Morgan for the California Wine Association. Courtesy Gail Unzelman Collection.

of San Francisco Bay, on the San Pablo peninsula, just west of the town of Richmond.

The building of Winehaven, as the new property was called, was the climax of Morgan's career, a monument to his executive ability. Everything about the place was to be in the superlative mode—the biggest, the most modern, the most efficient of all possible wine-making enterprises. And so it was. The buildings were constructed of steel, concrete, and brick—a safe haven for wine no matter what nature might do. The storage capacity was to be 5 million gallons immediately, with provision for an increase to 10 million. The winery itself was to be modest at the beginning, but was planned ultimately to handle twenty-five thousand tons of grapes annually—a quantity about equal to 4 million gallons of wine. After these essential facilities were built, a bottling plant, a cooperage shop, and a plant for the processing of by-products from grape skins, seeds, and stems were to be added. A wharf for oceangoing ships was built on the bay side; tracks from the mainline railroads led from the landward side; and the whole was threaded together by a private system of electric railroad. Eventually all this had added to it a distillery, a sherry-baking house, and a plant for the production of fresh grape juice—a concession to the increasing threat of prohibition. When it was complete, there were thirty-five buildings in the complex, dominated by the great crenellated, turreted, red-brick main building for offices and storage. This, "the biggest winery in the world," at once became one of the sights of the Bay Area, and has been vividly described in then-contemporary accounts: "There are hundreds and hundreds of tanks, so many that if you walk in front of each one of them you will have walked four miles," one reporter exclaimed, noting also that "they own their own wharf, 2000 feet long, and their own hotel for employees."[48]

AFTERMATH

Winehaven was ready to receive its first load of grapes in September 1907, but construction would not be finished until 1910. Before that, Morgan was exhausted by the extraordinary work that had been laid on him in the effort to keep the CWA on an even keel—as he did—through the disaster of the earthquake and fire and the labor of creating Winehaven. In 1909 he asked for a rest: "It was brought to the attention of the Committee that Mr. Morgan's medical advisor had expressed his opinion that it would be well for Mr. Morgan to take a rest and go away from San Francisco and be relieved of the daily responsibilities."[49] Morgan did go away but returned to work in 1910; then, early the next year, he finally retired from the CWA. The moment had come for his *nunc dimittis*.[50] He was gratified, he said, to think that he left the Association to his successor "in a better financial condition than it ever was before." And with that, Morgan was off to Europe with his family for the next three years. His days with the CWA were over.

The CWA continued on its prosperous way until the prohibition movement seemed to close off all prospects and to threaten what the wine men regarded as "confiscation." When Congress, in 1917, agreed to submit to the states a constitutional amendment for prohibition, the CWA directors gave up: their only course was to liquidate the company's assets before it was too late.[51] When national Prohibition went into effect in January 1920, the CWA had already managed to dismantle and dispose of most of its properties, though some parts remained. A final distribution of assets was made in 1936, and the company came to an end. Winehaven remained on the hands of a successor firm, the Calwa Corporation, until 1941, when the U.S. Navy took it over for use as a fuel depot. In 1995 the Navy pulled out; the property, listed in the National Register of Historic Places, now belongs to the city of Richmond; its fate remains unsettled.

FIGURE 19. Percy Morgan in an undated photograph, probably after his retirement from the California Wine Association. Courtesy Kelly Porter.

Percy Morgan returned to California in 1914 and marked his return by building a house, a huge, heavy, half-timbered pile of some fifteen thousand square feet in the Los Altos Hills. Called Lantarnam Hall, it was completed in 1915, but Morgan would live in it for only five years. In the morning of April 16, 1920, shortly before 9 A.M., he left his bedroom in his pajamas, went to the living room of his mansion, and shot himself in the head with a shotgun, dying instantly. Who knows why he did this? The family reported that he had been injured in an automobile accident some two months earlier and feared that the injuries would "permanently undermine his health."[52] Peninou and Unzelman, who have studied Morgan more thoroughly than any others have, suggest that the recent establishment of national Prohibition contributed to depress him.[53] He had evidently cared a great deal about the CWA and could hardly think of its annihilation with indifference. But he was still an active and wealthy man, a trustee of Stanford University and a director of many large businesses. Given the lack of any persuasive information, speculation seems idle.

What can be said in judgment of the CWA? It seems clear that it did bring a settled prosperity to the California wine trade in the years of its unhindered operation, say from 1900 to 1915. So long as those growers and winemakers who were independent of the CWA did not seek to attack it, they were welcome to share in the stability that it had created. Frank Swett, who operated a highly regarded winery near Martinez called Hill Girt, was emphatic in his opinion of Morgan's achievement: "Among some of the independent wine makers there is a tendency to criticise and carp at the California Wine Association. I am an independent wine maker and have no affiliation with the C.W.A., but I am not narrow-minded enough [not] to realize that the strong, intelligent, and far-seeing management of Mr. Morgan has been one of the predominant factors in the prosperity of both growers of wine grapes and makers of wine."[54]

When, after repeal, the renewed wine industry was struggling through the difficult years of the Great Depression, an organization in many ways reminiscent of the CWA was created to meet the dire situation. This was called Central California Wineries, a combine of some nineteen growers and winemakers backed by the Bank of America. It succeeded in raising the price of wine grapes in California, which had been hopelessly low, and in maintaining wine prices, but it then attracted the attention of the federal authorities. An antitrust suit was prepared against Central California Wineries, and though it was dropped, the mere threat was a sufficient scare: when the big distillers moved into the California wine trade in the early years of the war, Central California Wineries happily sold out to them.

Since then, there has been nothing like the CWA in California, though we live in an age of accelerating business consolidation on a global scale, and though there are now many wine-making enterprises far bigger than the CWA ever dreamed of becoming. Perhaps that is why another CWA is not likely: the scene is too large to be dominated by any one entity, especially now that wine is a thoroughly international commodity.

SEVEN

Paul Garrett

AMERICAN WINE FOR AMERICANS

IN 1904 PERCY MORGAN ATTENDED the annual meeting of the American Winegrowers' Association in Buffalo, New York. It was not usual for the California trade to pay much attention to such affairs, since they were mostly about the concerns of the eastern winemakers, but Morgan was not one to miss a chance to make defensive alliances. And his time was not wasted, for, as he reported on his return to California, there in Buffalo he had met "a very giant—Mr. Paul Garrett, of Norfolk, West Virginia." Morgan, an Englishman, had a somewhat shaky notion of American geography—Norfolk is of course in Virginia, not West Virginia. But his impression of Garrett agreed with that of many others. People called him "Captain" Garrett in instinctive recognition of his commanding way; or, as Morgan put it, the man was "a very giant."[1] Morgan added, in his usual cautious manner, that Garrett was "a little radical in some of his ideas," but he, Morgan, was nevertheless convinced that if those ideas were acted on, America would quickly become a wine-drinking nation.

When Morgan called Garrett's ideas "radical," what he meant was that Garrett had ideas about the future of wine in America that were bigger and more enthusiastically held than those anyone else had ever dared to have. Garrett believed, quite simply and without qualification, that America could and would be a country flowing with wine—American wine. And he would be the man to show how it was to be done. Twenty-five years after Percy Morgan first encountered Garrett, *Time* magazine published a story about Garrett to show how the wine industry was managing to survive under Prohibition. By that time, Garrett, now described as "portly" and "florid," had become a man of substantial wealth; nevertheless, as the *Time* writer put it, after fifty-one years in the wine business Garrett still had little thought for anything but grapes: "He ponders how to perfect grapes, how to blend grapes, how to sell grapes."[2] Since the country still lay under the blight of Prohibition in 1928, one could not talk about wine, though that of course was the meaning of all those grapes that so occupied Garrett. After repeal, *Time's* sister publication, *Fortune,* published an interview with Garrett; this was at a time when the just-renewed American wine industry was feebly groping about, trying to find its way under the most awful conditions: a market ignorant of wines, an industry without skilled winemakers, and a national depression of unprecedented severity. No matter: Garrett's ideas were just as big and confident as ever. "The wine industry," he told the *Fortune* writer, ought to be—*it can be*—bigger than the automobile industry, bigger than the steel industry."[3] Whatever others might think, to Garrett this was no exaggeration but a self-evident truth. If, he liked to argue, the authorities would only classify wine as a food and relieve it from the burden of taxation under which it suffered, then some 5 million acres of land would be planted to vines and would produce 2.5 billion gallons of wine while giving "pleasant and profitable employment" to 17 million Americans![4]

In his undeviating pursuit of this vision, Garrett accomplished a number of impressive things, but only three of his activities will occupy us in this chapter: how he sold great quantities of wine; how he successfully straddled the Prohibition years; and how he showed that east and west could be profitably combined.

ORIGINS

The beginnings of the Garrett story lie in what is almost the prehistory of wine making in America. Sidney Weller (1791–1854) was a Yankee, a graduate of Union College in Schenectady, New York, who, for the sake of his health, made his way south early in the 1820s and set up as a farmer outside of Brinkleyville, Halifax County, North Carolina. Weller had new ideas about farming in the south, where farmers had, for many years, carried on what was more like mining than farming, extracting the wealth of the soil in a few years of cotton growing and then moving on to new fields, leaving an exhausted land behind them. Weller would do no such thing. Instead, he would restore the worn-out four hundred acres that he had bought to a healthy fertility by crop rotation, by planting cover crops, by manuring, draining, and other newfangled ideas. He was always on the lookout for crops other than cotton that Southern farmers could plant, and he was quick to see possibilities in the grapes of the South—notably the muscadine variety known as Scuppernong.

The muscadine *(Muscadinia rotundifolia)*, a native of the coastal regions of the American Southeast, is not like other grapes. It has a different chromosome count, making it difficult to hybridize with other grape species; the fruit grows not in tight bunches but in loose clusters of a few large berries, which fall from the vine when ripe; it does not take to conventional pruning but prefers to ramble over large pergolas; it is remarkably disease-free and is the only grape known that shows any resistance to the attacks of Pierce's disease, which, like the muscadine itself, is native to the Southeast. Finally, it has a powerfully distinctive taste, sweet and musky, that comes through undiminished in its wine. Southerners, who know the grape as a fresh fruit and a source of jams, jellies, pies, and other desserts, are fond of this taste. Others may acquire it, or they may not. Like most other native grapes, the muscadine does not have a natural sugar content high enough to produce the alcoholic content necessary for a sound wine. The winemaker must therefore add sugar to the crushed grapes to bring the potential alcohol to the required level. This is an ancient practice, legal where the grapes need it (e.g., Germany), illegal where they don't (e.g., California).

Weller planted a vineyard of muscadines in 1828, and by 1835 he had begun commercial production of wine at what he proudly called the Médoc Vineyard—like most pioneers, he was not shy about making the highest claims for his enterprise.[5] The chances that the plains of eastern North Carolina could be made to resemble the Médoc were slim indeed; but no matter—Médoc it was.[6] The wine-making operation was not large, and, in a way, it was most improbable, for Weller, besides being an enlightened agriculturist, was an "ardent prohibitionist."[7] Probably he belonged to that class of prohibitionist that looked upon wine as the drink of temperance and saw no contradiction between drinking wine and opposing strong drink. In any case, Weller made and sold wine from a vineyard of some six acres, producing from forty to seventy barrels of wine annually—say, from twenty-five hundred to thirty-five hundred gallons.[8]

Sidney Weller died in 1854, but the wine making that he began continued under his son John, and the enterprise managed to survive the Civil War. In 1867, in the confused days of Reconstruction, Weller's Médoc property was bought by two brothers named Garrett: C. W. Garrett and Dr. Francis Marion Garrett. They changed Weller's exotic Médoc name to the more homely Ringwood Winery, Ringwood being one of the nearby hamlets.[9] But apart from that change, they continued to carry on what Weller had started, making muscadine wine and wine from the other small fruits of the region, particularly blackberries. And they greatly expanded what Weller had started and sustained.

BIRTH OF A SALESMAN

Dr. Francis Garrett, though a part owner of the winery, was not an active winemaker. That business was in the hands of his brother Charles, and after a time the enterprise was called C. W. Garrett and Company in recognition of this fact. Charles Garrett had lived in New York City before the Civil War, where he owned a successful clothing business. When the war broke out, Charles made his way back to the South. His business property was confiscated by the Yankees, but he kept his house on Murray Hill. After the war Charles sold the house, and it was the money from that sale that allowed him to join his brother in the purchase of the Weller property.

Dr. Garrett, though not an active partner in the work of the winery, nevertheless had an important contribution to make. This was his son Paul, born in 1863 to the doctor's first wife (he would have two more marriages, the third one most unlucky). Paul grew up in Halifax County, where he enjoyed the active, outdoor life of rural North Carolina but did not take kindly to school. He went to a country school where he was regarded as a dullard and then spent a miserable year at a military school. Paul begged to be allowed to return home and was finally allowed to leave with the understanding that he would work for his uncle Charles in the winery. This was in 1876, when he was thirteen years old (or 1877 and fourteen: the record is confused). Since his mother had died when Paul was only eight, and since his father had remarried unhappily, Paul, after leaving school, not only went to work for his Uncle Charles but lived with him as well. Charles's only son had died in infancy, so Paul became a second son to him. And for his part, Paul later acknowledged that he owed more to his Uncle Charles than to his own father.

He spent the next ten years learning the business in every detail. He was, he said, no good at growing things—"as a farmer, I have always proved myself a failure"[10]—but he worked enough in the vineyards to understand what went on there. It was in business affairs that he shone. In the quiet months between harvests, he kept the books, he carried on the correspondence (in an age without typewriters), he filled the orders, and he tended to all the other routine details of the winery operation. When the harvest and wine making began in September, he worked an eighteen-hour day, "keeping up my book-keeping, supervising the shipping, supervising and actually working in the winemaking," as well as bossing as many as three hundred men, women, and children who gathered the grapes, and another thirty or forty men—"colored employees"—who made the wine. "It was in this work of handling the labor and making the wine that I believe I became especially proficient."[11]

When his Uncle Charles died in 1886, Paul had every reason to think that he would have an important part in running the winery. But Charles died suddenly, without a will, and the direction of affairs went into the hands of his son-in-law, named Spooner Harrison. There was no love lost between Paul Garrett and Harrison, who, according to Garrett, was given over to "habitual intoxication." And so it happened that one day, soon after Charles Garrett's death, Spooner Harrison, "apparently quite under the influence of distilled spirits," came to the winery office and let Garrett know that he would "have to look for another job."[12]

By a lucky coincidence, two of the leading salesmen for the winery, the brothers Sy and June Wright, had paid their annual visit to headquarters shortly after Charles Garrett's death and, seeing the way things lay there, offered Paul a job with them at their home base in Little Rock, Arkansas. After some misunderstandings and delays, Paul accepted the offer and left familiar North Carolina for unknown Arkansas, where he would no longer be making wine but selling it.

The scene in the South at the time Garrett set out to sell wine could hardly have been more unpropitious. The South, even twenty years after Appomattox, was still dirt poor. Outside of a few coastal cities—Charleston, Savannah, New Orleans—there was no tradition of wine drinking. Whiskey—bourbon or moonshine—was the drink of the rural South. And muscadine wine—heavy bodied, musky, and sweet—has severely limited attractions. But it was under these conditions that Paul Garrett first set out to sell wine. To make his attempt even worse, he had, he says, no confidence in his abilities and no idea of how to go about selling wine. The Wrights would listen to no excuses, however, and told him to pack his bags for a three-month trip through north Texas to sell Ringwood wines. "I had never" he wrote, "been in a saloon in my life, had never taken a drink of whiskey";[13] nor, apparently, had he drunk much wine. Back home in North Carolina, "where the prohibition sentiment was steadily advancing," as Garrett recalled, the Garrett family "rarely served our own wine on our own table."[14]

Loaded down with all these disadvantages of innocence, young Garrett got off the train at Blossom Prairie, Texas, and timidly made his way to the less imposing of the town's two saloons. There he sought out the owner, a "lanky, rather unkempt man, with drooping moustache," and showed his little list of Ringwood wines. "I don't sell no wine, Sonny," was the response. "I wouldn't sell a drink in a month; in fact I don't remember that I ever heard a call for wine. Folks in this country want red 'likker'—the stronger the better."[15] Now desperate, his heart sinking, and wondering what to say next, Garrett "began to describe to him what a Scuppernong vine was like, what an unusual grape it was[,] and telling him of the vast acres we had in these grapes from which we made the finest wine in the world." Who knows where the inspiration came from? Where were those "vast acres"? Who had produced "the finest wine in the world"? And how? But Garrett saw that he had made an impression, and soon he had booked a substantial order—so substantial that he had to persuade his customer to cut it down a bit.

As it happened, that first customer paid his bills promptly and remained on the company's books for many years. And Garrett himself, after his first anxious, improvised encounter, never looked back. The Texas trip was a triumph. When Garrett met up with Sy Wright, the older of the brothers, by appointment in San Antonio at the end of his tour, the two compared their commissions and found that Garrett had sold more than twice as much as his boss. "It was my first great achievement."[16]

Back in Little Rock, Garrett and the Wrights set up agencies for the sale of C. W. Garrett wines throughout Arkansas under the name of the Standard Wine Company. To supply the trade that quickly developed, Garrett established a warehouse and bottling plant in Little Rock, broke in "a crew of colored boys," and worked the plant eighteen hours a day: "We did a wonderful business."[17] So wonderful was it, the company was in danger of running out of wine—the supply from North Carolina was limited, since Spooner Harrison was not interested in expanding production at that end.

Garrett was sent to California instead, where he first investigated Napa County but found no suitable wines there: "practically all of them being known as 'Dago Red' wines, consumed by Italians in the large Eastern centers."[18] He did better in Los Angeles County. There he contracted for 300,000 gallons of wine from the San Gabriel Winery, chiefly port and sherry, as they called the sweet fortified wines of the region. This is the earliest instance of Garrett's combining the eastern and the California wine businesses, as he would continue to do throughout his career. At some point not long after the deal with the San Gabriel Winery, Garrett bought another 350,000 gallons of California wine, this time from the Sunnyslope Winery in the San Gabriel Valley, founded by L. J. Rose and now owned by English investors who were hoping to profit from the phylloxera plague in Europe.[19]

Before all this, however, Garrett had suffered from the first of his many business encounters with the forces of prohibition. Arkansas was not yet a dry state, but there was a growing number of dry counties—twenty-four out of seventy-five by 1888—and a growing dry sentiment at work throughout the state. Local option put the wine trade at risk in many parts of Arkansas. Garrett's account of the episode is obscure and hard to follow, but the upshot is clear enough. He blames the misconduct of other winemakers for the trouble. But whatever the cause, Garrett and the Wrights, under pressure from the courts, agreed to wind up their business in Arkansas and leave the state before the end of the year 1888. The Standard Wine Company then removed to Memphis, Tennessee, and resumed its business of distributing wine in the South and Southwest. Garrett continued to travel, though he now made a specialty of what he called "missionary work, sounding out new territories."[20]

Then came a major change. In October of 1889 Garrett returned to North Carolina to marry Sarah Harrison (always called "Sadie"), the sister of his nemesis, the "permanently intoxicated" Spooner Harrison. Garrett had arrived at an understanding with the Wrights that, when he had returned to Memphis with his bride, he would no longer be called on to travel but would take charge of the office. When he got back to Memphis, however, he was told that he would, after all, have to travel, alternating with one of the Wrights from month to month. Faced with this prospect, Garrett determined to sell out his interest in the Standard Wine Company and return to North Carolina. And so he did.

Back in North Carolina, he was offered the exclusive right to sell the production of the Ringwood Winery, Spooner Harrison evidently thinking that he could now use the services of a man who had become his brother-in-law. But conflict between the two men was irrepressible. Garrett, in his own, not entirely clear, account of things, says that he sold large quantities of wine, but that Harrison, despite being bound by definite contracts, refused to pay him for his work. So, in or around 1890, Garrett made a deal with Harrison: the Ringwood Winery would supply him with wine in lieu of the money it owed him, and Garrett would sell it on his own account. To assist him in this, he was permitted to operate under the name of Garrett and Company.[21] He rented a small warehouse in Littleton, North Carolina, ten miles or so to the north of Spooner Harrison in Ringwood, and began traveling for himself. Thus began his independent operations, "with his father keeping his books, a little sister putting on shipping tags, and a reliable Negro boy taking care of the shipments."[22]

MAKING WINE

But Garrett was still tied to the Ringwood Winery for his stock in trade, and Harrison was still obstructive: when orders were sent in, they were often not filled. To break out of this impasse, Garrett first turned to New York as a source of supply, knowing that the wineries around Hammondsport in the Finger Lakes made "a line of wines somewhat similar to those I was selling." He contracted with the Urbana Wine Company for two or three carloads of wine to be sent to Littleton, "chiefly Catawba and Port."[23] Such wines, however, were not what he really wanted. The "backbone of my business," he wrote, was native wine—Scuppernong especially, but blackberry and fruit wines too—and if he wanted adequate supplies of these things, he would have to make them himself. So he did, at first by very primitive methods indeed. Perhaps to avoid the appearance of competing with his brother-in-law, Garrett's first wine making was carried out in Georgia, where a man named Robert Rockwell, in Columbus County, had some wine-making equipment, though it was "of the crudest kind." Knowing him to be an honorable man, Garrett engaged Rockwell to make wine for him from the Scuppernongs of the region. In order to insure a good response to his offer to purchase grapes from local growers, Garrett offered eighteen dollars a ton rather than the standard eight dollars, despite Rockwell's protests that he would be overwhelmed by the response to such an extravagantly generous offer. And so he was. Garrett was hastily summoned back to Georgia, where he found the road to the Rockwell place completely blocked by wagons and carts loaded with Scuppernong grapes. Garrett at once ordered an emergency supply of empty molasses hogsheads and whiskey barrels sent down from Wilmington, North Carolina, and the next day he, the Rockwell family, and such neighbors as could be recruited, crushed hundreds of barrels of Scuppernongs into the hogsheads and then transferred the juice to the whiskey barrels to ferment. Most of the grape pulp was wasted, but the resulting wine, most improbably, was, according to Garrett, "quality wine and in due time it helped materially in establishing the reputation for Paul Garrett's Scuppernong."[24]

FIGURE 20. Paul Garrett in 1896, aged thirty-three; he had already been operating independently as Garrett and Company for six years and owned a substantial winery in Weldon, North Carolina, from which he supplied a national market. Courtesy John Barden Collection.

From this improvised beginning, Garrett's wine making grew rapidly and without interruption. The small premises at Littleton were soon inadequate, so Garrett bought fifty acres on the outskirts of Weldon, North Carolina, on the banks of Chockoyotte Creek. Weldon, in Halifax County, was on the railroad and could provide Garrett with the transportation he needed as his production and sales grew. Here he built a solid three-story brick winery, which opened in 1893. Garrett, at the time he moved his business to Weldon, was said to be producing from 40,000 to 50,000 gallons of wine annually.[25] By the time he left it for Virginia, in 1903, the Chockoyotte winery had a capacity of 750,000 gallons. And the new winery at Norfolk was rated at a capacity of 4 million gallons—not a bad increase in barely more than a decade.[26]

Garrett had not yet hit on the name that would ever afterward identify his wines in the popular mind—that is, Virginia Dare. An advertisement from the Weldon years (1891–1903) lists instead the following wines from Garrett and Company, identified as "Wine Growers": Scuppernong, Escapernong (a variant of *Scuppernong*), Sacramental, Blackberry, Mish (another variety of muscadine), Catawba, port, sherry, claret, and champagne. The mixture of native names (Scuppernong, Mish, Catawba) with borrowed European names (port, sherry, claret, champagne) shows that Garrett had not yet decided to emphasize proprietary names with an American slant; nobody else did either, at the time. Scuppernong wine came first on the list, and that was no doubt the main product; Catawba very likely came from New York or Ohio, and, as a guess, the port and sherry came from California, where, as we have seen, Garrett had already had extensive dealings. Like most other substantial American wine producers, Garrett felt it necessary to provide a whole line of wines in order to give his customers what they wanted.[27]

The astonishing growth of Garrett and Company took place at the same time that the company was, paradoxically, in retreat. The enemy, of course, was prohibition. The state of North Carolina was not yet dry—statewide prohibition was not enacted until 1908—but so many straws were in the wind that anyone could see which way it was blowing. The dry sentiment was hardly a new thing: one remembers that Sidney Weller himself was an "ardent prohibitionist," and that Uncle Charles Garrett rarely had his own wine at table out of deference to the Drys of Halifax County. In 1903 North Carolina passed a piece of legislation called the Watts Law, providing for local option and prohibiting the manufacture and sale of alcoholic drink in all rural sections of the state. Garrett was not the sort of man to be caught out by such developments; doubtless he remembered his experience back in the 1880s, when he and the Wrights were forced out of Arkansas and took refuge in Tennessee. Now he prepared another move. In 1902 he bought a large piece of land at Berkley, Virginia, now a part of the city of Norfolk, which offered both rail and water transport. And there he built a monument to his own achievements, a splendid new winery crowned by a tower carrying, in Garrett's customary superlative style, "the largest clock on earth."[28]

When the Norfolk winery was in operation, Garrett achieved a volume of production that could not possibly have been supplied by the Scuppernong harvest of the coastal South, even though, as he said, "I was buying grapes from thousands of growers throughout the coastal region of Virginia and North Carolina." He still had the Chockoyotte winery, which alone was probably large enough to absorb the available crop of Scuppernongs. Obviously, he had to have supplies from other sources, mainly New York and California, and ultimately he bought large properties in both states in order to secure his sources. The grapes that he got from these new sources would not, of course, be scuppernongs but rather the native hybrids (e.g., Catawba, Isabella, Concord, Delaware) that grew in the New York vineyards, and the vinifera grapes that grew in California. How much of this alien fruit went into Virginia Dare wine is not known, but undoubtedly some of it—probably a lot of it—did. East and west met in Virginia Dare wine.

Garrett expanded his empire in various directions. An undated post-

FIGURE 21. Garrett and Company's Norfolk, Virginia, plant, constructed in 1906. The frieze at the bottom illustrates Garrett's wine-making properties in Saint Louis; Keuka Lake, New York; St. Helena, California; and three in North Carolina. Courtesy John Barden Collection.

card from the Garrett winery in Norfolk shows six other establishments then belonging to the firm. In addition to the Chockoyotte winery (capacity 750,000 gallons), there are the Tokay Vineyard (75,000 gallons, perhaps the winery established by Col. Wharton Green near Fayetteville, North Carolina); the Medoc Vineyard (130,000 gallons; the original family winery, no longer owned by Spooner Harrison); a winery at Penn Yan, New York (rated at 2 million bottles—this is where Garrett got his sparkling wine); a winery at St. Helena, California, of 250,000 gallons' capacity; and a distribution center in Saint Louis with a storage capacity of 1,250,000 gallons in bulk and 1 million bottles. With the 4 million gallons of the Norfolk winery, this series adds up to, say, about 7 million gallons of storage capacity. There were bigger wine-making enterprises in California then, but not many: and in the East there was nothing to approach it. Percy Morgan was right to call Garrett a "giant," for he was that, not only for the size of his ideas, but also for the size of his material means.

There was also a prudential motive behind this dispersion of things. Garrett had already been driven from Arkansas and North Carolina and would soon be driven from Virginia by the spread of prohibition. If he scattered his wine-making operations, he might always hope to have a producing facility in service for grapes from any source, even when other wine-making plants might be shuttered.

At some point, probably around the turn of the century, Garrett had come up with a new name for his white, sweet Scuppernong wine that gave it a special identity and a special fitness for promotion. Since the Scuppernong could claim to be the original white American grape, the first of the native grapes that the first English settlement knew, he would call its wine after the first-born white child in the new world: Virginia Dare. An artist produced the head of a pretty woman to stand for Virginia (who almost certainly did not survive infancy and of whom no picture of course exists): she wears a cap on her head, which is framed in long curls, and a puff-sleeved dress. This wholly imaginary young woman, in various forms over the years, appeared on the firm's stationery, on its wine labels, and in all its advertising, where she was identified as "the first lady of the land," and of course her wine was Garrett's Scuppernong.

One of the early promotional devices put out by Garrett was a preposterous book called *The White Doe or the Fate of Virginia Dare,* written by a woman from North Carolina named Sallie Southall Cotten, published by Lippincott in Philadelphia in 1901, and widely distributed as a giveaway by Garrett and Company. The story is composed of a few pages of "history" and some information about the Scuppernong grape, followed by a verse narrative too foolish to be summarized here. But Garrett evidently took the view that any ink was good ink, and so the book was passed out to visitors at the winery or at fairs and expositions stamped with this message: "Compliments of Garrett & Co. pioneer American wine growers, Norfolk, VA, producers of the famous Virginia Dare brand of Scuppernong wine."[29] It is possible, though there is no direct evidence, that Garrett's inspiration to call his wine "Virginia Dare" came from this book.

Garrett now had an American name to go with his American wine, and though he never ceased to produce wines with borrowed names (port, sherry, claret, etc.), he tried hard to follow up the line struck out by Virginia Dare, though without anything like the success that he scored with that one hit. An advertisement for Garrett wines in 1913 presents the following names, among others: Virginia Dare (white Scuppernong); Pocahontas (red Scuppernong); Old North State Blackberry; Hiawatha (red champagne); Minnehaha (dry Scuppernong). The Indians never enjoyed the popularity of the lone white girl, but that was not for any lack of effort on Garrett's part. His attempt to promote proprietary names was a step in the right direction, away from the

FIGURE 22. Garrett's famous "first lady of the land," Virginia Dare, created around the turn of the twentieth century to identify Garrett's white Scuppernong wine and synonymous with Garrett and Company thereafter. Courtesy Special Collections, California Polytechnic University, Pomona.

usual practice of appropriating European names. Originally, Garrett identified the grape that produced the wines (Minnehaha = dry Scuppernong), but gradually, as the proportion of Scuppernong in his wines dwindled and the proportion of wines from New York and California steadily increased, the proprietary name stood alone: Virginia Dare was Virginia Dare, never mind what it was made of. How much Scuppernong there might have been in a bottle of Virginia Dare before Prohibition is not known; after repeal, I suspect, it virtually disappeared from the mix. But there is no question that the wine was popular, and that at one time it was practically pure Scuppernong, showing that the taste for the grape can be created, just as that saloon keeper in Blossom Prairie, Texas, had discovered years earlier.

Another practice in which Garrett was far in advance of the rest of the trade was his insistence on selling Virginia Dare in bottle rather than in bulk. The dominant practice in the American wine business was for a winery to ship its wine in bulk to regional bottlers, who put their own labels on the wine and distributed it to their territories. Wine handled thus could have no identity beyond what the bottler chose to give it, and it was subject to all sorts of hazards: unsanitary conditions of storage and bottling, mislabeling, adulteration, and so on. These dangers were all the more present when wine was sold, as it often was, not in bottles but directly from anonymous barrels, drawn off into any sort of container that the customer might present. Garrett, by giving his wine a proprietary name and bottling it himself, could guarantee the purity of his product and at the same time give people something identifiable to ask for: not "some white wine, please," but "a bottle of Virginia Dare." These practices were essential to Garrett's success.

SURVIVING PROHIBITION

Garrett's retreat from a spreading prohibition continued: he had had to move from Arkansas to Tennessee in 1888; in 1903 he abandoned North Carolina for Virginia; and not very long after building his great winery in Norfolk the shadow of prohibition began to fall over Virginia. Under the formidable Bishop James Cannon, the Virginia branch of the Anti-Saloon League had been drying up the state at a rapid rate by various forms of local option. In 1910 the league announced that it was now determined to secure statewide prohibition. Garrett, as head of the Brewers, Wine and Spirit Merchants of Virginia, did what he could to assist the opposition, but they lacked heart and were divided among themselves, whereas the Drys were united in the zealous conviction of righteousness.[30] As though in quiet acknowledgement of certain defeat, Garrett himself moved to Penn Yan, New York, in 1912. There, on twelve hundred acres on the shores of Keuka Lake, he built a summer residence, complete with guest cottages, servants' quarters, and tennis courts. From this vantage he could survey his vineyards and the lake where, it was later said, he kept the fastest motorboat of all.[31] Virginia went dry by overwhelming vote in September 1914, though the enabling legislation was not passed until 1916. The main production of Garrett and Company's wines did not, however, move from Virginia until 1917, since extra time was allowed for established industries to relocate.

For this last of Garrett's moves, a winery was built in a part of the vast commercial development on the Brooklyn waterfront known as the Bush Terminal. The head offices of the company were also located there and remained there until the end. Garrett himself kept a Manhattan apartment as well as his Keuka Lake summer home. More and more of the firm's operations were concentrated in New York City, where grapes were sent from upstate New York or New Jersey to be converted into wine, or young wines from distant wineries were sent to be finished, bottled, and shipped.

But the wine-making operation did not have long to live. Congress voted to submit a constitutional amendment prohibiting the manufacture and sale of alcoholic drink to the states in 1917; under the pressure of the Anti-Saloon League, the main force directing the campaign in favor of the amendment, the necessary number of state ratifications was obtained by January 1919. The Volstead Act, spelling out the terms by which the amendment would be enforced, was passed that year; and early in January 1920, national Prohibition took effect.

As in the various state contests, so in the national campaign for prohibition there had been little organized opposition, and hardly any effective opposition at all: few of the people most concerned knew what to do besides protesting the innocence of their work. Garrett no doubt did what he could, but obviously to little effect. But after the damage had been done, he did succeed in opening an extraordinary loophole in the structure of the Volstead Act. When that Act was being prepared, Garrett called on its main architects, Wayne Wheeler and E. C. Dinwiddie of the Anti-Saloon League, and learned that they had no wish to cause a loss of crops to the American farmer or to harm the interests of grape growers, so long as the plan of prohibition was not affected. After several discussions of the issue, Wheeler drew up the paragraph that enabled home wine making throughout the Prohibition years (section 29, Title II of the Volstead Act): "The penalties provided in this chapter against the manufacture of liquor without a permit shall not apply to a person manufacturing nonintoxicating cider and fruit juice exclusively for use in his home, but such cider and fruit juices shall not be sold or delivered except to persons having permits to manufacture vinegar."

Originally, the word *wine* was used in this paragraph, but when that was objected to in the House debate on the bill, *fruit juice* was substituted for it. Garrett was far from satisfied with this formula: How did you "manufacture" fruit juices? And what had they to do with wine? Wheeler assured him, however, that this form of words would be satisfactory. As for *nonintoxicating,* that term was deliberately left undefined. And so, under this somewhat obscure and ambiguous provision, the grape growers of America were rescued: home wine-making grew to such an undreamed-of volume that, until overproduction burst the bubble, the early dry years were a time of unprecedented prosperity for the vineyardist. Garrett claimed at the time that the credit for this strange development was his, and he was not contradicted.[32]

During the nearly fourteen years of national Prohibition (January 16, 1920–December 5, 1933) a great many American wineries simply went out of business. But a considerable number of them went into a kind of hibernation, reducing their activity but staying alive in a quiescent mode. Wineries that owned vineyards could sell fresh grapes to home winemakers, and they could make and store wine from the leftover crop. Some wine could be sold for sacramental purposes, or for medical purposes, but neither of these markets, despite the many myths about them, amounted to much. Wineries could make grape "products"—such things as jellies, sauces, tonics, and grape concentrates. The latter item was the main product. People could make wine from concentrate at home at any time of the year, and millions did.

Garrett and Company stayed alive in this fashion, offering among other things, a grape concentrate that would make a "champagne" as fine, it was blandly said, as a genuine vintage champagne.[33] The company also developed a line of flavoring extracts, still being manufactured today under the Virginia Dare name, by a company spun off from Garrett and Company during the Prohibition years. Garrett managed to maintain production permits for all his varied properties during Prohibition; he kept a bonded warehouse in Chicago; and he installed a "de-alcoholizing plant" in the Bush Terminal winery to operate on the 10 million gallons of wine that he had in storage when Prohibition went into effect.[34] But little wine making could have gone on in his scattered empire. The letterhead of the firm in these years read: "Garrett and Company, Food Products."[35]

In 1929 a new prospect opened up. Overproduction had plagued American agriculture since the first World War, and the grape growers had also been led by the home wine-making boom into serious overplanting. President Hoover undertook to rescue American agriculture from its years of depression by an Agricultural Marketing Act; this created a Federal Farm Board, which managed a large fund to be used to "stabilize" the production of the major agricultural commodities: the growers would organize cooperatives, the Farm Board would lend them money, and with that money the co-ops would buy up surpluses, control production, and supervise marketing. Such was the plan, and to take advantage of it a group of big California growers—including Paul Garrett, who had been acquiring California vineyard property during Prohibition to add to the substantial property he already owned there—organized as Fruit Industries, Inc., a marketing co-op. Paul Garrett was chairman of the board and the leading public personality of the organization.

The Farm Board obligingly lent them a million dollars to start with, and Fruit Industries had then to think of something to do with the money. Their answer to the question was to push grape concentrate as it had never been pushed before. Calling it "Vine-Glo," Fruit Industries advertised its concentrate under eight different varieties: port, muscatel, tokay, sauterne, riesling, claret, burgundy, and—Virginia Dare! Garrett's hand was clearly evident there. To promote the sale of Vine-Glo, Fruit Industries offered a complete service: they would deliver the concentrate to your home, supervise its fermentation, and then bottle the wine. All the householder had to do was, first, pay for the concentrate, and second, drink the wine.

Garrett had another audacious scheme for selling Vine-Glo. In order to reassure the public as to the legality of making wine from the concentrate, Garrett proposed that Fruit Industries appoint a committee of referees who would publicly guide the sale of Vine-Glo. And who should they be? Garrett had a slate prepared: Mabel Walker Willebrandt, the assistant attorney general in charge of the enforcement of Prohibition; Lenna Yost, the legislative superintendent of the Woman's Christian Temperance Union; and Dr. E. C. Dinwiddie, who held the same office in the Anti-Saloon League. The Farm Board refused to accept this plan (though Dinwiddie agreed to serve), but its audacity says a great deal about Garrett.

Vine-Glo enjoyed a reasonable success for a time; it was not doing anything that other sellers of concentrate had not been doing, but it was doing those things much more noisily than the others and soon attracted hostile attention. This intensified when Willebrandt left the attorney general's office and became counsel for Fruit Industries, a move that set off much suspicious remark. The last straw was added when a Kansas City court determined that making wine from concentrate was illegal: if you bought fresh grapes you might, it was argued, use them for something other than wine. But if you bought concentrate, you had only one thing in mind, and that, the court said, was illegal. Section 29 of the Volstead Act was itself so unclear that it could be used both for and against home wine-making, so it offered only shaky support against the plain meaning of a court decision. In any case, the Prohibition Bureau, fearful of criticism, ordered Fruit Industries to withdraw Vine-Glo from the market.[36]

This all happened toward the end of 1931, when strong signs of approaching change were in the air. A number of wineries began producing wine again in the renewed hope that repeal could not be far away. The Democrats were already committed to repeal, and it was made certain by Roosevelt's election in 1932. Finally, in December 1933, the Eighteenth Amendment, instituting national Prohibition, was repealed by the Twenty-first. By that time the machinery for enforcing Prohibition had already been dismantled, and wine making was once again general—though much knowledge and experience had been lost and could be only slowly and painfully regained. Paul Garrett was one of the relatively few people still active at the dawn of repeal who had been prominent in the days before Prohibition. He *did* have the knowledge and the experience and, therefore, a great advantage. He did not fail to use it.

He had first to reclaim his right to the name Virginia Dare. Since he had merged his wine-making properties into the Fruit Industries co-operative in 1929, including the Virginia Dare name, described at the time as "perhaps the most valuable in the industry," the only way he could get it back was to buy it.[37] This he did in exchange for the large stocks of wine that he had accumulated in California and that were now eagerly sought as wineries scrambled to supply the pent-up demand that would be released upon repeal. The name Virginia Dare was worth the millions of dollars of wine that it cost him to recover it.

That name was probably the best-known survival from the pre-Prohibition days, and Paul Garrett's was the best-known name among the country's winemakers. As *Fortune* put it, "Everyone called Mr. Garrett the Dean of American Wine Growers."[38] He certainly deserved the recognition: no one else had his length of experience; no one else had the extent of his experience, covering as it did all the wine-growing regions of the country; and, for sure, no one else had anything approaching the splendor of his vision of what America's wine growing could become.

When, in Roosevelt's first administration, the federal government was desperately casting about for any ideas that might help a deeply depressed economy, Paul Garrett put forward a plan dear to his heart. The government should provide the means for the farmers of the South to plant muscadine vines on an unprecedented scale. Grape growing would help to restore the depleted soils of the region; the grapes would give the impoverished farmers a cash crop; and Paul Garrett would make wine from them to supply a demand that would grow without limit. He could get, he said, only about two thousand tons of muscadines for his current needs, at a time when he could use twenty thousand tons. If the scheme were carried out, Garrett prophesied, there was no reason why it should not extend to the entire country: 10 million acres might be planted, from which 5 billion gallons of wine would flow.

Wine making on that scale would solve the unemployment problem, and America would become a wine-drinking country.[39]

Nothing like that happened, though the government did give Garrett's plan a modest try.[40] Under the direction of the Federal Rehabilitation Agency, some six hundred thousand cuttings of muscadines were collected, and these were then distributed in quantities sufficient for a few acres each to farmers in North Carolina, South Carolina, Georgia, and Louisiana, including some at new communities, such as Pine Mountain Valley, Georgia, that had been recently created by the government. The plan was to plant five thousand acres in the first phase, beginning in 1934; but after a year only about two hundred acres had been planted. Garrett, who had undertaken to buy the produce of five thousand acres of muscadines for the next ten years, performed his part of the bargain, building a new plant in Atlanta and expanding his facilities in Virginia and North Carolina.[41] Then the work died, the victim of indifference and ignorance on the part of the farmers, and of Dry opposition back in Washington. Garrett was no doubt disappointed, but, needless to say, the result in no way dampened his enthusiasm.

There we may leave him. The fate of wine in America immediately following repeal was a disappointment for all concerned. Sales were far below what had been expected; the public taste was for sweet fortified wines called port, sherry, muscatel: dry table wines intended to be drunk with food had barely a quarter of the market and did nothing to attract a body of drinkers interested in seeing better wines. In these flat conditions, Garrett nevertheless managed to prosper; by 1939 he was selling 2 million gallons of wine a year, almost half of which was the old standby Virginia Dare.[42] At his death, of pneumonia, in New York City in March 1940, Garrett presided over an empire fully equal to what he had possessed before Prohibition: plants in New York City and in upstate New York, North Carolina, and California, and to supply these, thousands of acres of vineyards. His hopes for a direct succession, however, had been cruelly destroyed at the end of 1929, when his only son, Charles (named for the uncle who had been a father to Garrett himself) died of tuberculosis. The chapel that Garrett then built as a memorial to Charles still stands on Bluff Point, Keuka Lake, and it is there that Garrett himself is buried. Rather than any of his many wine-making properties, the chapel will perhaps be Garrett's most enduring material monument.

Since his death the wine business in America has been transformed beyond all recognition: fortified wines have virtually disappeared; table wines are made to a standard far surpassing anything that Garrett knew, and there are hundreds, even thousands, of winegrowers passionately competing to catch the attention and respect of an increasingly sophisticated class of wine drinkers. Paul Garrett's Scuppernong would have no chance at all amid such competition. Or would it? Would Garrett have changed with the times?

His successors did not. For a time the firm continued to grow; immediately after the war it had some ten thousand acres of vines, most of them in California. But by the late 1950s the firm's business was beginning to shrink: the New York plant was closed and all operations moved to Southern California. A few years later Garrett and Company, a family-held enterprise, decided to go out of business, figuring that its real estate was worth more than the family could hope to make by continuing in the rapidly changing wine business. The Virginia Dare name for wine was sold to the Guild Winery in 1961 and now belongs to the Centerra (formerly Canandaigua) Wine Company. The label, as of 2011, is not in use.

EIGHT

Ernest and Julio Gallo

CREATING NEW MARKETS

RETROSPECT

If, at the end of his long life, Ernest Gallo (1909–2007) troubled to look back over his career, what he saw was the whole extent of American wine history since its rebirth after the repeal of Prohibition at the end of 1933, the year that he went to work as a winemaker. He could take great satisfaction from the view, for what it showed was that, of all the many wine-making enterprises that had appeared in that dawn, his alone had survived and prospered: Roma, Petri, Italian Swiss Colony, Fruit Industries, Inglenook, Beaulieu, Larkmead, Christian Brothers, Paul Masson—all were gone or had been swallowed up and transformed by big conglomerates. Gallo himself now owned Louis Martini and Mirassou and Frei Brothers, though they were mere appendages to the huge body of his enterprise. The names of the big competitors that he had had to face at the beginning—mostly Italian Americans who, unlike Gallo, had enjoyed the backing of A. P. Gianinni at the Bank of America—no longer figured in the trade talk: Cella, Martini, Rossi, Petri, Lanza, Baccigaluppi, Cribari. All, without exception, had disappeared. The Gallo winery alone still flourished. And how it flourished!

Ernest Gallo, with his younger brother Julio,[1] had taken out a license to make wine in the last months of the Prohibition era, when the authorities, knowing that repeal was certain, handed out permits with a free hand. The repeal amendment, the Twenty-first Amendment, would not actually be ratified until December 5, 1933, and until then the manufacture and selling of wine "for beverage purposes" would continue to be illegal under the laws of Prohibition. But there was no law against making and storing wine against the day when it would again be legal to sell it for the purpose for

FIGURE 23. Ernest Gallo (left) and Julio Gallo in 1983, on the occasion of their fiftieth anniversary in business partnership. Copyright E. and J. Gallo Winery.

which it was made, and there was an eager rush to get ready for that day. The brothers received their license in September, set up in a small rented property along the railroad tracks in Modesto, and furnished it with equipment acquired on credit. They had a source of supply in the substantial family vineyards outside Modesto and at Fresno.[2] The original license permitted them to produce up to 50,000 gallons of wine, but they were already thinking bigger than that. They persuaded some local growers to send them their grapes, to be paid for after the wine had been made and sold, and by the end of the year they had made nearly 180,000 gallons of wine. They had to request an amendment to their original license to cover this irregularity, but no one was disposed to make trouble for them now that repeal had at last come to pass.

The history of the Gallo winery, from this promising starting point, is one of uninterrupted, rapid growth to a size undreamed-of since Noah planted the first vine. Ernest, showing the energy and enterprise in salesmanship that marked him to the end, flew to Chicago and the East Coast before the brothers' new-made wine had barely had time to settle out, and there he sold what they had made: his competitors, traveling by train, lagged far behind him. The brothers' profit for the year was thirty-four thousand dollars, a most impressive sum in Depression dollars for a small start-up firm.[3] In the next year they were not only making more wine but also buying wine in bulk from other sources in California[4] and, in order to deal with all that wine, had to increase the storage capacity of their rented premises. In the next year, 1935, the winery had reached a capacity of 355,000 gallons; but that was only a fraction of their volume, for in that year they sold 941,000 gallons, most of it obviously bought in bulk from other producers. Such growth made it clear that they needed a bigger winery; so a new one, on Fairbanks Avenue in Modesto, was built with a storage capacity of a million gallons.

In 1937, a distillery was added to the new Fairbanks Avenue establishment, and the Gallos, who had up to this point been making table wine only, were now able to produce a high-proof brandy with which to fortify the sweet wines that the market mostly demanded. The taste for table wines had been badly damaged by the Prohibition years, when a high-alcohol kick was all that had been asked of bootleg wines. As a result, fortified wines outsold table wines three to one throughout the first years of repeal, a fact that could hardly escape Ernest Gallo's notice.[5] So Gallo now made fortified wines. He did not neglect table wines, however, even if the market for them was slow, as other winemakers found to their cost. Georges de Latour, the founder of the highly regarded Beaulieu Vineyard in Napa County, had 400,000 gallons of unsold table wine filling his winery's tanks as the harvest approached in the summer of 1937. Ernest Gallo, confident of his ability to sell anything, bought the contents of de Latour's entire cellar for a laughable eight cents a gallon, blended it with his own wine to make what he called "a very good wine" and sold the lot. De Latour had made his wine, Gallo said, "too dry and tart," but still, he wondered, why was it that "a fellow like de Latour couldn't sell all his wine, when we could sell all of ours."[6] Why, indeed? By 1939, at a time when other wineries were desperately seeking relief from over-production, falling prices, and a sinking market, the Gallos quietly expanded their winery capacity to 3 million gallons.

So far their trade had been entirely in what is called bulk wine, as had that of almost every other California winery at the time. After the wineries had made and stored wine in a given year, they found buyers for it in the cities across the country. These buyers were called bottlers, people who operated bonded wine cellars, and it was their business to find supplies of wine (usually at the lowest possible cost) to store, blend, and bottle under labels of their own devising, and to sell it in their territory—regional, state, or local, according to the size of their operation. There were hundreds of these bottlers all over the country, and they were supplied mostly by means of railroad tank cars, each filled with 8,000 gallons of California wine. What happened to the wine after it reached the bottler was open to chance. The bottler might have adequate premises and machinery to handle the wine, or he might not. He might or might not advertise effectively and send out salesmen who knew what they were doing. The system gave the winemakers an advantage, since it made the bottlers negotiate the complex labyrinth of state and local regulations for the taxation and sale of alcoholic drink. But it also gave winemakers the disadvantage of having no control over their wines after they were shipped out and, most important, made it impossible to establish any identity. The wines that went out from the bottlers were labeled only as California or New York port, or sherry, or burgundy, with any brand name that the bottler might fancy—Old Monk muscatel, Chateau de Springfield sherry, Royal Secret port—names like that, of which there were literally hundreds, all of them meaningless. The buyer of such a bottle—and such bottles were the standard items of American wine commerce—had no way of knowing what was in the bottle, or what grapes it might be made of, or where it came from (apart from the state), or who made it.

Ernest Gallo saw clearly that the bulk wine business was not going to take an ambitious winemaker very far. As early as 1937 he began to think about changing his business, a change that would require three things: the creation of a brand; the means to do his own bottling; and control of distribution. He could not yet get any of these things, but he was thinking hard.

In 1940 he took a critical first step by buying a half interest in a New Orleans bottler, Franek and Company, that had run into financial difficulties. Gallo could now bottle wines for the New Orleans market under his own name as well as under those names already owned by Franek, and did so, though only in a small way. In the next year he acquired a Los Angeles bottler in the same way and now undertook to make a serious study of how wine was sold at retail in the Los Angeles market. He spent many days in Los Angeles learning what he had to deal with by the simple and direct method of visiting liquor stores all over the city, a method that he faithfully continued for most of the rest of his life. He thought about containers—he preferred clear glass to colored because it displayed the wine better. He thought about labels, about window and store-floor displays, about billboards and

JOLLY OLD GALLO

Sweet
Wines
20%
Alcohol
By Volume

Be Jolly! By Golly
BUY GALLO!

FIGURE 24. An early venture in brand-name advertising by Gallo, around 1940. From *Wine Review*, n.d.

other forms of advertising. And, applying his conclusions, he began to sell wine labeled "Gallo" in Los Angeles. "By golly buy Gallo," was an early advertising slogan, one of many false steps in those uncertain years.

The war years interrupted Gallo's plans, but not entirely. Every winemaker could readily sell all that he made in those years, when liquor was rationed, production limited, and demand high. Ernest Gallo was not content, however, merely to stand still. He secured a bottling line in a typical move. A New York bottler was in financial trouble, so Gallo, in exchange for the New Yorker's bottling machinery, made him a Gallo wholesaler.[7] The bottling line was, Gallo said, "ramshackle," but it was somehow shipped to Modesto over the wartime rails, accompanied by its own mechanic.[8] Now, though the line was primitive, Gallo could bottle his own wines under his own name at his Modesto property. At the same time, 1942, Gallo hired his first trained enologist, a breed that hardly yet existed in California. The few who did were now mostly in the armed services, but Gallo found one anyway. This was Charles Crawford, a graduate of Berkeley and Cornell, who came to run the Gallo laboratory and stayed until his death in 1999. As Crawford recalled it, Ernest Gallo, in hiring him, said that he wanted to improve his wines: "He wanted to make the best wine that could be made and sell it at a reasonable price."[9] Who could quarrel with that?

Immediately after the war a delusional euphoria swept over the wine business. Wartime conditions had forced Americans, at least those relatively few Americans who drank any wine at all, to drink American wine, since imports from the traditional sources—France, Germany, Italy—had been cut off.[10] Now, it was thought, they would continue to drink American wine, and, once wartime restrictions were lifted, they would drink it in quantities never before imagined. There had been considerable investment in California wine in the war years by the big distilling firms such as Schenley and National Distillers, since they were not allowed to distill whiskey for the domestic market and needed a product to sell. Now they hoped to make something out of their wine properties and set about buying up grapes at inflated prices and contracting for wine at even more inflated prices from wineries up and down the state.

Ernest Gallo, from his office in Modesto, looked at this overheated activity with a skeptical eye. He had large stocks of wine on hand, and instead of joining the rush to buy more grapes and make more wine, he prudently sold what he had at top price to his competitors. When the crash came, as it quickly did, he found himself flush with cash amid a scene of widespread gloom and distress. The big new wine market that had been predicted turned out to be a mirage, and the huge production from the year 1946 backed up on the winemakers' hands. The distillers, sorely bruised and thoroughly disenchanted, withdrew from the wine business. And the wine that Gallo had sold them at high prices he was now able to buy back from them at bargain prices.[11] In that same year of distress, 1947, Gallo wine became the best-selling wine in the state of California.

By 1948 the Gallo winery had reached a capacity of 12 million gallons, big but by no means the biggest in California. From this point on the numbers grew at a mind-numbing rate. In 1954 Gallo bought the big Cribari winery in Fresno and began expanding its 4-million-gallon capacity (forty years later the 4 million had swollen to 94 million gallons). By 1970 Gallo had run out of room at the original winery at Modesto. He therefore built a new winery and distillery at Livingston, thirty miles south of Modesto, where the firm had a large vineyard. Gallo wines were now made not at Modesto but at the two big wineries in Fresno and Livingston, which together had a storage capacity of 160 million gallons by 1978. By 1986 the three main properties—Fresno, Livingston, Modesto—had reached a storage capacity of 330 million gallons. Modesto remained the headquarters; wine was sent there from the producing wineries to be stored, blended, bottled, and shipped. The storage required at Modesto was on so vast a scale that the array of glass-lined steel tanks resembled nothing so much as a huge oil refinery.

The growth of sales matched the growth in production: 4 million gallons in 1948, 16 million in 1955, 30 million in 1960, 50 million in 1968, 100 million in 1971, and so on and on. In 1966 Gallo overtook its rivals—the main one was Louis Petri's United Vintners amalgamation—and became the number-one-selling wine in the United States. It has held that position ever since.[12]

ORIGINS

Ernest Gallo was the son of Giuseppe (Joe) Gallo, a native of the Italian Piedmont who came to California around 1905 and struggled through a variety of jobs—as day laborer, wine peddler, saloon keeper, and boarding-house landlord. In 1917, as the approach of Prohibition put the saloon business under a cloud, he bought a farm near Antioch, California, where, among other things, there were grapes growing. Ernest, then eight years old, was put to work on this unpromising farm, and so began a regimen of hard work that continued, practically, for the rest of his life, though the forms it took were varied. The family left the unprofitable Antioch farm for a twenty-acre vineyard in Escalon in 1922. This was, of course, the era of Prohibition, but by 1922, after the dire prophecies of the ruin of California's vineyards, it had been realized that a vineyard was now the equivalent of a small gold mine.

Home wine-making had created a powerful demand for fresh grapes shipped by rail to the big cities of the Midwest, East, and South. Grapes that could not be sold in the fresh market might go to one of the wineries that were still making "grape products" rather than intoxicating drink and there be converted into grape concentrate, a product also in demand for home wine-making. Prices for grapes were far better now than they ever had been when the commercial wineries were the only buyers, and many California growers were able to pay off their mortgages, buy new cars, and think of sending their children to college. Joe Gallo managed to get rid of his Escalon property and move to a larger vineyard—forty acres—outside of Modesto in 1924, where he and his family would remain. Ernest, with his younger brother Julio, continued to be burdened with most of the vineyard work for his father: plowing, planting, pruning, spraying, and harvesting. The boys were sent to Modesto High School, but as soon as the school day was over their services were demanded back at the vineyard: tardiness or absences were punished by beatings. They had no social life to speak of—no games, no casual hanging about, no parties: only work.

Joe Gallo was now in the business of shipping grapes to the Chicago market, grapes that came from the vineyards of his neighbors as well as from his own. Zinfandel, Carignane, and Alicante Bouschet were the favored varieties, especially Alicante, a grape whose thick skin held up well in shipping and whose dark juice could be stretched to make a lot of wine. It was a tough business. The carloads of fresh grapes, when they arrived after the long haul to Chicago, would be shunted off into big rail yards, where buyers would come to inspect the different lots and then bid for them at auction. Or they might buy directly, the shipper selling the grapes right out of the car to individual buyers. If the grapes arrived in good condition, and if the market were good that week, a shipper might expect to make a fair profit; but if the fruit had begun to spoil, or if the market were saturated, or both, he might not even recover his costs. It paid to know your way around: to have some acquaintance among the buyers, and to know whom to trust and whom to avoid. Buyers would of course haggle at the beginning of a deal; and if the market went down after they had made a deal, they would demand a rebate the next day.

When he ventured to Chicago to sell his grapes in 1926, Joe Gallo, the father, found that he had no taste for this tricky business. Back in Modesto he announced that he would never return to Chicago; at which point Ernest, then eighteen and still a high school student, begged to be allowed to go himself. His father was glad to say yes. Gallo recalled his first trip in the interview he gave to the University of California Regional Oral History Office in 1969:

> So at the age of eighteen I went back to Chicago and he [Joe Gallo] shipped me the grapes. I enjoyed the operation very much. There was a fundamental difference in my father's personality and mine. If he got into an argument with a man over a deal, why he'd just stop dealing with him forever. Whereas with me, every deal was a new deal. And if I thought I could make a profitable deal with a man, I would deal with him, regardless of what happened 15 minutes ago. . . . So I worked very well with those people. I'd make a deal with them, and if they came howling for a refund, a rebate, I may have given it to them, but at the same time I'd sell them another car for more profit.

He added that payment was typically in cash, and then, "If you could get to the bank with the cash before they could hold you up, you had a good day."[13]

Gallo bought a handgun, displayed it prominently, and so made sure that he had many good days.[14]

The market for fresh grapes, owing first to overproduction and then to the Great Depression, was not generally profitable after 1926, but it seems even then to have supported the Gallo family reasonably well. Ernest continued to travel east through 1932 to sell grapes; and his father acquired more vineyard property in those years. By 1933, when his parents' violent deaths put Ernest and his brother in control of the family vineyards, they totaled well over four hundred acres.[15] With repeal imminent, with a large vineyard property, and with a depressed market for fresh grapes, it was a reasonable proposition for the brothers to go into the wine business, even given their youth and inexperience.

Ernest Gallo liked to say that he and Julio knew nothing of wine making in 1933 and were saved from disaster only by the discovery of a couple of pamphlets on the subject published before Prohibition by the University of California and then hidden away in the basement of the Modesto Public Library during the dry years.[16] It is a good story, but wine making on one scale or another would have been going on all around them in the Modesto region, not just in the basement of their home. They would have had plenty of opportunity to observe and learn, and there were many people who had been in the pre-Prohibition business whom they might have consulted when in need. According to Charles Crawford, the two brothers, before they started making wine, went to Berkeley to consult Professor William Vere Cruess, the leading expert on wine making in California, "and spent a day with him asking, as Professor Cruess described to me years later, 'more questions than I have been asked in any day before or since.'"[17]

STAYING AHEAD

Once started, as we have seen, the brothers quickly prospered. They do not seem to have done things any differently from the rest of the trade in the early years, with the very large and important exception of Ernest's indefatigable exploits in salesmanship, an activity that certainly made a difference. But from the 1940s onward, they did a number of things that helped them to keep up with or even well ahead of the competition. Ernest Gallo's decision to build a brand was a crucial first step toward the development of an unmatched system for selling wine. We will return to that subject. His hiring Charles Crawford as an enologist—not many wineries at the time had such a person—was another step, one that would in time lead to the establishment of a large and comprehensive research laboratory. When he hired Crawford, Ernest Gallo told him not only that he aimed to make the best wine at a reasonable price, but also that he considered research like savings: "If you wait until you need it, it's already too late."[18] Gallo would stay ahead in that line; the number of distinguished names in the California trade who have passed through the Gallo laboratory—"the University of Gallo"—at one time or another is impressive.[19] One of these was Joseph Heitz, later the owner of a distinguished Napa Valley winery, who came in 1948 and was greatly impressed by the Gallo brothers' care for quality control. "They didn't have much money then," Heitz recalled, "and they worked the tails off of their employees, but they worked their own tails off."[20]

Good wine must come in the first place from the vineyards. Here, too, the Gallos were ahead of their competition. Their basic sources of grapes were Central Valley vineyards, from Fresno northward. The Central Valley is hot and is, traditionally, the home of fortified sweet wines rather than dry table wines, because grapes that yield a good dry table wine require, for the most part, a moderate climate.[21] We have already seen that the Gallo winery, from the beginning, bought large quantities of wine from Northern California vineyards, knowing that they would add a superior touch to the winery's basic Central Valley wines. For many years after the war, Gallo continued to be the largest customer for Napa Valley wines, taking the entire production of the Frei Brothers winery in Sonoma County, as well as from an array of other North Coast wineries.

But Gallo also undertook to learn what better varieties might be grown in the Napa Valley itself. In 1946 Julio Gallo, to whom the management of the vineyards and wine production had been confided, set out an experimental vineyard on the Livingston property; the original planting was of some four hundred varieties. The Livingston vineyard was also used to study fertilization practices, pruning, rootstocks, trellising, pest control, and cultivation and harvesting practices.[22] The Gallos let no opportunity for research elude them. One would suppose that studies on varietal selection had long since been done, but that was not the case. Prohibition had interrupted all experiments with wine varieties in California, and before Prohibition the dominance of inexpensive sweet wine production in the Valley had discouraged work with table wine varieties or even with superior varieties for fortified wines there.[23] After repeal, the University of California had been conducting

FIGURE 25. Charles Crawford (left), Julio Gallo, and Ernest Gallo in 1955. The caption to this photo, in a brochure called *The Story of Gallo Wines,* explains that the men, who "personally supervise every step in production," are tasting "the day's wines in the Gallo tasting room." Copyright E. and J. Gallo Winery.

important work in determining what varieties worked best in the different regions of California, but so far as I know, no winery other than Gallo was doing anything comparable.

A small winery was set up at Modesto to vinify the grapes from the experimental vineyards, and by the 1960s the wines from some 650 clonal selections had been tested.[24] Gallo now had a good idea about what varieties would suit the conditions of the Central Valley. Their choices were Sauvignon blanc, Ruby Cabernet, Barbera, Zinfandel, Chenin blanc, and French Colombard (choices that pretty closely paralleled those recommended by the university). The question now was how to persuade the Central Valley growers to plant them.

It was easy enough to get general agreement to the proposition that the Central Valley should grow better grapes. But it was another matter to get growers to make the switch. Replanting is expensive; it takes several years for a vine to reach commercial production, and meantime the grower has no crop to sell; there was little experience with the recommended varieties; they did not yield as big a crop of grapes as did the established varieties; nor was there any guarantee that growers would get the higher prices that alone would justify the costs of planting superior varieties. In this situation, what was there to do?

Gallo had an answer. The winery had established a grower relations department in 1965, itself a new thing in the industry. It worked by sending out trained viticulturists to advise those growers whose grapes were bought by Gallo on all the stages of grape growing. The unexpressed hope was that this sort of instruction and advice might help to persuade growers that they needed to plant better grapes. It did not, so the Gallo winery, in 1967, began to offer growers guaranteed long-term contracts if they would plant the recommended varieties. This scheme worked. Growers were offered, in contracts for ten or fifteen years, a guaranteed minimum price for their grapes, and if the market were higher than that minimum, then Gallo would pay the market price.[25] Many growers signed up, and the result was that the varietal composition of California's biggest vineyard region began to change for the better, the first such change in all the years since repeal. In the first five years following the Gallo move, the acreage of Barbera in the valley went from 1,840 acres to 19,781, and of Chenin blanc from 2,000 to 14,500; other varieties showed comparable changes.[26] The clout that Gallo, by its sheer size, had in California was exercised for its own advantage in this matter, but the result was for the general good.

Gallo's size allowed yet another development that helped to keep it ahead. When Ernest Gallo could not get the price he wanted for the millions of bottles his winery annually required, he built a glass factory at his winery in Modesto.[27] He already had a wholly owned truck line, the Fairbanks Trucking Company, that could haul supplies for his glass factory as well as carry goods and make deliveries for the winery.[28] Since all those bottles needed caps, and since no Gallo wine entered the market except under a screw-cap closure, Gallo founded the Mid-Cal Aluminum Company to manufacture them.

SELLING WINE

Most important, Gallo began, with his purchase of a couple of bottlers in 1940 and 1941, a campaign to control the distribution of his wine. It is more than doubtful that, without the success of this campaign, anything like the empire of Gallo could have been achieved. Bottling at the winery was the first requirement, and that had been met in the 1940s. Ernest Gallo's detailed survey of the liquor stores of Los Angeles had given him an idea of how to advertise his wines even when he could not yet afford conventional advertising. This was simply to make sure that his wines were placed at eye level (that, he knew, was where people looked first) in a prominent position in the store; if he could get the owner to allow this (and most owners were indifferent and made no objection), then Gallo had what he liked to call the owner's "silent recommendation"—pride of place implicitly meant something special.

Gallo hired his first salesmen in 1941 to cover Los Angeles and drilled into them the lesson of the "silent recommendation": not only were they to get the privileged position, but they were also to see that the shelves devoted to Gallo displayed the full range of types and sizes and to keep those shelves fully stocked; they were to dust the bottles to keep them clean and shiny and to put bottle tags on special items; they were to spot Gallo flyers and pamphlets around the store; and they were to set up special point-of-sale displays. Gallo salesmen were driven by the relentless example of their boss. One salesman said that he "spent three days in a flophouse trying to get the winos to buy Gallo."[29] And, according to hostile accounts, they were to do as much damage to the competition as they could get away with. They moved the bottles of competing brands to obscure shelves; they punctured the aluminum bottle caps to allow the wine to spoil; and they sprayed oil on competitors' bottles so that dust would adhere to them. Even dirtier tricks were alleged against them.[30] The system, with or without dirty tricks, worked; sales went up dramatically in Los Angeles, even though Gallo could not yet pay for a big advertising campaign. Gallo's salesmen could now assure a store owner that his profits would go up if he would display Gallo wines in the way that they wanted them displayed. The instructions to Gallo's salesmen, as time went on, grew into a legendary training manual that, by 1986, was composed of sixteen chapters spread over three hundred pages. It was jealously guarded against the prying eyes of competitors.

Gallo later, in his exhortations to his sales force, liked to talk about "total selling," or "total merchandising," the simple aim of which was to dominate every store in which wine was sold. As one of his salesmen remembered:

> Ernest called it total merchandising. One time he asked thirty of us what we thought total merchandising was, and we all did it differently. Finally, there

was one man from Ventura, California—his name was Conners—and he got up and said: "Ernest, I think what you mean is" (and this was supposed to be sarcastic) "if you have a great big supermarket, you open the door of that supermarket and you don't see any produce, you don't see any canned goods, you don't see any meat; all you see is Gallo wine." Ernest says, "*That's* total merchandising!"[31]

Gallo also insisted to his salesmen that they had a better wine to sell than did any of their competitors: "I know," he told them at a sales meeting in 1956, "and you know—that we have far better wine than our competitors."[32] He seems genuinely to have believed that, and he never ceased to repeat it as an article of faith. As he told Ruth Teiser in 1969, when he was at a restaurant where so-called premium wines were on the list, "I find that I have to be very careful in picking those wines to find one that I can enjoy, whereas my wines are always clean, fruity, fresh, pleasant."[33]

Gallo had certainly worked hard to get better grapes than had been the standard, and he had made a serious commitment to technical research. The leading idea behind his wine making, however, was that it should yield an absolutely consistent product: the consumer, he believed, wanted nothing so much as certainty. If he could count on Gallo to give him the same thing every time, he would buy Gallo. Or, as Charles Crawford, Gallo's first enologist, put it, "It's a religion with us that we give the consumer the same wine that we've given him in the past and that we want to give him in the future."[34] To achieve such uniformity Gallo had, in 1955, constructed a million-gallon blending tank, "the largest wine vat in the world." Its purpose, according to Julio Gallo, was "to assure constant uniformity in wines, so that consumers can rely upon every bottle of a given type being always identical with the last bottle purchased."[35]

The trade in alcoholic beverages in the United States presents an incredibly complicated scene. The repeal amendment declared in its first section that the Eighteenth Amendment, the prohibition amendment, was dead; but the second section undid the first, for it declared that the states could now do whatever they wanted about the trade—tax it, license it, own it, or prohibit it. As one winemaker ruefully said, prohibition was not really repealed, it was just amended. One thing that many states did was to prohibit the makers of spirits and wine (but not beer) from selling direct to the retail trade. This was done in order to prevent a return of the pre-Prohibition practice of allowing the distillers to control the retail market by direct ownership. Now there was to be a barrier between the producer and the retailer, a middleman called the distributor. Various regulations were laid down to protect the independence of the distributor and retailer, and so came into being the so-called three-tier system: producer, distributor, retailer.

Ernest Gallo saw that if Gallo wine were to dominate the American wine trade, as he meant it to do, he would have to circumvent or nullify the three-tier system, for an independent distributor would always be a bottleneck: he might treat Gallo wines as an afterthought; he might even favor a competitor's wines over those of Gallo. In California, where Gallo could sell direct, the independent distributor was not a problem: Gallo built his own corps of salesman there, all trained in the Gallo way. Other states required more circumspect procedures. A few states allowed Gallo to buy a distributor, and where he could, he did, as he had at the outset in New Orleans in 1939. In other states he set up subsidiary companies, legally separate from Gallo but practically not. Or, as he did in Texas, he persuaded a group of bottlers to give up their own trade and become exclusive Gallo distributors.[36] As his business grew bigger and more powerful, he could gain effective control of a distributor by putting his own men on the distributor's staff—the distributor would lose the Gallo account if it did not go along, and Gallo was the biggest-selling wine in the country. Or, by the very volume of the inventory he required to be maintained, he could make the distributor financially dependent on him. Legh Knowles, who worked as a salesman for Gallo from 1958 to 1962 recalls an episode from that time: "I started in Cincinnati. Ernest told me they take markets one at a time—'You go to Cincinnati; you be the distributor sales manager.' He said to the distributor, 'You don't know how to sell wine? I'll bring our sales manager in. You can hire him.' He brings me in there, and the distributor says, 'I usually hire all the people.' Ernest says, 'Fine. Hire this man.'"[37] That, or something like that, must have happened many times in the course of Gallo's steady march of conquest through the country's distributorships.

By 1971 Gallo's grip on the distribution of wine in America produced loud howls of protest from his competitors. The Federal Trade Commission looked into the charges and found, in a decision not issued until 1976, that Gallo was indeed guilty of what it called "exclusionary marketing policies," or in plain words, of squeezing out the competition by whatever means offered. The standard method was simply to get a financial hold on the distributor and then tell him what to do: hire Gallo men as salesmen and sell nothing but Gallo wine.[38] If he failed to obey, he would lose the Gallo line. Rather than contest these findings, Gallo agreed to sign a consent order obliging the winery to cease and desist from its "exclusionary" practices and allowing the FTC, for the next ten years, to monitor Gallo's transactions with its distributors. But the order also contained a proviso that Gallo's consent did not constitute an admission of lawbreaking.

Ernest Gallo was unrepentant. For him, the issue was simple: Gallo wines met every need, so why should anyone want to sell anything else? "I still think [he wrote] it is to the advantage of both our winery and the wholesalers for them not to take on competitive wine lines. We have a list of wines—generic table wines, varietals, sparkling wines, beverage wines, dessert wines, coolers, and vermouth, as well as brandy—that compete in each category, and I do not feel it is feasible for a distributor to sell and service two different brands in the same category effectively. We simply will not accept any distributor treating our wines as an afterthought."[39] When the Reagan administration took power in Washington, D.C., Gallo successfully petitioned to have the consent order lifted before its original expiration date. In Ernest Gallo's view, this reversal was a recognition that Gallo, rather than restraining trade by unfair practices, was really performing a public service by the very efficiency of its operations.[40]

It was all very well to improve the vineyards of the state, to make wine to the highest technical standard, to train a devoted and merciless sales force, and to manipulate the three-tier system. But as Ernest Gallo saw it, the one thing they most needed to do was to expand the market. The statistics were clear enough. There were hundreds of millions of Americans, but most of them drank no wine, never thought of wine, knew nothing about wine, cared nothing about wine. In Europe, the French, the Spanish, the Italians, took wine for granted and drank it regularly and without a second thought. The comparative figures were pitiful: twenty or thirty gallons per capita annually in France; one or two gallons in the United States—not the actual figures, but close enough.[41] If only one could stir up that inert American market, make it aware of wine and teach it to ask for wine, one would reach the New Jerusalem that Paul Garrett had preached about before and after Prohibition, a state of things in which millions of acres of vines yielded billions of gallons of wine—Gallo wine, if Ernest, with his total merchandising, had his way. Ernest Gallo's gaze was steadfastly and unwaveringly fixed on that goal from the moment he rented a warehouse to make wine in Modesto in 1933.

As he had studied the system of retailing in order to devise a better method, he also studied the tastes of the market that he had sworn to win over: find out what the public wants, and give it to them. That was not so easy when the public did not appear to want anything in the way of wine. The public did, however, show that it liked soft drinks, sweetened and fizzy confections that it drank in oceanic quantities. There were other special tastes to study as well—what women liked, what blacks liked, what college kids liked. Find the formulas that fit such tastes, and who could say what might follow?

One must not forget that Gallo continued to produce, in ever-increasing quantities, a line of standard wines under the usual names: port, sherry, burgundy, chablis, and so on, some of them perhaps a bit better than what the competition provided, none of them assuredly much worse. But Ernest Gallo was always searching for something different, for the magical something that would suddenly attract the great mass of Americans who knew not wine. In the course of this search, all sorts of trials were made, most of them probably unsuccessful. Something called "Gallo-ette," invented for a supposedly feminine taste in wines, failed in the late 1940s. Something else called "Scotty," a low-alcohol apple wine, fizzled as well.[42] There were many other such disappointments. But there were many successes.

The best-known, not to say notorious, instance is the flavored, fortified wine called Thunderbird, aimed specifically at the African American market, where it had an instant success. The way for Thunderbird (and for the many imitations that it immediately inspired) had been prepared by a change in the federal regulations for wine. Until 1955 the only wine allowed to have flavoring elements added to it was vermouth, a long-established compound.[43] The new regulations allowed "special natural flavors" to be added without altering the tax status of the wine, which would formerly have been treated as the product of rectification: such products were taxed at a higher rate and, besides, could not be produced in a bonded winery. Now the way was open to new possibilities. Gallo salesmen were the first to spot one of them. They saw in the liquor stores of Los Angeles that African American customers would buy a bottle of white port, open the bottle, take a swig, and then hand the bottle to the cashier, who had a container of concentrated lemon juice at his elbow and would pour a shot of that into the open wine bottle. When this was reported to Modesto, Ernest put his technicians to work. The lemon-flavored, sweet, fortified wine they came up with was named "Thunderbird" and at once flew through the ghettoes of American cities when it was brought to market in 1957. Production in that year was 32 million gallons.[44]

Thunderbird was an overwhelming marketing success, but it had the undesired effect of identifying Gallo with winos and ghettos; after a while the Gallo name was removed from the label, though the wine was not withdrawn from the market. Nor did Thunderbird attract new wine drinkers. One new product that did was called "Vino Paisano di Gallo," or "Paisano" for short, produced in direct imitation of a wine made by the Guild Winery called "Vino da Tavola." Both of these were so-called mellow wines, standard red wines slightly sweetened to appeal to the taste of the novice wine-drinker. Apparently they did. Paisano became the country's best-selling red wine in a short time after its introduction.

Another change in the regulations, made in 1959, permitted a mild carbonation in table wines, so the winemaker now had three lures with which to attract reluctant Americans: sweetness, as in Paisano; added flavors, as in Thunderbird; and now, carbonation. The third of these was especially pleasing to the trade, for was not carbonation the key principle in those soft drinks that Americans drank in wholesale quantities? Carbonated wines could also be of a low alcohol content—8 or 9 percent, another new permission in the regulations—so they were called "soda-pop" or "pop" wines. Gallo was quick to bring out one of these newly authorized wines: it was called "Ripple," and it did very well. But the success of Ripple was cast in the shade by yet another lightly carbonated "wine": Boone's Farm Apple Wine. This wine, if the fermentation of concentrated apple juice can be said to produce a wine, was introduced as early as 1961, at the dawn of the carbonated wine era, and had sold in only modest quantities, just enough to keep it alive as a brand. Then, suddenly, its sales exploded: 90,000 cases in 1968; 460,000 cases in 1969; 2.4 million cases in 1970, making it the largest-selling wine in the country. Other Boone's Farm wines were added to the line—strawberry, for example—and in 1972 Gallo sold 16 million cases of Boone's Farm wines.[45] The explanation for the popularity of the wine, according to Ernest Gallo, was that it appealed to the "young-adult market—ages twenty-one to thirty-four—who bought the new wines because they liked the taste, and because the wines were different and inexpensive."[46]

Gallo also kept plugging away at the job of making its basic table wines attractive to new drinkers. In the 1960s the winery introduced a "gourmet trio" with remarkable names (some arm-twisting at the federal agency regulating labels must have been required): Chablis Blanc, Pink Chablis, and Hearty Burgundy. They had been tweaked in various ways: Pink Chablis, for example, was lightly carbonated and sweetened. Hearty Burgundy had a base of Durif (Petite Sirah) from North Coast grapes and was quickly recognized as a real bargain among red wines. In the decade from 1957, beginning with Thunderbird and moving through a long line of new-style wines,

Gallo had immensely increased its own sales and had succeeded in expanding the market for American wines; if that expansion did not satisfy Ernest Gallo's aims, it was at least a very big step along the way. As a result of Gallo's efforts, many Americans who had not drunk wine now drank wine, and all of the Americans who drank wine now drank much more of it than they had before. And Gallo was the name they knew best.

Bigness brought some penalties with it. The Gallo winery did not have a particularly bad record in its relations with its vineyard workers; the record was not particularly good, either, but that might have been said, and could still be said today, about most growers. Two things made Gallo especially vulnerable to protest: its bigness, and the fact that it was privately held; instead of attacking a faceless corporation, protestors could hold up Ernest and Julio Gallo as villainous men of wealth who ground the faces of the poor. In the course of a struggle with Gallo over contracts for its field-workers, Cesar Chavez, the head of the United Farm Workers, declared a boycott of Gallo wines in 1973. The Gallos complained that they were the innocent victims of a turf war between Chavez's union and the rival Teamsters, as to some extent they certainly were. The conflict was settled finally to Chavez's satisfaction and the boycott called off in 1978, almost five years after it had first been declared. Whether the commercial operations of the Gallo winery had been much affected seems doubtful.

THE WINE REVOLUTION AND GALLO

From the late 1960s onward, more and more Americans, certainly in part as a result of Gallo's promotions, began to take an interest in wine. And when they did, they inevitably began to look for something more than what Gallo offered. "Chablis Blanc" could not long satisfy anyone who wanted to know more about white wines. With new experience came new demands, and many of these demands went directly against the practices associated with Gallo and other big commercial producers. People wanted varietal wines— Cabernet Sauvignon rather than burgundy, Chardonnay rather than chablis. But Gallo had no interest in varietal wines, only in such generics as burgundy and port; its vineyards were given over to Zinfandel at best, or to Chenin blanc, and were innocent of such exotic varieties as Cabernet Sauvignon or Chardonnay. Gallo scorned the idea of vintage-dating, holding instead that the consistency achieved through blending was the goal of good wine making. Gallo was not interested in barrel ageing when ageing in French oak became all the rage. Gallo had never closed a bottle with a cork, though now cork-finished bottles were seen as a mark of superiority. Ernest Gallo had long hoped to exploit the prestige of wine against the vulgarity of beer and whiskey,[47] but now that many Americans were at last acknowledging that prestige, his wines were seen as common, industrial, cheap.

Ernest Gallo might dismiss such judgments at first—after all, he thought his wines better than any others—but not for long. Just as he had thought when he sold grapes in the Chicago rail yards, a new deal was a new deal and you were foolish not to grab it. And there was no question that a new deal was now waiting to be grabbed. A first step, of great symbolic import, was made in 1974, when Gallo released its first cork-finished, varietal wines. Then a great underground cellar was dug at Modesto and filled with hundreds of wooden tanks of European origin. Gallo already had, and had had since almost the beginning of its operation, large sources of superior grapes and wines from North Coast vineyards, so that introducing varietal wines presented no special problem to the winery; only a change of mind was required. But the new demand for North Coast grapes meant that Gallo could not indefinitely expect to command the market, as it had for years. Facing this prospect, Gallo simply bought one of its longtime suppliers, the Frei Brothers winery in Sonoma County, giving Gallo some 750 acres of Sonoma property at one stroke.

Gallo's entry into the varietal wine business was a disappointment at first: sales in the first year reached only half of the target of eight hundred thousand cases.[48] But the effort persisted, and by 1988 Gallo had the "largest-selling line of varietal wine in the U.S., at two and a half million cases."[49] Gallo has in recent years greatly expanded its Sonoma holdings. By 1989 Gallo had four thousand acres in Sonoma and had begun construction of a major winery in the Dry Creek Valley, outside of Healdsburg. Today, Gallo of Sonoma, as it is called, produces high-market estate-bottled varietal wines that challenge comparison with the best that California makes; it also produces a range of midlevel varietals under several different labels (e.g., Rancho Zabaco, Turning Leaf). The Gallo winery has been renamed the Gallo Family Vineyards, and the name *Gallo* has been withdrawn from the inexpensive standard wines that are still the staple of the company: those wines now go to market under such names as Livingston, Carlo Rossi, and Vella. Ernest Gallo reinvented the public image of his winery to adapt to a changed market.

By any measure, Ernest Gallo's was a remarkable achievement, and the recognition and honors that came to him in his later years were without question deserved. No one, however, would have called Ernest Gallo a likeable man. As one reads the undisguisedly hostile book by Ellen Hawkes about the Gallo family and its quarrels,[50] one encounters an impressive accumulation of adjectives for Ernest, none of them flattering: "aggressive," "domineering," "suspicious," "paranoiac," "secretive," "mean," "grasping," "demanding," "selfish," "arrogant," "driven." It would be possible to document the case for each one of these epithets from the testimony of various observers, though of course not all of them apply with equal truth. "Secretive" is certainly one of the best-documented. The huge winery in Modesto, the biggest thing in town, is not advertised in any way in the city, and the property itself is well protected by fences, security cameras, and guards. There is no pandering to a curious public by providing a tasting room or a visitors' center: the traffic that other wineries in California eagerly promote is resolutely shunned by Gallo. When Ernest Gallo, against all likelihood, was persuaded to grant an interview in 1969 to Ruth Teiser, of the University of California's Regional Office of Oral History, he demanded that the transcript of the interview be kept confidential and inaccessible for the next twenty-five years, though it contains nothing that one could not learn from many other sources. Why seek to suppress it?

The term *driven* also seems well deserved. As he told Teiser in that long-inaccessible interview, "My day starts at about eight o'clock in the morning and I leave for home at six-thirty or seven o'clock, and I take the day's reports and mail with me, and, after dinner, why, I'm usually through by eleven. And either Saturday or Sunday will be spent on the work that I haven't had time for during the week."[51] When he was on the road checking up on his sales staff and distributors, he might visit thirty stores a day; that number, he said, would fill "a busy but normal day" for him, even when he was well into his eighties; and the more out-of-the-way the stores were, the better.[52]

Gallo paid, and more than paid, all the penalties entailed upon a long, long life. He outlived his younger brothers; he outlived his wife; he outlived his elder son. He was estranged from his brother Joe by a bitter legal contest; and he lived to see the day when the Gallo winery was no longer the biggest winemaker in the world. That distinction passed to Constellation Brands in 2003. But Constellation is a publicly held firm; its wineries are scattered around the world and are the creations of many different people at many different times; and they were acquired by purchase. Gallo remains the biggest winemaker in the United States and incomparably the biggest wine-making enterprise in private hands, an enterprise built in all its parts under the direction of a single man in one obsessively busy lifetime.

Could what Ernest Gallo did be done again? It seems unlikely. Some of the things that went into his achievement we might expect to see again: his hard work, his readiness to innovate, his careful study of markets and methods. His determination to keep the Gallo winery a privately held business, a condition that was undoubtedly critical in allowing him to go the way he wanted to go, might also be matched by a later entrepreneur.

But Gallo had advantages that were not of his creating. He began business when the market for wine in the United States was small, knowledge about it very limited, and expectations low: just the conditions for an enterprising young man confident in his ability to make a change. His competition was lethargic and unimaginative. As he told his salesmen in 1956, one of their main advantages had been the inaction of the competitors—"unbelievably inactive," Gallo called them. They had paid no attention to what Gallo was doing in the early years, and now were condemned to try to catch up, using the methods that Gallo himself had taught them.[53] Today, however, the competitive energy at work in the wine business in America might give even Ernest Gallo pause if he were starting out now.

Perhaps most important, today's wine business in America, far from being the small domestic affair that it was in the 1930s, is now global. A winemaker in California now competes with wines whose existence was not even suspected in 1933: wines from Australia, Chile, Argentina, and South Africa are now prominent on any store's shelves; Europe sends not only the familiar wines of Spain, Portugal, France, Germany, Italy but also those of Austria, Croatia, Rumania, Bulgaria, Moldavia. Portugal is no longer limited to Port but ships table wine from the Douro; Spain no longer means only Sherry but dry wines from all over the Iberian Peninsula. The range and variety is overwhelming.

In the United States itself, the conditions that Gallo knew at the outset have now been transformed. In 1933, California made 90 percent of the nation's wines; the remaining 10 percent was mostly supplied by New York State, with a few gallons coming from Ohio and a scattering of other states. Not today. Washington and Oregon are now West Coast powers. Texas has ambitious winemakers. So do Virginia and Pennsylvania and a reinvigorated Ohio. New York has a flourishing new wine-making territory on Long Island and a completely restructured industry upstate, around the Finger Lakes and elsewhere. It is not so easy to imagine "dominating" all this, as Ernest Gallo dreamed of doing eighty years ago. But he did so imagine, and he did dominate.

NINE

Frank Schoonmaker

A MASTER TEACHER

THROUGH EUROPE TO WINE

In 1923, Frank Schoonmaker, at the end of his freshman year at Princeton, dropped out of college. In the letter that he sent to the college administration explaining his decision, he said he could learn more by reading and travel than he could in a classroom.[1] But perhaps another element in his decision was the fact that he knew better than his teachers how to teach. He would spend the rest of his life teaching, and his subject, though he did not know it then, was to be wine.

Frank Schoonmaker was born in Spearfish, South Dakota, on August 20, 1905, the first child of his parents. Since they lived in Woodstock, New York, one must wonder why he was born in Spearfish, a small town in the Black Hills. Schoonmaker said that his mother had gone to that remote place to join a sort of early-day "commune," but that only raises other questions: What sort of woman was she? And why did she go to South Dakota to have her first child? I have no answer. The fact is, not much is known about Schoonmaker's personal history. The situation is confused by the fact that a good many misstatements have been made about Schoonmaker and his work, so that to the dearth of facts is added the problem of pseudofacts.

Presumably Mrs. S. did not long remain in Spearfish with the infant Frank but returned to her husband. He was Edwin Davies Schoonmaker (1873–1940); a number of misstatements have been made about him, too. One authority says that Edwin Schoonmaker was a professor of Latin and Greek in New York; another adds the specification that he taught at Columbia; a third says that he was employed by the State Department. None of this is confirmed by the elder Schoonmaker's brief biography in *Who's Who* or by his obituary in the *New York Times*. From these we learn only that he was a graduate of Transylvania University in Kentucky, that he taught "Ancient Languages" at little Eureka College in Illinois for the two years 1897–99, and that he then left for New York to devote himself to "research and literary work." No connection with Columbia appears, though he may well have lectured there informally, as thousands of specialists have at one time or another. The alleged State Department employment may be explained by the fact that Schoonmaker was a member of the official American mission to Russia in Siberia in 1918, an experience that left him convinced that the Soviet regime was a cruel despotism.

As for the "literary work," he published two of a planned four volumes of "racial dramas": *The Saxons* (1905) and *The Americans* (1913). A further two volumes, *The Slavs* and *The Hindoos,* if they were ever written, apparently remained unpublished. I have examined a copy of *The Americans* and can readily understand why the project was never completed. A "drama" of some three hundred pages of more or less blank verse about labor unrest in the Pacific Northwest is not exactly the sort of thing that would reward a commercial publisher. The elder Schoonmaker's other published books are also more political than literary: *Our Genial Enemy, France* (1932) and *Democracy and World Dominion* (1939) are representative. He wrote prolifically for the magazines on subjects of public interest and was, in fact, a man of wide experience who had traveled extensively in Europe (as his son later would) and who wrote and lectured about his work; in 1937 he interviewed Hitler. He died in 1940, leaving a widow who survived him by twenty-five years.

Mrs. Schoonmaker (1873–1965), née Nancy Musselman, was also a graduate of Transylvania and had studied at the Sorbonne as well. She was active in politics for most of her long life, on the state Democratic committee, in the League of Women Voters, and as an unsuccessful candidate for the House of Representatives in 1937. Frank Schoonmaker's remark that "my parents were fairly civilized people" is a modest understatement applied to people who were clearly experienced, active, and accomplished.[2]

Having left Princeton, Schoonmaker sailed at once for Europe on the French liner *Rousillon,* on which he was served wine: "And I liked it," he recalled.[3] In France, almost at once, he had his first serious encounter with wine: "When we docked I visited a region near Nice and stayed with the family of a Frenchman, a wine merchant who had lost his son. The first meal he put two glasses at my place and poured two wines. 'Which do you prefer?' he asked. 'This one,' I said. 'No wine for you,' he said and whisked away the glasses. Well, he kept this up for about a week, and I learned to tell the difference."[4]

After this vivid lesson in wine, Schoonmaker set out on his inspection of Europe on foot and by bicycle. He explored Burgundy, the region whose wines he came to love best of all in France. He visited Spain, Italy, Switzerland, Germany, Holland, and Belgium. Much of this is recorded in Schoonmaker's first book, called *Through Europe on Two Dollars a Day* (1927), a title that now evokes a lost world of security and cheapness. If nothing else, the book showed that Schoonmaker was a quick learner and an efficient worker. He had left Princeton only four years before and could now appear before the public as a well-traveled guide to a complex subject. The book is in fact an astonishing tour de force for a college-age writer who had only just come to Europe and who now confidently instructed Americans in how to get about, how to choose an itinerary, what and where to eat, and what to see. From the very outset Schoonmaker wrote, not as the Scribes and Pharisees, but as one having authority: he *knew*.

This first book pointed Schoonmaker toward a career in travel writing, and it was soon followed by a quick succession of travel books, each with a title beginning *Come with Me through*—whatever it might be: France (1928), Belgium and Holland (1928); Italy (1929); or Germany (1930). In 1932 he published *Spain* in collaboration with Lowell Thomas, then at the height of his celebrity as writer, traveler, broadcaster. The list of titles pretty well covers the countries with whose wines he would afterward be concerned.

Admirers of Schoonmaker's writings on wine have attentively examined these early books for signs of a developing interest in wine, and have been disappointed to find nothing of the sort. As Roy Brady concluded, after searching *Come with Me through France,* Schoonmaker, on the evidence of that book, "appeared to know no more about wine than any other American travel writer"; or as Brady wrote in another place, "In the beginning Schoonmaker was exactly where other Americans were at the time [of repeal] with respect to wine—nowhere."[5] This is too harsh: one remembers Schoonmaker's lessons in wine tasting at the hands of his French host in Provence; and it is hardly conceivable that, after years in Europe, he had not learned a great deal more about wine than the ordinary American could in the dry years of Prohibition at home. But he had not yet turned to it with serious attention.

That turn came toward the end of 1933, as repeal approached and stirred a renewed curiosity about wine, its kinds, its etiquette, and its history. For whatever reason—the connection is another one of those unexplained items in Schoonmaker's history—Harold Ross, the editor of the *New Yorker,* commissioned Schoonmaker to do a series of instructive articles for the magazine, and so he set out to learn his subject.[6]

He had at least two lucky encounters. Edouard Kressman, of the firm of Bordeaux shippers of that name, wrote many years later:

> I shall never forget when Frank Schoonmaker visited in Bordeaux with his wife, just about Repeal time. He came over to write a story about our wines for the *New Yorker,* which was probably the first American magazine to be interested in the new opportunity for gracious living which Repeal was offering to Americans. The young couple were both beginners in this field, and my father was among the very first to give them their initiatory lessons in Bordeaux wines in our tasting room. . . . I do not know if she developed such obvious gifts as well as Frank did his, since he has become one of the most knowledgeable wine experts in America.[7]

Back in Paris, and dining as he always did at the restaurant called Le Roy Gourmet, Schoonmaker encountered Raymond Baudoin, the editor of *La Revue du Vin de France.* Baudoin was highly respected in the trade, first as the editor of an influential journal and next as an expert taster and judge. He was also notorious for his rudeness and aggressive bad manners in his dealing with the wine trade. Schoonmaker was permitted to accompany Baudoin on several trips in France and was thus introduced to a number of small producers, especially in Burgundy, who would later supply his import firm. Baudoin encouraged small Burgundy producers to do their own bottling, a most unusual practice then, so that they could establish their own identity and avoid a complete dependence upon the big shippers in Beaune. This, too, would be an advantage to Schoonmaker in the business he afterward established, since it allowed him to buy directly from the producers.[8]

Meantime, the articles that Schoonmaker had been commissioned to write for the *New Yorker* began to appear in November 1933 under the running title of "News from the Wine Country"; they ran until December 1934, a total of eight articles that covered Champagne, Burgundy, Bordeaux, Cognac, the Rhine and Moselle, Vermouth, and the wines of Spain and Italy They were written in the clear, confident, expository style, mingled with advice, admonition, anecdote and historical reference, that Schoonmaker had already fully developed in his travel writing. The articles were obviously well-informed and expert, without snobbery or affectation. They stood out all the more clearly by contrast with the fumbling ignorance of the competition.

In a devastating article titled "New Decalogues of Drinking,"[9] Schoonmaker at this time enumerated some of the more sensational blunders committed by the swarm of self-appointed experts who broke into print at the dawn of repeal to instruct an innocent American public. One of these advised that a bottle of Champagne should be opened with a corkscrew; that writer also offered a list of "good recent years" in Cognac; another recommended the French brands of Sherry; yet another informed his readers that both rum and Spanish brandy are known as *aguardiente,* meaning "water for the teeth." Against a background of such nonsense, Schoonmaker's knowledge and good sense stood out vividly.

Even before the *New Yorker* series had finished running, Schoonmaker was at work on a book about the world's wines in collaboration with a journalist named Tom Marvel, who would be associated with Schoonmaker in his publications and his business for many years.[10] *The Complete Wine Book* (1934) is complete only in the sense that it covers the wine world as it was then conventionally understood: after those of France, Germany, Italy, Spain, and Portugal, the wines of the rest of the world are jammed in among "The Others," as one of the shorter chapters of the book is titled. As Schoonmaker later said, it took him many years to realize just how incomplete *The Complete Wine Book* was.[11] But it was far more "complete" than the ordinary American's understanding of the subject then. It was also notable for giving prominence to American wines, at the same time deploring the bad practices of American wine making, especially the dependence on inferior varieties of grape and on borrowed names—port, sherry, burgundy, and so on. Tom Marvel, according to Schoonmaker himself, was responsible for the American chapter, because Marvel, as a native Californian, "knew more about those wines than I did."[12] But Schoonmaker must certainly have approved what Marvel wrote and must have made his own contribution to the writing.

That was the first shot in Schoonmaker's long war against the sins of the American wine trade. One may also note that, at the head of the authors' acknowledgments, stands the name of M. Raymond Baudoin, "founder and editor of the *Revue du Vin de France,* who is not only one of the outstanding oenological authorities of Europe, but who has, for more than a decade, waged unrelenting warfare upon fraudulent practices in the wine business, and through whose kindness the authors found all doors open in the wine-producing regions of France."[13] Schoonmaker evidently saw his own role in Baudoin's example, without, however, copying the bad manners.

In March 1935, Schoonmaker set up in business as a wine importer under the name of Bates and Schoonmaker at 17 East Forty-second Street in Manhattan. Bates, a brother-in-law, soon disappeared from the firm, which then became Frank Schoonmaker and Company. Tom Marvel, as has already been noted, joined the business, and, early in 1938, so did the young Alexis Lichine, whom Schoonmaker recruited to be his sales manager and who proved himself a master salesman before he entered the army at the end of 1942.[14]

An early catalog (1936) of the firm, unmistakably written by Schoonmaker himself, emphasizes that all of the 116 wines listed (except the Madeiras) were personally selected by Schoonmaker himself. The theme of "personal selection" figures prominently in Schoonmaker's business practice thereafter:

> We have never [Tom Marvel wrote in 1940] felt it necessary or wise to change the ideas or opinions which we held at the start—that, whenever possible, it is best to buy wine from the man who makes it, bottled by the man who makes it, and under a label which carries the maker's name. We have never bought and listed a bottle of wine from a person that we did not know personally, nor a bottle of wine from a vineyard that we have never seen. We have never put on sale a bottle of imported wine that we had not tasted in Europe before it was purchased, nor shipped a wine which we had not tasted in America after it had arrived.[15]

"A Frank Schoonmaker selection" printed in yellow on the green neck label on countless bottles in later years was a reassurance to timid wine buyers that they would be safe if they chose to buy something "selected" by Frank Schoonmaker.

In the early years of the firm, small Burgundy producers, such as the ones Schoonmaker had met on his tours with Raymond Baudoin, figured importantly in the list; it has been said, indeed, that it was these producers who had originally suggested that Schoonmaker go into the import business.[16] They included Pierre Gelin (Gevrey-Chambertin), Jean Grivot (Vosne-Romanée), George Roumier (Chambolle-Musigny), (Chassagne-Montrachet), and others.[17] Schoonmaker would visit these and other producers on a twice-yearly basis, make his selections, and for Burgundy at least, leave the red tape required for shipping the wine to the Marquis Jacques d'Angerville of Volnay, who was his supplier, agent, and friend. By this practice of personal attention, and by the evidence of his abilities as a judge, Schoonmaker acquired a high

FIGURE 26. Frank Schoonmaker at his familiar work of leading a wine tasting. Courtesy Gail Unzelman Collection.

reputation among the winemakers of France. It also helped his standing that Raymond Baudoin acted as his broker in many transactions.

Frank Schoonmaker the importer appears to have developed a decent business even under the difficult conditions of the 1930s—economic depression and a market ignorant of wine, a market that he was eager to teach. He began to publish informative pieces for his clientele just as soon as he opened for business in 1935: the first of his series of *Vineyard Reports* that I have seen, a neatly printed pamphlet of four dense pages, is dated from the Grand Hotel d'Europe et d'Angleterre, Mâcon, April 24, 1935, followed by another from Bordeaux on May 8.

He continued to write for his immediate customers and, in the magazines, for a wider audience. If one trolls through the periodical indexes for the 1930s, one finds pitifully little writing about wine in American magazines; Schoonmaker was by far the best among the few writers, and his was the name most frequently found on such articles as were published. He wrote for the *New Yorker* occasionally; more frequently for *House Beautiful, House and Garden,* and *Harper's*. When, in 1941, *Gourmet* was founded, he had a useful forum in that magazine; even better was *Holiday,* from the 1950s onward. What he wrote were not exercises in appreciation but essays in instruction. What was, for example, Burgundy, properly understood? Who were the good producers? What were the conditions under which they worked? How much should one expect to pay, and what should one avoid? And so on. In Schoonmaker the American public had a teacher in whom it could place confidence—and was lucky to have him.

DEALING IN AMERICAN WINES

Frank Schoonmaker and Company did not deal in American wines in its first years for the simple reason that Schoonmaker did not think well of them. He had made it plain in *The Complete Wine Book* why he thought thus, and he was fully prepared to defend his position against the querulous complaints of the domestic winemakers—both eastern (New York) and western (California). The Californians especially resented Schoonmaker's charge that selling California wine as port or burgundy was fraudulent: everyone, they said, knew that those terms were generic and, besides, the word *California* always appeared on the label as well. They were honest men, and it was unconscionable to charge them with an intent to deceive.[18] But there was really no defense against his main objections: that California wines came from inferior or unsuitable grape varieties and were given labels that either did not inform or misled or both. To put it as simply as possible, until California planted better grapes and used honest labels, the wine trade there would never realize its possibilities.

The first flurry of conflict between Schoonmaker and the American winemakers over these issues followed immediately upon the publication of *The Complete Wine Book* in 1934. When the fight was renewed around 1940, the situation was very different, for Schoonmaker not only was now interested in the reform of California wine practices but also had become a dealer in California wines himself. This shift had, of course, been brought about by the approach of war in Europe. Schoonmaker's main business was in the wines of France and Germany, countries certain to be combatants; both Spain and Italy, also important in his business, were uncertain quantities. As a prudent businessman, Schoonmaker had to look to his supplies, and so, beginning in 1939, he undertook the study of California wines as, a decade earlier, he had studied the wines of Europe.

He began his first tour of inspection of California by consulting such experts as could be identified: the Wine Institute, in San Francisco, though helpful, was a prejudiced source, but other points of view could be found among the members of the San Francisco Medical Friends of Wine and the San Francisco Wine and Food Society. Armed with recommendations and introductions from these sources, Schoonmaker set out in May 1939 on a monthlong, thousand-mile trip through California's North Coast counties, looking for wines that he could sell without apology, tasting some five hundred of them, and choosing five wineries to represent back East: Wente, Inglenook, Larkmead, Fountain Grove, and Paul Masson. That, at any rate, was the first report, though, as we shall see, Paul Masson was soon dropped from the list.[19] In hindsight, Schoonmaker's choices appear to have been unexceptionable; though only one of the list (Wente) still survives as anything more than a mere name today, they were all of the highest repute then.[20] And the Californians greatly enjoyed the spectacle of their much-resented critic now reduced to seeking his wines at their hands.

Schoonmaker, however, would make his own rules. The wines that he selected to sell under his name would be labeled according to the arguments that he had been urging on the Californians since 1934. What these arguments were, he carefully rehearsed in an article published in *Wines and Vines* in 1940. California wines, he wrote, could have no identity until they were labeled in a way to show what grapes they were made of ("varietal" labeling)[21] and the region they came from (Napa, Livermore, Santa Cruz Mountains). California's vineyards would have to be planted to superior varieties of grapes if California's wines were to rise to a new level of quality: Cabernet Sauvignon and Pinot noir in place of Alicante Bouschet and Carignane; Chardonnay and Sauvignon blanc in place of Burger and Thompson's Seedless. And in order to get superior varieties the winemakers would have to pay a premium price for them.[22]

A brief account of the history and logic of the "varietal" labeling for which Schoonmaker was campaigning may be useful. The principle of naming in Europe was geographical: wines were named for a town, such as Jerez, Oporto, Bordeaux; a river such as the Rhine, Moselle, Rhone; a region such as Burgundy or Alsace. Wines with such names had, by long tradition, achieved clear identities: one knew where they came from, how they were grown, what they were made of. In the new world, obviously, no such long tradition existed, so naming by place alone was not a useful option: Longworth's Catawba would not have been much helped by calling it Cincinnati White. By the time that Schoonmaker began his campaign, however, there was something like a tradition of American wine growing. California was understood to make wines very different from those of New York or Ohio; within New York or Ohio it was known that the Finger Lakes and the Lake Erie shore were privileged places for wine. And within California there were a number of recognized distinctions: the Bay Area was clearly different from the Central Valley; Cucamonga was one sort of place, Sonoma quite another, and so on.

But such regional names could only be the vaguest sort of sign as to what was contained in a bottle of wine. The name of the grape variety used would make everything clear: *Cabernet Sauvignon* instead of *burgundy; Sauvignon blanc* instead of *chablis,* and so on. This practice would mean that the American public would have to acquire an elementary knowledge of what foreign names such as these stood for (and overcome anxiety about how to pronounce them); but once that hurdle had been cleared, the way was open for an honest scheme of labeling.

Thus it made sense, as Schoonmaker argued, to combine varietal and regional naming: *Napa Cabernet Sauvignon* rather than *California burgundy; Livermore Chardonnay* rather than *California chablis.* And this practice would be not just a bow to honesty but also a way to make more money: wines made from superior varieties and of clearly identified origin would earn higher prices for all concerned: the grower, the winemaker, the merchant. QED.

These now seem almost transparently obvious propositions, so that it is difficult to imagine the violence with which they were opposed at the time; the debates over the question, as Schoonmaker discreetly said, were "acrimonious."[23] That was putting it mildly. Why was this man stirring up trouble? Why did he want to disturb long-established practices? He was accused of, among other things, seeking to confuse the American public by a barrage of unfamiliar names so that he could obstruct the California trade and sell more of his imported wines.[24] And was he not slandering the entire industry by calling for "honest" labeling? If he were honest, what did that make the rest of them?

One objection, at least, did have some force. Varietal labeling does not allow for blending: a Bordeaux-style red would have to be labeled Cabernet Sauvignon, Merlot, Malbec, Petit Verdot, and Cabernet Franc—a heavy burden to carry on a label. A Rhone-style wine would have an even more elaborate statement of contents to make. Once the varietal idea has been established, it quickly leads to the further idea that a varietal wine should be "pure"; that is, 100 percent of the variety named. Anything else would be regarded as adulteration. Yet a judicious blending of wines from different varieties is the means whereby some of the world's best wines are produced. It is a distinct weakness of the system of varietal labeling that this method is not provided for.[25] It is true that, at the time Schoonmaker was seeking to make converts, the federal regulations required that only 51 percent of a wine carrying a grape name need be actually the juice of that grape, so that a whole lot of blended wine might go into a varietally labeled bottle. In 1983 the rule was changed to require a 75 percent minimum. But even this requirement is thought by many critics to be too permissive.

Another defect of a simple varietal system arises from the fact that a vast range of characters and qualities is concealed behind the single varietal name: a Cabernet Sauvignon grown in the Niagara Falls region of Canada will have little in common with a Cabernet Sauvignon grown on the coast of Tuscany or in the San Joaquin Valley of California. But of course Schoonmaker also required a geographical designation to complement the varietal name: Livermore Semillon, Napa Cabernet. There can be no doubt that at the moment Frank Schoonmaker entered the business of selling American wines, his scheme of varietal and regional labeling was a clear advance beyond the bad old practices then prevailing.

Schoonmaker was reported in June 1940 to be "engaged in a comprehensive survey of the vineyards of northern Ohio and of the Finger Lakes district of New York State."[26] By the end of that year he had added several wines from these regions to his list, all of them white and all of them from native hybrid varieties. They were Catawba from Engels and Krudwig from the Lake Erie shore of Ohio; and Elvira, Delaware, Diamond, and other varieties from Widmer in the Finger Lakes region of upstate New York. The inclusion of these wines required an even greater change of taste in Schoonmaker than anything from California did, for, like all wines from native grapes, they had strange and sometimes startling flavors. Eastern winemakers had no choice but to use such grapes, for they alone would survive the assaults of disease and weather that made it impossible, at that time, to grow vinifera vines in their regions. Schoonmaker saw to it that his selections of eastern wine were identified according to his principles by labels of his own design.

By 1941 Schoonmaker was well on his way to educating the American public in the virtues of American wines—that is, the virtues of those wines chosen to be Frank Schoonmaker selections, which were, without doubt, among the very best then available. The catalog of Frank Schoonmaker and Company in the fall of that year lists a great many American wines: to his original selection, Schoonmaker had added such names as Scatena Brothers, Korbel, and Martini. He also undertook to have wines made to his personal specifications: instead of being merely a passive buyer of wines already existing, he would direct the winemakers of California onto new— or rather, traditional—paths. It was reported in 1941 that Korbel had made, at Schoonmaker's suggestion, a "brut" sparkling wine from the vintage of 1933 that Schoonmaker was successfully selling in the East, "where the taste for an extremely dry champagne seems to be predominant."[27]

Earlier, he had commissioned Martin Ray to make, "in accordance with definite specifications," twenty-five hundred gallons of Folle Blanche: "The wine is to be made from grapes picked early; it is to be stored in small oak barrels, bottled when fifteen months old, and put on the market in the fall of 1942." And of course it would be labeled under a "distinctively American, rather than a European name."[28] In 1942, at Schoonmaker's suggestion, there were plans to produce a rosé at Almadén.[29] That people now began to notice what Schoonmaker was doing is evident in a letter by H. L. Mencken written in 1941. "The best red wine that I have found so far," Mencken wrote with his usual energy of expression, "is Fountain Grove Sonoma Pinot Noir, marketed by Frank Schoonmaker. It has no bouquet whatsoever, but its flavor is not bad, and I have drunk it without gagging. It is certainly much better than the ordinary French table wine."[30] That last sentence is just what Schoonmaker himself might have written.

The next step in the campaign was the publication, in 1941, of a new book by Schoonmaker and Tom Marvel called simply *American Wines*. This is, in part, a recapitulation of themes that Schoonmaker and Marvel had set forth in *The Complete Wine Book*, and that Schoonmaker had repeated in his periodical writing. It was also, to some extent, a work of propaganda for the wines that Schoonmaker was now selling: Roy Brady, with an eye on that side of the book, called it "a purely commercial undertaking."[31] But it was more than that. It was, to begin with, the only book devoted to American wines that had appeared since repeal, so its mere publication was a landmark in American wine history. It was written with Schoonmaker's usual assurance, clarity, and distinctness. And it presented an honest picture of the state of wine growing in America.

American Wines, after a brief sketch of the historical background, surveys California (Schoonmaker accepts the fictions about Agoston Haraszthy,
but they were received truths at the time). The chief theme, introduced over
and over again, is the great promise of California and its disappointing performance. The book, since it predictably stresses the importance of variety,
devotes a long chapter to an enumeration and description of all the vinifera
varieties that Schoonmaker considered worth knowing.[32] It then turns East,
sketches in the history of that region, describes wine growing in New York,
and touches briefly on Ohio, New Jersey, Missouri, and Virginia. Again, the
theme is of opportunities missed or of possibilities just beginning to be realized. A long list of native American grape varieties follows. At the end, in
the chapter "How to Buy Wine," the reader is instructed to seek out wines
labeled, according to Schoonmaker's well-established principles, with the
region and the grape variety.

The tone of Schoonmaker's account of things might be illustrated by a
thousand examples, but this one will have to suffice. Writing of an "agree-
able" white wine from Inglenook labeled "Pinot de la Loire," Schoonmaker
notes that, "as a matter of fact," the grape called by that name "is the excellent
grape from which Vouvray is made—its true name is the Chenin Blanc and
it is no more a Pinot than a Welsh Rabbit is a quadruped or a Scotch Wood-
cock is a bird."[33] Thus did the correction of popular error proceed.

Though the burden of the book was that California (and the rest of the
United States) was not even remotely approaching its potential, Schoonmaker remained optimistic (he had, one remembers, California wine to sell):
"The vine," he wrote, "at long last, is beginning to receive, in the better California vineyards, the respect and study and loving care which it deserves and
which it can so richly reward." How great was the promise of California in
Schoonmaker's judgment may be gauged from this remark on the vineyards
of Santa Cruz County: "It is possible to make, out of the great, traditional
European grapes—the Cabernet, the Pinot Noir, the Pinot Chardonnay—
grown on foothill vineyards, cultivated, picked, sorted, crushed, fermented
in the slow, meticulous European way, wines which will, within a few short
years, be able to hold their own against the better classed growths of the
Médoc, and against all but the very best red Cortons, for example, and white
Meursaults."[34] Two things stand out in such a passage: the confidence in the
potential greatness of California wines; and Schoonmaker's thoroughly con-
servative view of wine making, a view that assumes that French standards
alone are those to be aimed at.

Since the book laid such heavy stress on the failures and omissions of the California winemakers, it produced loud cries of pain from that quarter: it was all very well to talk of the promise of California—the criticism of present reality was what hurt. One winemaker, however, had cause to resent the book not for what it said about him but for what it didn't. This was Martin Ray (1905–76), the fanatical, impossible owner, at that time, of the Paul Masson Champagne Company, high in the hills above the Santa Clara Valley. Here Ray had been making wines from Cabernet, Chardonnay, and Pinot noir since 1936, wines for which he asked what were then astronomical prices and which had attracted a cult following. Schoonmaker was much impressed by them, so much so that in 1940, as has been noted already, he commissioned Ray to make a special lot of wine for Schoonmaker's firm. Toward the end of 1940 Martin Ray wrote, doubtless with considerable exaggeration, that Schoonmaker was then "determined to get a monopoly on the top grade wine industry of the country through purchase of the necessary vineyards and cellars in California."[35] In pursuit of this grand scheme, Schoonmaker offered to buy a half interest in Ray's winery, but when the time came in April 1941 to produce the money, Schoonmaker was unable to do it. Ray then killed the deal, and the two men parted in anger.

When Schoonmaker had arrived at Ray's winery on that fateful April day, he bore with him the galley proofs of *American Wine,* which then contained an entire chapter devoted to Ray and his exemplary wines. But when the two men quarreled over the botched deal, the chapter was torn from the book—by Schoonmaker, according to one account, because he was angry with Ray; by Ray, in another account, because he would not be bullied by Schoonmaker. What is certain is that Martin Ray does not figure in *American Wines,* though a few references to the vineyards of the Santa Cruz Mountains remain.[36]

Schoonmaker failed to make a partnership with Martin Ray, but he soon had another opportunity to establish himself in California. The Almadén winery, south of San Jose at Los Gatos, went back to the 1850s, the primitive era of Northern California wine making. It had a long and distinguished history and was particularly celebrated for its sparkling wine. During Prohibition it had changed hands, and, after renewing production upon repeal, the owners had found tough going in the Depression and went bankrupt in 1938. The vineyards and winery were bought and revived in 1941 by a San Francisco financier named Louis Benoist, who then allowed (or encouraged) Frank Schoonmaker to buy a controlling interest in the winery. Schoonmaker, it is said, had recommended the purchase to Benoist in the first place. This arrangement did not last, as we shall see, but it began a relationship between Schoonmaker and Almadén that *would* endure until 1973.

One reason that Schoonmaker had confidence in the future of California was his acquaintance with the work that Maynard Amerine and Albert Winkler of the University of California, Davis, were doing in the analytic study of grape varieties (to be discussed in the next chapter). In Amerine's recollection, Schoonmaker called on them at Davis around 1941, and he and Amerine were soon on friendly terms. On this and other visits to California, Schoonmaker had, in Amerine's words, "proved that he could pick out the good wines, that he could do it time after time and that they couldn't fool him. If he liked bin 34 and they brought it to him as bin 74, he'd say[,] 'This is bin 34, and this is the wine I want." He had great confidence in his ability.... He was a very good conversationalist and a very good person to be around, unless he got in an argumentative mood. Then he was not very much fun any more."[37]

Schoonmaker's business affairs were more problematic than his tasting abilities. A Dun and Bradstreet report on Frank Schoonmaker and Company in 1940 concluded that the firm was "undercapitalized" and its payments to creditors "irregular," but that, on the positive side, its business was expanding.[38] Dun and Bradstreet seem to have gotten it right. As Schoonmaker's business affairs had grown bigger they had also grown more and more burdened; the expanding business was evidently not enough to compensate for a perennial lack of money. Each of his four major suppliers of American wines—Korbel, Martini, and Wente in California, Widmer in New York— had put ten thousand dollars into the business, as well as extending large credits for wine delivered. By 1942 the wineries were not inclined to give him any more. As Louis Martini put it: "I like him. Very intelligent man. And he knows wine. He has a good palate. He is a good writer, and he is a good promoter. He is idealistic and very honest, but he is unfortunately not a good businessman."[39] Or as Peter Sichel put it even more succinctly, Schoonmaker was "erudite, opinionated and not a good businessman."[40] Early in 1942, Schoonmaker lost control of his company to "21" Brands, a firm of distributors; he continued as president, on salary, but only because the prestige of his name was wanted. When, at the end of 1942, he went into military service in the Office of Strategic Services and was sent to Spain, Schoonmaker simply left his liabilities and his assets to his main creditors. They nominally continued to run Frank Schoonmaker and Company, but they were concerned exclusively with paying off its debts. The main asset of the idle company was its stock in Almadén, and this was sold to Louis Benoist in 1944. Frank Schoonmaker and Company was now a firm without assets; as for business, that had all been taken over by "21" Brands.

Meanwhile, what of Schoonmaker? Here, again, one encounters some confusion and misstatement. Schoonmaker said that "two days after Pearl Harbor I was in it" (the war),[41] but if so it must have been on some very special terms, for he was in California buying wine in June 1942; and in September 1942, he is reported as having "just returned from his fourth trip to the West Coast this year."[42] Some things do seem to be certain. He *was* sent to Spain, and there, according to his own account, "was trying to find out whether the Germans were planning to invade Spain."[43] His cover was as a wine merchant, and, he said, "I made as much noise about my business as possible."[44] All went well, he said, until he was caught near the Spanish-French border carrying a hundred thousand dollars in francs for the French resistance: he was taken back to Madrid but allowed to stay in the house of the American ambassador "until passage could be arranged to Gibraltar."[45] But what difficulty could there have been about arranging "passage" to Gibraltar? The Spaniards could have had no trouble with that. From Spain he joined the planning staff of the Seventh Army and was at least for some time in Algiers.[46] Schoonmaker then followed in the wake of the American invasion of the south of France in 1944. He did not escape quite unscathed. A jeep in which he was riding near Lyon hit a landmine and flipped over. Schoonmaker hurt his ribs and was in great pain. Since he had no morphine or other painkiller, he called a restaurateur friend in Lyon, who brought him a bottle of cognac and "quite a bit of Champagne" to serve as anesthetics.[47] Schoonmaker left the service toward the end of 1945 with the rank of colonel, decorated with the Bronze Star and the Croix de Guerre.

There is some evidence that he actually did buy wine while posing as a wine merchant in wartime Spain, and that he continued to perform jobs for the company to which he nominally belonged back in New York. Julian Street, writing in early 1943, reports that Schoonmaker, while unable to "get his claws on company funds or to have to do with management," was still able to "select wines (and has been doing so abroad just lately) and write advertising."[48]

After the war, Frank Schoonmaker and Company was beyond restoring. When Alexis Lichine, also back from the army, applied to take up his old job with the company, there was nothing there for him to join. But the irrepressible Schoonmaker himself was soon back in action. First he scolded the California wineries in print: he had come back from the wars to find that they were still unwilling to pay premium prices for premium grapes, with the result that no premium grapes had been planted, and so the growing demand for good wine could not be met. What was the good of having created a demand if the people most concerned did not respond to it? The wineries really ought to wake up to the situation, Schoonmaker wrote, and he concluded by hoping that they would.[49] Then, in 1946, he set up in New York as the F. S. Importing Company, a base from which he could renew connections with his prewar suppliers. He resumed his California connections as well, in an "advisory and promotional capacity."[50] His clients included his old associates Wente, Korbel, Martini, and Almadén—especially Almadén. Schoonmaker was no longer a shareholder, but as an advisor he had an active and practical influence on the company's policies, which followed Schoonmaker's principles.[51]

ALMADÉN AND AFTER

In the immediate postwar years, Almadén resumed the work that Schoonmaker and Benoist had planned before Pearl Harbor. The company planted superior varieties in vineyards of large acreage, bottled varietal wines, and labeled them with the names of the grape and the region. The Grenache rosé wine that Schoonmaker had suggested in the early 1940s actually came on the market in 1945. Almadén sherry had a deserved success, for it at least approached the idea of genuine sherry as no other wine by that name did in California. It was made under *flor* yeast and put through a solera system.[52] The company also sold standard wines under the modest labels of "red" and "white," to which Schoonmaker added the word "mountain": Almadén's "mountain red" and "mountain white" had an appeal that no flatland generic could match—though the mountains in question were wholly poetic.[53]

The importance of the Almadén enterprise under Schoonmaker's direction can hardly be exaggerated. For many, many Americans, Almadén's wines provided a first encounter with a wine that aspired beyond the level of generic burgundies and that had a clear identity. It was a distinctly interesting experience to have a Santa Clara Valley Sauvignon blanc instead of a plain chablis. Moreover, Almadén wines were not expensive, and—most important—they were available. One did not merely read about them; one could buy them. The wines did not always live up to the exciting promise of Schoonmaker's back-label descriptions, but they were good enough; one could enjoy them, and they helped greatly in learning about wine.[54]

Schoonmaker's original series of articles on wine for the *New Yorker* had appeared under the general title of "News from the Wine Country"; he now began a lively and informative newsletter for his new firm of the F. S. Importing Company under that old title; it was, like everything that Schoonmaker wrote, clear, interesting, informative.[55] It had also the added virtue of cartoon illustrations by a Chilean artist named Oscar Fabrès, who thus began an association with Schoonmaker, and later with Almadén, that lasted for many years. When Schoonmaker began writing the back labels for Almadén wines, they, as well as the company's ads, were adorned with drawings by Fabrès, drawings whose charm made them a worthy accompaniment to Schoonmaker's prose.

From the 1950s on, Schoonmaker was easily the most familiar American presence to people who took an interest in wine. He published a small but important book, *The Wines of Germany,* in 1956. Just as his *American Wines* had been a useful promotion in 1941, so now *The Wines of Germany* was a useful promotion for the German wines that were an important part of Schoonmaker's importing business. But more to the point, Schoonmaker loved German wines, had a thorough knowledge of them, and of course wrote well about them. It was also, as James Gabler has pointed out, "the first book published by an American author in the U.S.A. dealing exclusively with German wines."[56]

But it was not by his books that Schoonmaker's presence was most widely felt; one encountered his name constantly in a vast output of ephemera. The back labels on Almadén wines have been mentioned; so have the newsletters: these had a press run of seven hundred thousand copies by 1969. Schoonmaker was the most prominent of wine writers for *Gourmet* and *Holiday.* He produced brochures and flyers to be given away at liquor store counters. And he regularly issued little pocket-sized booklets on the vintages of European and California wines, with commentary; these would then be gathered up into decennial collections as "Frank Schoonmaker's Report from the Wine Country" or under some other, comparable title. In the forties, the fifties, and into the sixties, he really had no competition for the role of America's expert on the world's wines.

Something of the awe Schoonmaker aroused among his faithful readers may be seen in what Roy Brady has written about him. Brady, then a graduate

FIGURE 27. Back label, Almadén Pinot noir, from 1972. Schoonmaker's association of this modest California varietal with Chambertin, Pommard, and Romanée Conti is an unusually bold implicit claim, though literally he says nothing beyond the simple fact that Pinot noir is common to all of them. Courtesy Gail Unzelman Collection.

student of mathematics at the University of Chicago, came across *American Wines* at a bookshop in 1947, opened it casually, read in it, and was at once smitten by the desire to become, as he put it, a "student of wine." He began to collect wines, to read all the literature he could find, and to seek connections with any knowledgeable sources about wine in Chicago. He became a wine consultant to one of Chicago's best stores, not for the money but for the experience, and was rewarded, in April 1949, by an invitation to a tasting in Chicago presided over by Schoonmaker himself. The tasting, held at the fashionable Bismarck Hotel, showed Schoonmaker's two sides: California wines either from Almadén or from his own line of selections that he was then promoting (Sonoma Pinot Blanc, Santa Clara Cabernet, and so on), and the Moselle wines that he imported from the ancient estate of the Counts of Kesselstatt. The reverent young Brady was gratified by the opportunity to meet and pay discreet homage to the man whom he then regarded as a "demigod, or at least a hemidemigod . . . wearing his inevitable bow tie."[57] Brady continued for the rest of his life to be a serious student of wine, and he never lost his respect for Schoonmaker as a writer on the subject.

Brady's high estimate was confirmed by Schoonmaker's most substantial book, appropriately enough an encyclopedia: *Frank Schoonmaker's Encyclopedia of Wine* (1964). This covers, in some four hundred pages, the world's wines and their lore as seen by Frank Schoonmaker in the 1960s, from Abboccato to zymase. The scene has greatly changed since then; we have many reasons to alter our judgments about the world's wines and their relative merits, and we recognize many things that were hidden over time's horizon then. But for all that, the book is still immensely readable and, I would venture, still immensely authoritative. It is a good place at least to begin a serious inquiry into almost any matter pertaining to wine. The entry on California is a masterful summary of the good and the bad elements in that state's wine making, though at the time—the so-called wine revolution was still to come—Schoonmaker might have been suspected of special pleading, as in his remark about the California winemakers who were then trying to make good wine: "The California producers who have undertaken the difficult and often unprofitable and thankless job of turning out this country's best wines and marketing them under honest but relatively unknown varietal names, deserve well of all wine-drinkers and of their country." They are, he added, "people of good taste and good will" who will need "all the encouragement they can get."

Outside of California, the Finger Lakes of New York, and Washington State (a brief mention), the *Encyclopedia* has nothing to say about other American wine-growing regions, for the good reason that there were none in 1964. The situation has been entirely transformed since then, in part because of Schoonmaker's work in teaching Americans about wine. He thus contributed to the obsolescence of his own book. There were, however, six editions between 1964 and 1975 and translations into six languages. Since Schoonmaker's death the *Encyclopedia* has been twice revised: first by Julius Wile (1978), then by Alexis Bespaloff (1988). There was also an English edition with a foreword by Hugh Johnson, who, after noting that Schoonmaker was a household word in America, wondered why "Frank Schoonmaker has not been a household name in Britain, too?"

The publication of the *Encyclopedia* marked the high point of Schoonmaker's reputation. About this time the first distant rumblings of the wine boom began to be heard. Robert Mondavi put up his bold new Napa Valley winery in 1966 in a bid to match the world's best wines; in 1967 the sales of table wine in America surpassed those of fortified wine for the first time since repeal; new wineries began to sprout up all over the map as people new to the wine trade began to make wine; new vineyards in new regions were planted, and already-established regions expanded to their limits. By 1972 the noise of the boom was loud enough that *Time* magazine could put the Gallo brothers on its cover and proclaim, "There's gold in them thar grapes."

Even before that, big corporations, sensing the money to be made in the new American taste for wine, eagerly bought in to the business—Coca-Cola, Heublein, Norton Simon, Nestlé, and many others. A new California gold rush was on. Where there had been only a few relatively small wineries aiming at wines of distinction before, there were now dozens and scores. Where there had been only a few voices offering advice and instruction before, there was now a noisy babble.

For Schoonmaker, the change came in 1967, when Almadén, with which he had been closely associated since 1941, was sold to National Distillers and its sales policies changed. Almadén had been steadily expanding under Louis Benoist, but that expansion was now accelerated at the cost of whatever quality remained. In 1969 Almadén was selling 2 million cases of wine annually; by 1980, 12 million.[58] Schoonmaker himself was now in poor health. Around 1967 he had a pacemaker inserted to regulate an irregular heartbeat; in 1969 he had surgery for intestinal cancer. You would think, one of his business associates said, "that he was a very magnificent, athletic, healthy man, but he never was."[59]

In 1972 he was approached by Pillsbury, the Minneapolis flour miller, which wished to get into the wine business. Pillsbury had already acquired the name of the small, distinguished Souverain Winery in the Napa Valley and had grandiose plans for expansion. The company wanted the prestige of Schoonmaker's name and was willing to buy his import company in order to get it. In 1973 it was announced that Frank Schoonmaker had sold his business to Pillsbury, had ended his long connection with Almadén, and would now consult for Pillsbury's wine interests. But this was the briefest connection; no sooner had Pillsbury gone into the wine business than it got out again. It was losing money heavily as a winemaker and had no prospect of ever making any. Pillsbury, confronted by this bleak prospect, put all of its wine properties, including Schoonmaker's firm, up for sale in 1975.

Schoonmaker himself barely lasted into the next year, dying at his New York home in January 1976.

His first and enduring love was no doubt for European wines—those of Burgundy and Germany especially—but, as Hugh Johnson has written, Frank Schoonmaker "as much as anyone . . . pointed California towards making fine wine."[60] That is a fair epitaph.

TEN

Maynard Amerine

APPLIED SCIENCE

If you don't know biochemistry,
you don't know anything about wine.

MAYNARD AMERINE, *1985*

SCIENCE OR ART?

Is wine making an art or a science? The question is a false one, since the answer is obviously "Both." But people still argue endlessly about it. It can hardly be a science, one side says, since wine has been made for thousands of years, and most of those years were, by any definition, prescientific. "Ah, but what kind of wine was it?" the other side asks. Spoiled wine, adulterated wine, flavored wine, doctored wine, watered wine, undrinkable wine. Only since scientific understanding has been brought to the vineyard and the winery has the world had a reliable supply of sound wine. If I had to choose, I, for one, would choose to put the scientists in charge of the business, just because they could certainly provide that reliable supply of sound wine. But of course one does not have to choose. The scientists contribute their indispensable part, and the individual artist remains free to do things in his or her own way.

EARLY RESEARCH IN CALIFORNIA

In California the beginnings of scientific study occurred in 1880, when the legislature passed a bill to support research in viticulture and enology. The immediate motive for this act was the threat of phylloxera, first discovered in California in 1873 and, by 1880, a danger that could no longer be ignored. The act created a public agency called the Board of State Viticultural

Commissioners and, at the same time, assigned research and instruction in viticulture to the College of Agriculture in the University of California. The act provided the university an initial grant of three thousand dollars, which was used to establish a cellar and laboratory. This dual arrangement of board and university inevitably led to quarrels between the two bodies; ultimately the university prevailed, and the board was suppressed.

Even before that, however, the university had undertaken important work under the direction of Eugene Hilgard, dean of the College of Agriculture. Hilgard's first order of business was to determine what were the good grape varieties for the state, whose vineyards were then dominated by the Mission, Zinfandel, and Burger. To do this, he proposed to make a "systematic investigation of grape-varieties with respect to their composition and general wine-making qualities in the different regions of the state."[1] This plan, apparently so modest, has been described by a later expert, Maynard Amerine, as a "remarkable project," having the "insight and comprehensiveness of a modern scientific agricultural project. For its time it was extraordinary."[2] In a series of bulletins and reports published between 1882 and 1896, Hilgard reported on the wines made at Berkeley and the grape varieties from which they were made, so that, to quote Maynard Amerine again, "a beginning was made in the classification of the many varieties of wine grapes based on the qualities of their wine."[3]

Hilgard was succeeded in his work on wine at the university by Frederic Bioletti (1865–1939), an Englishman despite his Italian name, who had been hired by Hilgard to supervise the cellar at Berkeley. Bioletti had thus been deeply involved from the beginning in the varietal studies directed by Hilgard. His enological research was obstructed by Prohibition, but he lived long enough to see repeal and to publish an ampelography of California.

In 1908 the College of Agriculture established an outpost at Davis, California, near Sacramento, on a farm that had been purchased by the university. At first, most of the work carried on at Davis was in practical teaching through nondegree courses, all activity being closely directed from headquarters at Berkeley. Viticulture—but not wine making—was one of the subjects offered at Davis, and even after Prohibition it continued to be taught, though now without any mention of the indissoluble relation between grapes and wine—another of Prohibition's many falsehoods. At Berkeley, where research and teaching about wine making had been carried on, Prohibition had severe effects. The staff there turned to the study of food processing, and the now-forbidden work on wine was abandoned. The change was clearly marked by a change in name: what had been the Division of Viticulture and Enology was now (and thereafter) the Division of Viticulture and Fruit Products.

When repeal came about at the end of 1933, the people at Berkeley resumed their work on wine, though now as only a part of their business rather than the whole. Under William Vere Cruess, the chairman, the department performed an essential service in instructing the revived wine industry, ignorant, confused, and uncertain as it was, in the elements of sound wine making. Cruess and his associates published pamphlets and books on all the procedures of wine making, organized instructional meetings, traveled up and down the state visiting wineries to help with their problems, and stood ready at all times to answer questions and solve problems.

Teaching basic wine making to an industry that had forgotten how to make wine was the first necessity, and it was Berkeley's notable achievement to do just that. Davis had equally important but less immediately pressing work to do. That was to thoroughly investigate what may be called the varietal question, continuing the work that Hilgard had begun. There are literally thousands and thousands of grape varieties scattered around the world: some are good for the table; some are good for raisins; some are good for wine; some are good for nothing, humanly speaking. And as there are thousands of grape varieties, so there is a near-limitless number of varied sites on which grapes may be grown: hills, valleys, flatlands, cold country, hot country, dry country, wet country, clay country, chalk country, and so on through all the combinations and changes. How, in all this multiplicity, can one expect to find just the right variety to match with just the right location?

In the traditional wine-growing regions of the world, that question has been settled in a practical way by trial and error over a long time: in Bordeaux the traditional choice is Cabernet Sauvignon; in Burgundy, Pinot noir; Riesling in Germany; Sangiovese in Tuscany; and so on.[4] But obviously no long-continued process of trial and error had gone on in California, where, at the time of repeal, significant commercial wine-making was not yet a century old. Old-world experience was of course useful. But the controlled study of how varieties performed in California, and where they performed best, had not been carried on after Hilgard, and all possibility of doing so had been cut off by Prohibition. Now A. J. Winkler, the professor of viticulture at Davis, was preparing to renew and extend this project, which would obviously be the work of years and would require competent help.

In rough outline, this was Winkler's plan: he would, each season over a course of years, gather samples of every variety of wine grape grown in California from every grape-growing region in the state, from Oregon to Mexico and from the Pacific to the Sierra. From these samples he would make wine under conditions as uniform as possible. These wines would then be analyzed according to the usual methods to determine such things as total acid, pH level, residual sugar, mineral elements, and so on. But then—a bold idea— after the objective analysis, a subjective test: they would taste the wines and rank them according to a scoring system worked out at Davis.

It would also be necessary to devise a classification of California's grape-growing regions. If the right variety were to be matched to the right site, one needed to know not only the qualities of the grape but also the character of the site—ideally through a comprehensive study of climate and soil. That, however, would be work for generations to come. Winkler decided to make temperature the defining condition, since temperature was not only of primary importance but also easily measured. From recorded information and continued observation, Winkler described five different temperature regions in the state, region I being the coldest and region V the hottest.[5]

THE EDUCATION OF AN ENOLOGIST

Once the outlines of this ambitious project were drawn, the next question was: Who could help carry it out? The job was given to a young graduate student, Maynard Amerine. Amerine (1911–98) was a farm boy who grew up on a fruit farm north of Modesto, California. He attended Woodside High School in Modesto (Julio Gallo was a classmate, but their acquaintance was slight), went on to Modesto Junior College, and then went to the Davis branch of the University of California, where he took a bachelor's degree in plant science in 1932. Davis was then still administratively part of the University of California, Berkeley, where Amerine next went in order to take a doctorate in plant physiology under teachers he had already known as a Davis student.

Professor Winkler had evidently taken note of Amerine while the latter was still in residence at Davis, and now, in 1935, before Amerine had finished

FIGURE 28. Maynard Amerine, photographed by Ansel Adams, c. 1967. Contemporary print from original negative by Ansel Adams. UCR/ California Museum of Photography, Sweeney/Rubin Ansel Adams FIAT LUX Collection, University of California, Riverside.

his work at Berkeley, Winkler invited him back to be his research assistant in the big varietal project. In the next year, when he had PhD in hand, Amerine was promoted from research assistant to junior enologist. He had had no thought of going into enology before the Davis offer came, but, as he said, jobs at that time were scarce.

Here one must say something about the status of wine in California in general and at Davis in particular at the moment of Amerine's entrance upon the scene. At the end of 1935 there had been only two postrepeal vintages, and these had made a sorry showing: wines spoiled by improper fermentations and by infections were made in wholesale quantities; wines were made from inferior varieties; wines were shipped to market too early—one might go through a whole litany of errors and bad practices. Enough to say that wine making in California was then a naive and struggling business, attracting little attention and earning little respect.

A major problem, one that the winemakers themselves were reluctant to admit or even to recognize, was the lack of good grapes. There had never been large numbers of superior varieties in California, but before Prohibition the supply of such varieties—Cabernet Sauvignon, Riesling, Semillon, Pinot noir, and the like—had been growing. Prohibition reversed that trend. The vineyards of the state, as has been said, flourished under Prohibition because of the demands of home winemakers. But the only consideration in that business was quantity, so out came the superior varieties and in went the coarse, big-yielding kinds that shipped well and looked good at the end of their long journey to market. The great favorite of growers and home winemakers alike was the Alicante Bouschet, a robust and handsome grape but a poor choice for wine.[6] Since white wine varieties were in little demand, whatever small acreage of fine white varieties there may have been in California effectively disappeared during Prohibition. If white wine were wanted (and most of it would have been in the form of California sherry), there was plenty of Thompson Seedless around to provide a pale, neutral wine—nearly two hundred thousand acres of it, in fact, making it the most widely planted grape in the state. Such varieties—Alicante Bouschet, Thompson Seedless, the sturdy Spanish variety called Carignane by the French and Kerrigan by the Californians, all big producers—were the staple of California's vineyards, and most of those vineyards were in the hot Central Valley, where it was difficult to grow grapes with the balance of sugar and acid needed to make good wine. If the dominant varieties were ever to be pushed out in favor of better grapes, it would be essential to show that better grapes, making better wines, existed. Hence the necessity for Winkler's varietal project, which aimed to make objective and demonstrable distinctions among good, bad, and indifferent varieties for California and to suggest where the good ones might best be planted. As Amerine put it many years later, "My job in 1935 was to try and get the California wine growers back on the straight and narrow path of planting good wine grape varieties."[7]

At Davis, where viticulture had a respectable history, but where wine making had been unknown, things were not much better. The business manager at Davis, Ira Smith, was friendly toward viticulture but disapproved of wine and did not want to support enology. Strange as it may seem, Professor Winkler himself did not care for wine, though he did not, like Smith, disapprove of it. Whenever Winkler was given a bottle of wine, as might often happen to a man in his position, he at once sought to give it away again.[8] Strangest of all, Mrs. Winkler, the wife of the man who was soon to take over the direction of all viticultural and enological work at Davis, was an ardent prohibitionist, the head of the local chapter of the Woman's Christian Temperance Union![9]

As for Maynard Amerine, now the junior enologist at Davis who was to assist in the gigantic task of making and assessing thousands of sample wines from California grapes, he knew no more than the others—that is to say, almost nothing. He would have been surrounded by vineyards around Modesto, where he grew up, and he no doubt saw plenty of home wine-making there. But perhaps not in his own home, for when he was five years old he was enrolled in the WCTU by his grandmother![10] He was only nine years old when Prohibition went into effect, and it had been repealed for only two years when he joined the staff at Davis. He thus had had no means of learning anything about the qualities of wine, about its countless variet-ies, about its long traditions, about its vast literature. The situation was the sort of thing belonging to fairy tale, where the princess, charged with some impossible task by the wicked witch, can only sigh and weep until the fairy godmother appears.

The fairy godmother in this case was a gentleman named Edmund Henri Twight (1874–1957), the son of a French mother and an English father, edu-cated in France and employed in teaching about and making wine in Califor-nia since the turn of the century. He had been the first professorial appoint-ment in viticulture at Berkeley in 1901 but had left the university after a few years to work for commercial wineries. Now he returned to the university, or to its branch at Davis, to teach wine again. His main pupil was Amerine. As Maynard Joslyn, one of the scientists in the Division of Viticulture and Fruit Products at Berkeley, recalled, when Amerine took the Davis job he had

no personal knowledge of grapes or wine making.... So to train him in the art of appreciating wines and wine making ... E. H. Twight, who had been professor of enology before Bioletti, was hired to live with and to work with and to train and to influence Amerine.... Twight's talent and knowledge of viticulture and wine making was used in the training of Maynard Amerine, because for a year or more he lived with Amerine, and they discussed grapes and wines and tasting, so that Amerine was trained by the University for wine appreciation and wine making.[11]

Amerine paid tribute to Twight and his tutoring in an obituary note pub-lished in 1957: "In viticulture and enology," Amerine wrote, "he was a true master."[12] If there were a pantheon of California wine deities, Twight would surely deserve to have a least a minor place within it.

Winkler and Amerine, having been trained, now went into action ("I never did develop a very sharp palate," Winkler admitted; "never equal to Amerine").[13] Beginning in the fall of 1935, they visited vineyards all over the state, picked grapes of every variety (they usually got them free, but not always), took them back to Davis and made wine from them in five-gallon lots. Their means were at first primitive—they had little wine-making equipment and no proper place in which to make or store their wines until 1939, when a new building was put up expressly to house the work in enology.[14] As Amerine recalled this time: "We would go in the evening to San Jose, pick grapes at five o'clock in the morning and have them here [Davis] at four in the afternoon, crush them, and take care of the other lots that were fermenting, and the next morning at five o'clock go to Napa and pick grapes. This went on for a period of six or eight weeks. Every fall, '35, '36, '37, '38, '39, '40, '41."[15]

In the first year of the project, 1935, they managed to make 556 wines, even though they had no destemmer and had to do all that work by hand, forcing the grapes through a screen at the cost of skinned knuckles.[16] By 1939 they had made some three thousand sample lots of wine and were doing their best to advertise their work and its results to the people in the trade. They held a series of meetings up and down the state for three weeks every year, "teaching about varieties" and doing "an enormous amount of field work telling the growers what we had done."[17] What they hoped to show was that the belief then common in California, that "a grape is a grape," was profoundly wrong. As Amerine said of that time: "People just didn't know anything about grape varieties."[18] The Thompson Seedless dominated California. "The three-way grape," it was called, because you could sell it as fresh fruit, or dry it into raisins, and then send whatever was left over to the wineries, who turned it into white wine, or sherry, or distilled its wines for high-proof spirit.

This was the state of things that Winkler and Amerine were devoted to changing, against very heavy odds in the depressed decade following repeal. Then the war effectively put a stop to their progress: Amerine went into the army in 1942; Winkler remained at Davis, but the experimental wine making came to a halt. By this time, however, they had made wines from dozens and scores of varieties from every region of the state and had accumulated fifteen thousand tasting notes in addition to their analytical data. This information was at last published during the war years, in 1944, under the colorless title of "Composition and Quality of Musts and Wines of California Grapes."[19]

This document, a publication of seminal importance in the history of American wine, reports on the many different lots of wines made from 139 varieties from all five climate regions of the state. The assessments included detailed analysis of such elements as sugar content, total acid, pH, tannin, and so on, to which were added the results of a series of tastings, scored according to the Davis twenty-point system.[20] When, on the evidence of such accumulated knowledge, Amerine and Winkler recommended a particular variety for a particular region, they knew what they were saying. And so did they when they withheld their recommendation, as they did for many varieties long grown in the state. Some varieties, in some regions, consistently scored well; others did not, and for reasons that were plainly set forth. The Alicante Bouschet, then planted everywhere in California, "fails to retain much acid and the wines are frequently flat," or they are "rough and somewhat harsh"; they had an attractive dark color, but, "unfortunately, the color is not stable." The conclusion was clear: "Alicante Bouschet is not recommended for California because of low quality and unstable coloring matter." Cabernet Sauvignon, on the other hand, then only rarely planted in California, when grown in regions I, II, and III proved "well-suited for table wines of superior quality. . . . The wines were distinctive in aroma, full flavored, soft, well balanced, excellent in quality." If one turns to the tasting notes provided for each variety, one finds that the wines of Alicante Bouschet were "harsh," "flat," "common," "very poor," or at best, "very ordinary." Cabernet Sauvignon yielded wines of "excellent quality," "soft," "rich," "fruity," "well balanced," and having "distinct aroma."[21] The recommendations that Amerine and Winkler made on this kind of evidence were not final, nor were they intended to be; but they put the understanding of varietal choice on an entirely new basis.

The timing of the report was inauspicious. Wineries in 1944 could sell all that they made under wartime conditions, so why bother to change? In any case, supplies and labor were difficult to get, so if any growers had plans to invest in better varieties, their plans remained just that—plans. After the war, when one might suppose that new practices would be welcome, the wine business went into a slump. The hope that Americans would drink more wine when more wine became available turned out to be a delusion. Americans happily went back to bourbon after the war, and wine, in oversupply now, backed up on the producers' hands. Prices crashed, and it was years before anything like a balance between supply and demand was reached. In this situation, an improvement in the varietal composition of California's vineyards, following the recommendations of Amerine and Winkler, might have had a good effect on the fortunes of wine, but few were in any mood to try. As late as 1965, more than twenty years after Winkler and Amerine's recommendations had been published, the visible results were so meager that Amerine felt he had wasted his time on the work: so discouraged was he that, as he later wrote, he would have left the university for "the right biochemical job" if one had been offered then.[22]

The work was having its invisible effects, however; what had been a gradual and scattered development for years at last gathered momentum in the late 1960s, when, as part of a general change in the fortunes of American wine, Californians took to planting superior varieties as a matter of course. Amerine and Winkler, though their work needed some modification in the light of further experience, were now regarded as authoritative guides—and still are. Of their work it may be said that no more important contribution to American wine making has been made in the years since repeal.

BECOMING AN AUTHORITY

The transformation of California's vineyards was a slow process; the transformation of Maynard Amerine from raw graduate student, uninstructed in wine, to finished and sophisticated professional was astonishingly rapid. The popular notion of the laboratory scientist as a narrow-minded technician is doubtless wrong, but Amerine seems to have had a much greater variety of interests than is usual. He was interested in music performance: he played the French horn in high school and remembered his music teacher—Frank Mancini—with special regard.[23] He was interested in painting, opera (he was a faithful patron of the San Francisco company), and theater (he was in the Drama Club at Davis as an undergraduate). He liked to dance. He reported from Madrid, where he was on sabbatical in 1954, that he had been "going out a lot. Three or four wonderful dance halls here. Of course all prostitutes but not bad looking if you look and choose carefully."[24] He enjoyed literature, both classic and contemporary. His bookish interests extended to collecting as well, and from collecting to bibliographical description. The extensive holdings of viticultural and enological literature in the university library at Davis owe much to his care and advice, and he saw to it that the library acquired not only the technical publications but the historical and literary items as well.[25] The collection is now, most appropriately, housed in the Amerine room of the library.

At an early point in his Davis career, in 1937, Amerine joined the Wine and Food Society of San Francisco, a branch of the London society, founded by André Simon on his American tour in 1935. Amerine was a good cook,[26] and a notably good host, attractive virtues in a young man living a bachelor life. Through friends that he made in the Wine and Food Society, he was soon made a member of San Francisco's Bohemian Club, and it was not long thereafter that he was put in charge of the club's notable wine cellar. Not bad going for a young man who, a few years earlier, had no knowledge of wine.

He was also beginning to make a name through publication, mainly in the trade press at the outset; by the end of his career he had appeared in an impressive variety of publications directed toward audiences of all kinds. His first article, a report on the wines at the Paris International Exposition, appeared in the trade journal *Wines and Vines* in 1937, and this was followed by an unbroken stream of further publications continuing almost to the end of his life. By 1942 he was writing for André Simon's elegant quarterly, *Wine and Food,* further evidence, if any were needed, of his rapid rise to authority.

When the wine judgings that had been a feature of the California State Fair were reinstated in 1934, following the hiatus caused by Prohibition, Professor Cruess at Berkeley was at first put in charge of them. After a few years this position was handed to Amerine, a position in which he became even better known to the trade, although in a difficult way: it was hard to avoid offending competitors who won no prizes. But the position confirmed Amerine's quickly earned status as a leading expert. When a judging of California's wines was planned for the San Francisco world's fair—the Golden Gate Exposition—in 1939, Amerine headed the jury, which included his old mentor E. H. Twight. This judging, Amerine thought, was the best that had been held in postrepeal America; it was an affair that "really meant something" and that had "a really lasting influence."[27]

Before that sort of recognition came, however, Amerine had seen clearly that, if he were to be kept on at Davis, he would have to visit Europe, especially France, to extend his knowledge of wine beyond what California offered. By an extraordinary indulgence, he was granted a special leave in the summer of 1937—he had been on the faculty only for a couple of years, he held a very low place on the academic totem pole, and money for such things was hard to come by in those years. But Dean Claude Hutchison, of the College of Agriculture, and Professor Winkler thought so well of their promising young man that they contrived the means to send him abroad.[28] Amerine did not need to be told that this was a big chance. The journal he kept of this trip survives among his papers and is a highly interesting account of what a rising young enologist could see and learn in those days.

He sailed on the *Normandie* and, once in Paris, did the things that Americans in Paris do: the Opéra, the Opéra Comique, the Café de Flores, and all that. He then toured the *chais* of Champagne, called on the big merchants of Burgundy, attended the Congrès International de Viticulture assembled in Paris, and then went south to Bordeaux, where he was treated generously. He called on the *négociant* firm of Kressman—"very nice people here," he noted—and then, in rapid sequence, visited Chateau Margaux, La Mission Haut Brion, Haut Brion, Smith Haut Lafitte, Olivier, and Yquem, where he had lunch: "Excellent lunch (dinner) beautiful organization, modern equipment used properly—this is undoubtedly a high light of fine living for me."[29]

From Bordeaux he went over to the Rhone, visiting Chapoutier at Hermitage, made a side trip into Switzerland (where his hosts gave him a marvelous Volnay '29 and a "perfectly marvelous" Chateau Cheval Blanc '28), and then returned to Paris. On the twenty-first of July he sailed on the *Île de France* and ten days later was back in Davis. As he said, some forty-five years later, about his return from France, "I probably thought I knew more about wine then than I ever did."[30]

On his return to Davis, Amerine found himself caught up in a squabble between the Division of Viticulture and Fruit Products at Berkeley and the Division of Viticulture at Davis. The Davis people looked at some of the Berkeley activities with suspicion, not to say horrified disapproval. Berkeley, they thought, was giving bad advice to the California wine industry, advice that, if followed, would do damage to the reputation of California's wine.[31] The Berkeley people, conscious of their key role in saving the California wine industry by teaching it sound methods, hotly resented the accusation. The dean of the College of Agriculture, to which both departments belonged, then stepped in. The principals of the two departments ("divisions" they were then called) were summoned and told that they must speak to the California wine industry with one voice, from a unified point of view. To do this, they were instructed to cooperate on publishing a series of instructional bulletins that would present a comprehensive account of approved wine-making practices. Amerine was, as he put it, the "fall guy" from Davis assigned the task of writing these bulletins. The other fall guy was Maynard Joslyn, from the Berkeley side. Despite the coincidence of their rather unusual first names, Amerine and Joslyn had very different origins—Amerine a farm boy from Modesto, Joslyn a Russian Jew. But they managed to cooperate successfully, producing between 1940 and 1941 a series of three substantial treatises on the production of table wines, fortified wines, and brandy.[32] These were surveys of accepted practices and were at once received as the last word on their different subjects. Amerine did not pretend that the work was the outcome of any original scientific inquiry; it was, rather, a survey of what was known and thought; or, as Amerine said of it: "Well, this is the literature: take your choice."[33]

In the year after the publication of the last of these three bulletins, Amerine disappeared into the U.S. Army, which assigned him to the Forty-fifth Chemical Laboratory Company. It was while he was in camp in Tennessee, Amerine remembered, that he read the proofs of his report with Winkler on the results of their long investigation of California grape varieties. That was in effect the end of a long experiment; he could also look with satisfaction on the work that he and Joslyn had successfully completed on the three comprehensive bulletins. But war service interrupted much other work with which Amerine had been engaged. With E. H. Twight and A. J. Winkler, he had published a long series of articles analyzing the whole range of California wines, mostly with the result of exhibiting their many defects.[34] From his experience as a wine judge, he wrote on wine-judging methods, a subject to which he was later to return in a more sustained and scientific way. The subject of color in wines—a matter of some concern in hot-country wines—produced a series of studies between 1940 and 1947. Amerine and Winkler together studied the question of grape maturity or, rather, the problematic question of how best to determine the point of optimum maturity, and published articles about it in 1940 and 1942.[35]

It should be noted that all of this work had an immediate, practical bearing on the concerns of the California wine industry. Neither Amerine nor any other of the scientists employed at Davis was engaged in what is called "pure" research; they were dealing with questions affecting the daily practice of wine making in California, bringing scientific understanding and scientific measurement to making California wine. Who can doubt that this was an essential service? Amerine was at Davis from 1935 until his retirement in 1974, a span of nearly forty years, minus the three years of army service; for all of those years, the character of the research carried on at Davis was largely determined by the practical needs of the wine industry. Davis was its lab. As Amerine put it, probably no other department in the university had such an intimate relation to the industry it served as viticulture at Davis did with California wine making.[36]

It is different now: the scientists in today's Department of Viticulture and Enology, while still in close touch with the industry and its problems, are free to experiment in ways that have no necessary practical application. This is sometimes regretted by people who remember what it was like in an earlier day. But the change is probably irreversible, since it is the product of many other changes. The big, well-heeled wineries can do their own research, and there are now commercial laboratories that can answer questions of the sort that Davis and Berkeley, in more innocent days, had to deal with. Funds dedicated to sponsoring research, such as those of the American Vineyard Foundation, can be directed to a number of institutions prepared to take on such work; the federal Department of Agriculture and the various state departments are more and more prepared to undertake research in viticulture, especially in those states where wine making is newly flourishing—in Washington, Oregon, Texas, and Virginia, for example. Davis is no longer alone, and so it can go off in directions where it could not venture before. It is also the case that the work already done by Davis does not need to be done over again.

THE POSTWAR SCENE

Amerine had been drafted into the army as a private soldier; the army is, of course, notorious for its inability to put the right peg in the right hole, but in this case it came close enough. Amerine went into the Chemical Corps and was then sent to Officers' Training School, emerging as a second lieutenant. The training for this work was useful to him: it was, he wrote to Winkler in 1943, "a good review of analytical chemistry."[37] He seems never to have lost his professional interests throughout his particular experience of the war. His unit was first shipped to Algeria, late in 1943, and set up camp in the midst of vineyards and in the neighborhood of several wineries. Amerine studied the vineyard practices and visited the *caves* as soon as he was free to do so, then reported his observations to Winkler back in Davis.[38]

His company was then sent to a remote corner of India, Chabua in Upper Assam, where India, Tibet, and Myanmar converge. It is hard to imagine a place more remote from wine making, but Amerine still managed to keep up his professional interests, as illustrated by a story that appears to be substantially true. A fellow soldier in the Forty-fifth Chemical Laboratory Company, August Haschka, later a doctor practicing in Malibu and an enthusiastic home winemaker, recalled that his first interest in wine was aroused by Amerine in India. "I knew nothing of his background," Haschka said. "Amerine was always asking me to bring back wines from Calcutta, even providing the name of the wine shop at which to make the purchases. When he received the wine, Amerine would disappear into his thatched-roof hut, not to be seen for perhaps a week." Haschka naturally concluded that Amerine was enjoying a heroic drunk, but he was wrong: "Actually, Amerine was compiling a very careful scientific analysis of Asian wines while doing sensory studies on them. In addition he checked the alcohol content, potassium content, and intricate chemical breakdowns of the beverages. Upon returning to the U.S. following the war, Amerine published a definitive treatise on Asian wines as a result of his studies in Upper Assam."[39] By the time of his discharge from the army, Amerine had risen to the rank of major. He remained active in the Army Reserve for the next twenty years, retiring as a lieutenant colonel. When asked about his army experience, he replied in the laconic style that he typically used in response to personal questions: "I probably learned a little chemistry."[40]

What he found on his return to civilian life in 1946 was not particularly encouraging. The wine industry was in trouble. It had been confidently supposed that the sale of wine would go up after the war, but it did not, and there was soon a severe problem of overproduction. Prices fell, new developments stalled, and the mood of the industry resembled that of the bad old days of the Depression. This state of things was reflected at Davis, where few students were attracted to wine making, and, of those who were, most were likely, on graduation, to take better-paying jobs in other businesses. These were not exactly locust years, but for a decade and more following the war the pace of change was slow. As Amerine wrote to Martin Ray in 1953: "Registration is here—little interest in enology. Perhaps we make it too difficult? But the industry is certainly not prosperous enough to attract new students. The veterans who came in 1946–47 have nearly all left the wine industry now. Perhaps our teaching did not inspire them enough to continue? Or maybe we should have a course in marketing."[41]

As for Amerine himself in these years, he had never been busier. In the ten years from 1946 through 1955, he added sixty-one published items to his bibliography (including some translations). The number is impressive, but even more impressive is the variety of his topics and the diverse character of his audiences. That is what made Amerine so unusual. Doubtless there have been, and are, many scientists who have done as much work, and no doubt some of that work is more original than anything that Amerine did. But very few have been able to get across to so many different audiences at so many different levels of knowledge and interest, from the Sunday supplement reader to the student of the most rarified technical journal.

One of the subjects that attracted Amerine after his return to Davis was the matter of wine tasting and wine judging—organoleptic or "sensory" evaluation, in the language of the initiated.[42] He had been compelled to think about this elusive business from his experience in presiding over the California State Fair judgings before the war, and of course from the very beginning of his work at Davis, when he and Winkler set out to discover what was good and bad in California wines under the tutelage of Ned Twight. After uncounted thousands of tastings, Amerine badly wanted to understand what was involved. As early as 1939 he had published an article on the subject, "Wine Judging Methods."[43] Now, beginning in 1948, he published a series of items that show his varied approaches. First was an article in the trade journal *Wine Review,* "An Application of 'Triangular' Taste Testing to Wines,"[44] treating one of the methods for controlling the wayward subjectivity of tasting. In the next year he produced a study called "The Influence of the Constituents of Wine on Taste and Application to the Judging of Commercial Wine," originally given as a talk to the Wine Technical Conference at Davis.[45] In 1950 came a more casual return to the subject, "A Matter of Taste," published in the trade journal *Wines and Vines.*[46] All this was merely a warm-up. In 1952 came the formidable "Techniques and Problems in the Organoleptic Examination of Wines," produced in collaboration with the mathematician Edward Roessler and published in the *Proceedings of the American Society of Enologists.*[47]

The experimental and analytical work that Amerine carried out in collaboration with Roessler produced, in the years following, a series of articles and, ultimately, the book called *Wines: Their Sensory Evaluation,* in 1976.[48] The book was an examination of wine-judging practices and a guide to establishing methods that would yield statistically valid results. "The statistical part of the book," Amerine recalled, "frightened many people";[49] but here he was aiming at a very special readership.

Another part of Amerine's work in these years produced a series of analytical studies: "Hydroxymethylfurfural in California Wines" in 1948; and "The Acids of California Grapes and Wines. I: Lactic Acid" (1950) and "The Acids of California Grapes and Wines. II. Malic Acid" (1951), for example. Such studies were given semipopular treatment in 1953 in the article "The Composition of Wines" in *Scientific Monthly*.[50] But even before that he and Maynard Joslyn had transformed their bulletin on table wines from 1940 into the nearly four hundred pages in *Table Wines: The Technology of Their Production in California,* published not as an agricultural experiment station bulletin but as a trade book by the University of California Press.

And then there were the bookish interests, literary, historical, and bibliographical. Amerine had been reviewing nontechnical books on wine for André Simon's quarterly *Wine and Food* starting in 1942 and, from that beginning, went on to publish many articles on wine history (e.g., "An Historical Note on Grape Prices"), wine literature (e.g., "Some Early Books about the California Wine Industry"), and wine appreciation (e.g., "Bordeaux and Burgundy").[51]

Bibliography was perhaps an inevitable outgrowth from Amerine's collecting habits. As his personal collection grew, so did his interest in the literature of wine in general. In the course of his many travels he regularly visited not only the local bookstores but the libraries as well so that he could add to his knowledge of publications in most of the languages of the wine-growing world. At Davis, he was an notable patron of the university library. The first fruit of this interest was *A Check List of Books and Pamphlets in English on Grapes and Wines, and Related Subjects, 1938–1948* (1951), compiled in collaboration with the Davis librarian Louise Wheeler and intended to supply information about the decade of the 1940s, much of which remained unknown because of the gaps created by the war years. This was only a beginning; before he ceased to be active, Amerine published at least seven more bibliographical lists, usually in collaboration.[52]

One of Amerine's goals was to make the training of enologists fully professional and to have this status recognized by the wine industry; only then would Viticulture and Enology at Davis begin to attract and keep good students. His ideal enologist was described in a speech given to the newly founded American Society of Enologists (later the American Society for Enology and Viticulture) in 1951.[53] The key was that the budding enologist must have "an intelligent interest in the scientific aspects of his chosen profession." If he had this (there were no "she's" in this category in 1951), then he would naturally seek to keep up with the current literature, to follow advances in the field by attending conferences, and to learn a foreign language or languages (especially French), since "far more scientific work on grapes and wines is being produced abroad than in this country"; and he would seek to acquire a "familiarity with all phases of the industry." A winemaker should know all about grapes, as a viticulturist should know all about wine making. Then he would be fit to carry out genuine research, rather than performing mere routine analyses and solving immediate small-scale problems. Amerine also showed in his lectures to students at Davis that the study of enology was broader than the simple technical side. As one of his assistants recalled, in these he included material on world wine history whether they cared to hear it or not.[54] How close the training at Davis came to Amerine's ideal I do not know, but there is no question that the Davis-trained enologist came to command respect.

Amerine had comparable hopes for the wine-growing industry in California, and he did what he could to move it out of the doldrums. The same poor varieties that dominated in the 1930s still dominated in the 1950s, and the wineries continued to make out of these grapes "ports" that were not Ports, "sherries" that were not Sherries, "burgundy" that was not Burgundy, "rieslings" that contained no Riesling, and so on through a long list of sins.

In an unpublished talk that he gave in 1955 to the Technical Advisory Committee of the Wine Institute, Amerine reviewed these things with unsparing frankness. The promotional talk that one familiarly heard about California making "the world's finest wines" was, he told his audience, simply baloney. Worse, it was self-deluding; California winemakers flattered themselves that they were making distinguished wines when in fact they were making, at best, mere standard wines and, at worst, mere plonk. "What is needed is a regular supply of high quality grapes," he told the assembled technicians. "This we do not have." The situation could not be described more plainly. And the standard industry practice of labeling wines with so-called generic names—"burgundy" for any sort of red wine; "chablis" for any sort of white wine—was a self-defeating practice. The meaningless names applied in California were matched by wines that might be anything. Until California made wines with genuine identities, honestly labeled, the trade would go nowhere.

He then went on to scold his audience for their failure to develop expert tasting skills—"Practice. Study. Practice," he told them—and for their indifference to technical standards and developments. Only nine hundred copies of the Amerine-Joslyn *Table Wine* book had been sold in the four years since its publication, and many of those copies had been sold outside of California. In the light of what Amerine had written about the "educated enologist," the California winemakers looked like a pretty barren lot, though he did not say that in so many words. How many showed any imagination? How many cared to keep up with the field? How many had the patience to learn at least a reading knowledge of one foreign language?

What Amerine told the California wine men about their wines was nothing new—they had been hearing the same thing from Frank Schoonmaker for a long time; but Amerine was in a more delicate position, and he was therefore all the bolder to speak out as he did. The department at Davis could not be seen as hostile to the industry that it was meant to serve, so Amerine ran a real risk in speaking plainly. And some bad feeling certainly followed. Allowing for the large measure of exaggeration in nearly everything that he ever said or wrote, Martin Ray was perhaps not wholly wrong in what he wrote of Amerine in 1956, a year after that talk to the Technical Advisory Committee. After noting Amerine's disappointment over the poor sales of the book on table wine, Ray went on: "He is currently a very bitter man too! He has broken with most of his friends, is under a doctor's care, and recently told me on the telephone that practically nobody in the industry will any longer speak to him and that he didn't want to hear any longer from me either!"[55] Disappointed Amerine certainly was: we have seen already that, even a decade later, he was, on his own saying, so discouraged by the apparent failure of his work to make any difference that he thought of leaving Davis for work elsewhere. But he went on working. The decade from 1955 to 1965 saw the usual flow of research papers, popular articles, books, and speeches.

A recollection of Amerine at work in these years by one of his research assistants throws a very different light on him than that cast by Martin Ray's lurid glare. Clare Bailey, a young microbiologist hired as Amerine's laboratory assistant in 1957, remained with him for the next two years. Her memories are all positive. Amerine, she found, was a hard worker—she never got to work before he did. One of her regular assignments was to analyze the experimental wines that continued to be made at Davis, and of these Amerine tasted twenty each morning and twenty each afternoon. He was always pleasant to work for: he never criticized her work, nor did she ever hear any complaints about his treatment from others. Nor was it all work. He entertained the staff at his home, where he could exhibit his gifts as a cook and host—there were, she remembered, wines with every course.[56] In short, he behaved as one would expect a hardworking, productive professional to do: whatever pressures might trouble him, he kept to himself.

The changes in the fortunes of American wine that had been in long and invisible preparation began to be clearly visible in the 1960s. Better variet-

FIGURE 29. The experimental wine cellar in the enology building at the University of California, Davis, 1967. Begun by Winkler and Amerine in 1935, it has never ceased to grow. It has now been transferred to the new Robert Mondavi Institute at Davis. Contemporary print from original negative by Ansel Adams, UCR/California Museum of Photography, Sweeney/Rubin Ansel Adams FIAT LUX Collection, University of California, Riverside.

ies of grape were planted; new wineries were built, new people came into the business, a new public interest began to develop. The weather was changing. There had already been immense changes at Davis, which was transformed from an agricultural college to a full-scale university in 1959 in response to the swelling population of the state. The Department of Viticulture and Enology began to exhibit a new self-consciousness. As Amerine remembered, it had had only a modest opinion of itself when he joined it: it had, after all, only recently been revived, and its work was all before it. But by the 1950s the department began to earn recognition of its leadership in the field: more and more of its graduates were working with distinction in the wine-making business; it attracted foreign students; its teachers and researchers were sought as judges and consultants in the wine-making countries of the world; and in California, Davis was the unchallenged authority on all points of wine and wine making.

In the early 1950s Amerine had lamented the lack of students attracted to viticulture and enology. Not now. Enrollments ballooned. To help manage the swollen numbers that now crowded his introductory course, Amerine enlisted his colleague Vernon Singleton. The lectures that they developed for the course were edited and published in 1965 as *Wine: An Introduction for Americans.* To every one's surprise, the book, intended only as a modest textbook, became a popular success: there was now an audience in this country eager to learn about wine. At this point, Amerine, though hardly a national figure, was at least a name to conjure with among the growing body of Americans who cared about wine. No one else presented such a combination of qualifications: scientist, teacher, writer, lecturer, connoisseur.

YEARS OF DISTINCTION

A sampling of the talks that Amerine was now constantly sought after to give to different audiences provides some idea of how flexible and adaptable he could be. To the Pacific College Health Association, he delivered the lecture "Wine and Health" (1976); to an unidentified group of physicists, he presented "What We Know and Don't Know about Wines: Leptons and Quarks" (1977); the San Francisco Wine and Food Society heard their founder (and Amerine's friend) discussed in "André Simon" (1977); while the New York Wine and Food Society listened to "The Appreciation of California Wines" (1977). The Friends of the Los Angeles Junior Arts Society heard "Wine and Aesthetics" (1977); to his fellow Bohemians at the Bohemian Grove, he presented "The Pleasures of Drinking Enough" (1977); and the California Academy of Sciences listened to "The Natural History of Wine" (1978). These different titles were not merely cosmetic changes: Amerine really had different things to say to different audiences, though of course he held consistent views about his essential subjects, the history and technology of wine in general and of wine in California in particular.

His standing as America's wine expert on the scientific side meant that he was, by the end of his academic career and after, much in demand as a distinguished presence: he judged wines in Yugoslavia, Hungary, and Russia; he consulted in Venezuela, Chile, Algeria, and Japan; he lectured in Germany, France, Algeria, South Africa, India, and Japan. Honors and distinctions accumulated: the French gave him the Croix d'Officier de l'Ordre National du Mérite; the Italians made him a member of the Accademia Italiana della Vite e del Vino. Back home, he was a founder and president of the American Society for Enology and Viticulture, the winner of the American Wine

Society's Award of Merit, and the Wine Man of the Year for *Wines and Vines*. He was a member of innumerable committees—advisory, steering, editorial, program—of official bodies, academic and otherwise. In 1979 Ernest Gallo endowed the Amerine Chair of Enology at Davis. And all of this is a mere selection from a long, long list. The junior enologist of 1935 would scarcely have recognized the eminent elder statesman of American wine who retired from Davis in 1974 and withdrew to a house in the hills high over St. Helena, in the heart of the Napa Valley, where he continued to be sought out by experts and amateurs alike.

Like any man of distinguished achievement, Amerine has been the subject of the usual exaggerations. Ernest Gallo declared for public consumption that Amerine had "contributed more to the science and art of winemaking than any other living person."[57] Such extravagant statements are impossible to prove or disprove, but Amerine himself would have been the first to scoff at the claim. He had a much more modest and measured view of what he and the department at Davis had accomplished. As he put it in his interview for the University of California's Regional Oral History Office, conducted in 1985, the Davis people had done three important things: they had changed the varieties planted in California's vineyards; they had trained a stream of professional enologists and viticulturists; and they had provided a body of reliable technical literature.[58] These things were of critical importance in the transformation of the California industry in the years since repeal. Amerine did not say, as he well might have said, that he had had a leading role in each one of these three essential activities.

There was yet another important change: as he reviewed his career for *Wines and Vines* on the occasion of his retirement, Amerine noted that "the wine industry has become respectable in my time."[59] That was the biggest change.

Despite the modesty of his personal claims, Amerine had the pride of his profession. In a speech to the Institute of Masters of Wine in London in 1969, he listed some of the advances in viticulture and enology that had been entered into modern wine making, advances that had come from sources all over the world—from Germany, Switzerland, France, South Africa, South America, Australia—as well as California. Vines were now planted in regular rows, rather than in the helter-skelter confusion of the prephylloxera era; the vines grew on resistant rootstocks, and they were of superior varieties; they were trained and pruned to achieve a satisfactory balance between crop size and vine vigor. The control of diseases and pests, never complete, was at least better than it had been. Production had been increased without sacrifice of quality through clonal selection, and the crucial question of determining grape maturity was now better understood. What was true in the vineyards was also true in the winery: a winemaker now had improved machines: new crusher-stemmers, presses, and tanks made control at every step easier and more precise; pure yeast cultures and temperature-controlled tanks guaranteed clean and sound fermentations—and so on through a substantial litany of improvements.

"There are a lot of people," Amerine told the Masters of Wine, "who think that growing grapes and making wine is carried on by God." But what God apparently has in mind, if left to his own devices, "is to over-crop the vines, produce low-sugar must and make vinegar from the new wine." If you want sound wine, you need human intervention, and that must be guided by scientific understanding. We have that understanding now, so that Amerine could state simply, "There is no excuse for spoiled wine." Not only is spoiled wine no longer excusable, more fine wine is being produced around the world than ever in the past. Amerine's confident conclusion? "Now is the Golden Age of wine."[60]

Since those proud words were spoken, there has been a growing reaction against the regime of scientific control in grape growing and wine making. It is commonplace now to hear people say that wine is "made in the vineyard"—the unspoken assumption being that what nature provides can only be injured by human manipulation. Instead of using pesticides and herbicides and chemical fertilizers, growers are urged to practice "sustainable" or organic or even biodynamic agriculture, all of which have in common an appeal to natural processes. So with the current vogue for exalting the notion of "terroir," which, when it means anything at all, means just those things about which one can do nothing: the location of the vineyard site, its exposure, its soil, and the local conditions of rainfall, sunshine, and so on. And so with winery practices: whole clusters go into the fermenting vat, not the crushed and destemmed grapes that have passed through a machine; the "natural" yeasts on the grapes as they come in from the vineyard are encouraged to do their work rather than being killed by disinfectants and replaced by scientifically purified strains; the new-made wine flows from the fermenting vat to the storage vessel not under the artificial pressure of a pump but by the gentle pull of gravity, and so on. What all this means, however, is not a return to "natural" procedures, but only that the work of the scientific revolution in wine making that began with Pasteur is now fully assimilated and can be taken for granted; the security that it provides allows winemakers to return safely to certain traditional practices. If we are not now in the true Golden Age of wine making—however that might be defined—it is certain that, without what science and technology have added to the practice of wine making, we would be back in the Dark Ages.

ELEVEN

Konstantin Frank

ZEALOT AT WORK

A GERMAN IN RUSSIA

Wine making has always had an international flavor in America. This book has so far included the Swiss Dufour, the Germans Husmann and Kohler, the Italian Sbarboro, and the Englishman Morgan, but the list of such names among the pioneers can easily be greatly extended. The French Legaux in Pennsylvania, the Italian Mazzei in Virginia, the German Rapp in Indiana, and the Hungarian Haraszthy in California are among the pioneer names, and to them one might add the Irishman Keller in Los Angeles, the Costa Rican Gallegos in Fremont, and the Japanese Nagasawa in Sonoma, not to mention the uncounted, nameless Indians, Mexicans, and Chinese who did the work of vineyard and winery up and down California throughout the nineteenth century.

What was true in the early days continues to be true today: the Italian Luca Paschina in Virginia, the German Herman Wiemer in upstate New York, and the Croatian Mike Grgich in California are representative of a large and varied group currently active in American wine making. Konstantin Frank is thus not really an exotic but part of a tradition.

Still, his is a striking story, beginning with his birth near Odessa in what was then the Russian Ukraine. Germans have been settled in Russia for many centuries, but large-scale immigration began in the time of Catherine the Great, who, in a policy intended to assist the technical and cultural development of the country, issued a proclamation of free entry into Russia in 1763 and attracted many thousands of Germans. Later, in the period of the Napoleonic wars that convulsed Europe, Alexander I reissued Catherine's proclamation and another large immigration followed. In the nineteenth century there were Baltic Germans, Volga Germans, Black Sea or Ukrainian Germans, Crimean Germans, and so on through a long list of territories. The Germans in these settlements remained unassimilated: they enjoyed special tax privileges; they did not have to do military duty; and they continued to be German-speakers. By the time that Konstantin Frank (1899–1985) was born, as a fifth-generation German in Russia, most of these privileges had been withdrawn, but the Germans, who now spoke Russian as well as German, continued to retain their German identity. Frank's great-grandfather, who came to Russia in 1812, in the time of Alexander I, had settled near Odessa, and so the Frank family were among the Black Sea Germans.

Frank's father was a prosperous civil engineer who, as a sideline, raised stock on a farm outside Odessa. There was also a vineyard on the property, and here Konstantin Frank had his first experience of working with grapes, though not commercially. By 1917, at the beginning of the Russian revolution, he was studying viticulture at a local agricultural institute. The German communities in Russia could not escape the revolution but, like all the other residents in that unhappy country, were compelled to choose which of the warring factions they would support; the situation in the Ukraine was especially complex, because it was not merely a question of Whites versus Reds but of Ukrainian nationalists against both. The Franks chose to side with the White Russians against the Bolsheviks in the years of civil war, 1918–20, and so were on the losing side. Konstantin Frank remained at home, but two brothers fought alongside the Whites and were killed.

After this disastrous episode Frank was allowed to resume his studies, probably around 1919. In 1924 he was appointed assistant professor of plant science at the school. Two years later he was assigned the task of restoring the vineyard originally established on Prince Trubetskoy's estate by the prince in the reign of Catherine the Great. The estate was a vast affair, covering some thirty-six square miles along the Dnieper River, and the vineyard was of a matching scale—two thousand acres. It was in derelict condition when Frank took over the management, owing first to the devastations of phylloxera and then to the anarchic conditions of revolutionary Russia. Faced with this task, Frank, as he later said, learned how to grow grapes.

The first, essential, step was to replant the vineyard with such varieties as Pinot gris and Chardonnay, which had been there before but were now to be grafted to phylloxera-resistant rootstock. The vineyard would also have contained such old-time Russian varieties as Rkatsiteli, Sereksia, and Saperavi, and these, too, were renewed. The vineyard would not, however, have con-

FIGURE 30. Konstantin Frank in his vineyard above Keuka Lake. Courtesy Dr. Konstantin Frank Vinifera Wine Cellars.

tained any of the modern French hybrids, which were then making their way into the world's vine-growing regions. Frank would have nothing to do with them, then or at any time afterward.

The next step in Frank's history was his entrance at some point in the late 1920s as a PhD candidate in agricultural science into the Odessa Polytechnic Institute, where he studied both viticulture and enology. The title of his thesis, prophetic of his work in New York, was "Protection of Grapes from Freezing Damage," for which he was awarded his doctor's degree in 1930. It is said that one of his professors was Trofim Lysenko, notorious for his discredited doctrine of the inheritance of acquired characteristics, a doctrine that became the official Soviet line when Lysenko was made president of the All-Union Academy of Agricultural Sciences.[1] Presumably Frank's thesis did not have to deal with the truth of genetic theories.

In the years between the completion of his studies in 1930 and his flight from Russia in 1941, Frank continued his teaching and his practical vineyard work. At some point in the 1930s he was made senior agronomist on a collective farm where there were extensive vineyards. Here, his most notable contribution was his design for a vineyard plow that would bury grapevines under soil as a protection against winter cold; such burying was a traditional practice in cold countries, but one that was always carried out by hand labor—mostly that of women—and was economic only where the cheapest labor was available. Frank's plow mechanized the business. Having designed a plow that would cover the vines, he next had to design one that would uncover them, and so he did. His first prototypes were tested in 1935; by 1939 the designs were perfected and some forty-five thousand of the plows were eventually made.[2] Frank, in later years, somehow managed to bring one of these Russian plows to his farm in upstate New York, where, according to one visitor, "it always seemed to break down in our inhospitable Finger Lakes soil. He gave up using it but used to enjoy sitting on it from time to time."[3] There had to be other ways to cope with New York's winters.

When the Germans invaded Russia in the summer of 1941, their armies quickly spread over the Ukraine. The situation of Frank was more than awkward: if he were to flee the Germans to the protection of the Russians, he would in all probability be deported to Siberia or conscripted into one of the "labor armies," as most of the Germans long settled in Russia were. If he were to remain under the Germans, he would be seen as a Russian. The solution was to leave Russia, which Frank, now with a wife and three children, somehow managed to do in 1941.[4] One authority says that this was managed by desperate means, the family "hiding in the coal in a tender behind a steam locomotive."[5] Another says merely that they "were sent."[6] However it was done, the family arrived in Vienna and lived there while Frank managed an estate devoted to food production. The approach of the Russian army in 1945 sent them fleeing to the American zone of occupation in Bavaria. Here he was appointed by the American authorities manager of a large Bavarian estate confiscated from the Nazis.

THE STATE OF NEW YORK

In 1951 Frank resumed his westward movement by sailing with his family to New York. This had to be quite as anxious a move as either of their flights in wartime Europe, for, in the received account, Frank arrived "penniless." Though he spoke five languages,[7] English was not among them. He found a slum residence, under the Brooklyn Bridge, and a job washing dishes at one of the Horn and Hardart Automats. Since, at the time, an emigrant like Frank had to have a sponsor and a guaranteed job before he could enter the United States, Frank evidently did not act entirely alone. But the situation was sufficiently dire. From this low point, one could only go upward, which Frank proceeded to do over a very rough road.

Early in 1952 Frank made his way to the Finger Lakes town of Geneva, New York, the site of the New York State Agricultural Experiment Station. Research on grapes had been carried on for many years at Geneva, and Frank hoped to be employed in that work. His timing was unlucky, for the conditions were all wrong in New York at that time. Frank was keen on vinifera grapes and wine: the staff at the Station, through no fault of their own, were not. The state's vineyards were (and are) overwhelmingly dominated by the Concord grape, a source mainly of pasteurized grape juice, of grape jelly, and, to some extent, of sweet kosher wine. Such wine making as was carried on was based either on the Concord or on native American hybrids—Catawba, Delaware, Niagara, and the like. New York State wine making also depended upon large additions—up to 25 percent—of neutral California wine. This was not only vinifera wine, it was also much cheaper and more reliably available than any wine New York could ever hope to provide. Furthermore, the fear of arousing prohibitionist sentiment, still powerful in places where budgets were made and passed, discouraged any work at the Station with grapes that were meant for wine. As Hudson Cattell has put it, "Major funding for wine-related activities at the Station was still years in the future."[8]

Work on vinifera in the East had never been wholly given up. The U.S. Department of Agriculture had a vineyard of vinifera at the Arlington Experiment Farms, near Washington, and reported on the results there in a bulletin published shortly after repeal, at the beginning of 1934. The report was cautious but encouraging: though many varieties failed to ripen or to produce any fruit, a few were "worthy of trial," including some varieties suitable for wine, such as Blauer Portugieser, Chasselas Doré, Cinsaut, Valdepeñas, and Zinfandel. These, it was said, "have matured regularly and have produced well."[9] Some work with vinifera had long been carried on at the Geneva Station too; a small experimental planting of vinifera vines had been made there in 1902, and this was expanded in the following years, mostly with cuttings sent from California by George C. Husmann and by Frederic Bioletti. By 1917 the results were clear enough to justify the publication of a bulletin titled *Vinifera Grapes in New York*.[10] This report cautiously recommended certain vinifera varieties to home gardeners, to specialist growers of fresh fruit, and to plant breeders—but not to winemakers. The risks of winter damage were too great for a commercial enterprise, the bulletin cautioned, so that "it would not be wise to attempt growing [vinifera] on a large scale commercially until we have had more experience with them and wider knowledge of the requirements of this species."[11]

The onset of Prohibition only three years after the publication of this bulletin made it impossible to acquire the "wider knowledge" that would be required before the Station could make a confident recommendation. During Prohibition there was no encouragement to plant anything but the innocent Concord; and when repeal came, New York's vineyards were essentially Concord vineyards. Genuine wine grapes were a marginal interest at best; the scientists turned to work with other crops, and the official word about vinifera in New York remained what it had been in 1917: *not* a commercial proposition.

The Station did, however, give Frank a job as a laborer, beginning in April 1953; we hear that he hoed blueberries and swept floors, but also that he grafted vines, so that some part of his abilities may have been recognized. He would also have seen the vinifera vines growing in the experimental plantings at Geneva; at least some of the vines, among those that had been planted back in the early years of the century, were still growing as late as 1960.[12] One wonders what their condition was: Were they fruitful? What scars of winter damage did they show? As one writer observed of these vines, they were "successfully" grown only if "one is willing to accept the erratic cropping, erratic ripening, and abnormal maintenance techniques" that went with them (the vines were buried each winter).[13] Whatever their condition, they did nothing to discourage Frank.

Frank's decisive moment came not long after his arrival in Geneva. The Geneva Station was holding a conference of growers and winemakers at which Charles Fournier, the head of the Gold Seal Winery at Hammondsport, on Keuka Lake, was among the conference-goers: this was in 1953. Whether Frank knew anything about Fournier is not said, but presumably he did, for Fournier's was just the sort of interest Frank needed to attract. A Frenchman from the Champagne district, where, before repeal, he had made wine for the celebrated firm of Veuve Clicquot Ponsardin, Fournier had been lured to the Finger Lakes in 1934 to take over the renewed wine making at Gold Seal, where sparkling wine was a specialty, as it was at the two other big Hammondsport wineries, Taylor and Great Western (Pleasant Valley).

The first thing that Fournier had been told when he arrived in the Finger Lakes district was that "you cannot grow [vinifera] here[;] ... it cannot be done."[14] Vinifera grapes had been planted in every colonial settlement since the first permanent settlement early in the seventeenth century, and after

FIGURE 31. Konstantin Frank (left) and Charles Fournier.
Courtesy Dr. Konstantin Frank Vinifera Wine Cellars.

more than three centuries of unbroken failure in the attempt to grow vinifera, it was certainly reasonable to conclude that the thing could not be done. After nearly twenty years of turning native grapes such as Catawba, Elvira, Diana, and Delaware, into an acceptable sparkling wine, no one knew better than Fournier that New York needed better grapes. Through long experience the winemakers of New York had managed to get everything they could out of the native grapes used in their sparkling wines. Fournier himself stood at the head of their ranks. His Gold Seal New York State Champagne won the gold medal in open competition at the California State Fair in 1950—the first and only time that non-California wines had been invited to enter the fair's wine judging. The California people were too embarrassed to venture the experiment again. But despite such triumphs, Fournier wanted something better.

As he listened to the eager discourse of Dr. Frank that day of their first meeting in Geneva (the conversation was in French), assuring him that he,

Dr. Frank, knew positively that he, Dr. Frank, could make vinifera grow in the Finger Lakes, Fournier may well have thought that he saw here the hand of providence. In Fournier's own version of this meeting, "Dr. Frank told me he had developed a big vineyard in the Ukraine in Russia in a continental climate similar to the climate of New York State[,] and that he had been very successful in growing most of the grapes of the northern viticultural zone of Europe."[15]

Fournier, so the story goes, hired Frank on the spot: the floor sweeper was at a stroke transformed into the director of research for Gold Seal. But the story needs a little modification. In a more sober version, Frank did not leave the Geneva Station for Gold Seal until February or early March 1954, just under two years after he had gone to work at Geneva; in another version he went to work at Gold Seal at some time in 1953.[16] Once he had left it for Hammondsport, Frank never ceased to be the sworn enemy of the Geneva Station as the citadel of a reactionary ignorance. And so began what has been described as a relationship "fruitful but stormy" between Frank and Fournier.[17]

LOOKING FOR A ROOTSTOCK

In his search for a better sort of grape than the native hybrids of New York, Fournier had already begun work with some attractive alternatives. These were the so-called French hybrids, given that name not because they were combined out of specifically French elements but because most of the hybridizers, working from the late nineteenth century onward, were French—men with names such as Seyve-Villard, Seibel, Couderc, Landot, Ravat. As earlier hybridizers had done, these men sought to combine the fruit character of vinifera with the pest resistance of the native American species—riparia, rupestris, berlandieri, aestivalis, and so on. But in a post-Mendelian age, they worked with a much better understanding of genetic principles, and they were producing hybrids of a new level of complexity and a new level of elegance. These hybrids were now, in the 1950s, widely grown in vineyards all over Europe and were just beginning to make their way in the United States. Their main sponsor and promoter was Philip Wagner, an editor with the Baltimore *Sunpapers* by profession, and a greatly accomplished viticulturist, winemaker, and writer on viticulture and wine making by avocation. From his Boordy Vineyard nursery outside Baltimore, he distributed cuttings of the French hybrids to customers all over the country. And by his gracefully written books, he made their attractions known to a growing number of interested readers.[18]

Wagner had long been in touch with the Finger Lakes wineries about his work, and with the people there he had held a series of annual tastings comparing the wines of the French hybrids with those of the native American hybrids, almost always to the distinct advantage of the former. Charles Fournier had shown a special interest in Wagner's results, and in 1947 or thereabouts—the date is uncertain—he established a vineyard of French hybrids on the shores of Keuka Lake with cuttings furnished by Philip Wagner. The first commercial French hybrid wine from Gold Seal appeared in the early fifties.

Frank, as has been said, would have nothing to do with the French hybrids, which were already known in Russia in his day. He had no patience with what he saw as compromises, the French hybrids. Why palter with half measures? Vinifera, and only vinifera, was what was wanted, and in this dogmatic conviction he never wavered. He would listen to no doubts. Prudent arguments about risk, such as guided the recommendations of the Geneva people, had no effect upon him. In the course of his campaign for vinifera he displayed all the rigid qualities of the bigot: whoever was not with him was against him; all alternatives were not merely worthless but positively harmful. Philip Wagner, who was urbane in contrast to Frank's bluntness, and who was gracious in controversy, in contrast to Frank's dogmatic certainty, became, together with the scientists of Geneva, among the demons in Frank's mythology. Wagner promoted the French hybrids; the French hybrids were evil; therefore Wagner was evil. As Wagner himself put it in his soothing way:

> The supposed antagonism between us was strictly one-sided. A visit with Konstantin Frank was something I used to look forward to on trips to the Finger Lakes. The meeting might be in the experimental vineyard or in the Fournier kitchen while Charles went about cooking one of his fabulous dinners.
>
> These encounters were always stimulating, and entertaining too. I never ceased to marvel that anyone could be so totally sure of himself.[19]

Perhaps someday some enterprising scholar will find and translate Dr. Frank's dissertation, "Protection of Grapes from Freezing Damage," and then we may get a clearer idea of what his ideas on the subject were.[20] So far as I know, Frank published hardly any technical description of his findings and recommendations.

Burying the vines is a traditional method, and though Frank may have successfully mechanized it in Russia, it was not a practice that he followed in New York. Frank's main object, according to Fournier's account, was to find a rootstock that would restrict the vigorous growth of the vine and at the same time hasten the maturity of the fruit.[21] Vigorous growth needs to be restrained in cold-country viticulture because canes need to be fully mature—hardened off—before the cold weather sets in; the more vigorous canes that a vine produces, the more slowly will they mature and the more vulnerable they will be to cold damage. And early maturity of the fruit is of course highly desirable in a region with only a short growing season. So the ideal is to secure these seemingly contradictory qualities: reduced vigor and accelerated maturity. Frank and Fournier together set out to find a rootstock that would do the job.

Frank scoured the state and neighboring Canada for the right stock. With Charles Fournier at the wheel of his Alfa-Romeo, they penetrated as far as the province of Quebec, where they found what they were looking for in the garden of a small convent. There, Fournier wrote, "we discovered that the monk in charge of the gardens was growing Pinot grapes[,] and he told us that one year out of three he would make a fairly good wine in spite of the extremely short growing season. He gave us some of the rootstocks he was using. With these, and with some interesting Riparia we found right in our own backyard at Gold Seal, the great experiment started."[22]

Frank now set to work with the dedication of the zealot. In the next eight years, 1953 to 1961, he made, according to Fournier's report, "over 250,000 grafts representing thousands of combinations of 58 rootstocks with 12 V. vinifera varieties and many clones of each of them in 9 soil conditions."[23] If Fournier's numbers are right, Frank was making 85 grafts each day over an eight-year period, as well as producing his material from a nursery and carrying out the experimental planting, cultivating, and testing of thousands of grafted cuttings. How much help he may have had I do not know, but he must have labored like one possessed no matter how many helpers assisted him.

The winter of 1956–57 in upstate New York was marked by a more-than-usually-severe cold spell: for three nights running, the temperatures along the slopes of the Finger Lakes dropped to between ten and twenty-five degrees below zero. Some of the old standby native hybrids—Dutchess and Isabella, for instance—were so stricken that they produced no crop that year; others, like the Concord and the Catawba, lost up to a third of their buds. Frank's vinifera plants suffered damage to less than 10 percent of their buds. Looking at these results, Fournier wrote, "I did not need to be convinced further[,] and planting was then started commercially as fast as we could get enough rootstock in our nursery."[24]

A first, experimental, wine was made from Frank's plantings of Riesling and Chardonnay in 1957. Wine from Gold Seal's vinifera vineyard was first produced in 1959, and in the next year a small commercial quantity—"several thousand gallons"—was produced.[25] Frank's zeal was now unchecked. According to Alexander Brailow, a fellow Russian who was the head winemaker at Gold Seal, Frank had already "jeopardized the entire operation" by his demands upon the facilities of the winery. Now, again according to Brailow, Frank, having found the way to success, demanded that "all our labrusca and hybrid vines be ripped out and replaced with vinifera."[26] The management at Gold Seal, unwilling to commit commercial suicide, refused the demand. Frank left in early 1962. Gold Seal did in fact plant a vineyard of vinifera and did release a little vinifera wine—Riesling and Chardonnay— in 1961, but soon decided that (as the Geneva Station already had told them) the enterprise was uneconomic. Fournier's enthusiasm was powerless against the doubts of the managers.[27]

One should note here that, just as experimental work with vinifera was never quite given up in New York, so it was kept alive across the border in Canada. In fact, the first commercial vinifera wine produced in eastern North America was a Pinot made in 1955 by Bright's Winery of Niagara Falls, Ontario, from vines planted in 1951, the year that Konstantin Frank arrived in New York.[28] But the Canadians' work is another story.

GOING IT ALONE

Frank, having left Gold Seal, was prepared to go it alone, though now, at the age of sixty-three, he was approaching not an end but a new beginning. In 1956, with Charles Fournier guaranteeing the loan, he had bought a property of 118 acres, complete with brick house and a few acres of vines for six thousand dollars high above Keuka Lake on its western side. Here he did much of his experimental work for Gold Seal, at his own expense and without occupying vineyard space that was commercially valuable to Gold Seal. The site was almost exactly that of the earliest commercial viticulture in the Finger Lakes and was therefore a highly symbolic place in which to make a new start. The vines already growing on the property were the despised native hybrids, but selling their crop gave Frank some needed cash. And he could now begin to plant his own vinifera, which he did—mostly Riesling, Chardonnay, and Gewürztraminer obtained from the nursery at the University of California, Davis.[29] They were grafted, of course, on Frank's rootstock (riparia? We don't know) from Canada and from upstate.

His winery was bonded in June of 1962, only a few months after he had left Gold Seal. It was called, with unmistakable emphasis, Dr. Konstantin Frank Vinifera Wine Cellars. Frank's first wine to be released commercially, a Riesling *trockenbeerenauslese* from 1962, was put on the market in 1965, though only in a very small quantity, more symbolic than commercial. Such a wine was more than a little surprising. Only by letting the grapes remain on the vine for the longest possible time, under the constant danger of a freeze, could Frank have obtained grapes ripe enough for this style of wine— made from grapes that were near-raisins and that had been hand-selected. It also requires the action of "noble rot" (the French call it *pourriture noble;* the Germans, *Edelfäule*) to concentrate the sugars of the grape; the presence of this noble rot is a condition unusual in American vineyards, though not unknown in upstate New York vineyards. Altogether, this was not just a special but an extraordinary introductory wine, probably the first of its type ever made in this country.[30] It was evidently intended more for arousing attention than for ordinary commercial purposes.

The label that decorated this first wine was itself a curiosity. It showed what might have been a staged scene in the Finger Lakes—an autumnal vineyard on the slopes above a deep, narrow lake, like Keuka Lake. But in the foreground were three very un-American figures, two women in peasant dress flanking a young man carrying a grape-filled *Hotte* on his back. The scene was in fact from the Rheingau, and the labels had been printed in Germany. Did this mean that Frank lacked confidence in the wine's New York origins and sought to conceal them under a German image? Or was it a proud statement that his wine was equivalent to Germany's finest? One inclines to the latter answer.

Frank, it is said, was not a good businessman: he was more interested in experiment than with business routine. He is reported to have planted in his own vineyard, by way of experiment rather than with any commercial purpose, not only the three staples of Riesling, Chardonnay, and Gewürztraminer but also Pinot gris, Cabernet Sauvignon, Pinot noir, Gamay Beaujolais, Pedro Ximenez, and the Russian varieties Sereksia and Rkatsiteli.[31] But he had a flair for promotion, perhaps owing in part to his unshakeable belief in his mission—to bring vinifera to the East. His wines began to attract

FIGURE 32. Label of Dr. Frank's first commercial release. The scene is of the German Rheingau rather than of New York's Finger Lakes. Courtesy Dr. Konstantin Frank Vinifera Wine Cellars.

newspaper and magazine attention, and then to attract influential customers; the governor of New York may be suspected of a political motive in patronizing Frank's wines, but Jimmy Carter and his wife presumably had no such thought when they ordered Frank's Chardonnay when dining out in New York City in 1978.[32] The curiosity interest was, of course, very strong at the outset: who would believe that New York could make a vinifera wine?

At first it was enough to be a curiosity. But in a very short time the attention became more serious: Frank's Riesling (always the signature grape) was found to be surprisingly good in and of itself—never mind the curiosity interest. Good judges began to speak well of it. In 1965, the first year in which Frank's wines were commercially available, they were the subject of a substantial article in *Holiday* magazine, then a popular national publication. Leon Adams, who spent most of his life promoting California wines, said that Frank's Chardonnay was "equal to the best French white burgundies."[33] Sheldon and Pauline Wasserman, writing in the *Wine Spectator,* described

Frank's 1975 Riesling as having a "delicate, flowery scent[,] . . . outstanding balance; quite rich and full in the mouth, good long finish—exceptional quality."[34] Such enthusiastic press notices began to add up to create a distinctly interesting reputation.

Back home in the Finger Lakes, among the people whose living depended on the vines and wines of the region, the response was much more cautious, to Frank's unconcealed exasperation. The general feeling in his home region reflected the official caution of the scientists at the Geneva Station. There had been short-term success, granted; but what about the long term? Frank's experiments were welcome, and his willingness to risk everything on vinifera when no one else dared venture was an admirable work of public spirit. But did Dr. Frank really have the answer to the problem of winter kill? Could a rootstock really make that much difference to the crucial stages of a vine's seasonal performance? The authorities all said No. A fifteen-year study by the U.S. Department of Agriculture published in 1939 concluded that different rootstocks made only slight differences to the times at which the vine began to grow, to blossom, and to mature its fruit.[35] The Geneva Station issued a bulletin in 1968, six years after Frank's first vintage, reporting that "in trials [of vinifera] conducted by the Geneva Station, the various rootstocks did not differ in affecting the winter cold hardiness of the vines."[36]

So what was a grower to do? There, on the one side, stood Dr. Frank, happily producing vinifera wine and beckoning all the others to follow him; and there on the other side stood a whole phalanx of doctors urging caution and warning that vinifera could never be economic. It is said that the design of the bumblebee is aerodynamically unsound, so that it is impossible for the bee to fly, while at the same time the bumblebee is well known to fly. The status of vinifera in the Finger Lakes was like that of the bumblebee: it couldn't, and yet it could. Frank took a simple, impatient view of the situation: "They hated me when I came," he said; "now they hate me more because I have showed them up."[37] But this is surely exaggerated. His neighbors may have been a little sore at being "shown up," but uncertainty rather than resentment explains their reluctance to follow Frank's lead.

SPREADING THE WORD

But a prophet is not without honor outside his own country, as Dr. Frank soon began to find. Word of his work with vinifera began to circulate among people who were interested in the matter, some of whom took the trouble to seek him out. One of these was an industrial engineer from Ohio named Arnulf Esterer, who came not only to call on Frank but also to serve an apprenticeship under him, working in the vineyards. There, as Leon Adams put it, Esterer "learned Frank's secrets of growing Vinifera in the East."[38] *Secrets* is perhaps too strong a word: though Frank published little about his experiments,[39] so that skeptical scientists had no certain means by which to replicate them, he was prepared to advise and instruct those who came to him and were willing to listen. On his return to Ohio, Esterer planted a vineyard of vinifera near Conneaut, in the northeastern corner of the state, and has been successfully making wine there from vinifera for the last forty-one years at his Markko Vineyards. Unlike Frank, Esterer does not reject the French hybrids, but his reputation and his effect are both founded on his production of vinifera wines.

Another postulant at the shrine was Douglas Moorhead, who came from the established Concord-grape-growing area of the Lake Erie shore of Pennsylvania, not many miles east of Arnulf Esterer at Conneaut. Moorhead farmed a big Concord vineyard and dealt in wine-making supplies, in fresh grapes, and in juice for home winemakers. But he was ambitious to make good wine and had already experimented with vinifera when he heard of Dr. Frank's work. A visit to Frank confirmed his purpose and, presumably, provided him with vital information. At any rate, his Presque Isle Wine Cellars, at North East, Pennsylvania, has been producing vinifera wine since its founding in 1968. Moorhead grows far more Concords than anything else (they go into grape juice) and makes a variety of wines from French hybrid grapes, but, like Esterer in Ohio, his vinifera wines are what distinguish his enterprise.

Another sort of disciple was Elizabeth Furness, of Fauquier County, Virginia, who, inspired by Frank's example, planted Virginia's first modern vineyard of vinifera in 1973 at Piedmont Vineyards (there had been plenty of failed Colonial vineyards). She brought the social cachet of Virginia's Hunt Country squirearchy to pioneer wine making, a distinct asset to a work that needed all the help and attention it could get. Virginia offers some advantages to vinifera vines: it lies, as Lucie Morton has put it, "north of Pierce's disease and south of the deep freeze."[40] Protected by modern pesticides, assisted by clonal selection and modern methods of training and cultivation, vinifera grapes now dominate the three thousand acres of the state's wine grapes.

Virginia also produced a missionary devoted to spreading the word of

Dr. Frank's revelation. This was Robert de Treville Lawrence, a retired State Department officer who planted a small vineyard of vinifera at his home in The Plains, Virginia, near Furness's Piedmont Vineyards. More important, when a group of enthusiasts in Virginia came together to found the Vinifera Wine Growers Association in 1973, Lawrence took on the job of editing its journal. For the next fifteen years he made it a lively means of instructing, amusing, and annoying its readers with information about the fortunes of vinifera in the eastern United States. Some of the information was useful, some of it was doubtful, and some of it foolish, but the mix was always interesting. Lawrence had the true missionary temper: he entertained no doubts; he admitted no alternatives; he treated all skeptics and naysayers with unwavering severity; in short, he was a faithful disciple of Dr. Frank.

Frank was of course pleased to see his example being followed, but he wanted it known that it was *his* example that did the leading. When Hermann Wiemer, who had made wines from French hybrid grapes for Walter Taylor, established his own vineyard of Riesling on Seneca Lake, Frank paid him no attention. When, by a ruse, he was at last brought to inspect Wiemer's vines, his only comment, at the end of the visit, was to say, "So now we see how wrong I was when I said we can grow vinifera."[41] Louisa Hargrave, who with her husband had planted the first vineyard of vinifera on Long Island, recalled a visit from Frank in the early days: "He was excited that we were growing European wine grapes, but, since we had visited him before coming to Long Island, he wanted to take the credit for our new planting. He wandered from plant to plant, stooping over to make his inspection as if we were trying to fool him. 'Yes,' he announced in broken English, 'is Cabernet Sauvignon. Yes, is Pinot Noir.' He drew himself up, looked around to make sure we were listening, and said, 'You could never have done it without me.'"[42]

The stream of pilgrims to the Frank home on the slopes of Keuka Lake continued to grow; there they could be sure of hearing the doctrine of vinifera set forth at length and with assurance from Dr. Frank himself; his favorite places for holding forth were, it is said, the back porch of his house in summer and the kitchen in winter, "enological shrines where visitors sipped wine and heard almost as much partisan oratory as in the Houses of Congress."[43] After a considerable experience of this sort of attention, Frank concluded that it might well be organized to good effect. He invited a group of friends and well-wishers to a meeting at his home in December 1967 and there proposed that they found a society to promote the new American (that is eastern vinifera) wines. Thus was founded the American Wine Society, still active but long since strayed from the path that its founder would have had it follow.

The constitution of the new Society declared that it was not "anti fine imported wines," but that it would be devoted to the cause of American wine, since "America can and is producing wines which are among the best in the world." What this meant, being interpreted, is that Dr. Frank, a mere two years after releasing his first wines, had found a group of enthusiasts ready to proclaim them "among the best in the world." The "American wines" in question were the vinifera wines then being produced in the East only by Frank and Gold Seal, and in quantities so small as to be nearly invisible. But no matter: promise was equivalent to performance. Frank at first was able to control the behavior of the American Wine Society—its original concern was exclusively with eastern American wines from vinifera—but as it grew, its membership included many who knew not Frank, and its interests inevitably came to include all sorts of wine. The constitution was modified to say that the purpose of the Society was simply to promote "the appreciation of wine, especially American wine," rather than only such wines as Dr. Frank produced. Frank resigned.

The same intransigence appears in one of his more notorious doctrines. The published results of German experiments in 1959 and 1967 had shown that hens fed with grapes and wines from French hybrid vines produced malformed chicks. Frank seized on this "evidence" to assert that French hybrid grapes were toxic and would "cause grave damage to human kidneys, livers and embryos due to the diglucosides they contained."[44] The methods and the conclusions of the German experiments were soon discredited,[45] but that did not disturb Frank's conviction: he continued to assert that hybrid grapes were toxic and to agitate against them in any way that he could, long after such charges had been shown to be baseless.

THE FORTUNES OF VINIFERA

On the positive side, Frank's success with vinifera in New York stimulated trials everywhere in the eastern states, or at least in all those places where it was possible to imagine successful grape growing. In New York State, the unqualified success with vinifera has been on the eastern end of Long Island, on land formerly devoted to potatoes. No one here thought of wine growing until Alexander Hargrave set up his Hargrave Winery in 1973. Hargrave, and those who soon followed him, discovered two great advantages. The first was that red wine varieties—Cabernet Sauvignon and Merlot especially—did well on Long Island. The eastern states have always produced far better whites than reds from the traditional varieties, so good red wines from Long Island were a welcome surprise. So too was the success of Long Island wines in the metropolitan New York market, where, historically, the native wines of New York State had been neglected, not to say condemned.

Cautiously and tentatively, experiments with vinifera began to spread. Virginia, Pennsylvania, and Ohio have already been mentioned. Maryland, North Carolina, Michigan, and Texas all have significant production of vinifera wines now. The statistics are modest, compared to the scale of things on the West Coast, where vinifera is at home. But if modest, they are not negligible; there are approximately twenty-five hundred acres of vinifera in Virginia, three thousand in Texas, two thousand in Michigan, and smaller numbers in a wide scattering of eastern states.[46] The possibility of making good wine in places where such a thing was unthought-of before has created much excitement about wine making wherever these new beginnings have been made.

Of course, vinifera, despite its recognized superiority over other species of grape for wine, does not automatically give good wine in the eastern states—or anywhere else, for that matter. Mistakes have inevitably been made, as growers and winemakers have tried to learn what they can do under the conditions that they must work with. Since Cabernet Sauvignon and Chardonnay have become pretty much the default wines of the American market, those varieties have been hopefully planted in regions entirely unsuited to them—regions where they could not properly ripen or develop their proper flavors. Other, less fashionable, varieties might well do much better in such regions, but only continued experiment will show what works and what doesn't. It will be a long process to discover what the right combinations of site and variety are, and then to develop a market that appreciates what is grown. But it is certain that not every sought-after variety can be successfully grown all over the East.

We speak of "the East" as though it were a simple category, but of course it is a very big space—everything from the Rockies to the Atlantic and from Canada to the Gulf, exhibiting an immense variety of sites and local climates. If Minnesota is part of "the East," so too is Florida, and yet they are obviously utterly different places. Many regions, given our current abilities, remain unsuitable for or hostile to vinifera; in the coastal regions of the deep South, Pierce's disease is fatal; in states such as Missouri, otherwise favorable to viticulture, the combination of winter cold and summer humidity creates too great a risk for growers to rely on vinifera. The expanding wine industry in Missouri, a renewal of the important industry there in the nineteenth century, is firmly based on native American and French hybrid varieties, old and new. And in all the states in which vinifera has been established more or less successfully, the French hybrids continue to be a dependable resource. Behind all the noise that has surrounded the spread of vinifera through much—but not all—of the East, a careful listener might always hear the cool voice of Philip Wagner, advising that the course of prudence is to go with what works: hybrid grapes.

Konstantin Frank had no patience with the merely prudential, but others did and do. While Frank was developing his vinifera vineyard, a handful of enthusiasts were pioneering new wines from French hybrids in New York. Everett Crosby, with vines obtained from Philip Wagner's nursery, planted a vineyard of French hybrids in Rockland County, on the western shore of the Hudson, in 1952 and made wine at his High Tor Winery, wines called simply Rockland Red and Rockland White. Walter Taylor, of the wine-making Taylor family, having been cut loose from the Taylor Winery after loudly criticizing New York's standard practice of adding water, sugar, and California wine to the juice of its own grapes, founded Bully Hill Vineyards on the old Taylor property outside Hammondsport. Here he produced wines from such French hybrids as Aurora, Baco, Chelois, and Seyval. At first he used some of the old native hybrids, but he soon went exclusively to the French hybrids and became as passionate an advocate for them as Frank was for vinifera.

These were only the first of many other new wine-making enterprises in New York State, which now boasts some 169 wineries, many of which, if not most, produce wine from both hybrids and vinifera. These grapes are not, as Dr. Frank would have had it, mutually exclusive quantities. Compromises, he would certainly call them: but they are viable compromises. And it remains true that vinifera in the East is still very much a minority proposition. The revolution begun by Frank is still, nearly half a century later, in its early stages. But it is a revolution.

Frank died in 1985, and for some years before that, ill-health had greatly slowed him down, without diminishing the strength of his convictions. One of his late public appearances was at a meeting of the Vinifera Wine Growers Association to accept an award from that group, a group that had remained undeviatingly true to his gospel: vinifera exclusively. Dr. Konstantin Frank Vinifera Wine Cellars has continued to flourish, first under Frank's son

Willibald (Willy) and now under his grandson Frederick. Willy introduced a line of sparkling wine under the Chateau Frank name, and Frederick has introduced a line of popularly priced wines made from purchased grapes under the Salmon Run label, but both have remained true to the vinifera-only principle, and they have kept the founder's name prominent on the now much-enlarged roster of New York winemakers.

The general opinion seems to be that, as Hudson Cattell has written, "vinifera would sooner or later have been widely planted in the East"; but, Cattell adds, "Dr. Frank's work advanced that date by many years."[47] Herman Weimer, who founded his all-vinifera winery on Seneca Lake in 1979, speaking of Dr. Frank's achievement, put it another way: "I would never," he said, "have had the patience and determination to go it all the way alone."[48] Konstantin Frank did have those things, the determination considerably outweighing the patience; and he showed great courage in staking his all on what was seen as a desperate enterprise. Without question, he changed things for the better.

TWELVE

Robert Mondavi

AIMING FOR THE TOP

ROBERT MONDAVI (1913–2008) began as a maker of anonymous bulk wines and ended as the best-known, most widely publicized maker of American premium wine, the national icon of fine wine. Mondavi's career, to some extent, is the story of California wine itself as it underwent its Cinderella transformation in the last half of the twentieth century, from neglected obscurity to glamorous prominence. Though many shared in this change, Mondavi stood out beyond all the rest, a distinction that he had earned by an indomitable ambition to be among the very best and a readiness to do whatever that might require.

SUNNY ST. HELENA WINERY

The Mondavi story begins in the Iron Range of remote northern Minnesota, a strange and intimidating place: even in summer one feels the threat of the winter that will, too soon, overwhelm the region; the landscape of endless conifers is pockmarked by huge pits scooped out of the red soil where the rich iron deposits lay (the easy stuff is now long gone and the mills have to process the diamond-hard taconite to get at the ore). One would suppose that only the hardy Swedes and Norwegians of Minnesota would live here, but one would be wrong. In the days of prosperous open-pit mining, the countries of Europe were scoured by the mining companies in their search for laborers, so now the Iron Range is home to Croatians, Czechs, Poles, Finns, Cornishmen, and—most incongruous of all in that dire northern place—Italians.

One of these was Cesare Mondavi, who, after emigrating from Italy in

FIGURE 33. Robert Mondavi in the 1980s, when he and
his winery were at the top of the California wine world.
From Cyril Ray, *Robert Mondavi of the Napa Valley.*

1906, worked in the mines for a time but then ran a saloon for his fellow
Italians in conjunction with a boardinghouse managed by his wife in the
Iron Range town of Virginia.[1] When Prohibition descended upon the country, Cesare Mondavi, who was a man of high consideration in his community, was sent by his wine-loving compatriots to California to buy grapes to
be shipped back to the Iron Range. There they would be made into wine and
so sustain the Italian community in its wonted style.

Mondavi's first venture to California was made in 1919, after the passage
of the Eighteenth Amendment but before the Volstead Act became law in
January 1920; thereafter he traveled to California each year until 1923, when
it occurred to him: Why go back? Why endure Minnesota's long hard winters
when California offered year-round sunshine? And a good business opportunity as well. These were boom years for the California wine grape trade, when
the demand for grapes for home wine-making sent grape prices to unprecedented heights and when the planting of new vineyards doubled the size of

California's grape acreage. So Mondavi brought his wife and young family—Robert, the eldest, was then ten years old—to Lodi, then as now the biggest source of wine grapes in California and the center of Mondavi's operations.[2]

The coming of the Great Depression after the panic of 1929 and the passage of the repeal amendment in 1933 greatly changed the markets that Cesare Mondavi served, but he continued to prosper under the new conditions, shipping vegetables as well as grapes. Immediately following repeal, in 1934, he helped to organize the Acampo Winery, just north of Lodi. In the next year he suggested to his two sons, Robert and Peter (b. 1914), that they should consider going into the wine business, particularly the table wine business, for which he saw a promising future. A suggestion from Cesare was, perhaps, rather more a command than a mere suggestion. At any rate, both boys dutifully entered the wine business and remained in it for the rest of their lives.

Robert, then in his junior year at Stanford, at once set about preparing himself to be a wine man by enrolling in a chemistry class for his senior year. Upon graduation he spent the summer being tutored by a University of California chemist in the chemical analysis of wine and then, fortified by this training, went to work, through his father's arrangements, at the Sunny Hill Winery in St. Helena, Napa Valley. Sunny Hill was owned by an Italian, Gioachino "Jack" Riorda, who, after struggling for a few years, had turned to Cesare Mondavi for financial support. Mondavi took a controlling interest in the winery and in 1937 reorganized it, renamed it Sunny St. Helena Winery, and sent his son Robert to work there under Riorda. The winery, rather small under Riorda, was at once greatly expanded under Cesare Mondavi. The business was entirely in bulk wine, shipped out in tank cars to bottlers all over the country. Such was then the practice of almost all wineries in California—only a few, very few, wineries bottled any part of their own production under their own labels.

Robert Mondavi's entrance into the Napa Valley was of course unnoticed at the time, though it was big with importance for the valley's future: no one would do more than Mondavi to promote the valley and its wines and to establish it as the palladium of American wine over the next half century. Like Ernest Gallo's and Maynard Amerine's, Mondavi's entry into the business of California wine took place at a low point in its fortunes, the beginning of a career that, like theirs, would follow the whole trajectory of the trade's rise from troubled obscurity to splendid prosperity.

Riorda, Mondavi recalled, "was a very knowledgeable wine man" who, though without scientific training, made good wines. "He taught me a lot."[3]

Mondavi's pupilage did not last long. Riorda died at the end of 1939, after which Robert Mondavi took over the management of the winery. He was the salesman as well as the production man, and so began his travels to markets all over the country. "We were selling," Mondavi recalled, "bulk wines to people in New Orleans, in New York, in Boston, Chicago, Minnesota, and places like that." And, he added, "I met all the people."[4] By the time of Riorda's death, the expansion that had begun under Cesare Mondavi's direction had made Sunny St. Helena one of the largest in the Napa Valley, and it continued to grow.

Robert Mondavi, however, had aspirations that the bulk wine business, no matter how prosperous, was unable to satisfy. He was always competitive, always wanting to excel, no matter what he did. Now that he was in the Napa Valley, where wine was the main enterprise, he wanted to make, not just wine, but the best wine. "When I came here," Mondavi said years later, "I was tremendously impressed by what I called the big four of the California wine industry. The big four at that time were Inglenook [of John Daniel Jr.], B. V. [Beaulieu Vineyard], Beringer Brothers, and Larkmead. And frankly, I was so inspired by them, especially John Daniel, that I bowed my head as I went by Beaulieu and Inglenook."[5] Both the Beaulieu and Inglenook wineries stand on Highway 29 leading south out of St. Helena, as did the Sunny St. Helena Winery, so Mondavi would have had many occasions to drive by them and to bow his head. The gesture was richly expressive, at once a sign of reverent humility and of bold aspiration. Making bulk wine would never allow Mondavi to reach the level of excellence that his competitive spirit demanded.

THE CHARLES KRUG WINERY

The war years brought him his first opportunity. The war had stirred up the somnolent wine business, because the big, prosperous eastern distillers wanted wine to sell. They were no longer permitted to produce whiskey but were compelled to divert all their production to industrial alcohol for the war effort. If they could get wine, they could keep their sales lines open. The California wineries suffered restrictions too, especially in the loss of the Thompson Seedless crop, the mainstay of the fortified wine trade, now by federal rule wholly devoted to the production of raisins. But wine was still made from the state's remaining grapes, which were not required for any wartime purpose. In this situation, every California winery of any size became a valuable object. Schenley bought the Cresta Blanca, Elk Grove, and Roma wineries in 1942; National Distillers bought Italian Swiss Colony in the same year; in the next year Seagram's bought Paul Masson, and Hiram Walker bought the Valliant and R. Martini wineries. The large bottling firms who had been the main customers for California wine now found themselves in danger of being shut out from their supplies and began to scramble to save themselves by buying wineries. Cesare Mondavi, by then the president of the Acampo Winery that he had helped to found in 1934, was glad to sell the property, now grown to a capacity of 2.25 million gallons, to the Gibson Wine Company, a bottling firm in Covington, Kentucky. By a happy coincidence, just when Cesare Mondavi was flush with money from the Acampo sale in 1943, the venerable Charles Krug Winery came up for sale.

The Krug Winery was one of the great names of the Napa Valley. Charles Krug, a liberal journalist, had had to flee reactionary Germany after 1848 and had come to San Francisco in 1851. He bought property in Sonoma County, learned to make wine, and ventured into the Napa Valley, where he first made wine for others and then, in 1861, for himself. By the time of his death in 1892 his substantial winery had the highest reputation, and he himself was one of the patriarchs of the Napa Valley, esteemed for his integrity and his wise leadership of the wine industry. During Prohibition the winery was idle; upon repeal, in 1934, it was leased by Lou Stralla to make bulk wine, but Stralla moved out in 1940 and the place was again idle. In 1943 its owner, J. K. Moffitt, in whose family it had been since Krug's death, determined to sell the winery.

When Robert Mondavi learned of this development from his local banker, he leaped at the chance that it offered. He went at once to his father in Lodi, somehow persuaded him to inspect the property, went with him to Moffitt's San Francisco office, where, to Robert's inexpressible delight, Moffitt at once agreed to sell the place to the Mondavis. The price was seventy-five thousand dollars, which seems a derisory figure to us now.[6] But one must consider that the winery was seriously run down, the 150 acres of vineyard that went with it in degenerate condition. The labor of renovating the Krug Winery would be long and very expensive, especially under wartime conditions. But Robert was elated by this new possession.

What, exactly, did the Mondavis receive for their seventy-five thousand dollars? There were a couple of houses on the property and a famous carriage house and stable, one of the landmark buildings of the Napa Valley. For wine making there was Krug's old winery building, now in advanced decrepitude: the second and third floors were ruinous and would have to be rebuilt; the floors were of dirt, the walls cracked by earthquakes, the cooperage old and contaminated, so that it was a burden rather than an asset. The Mondavis had also bought a once-famous name, but no wine under that name had been made and sold in the near quarter-century since the onset of Prohibition. If the Charles Krug name were to stand once again for distinguished wine, that reputation would have to be earned by the Mondavis. Finally, the 150 acres of vineyard were like the other properties: whatever they had once been, they would now have to be restored. "The vineyard was completely run down," Peter Mondavi recalled: "there were mixed plantings of this and that. . . . All I recall is a Carignane, some Zinfandel, and there may have been Gamay in it."[7]

Any person of ordinary common sense would have seen all the drawbacks and difficulties in the way of restoring Krug, especially under wartime conditions. What Robert Mondavi saw was a splendid opportunity: to bring back to life a great old name by making and bottling fine wine from a fine site. Here was a chance to excel—the most attractive part, to him, of the whole deal. Before the sale was made, Mondavi recalled, "I couldn't sleep . . . because I was so excited"; and afterward, "it took me a long time to calm down."[8]

Meantime, it would be necessary to sell wine of some sort, and here the Sunny St. Helena operation provided the answer. The Charles Krug Winery bought the decent but undistinguished bulk wine produced by Sunny St. Helena and bottled it under the CK label in half gallons and gallons. The Krug winery had started to make its own wine in the season of 1943—but no wine called Krug yet. That name was reserved for the fine wines that, some years hence, would be produced by the restored vineyards and winery.

The work of restoration fell almost wholly on Robert Mondavi's shoulders. His younger brother, Peter, who had been at work as a winemaker in the Acampo Winery, and who would join his brother at the Krug winery later, went into the army in 1942; Robert, as an "agricultural worker," was exempted. By persistent visits to the authorities in San Francisco who handed out priorities for building materials, Mondavi succeeded in getting a double-A priority, and with that he could buy cement, building materials, and materials for a new cooperage. Work went on at high pressure in that first year. Cement floors were laid over the old dirt ones; the earthquake-cracked walls were reinforced; the upper floors were rebuilt; new redwood fermenting tanks were erected, and as soon as each new one was finished it was filled with crushed grapes from the 1943 harvest.

Restoring the vineyards was necessarily a slower business, but, as Mondavi recalled, "little by little we began to replant all the vineyards" with "the right varieties that we wanted."[9] These included Cabernet Sauvignon, Pinot noir, Chenin blanc, and Riesling.[10] Chardonnay, one may note, did not yet figure in Mondavi's plans, being practically unknown at that time in California.

The rise of the Charles Krug Winery to leadership among Napa Valley's wineries was, after its renewal under very difficult conditions, quite rapid. Robert Mondavi was always ready to experiment, and he was fertile in ideas for promotion. When, in 1944, Louis Martini formed a group to discuss the problems common to the wineries of the Napa Valley, Robert Mondavi was among the original members.[11] When André Tchelistcheff, most eminent of Napa Valley winemakers, grew restive under his unresponsive owners at Beaulieu Vineyard, who took little interest in Tchelistcheff's ideas for change and improvement, Robert Mondavi was glad to employ him as a consultant: "Whatever he wanted to do, I listened to it."[12] When Tchelistcheff organized a Napa Valley Wine Technical Group for the exchange of practical information, Mondavi (who thought the idea was his) joined at once.

Experiment and innovation ruled at the Charles Krug Winery. Peter Mondavi, now out of the army, joined the business in 1946 as winemaker and at once began trials of cold fermentation of white wines, a subject that he had first studied while a student under W. V. Cruess at Berkeley. The practical commercial application of the technique in this country was first carried out at the Krug Winery and greatly helped to establish the high reputation of its white table wines. Among other matters of research pursued at Krug in the next years were acid correction, sterile bottling, vacuum corking, experiments in length of skin contact, and the use of small French oak cooperage.[13] The results of the work were demonstrated in the judgings held at the California State Fair, judgings that had been interrupted by the war but that had been reinstated in 1947. That was the first year in which the Mondavis offered wine for sale under the Charles Krug label, wines that were not yet ready to challenge the best. A short two years later, however, they took four gold medals at the fair and so began a long run of triumphs—gold medals for Traminer, Semillon, Sauvignon blanc, Pinot blanc, Chardonnay, White Riesling, Grey Riesling, Gamay, Cabernet, and Zinfandel.[14] Charles Krug Chenin blanc, a spectacularly successful wine in its time, won a gold medal in 1955; it was a demonstration of the results achieved by cold fermentation and (since it contained residual sugar) sterile filtration.

Mondavi was also an innovator in the promotion of his wines. After an unproductive trial of conventional print advertising, he turned to what we call public relations, but which he called "being honest": inviting people to come to his winery to taste his wines and informing them about wines in general as well as about his in particular.[15] We think now of the winery tasting room as a standard fixture—almost every winery has some version of it, ranging from a bare-bones counter and chairs to an opulent mansion provided with every luxury for entertainment. But things were different then. Beringer had a tasting room as early as 1934, but the example was not followed. The Mondavis opened their tasting room in 1950, and that was only part of a wider scheme of drawing the public to the winery: tastings were also held outside on the spacious lawns and under the venerable oaks of the property, and to these were added picnics, barbecues, group parties, and entertainments such as the "August Moon" concerts held every summer from 1965.[16] The concept of the winery as a public attraction, combining park, restaurant, gallery, shop, and other amenities, now so widespread, owes much to the model that Robert Mondavi created at Charles Krug in 1950.

Another form of public relations that Krug managed remarkably well was the publication of a newsletter called *Bottles and Bins*. This was begun in 1949, under the editorship of Francis "Paco" Gould, a retired wine merchant who had an attractively understated style of promoting Charles Krug wines with a mixture of wine lore, anecdotes, and recipes: the publication ran for thirty years and was read by a devoted and growing list of subscribers. For the many people whom the Krug Winery was able to reach through tours, tastings, concerts, and newsletter, Krug wines had a distinct personality, confirming Robert Mondavi's often-expressed belief that "wine is a living thing."

The winery needed all the promotion it could get. The Charles Krug Winery, unlike the Gallo winery but like most of the other California wineries, was hard hit by the collapse of prices that devastated the California wine trade in 1947. It was just bringing its first premium wines under the Charles Krug label to market in that year and had signed an agreement with the well-known firm of McKesson and Robbins to distribute them. When the bottom fell out of the market, McKesson fired its entire sales staff and broke the contract with the Mondavis. Years of struggle to stay afloat followed: "We were badly hurt," Mondavi remembered. "We barely hung on because it was so tough. . . . All of us worked very, very hard, and it was a strain."[17] The wines, however, continued to improve as the replanted vineyards matured and the supply of superior grapes around the Napa Valley increased. The volume of production also grew, passing the million-case mark by the end of the 1960s. Charles Krug wines, as we have seen, were consistent prizewinners and steadily added to their high reputation. By the 1960s it was possible to see the Charles Krug Winery, in James Lapsley's words, as "the state's leading premium wine producer, both in quality and quantity."[18] Robert Mondavi, who had dreamed of joining the company of Inglenook and Beaulieu, had now done just that; and he was no mere guest but rather a host at the party.

This achievement had a high cost. The winery was the property of C. Mondavi and Sons, a partnership in which the elder Mondavis, Cesare and his wife, Rosa, held 40 percent of the stock; the brothers, Robert and Peter 20 percent each; and the two Mondavi sisters, both married, 10 percent each. Cesare was an important presence until his death in 1959, but the dynamic Robert was the leading spirit, and his unrelenting pursuit of excellence was a strain on the others, Peter Mondavi included. All through the lean years following the collapse of 1947, Robert had insisted on plowing profits back into the development of the winery. He was also the public face of the company, and his flamboyant extravagance in this role troubled the members of his family. "I was working like a dog," his brother, Peter, remembered, "and he'd come back from a trip and tell me that I was doing everything wrong. Meanwhile, he was out promoting, overspending, overprojecting, never catching up with any of his big projects."[19] How their smoldering resentments eventually erupted was a sensational story at the time and is now one of the fixed legends of the Napa Valley. The disagreements between Peter and Robert Mondavi about policy and about Robert's style came to a climax in 1965 in a fistfight, brief but violent, between the two brothers. No bones were broken, but the management of the Charles Krug Winery had been shattered.

Rosa Mondavi, who, after Cesare's death, still held 40 percent of the stock of C. Mondavi and Sons, had to pick up the pieces. She sided with Peter, put Robert (who continued to hold his 20 percent of the company) on a leave of absence, and let him know that Robert's elder son, Michael, would not have a place at the Charles Krug Winery. Robert, now in limbo, contrived to keep busy by consulting for two other wineries, Mirassou in the Santa Clara Valley, and the big co-op called Guild in Lodi, but he was deeply troubled by the thought that his son would be excluded from what was, after all, a family enterprise. If that was the case, then he, Robert, would start up a modest new winery to be handed over to Michael. When word of this development reached Rosa and Peter, they asked no questions but fired Robert at once. He could not, they argued, work for Krug and compete with it at the same time.

Krug was still a Mondavi business, but Robert Mondavi and his sons would have no direct part in it.

THE ROBERT MONDAVI WINERY

At the end of 1965, at the age of fifty-three, Robert Mondavi found himself forced to make a new start. Most men at that age would have found this a deeply depressing prospect, but for Mondavi, much as he was troubled by the family conflict, the thought of beginning anew appeared as an exhilarating opportunity. He would now aspire not just to join the elite of the Napa Valley, as he had dreamed of doing in 1937: he would make wines that would take their place among the world's best.

The ambition was not new. Mondavi had gone to Europe in 1962, by which time, he said, he was already "producing wine that belonged in the company of the finest California wines." In Europe, where he "began to drink and taste the Bordeaux and Burgundies," he "aspired to produce wines that belonged in the company of the greatest wines in the world."[20]

Mondavi singled out a particular moment in his first journey to Europe as a "revelation": this was a lunch at Fernand Point's celebrated restaurant, La Pyramide, in the town of Vienne, on the Rhone. Food, wine, and setting all combined in beautiful harmony, revealing to Mondavi a new level of achievement beyond what he had known. He thereupon made a vow. Since he was a winemaker, he would make wines worthy of La Pyramide, "wines that have grace and style, harmony and balance."[21] Vivid as this moment was, it had been long prepared-for and would certainly not have been effective had it been otherwise; the young man who had bowed his head when he passed the Inglenook and Beaulieu wineries was still very much alive in the middle-aged man eating lunch at La Pyramide. He would excel; he would be among the best.

The unfolding of Mondavi's plan was remarkably swift. He found local investors to back him, managed to buy a twelve-acre section of the famous To Kalon property, and in July 1966 ground was broken for the new winery along Highway 29 in Oakville, south of St. Helena, in the same region long dominated by Beaulieu and Inglenook.[22] Wine was made while the building was still under construction, and by 1967 Mondavi had white wines for sale—Chenin blanc and Sauvignon blanc, labeled as Fumé blanc, a name of Mondavi's invention that has since been widely copied. He also had a Gamay rosé that, in the early years, constituted as much as 20 percent of the winery's production.[23] These wines, made by the techniques that he and his brother had developed at Charles Krug, made a hit, as did the red wines that soon followed them in 1969: Cabernet Sauvignon, Pinot noir, Zinfandel, and a Chardonnay.[24] Within a decade the Robert Mondavi Winery was one of the Napa Valley's established successes, perhaps the best known of them all. The name and image of Robert Mondavi were ubiquitous in the wine world, his wines were regarded as models of California's best, and his winery had become a place of pilgrimage for all who took an interest in wine. That success would never have been achieved without Robert Mondavi's vision and energy, but he was lucky too: the time was right.

Mondavi had launched his new winery on a rising tide. The sales of California wine had been slowly growing since the industry went back into operation at the beginning of 1934, following the repeal of Prohibition. But that growth had been irregular as the trade passed through the depression years, through the disruptions of the war, and into the difficult postwar years. There was much that needed to be changed. The market was dominated by sweet, fortified wines, mostly made from indifferent varieties of grape. The quality of California's table wines was limited—to put it politely—by an oversupply of inferior grape varieties, an undersupply of desirable varieties, and a habit of unimaginative, unambitious wine making. Production techniques were, in many cases, outmoded and unsatisfactory. Nor did the American market, content as it seemed to be with sweet, fortified wines, show that interest in table wines that might have led to improvements. Enterprise and imagination were not much encouraged among the big wineries, with the notable exception of Gallo.

The professors at the University of California were actively striving to improve this state of things, and they were aided to some extent by the Wine Institute, the trade organization of the California winemakers. The Inglenook, Beaulieu, and Krug wineries in the Napa Valley continued to set a good example for quality wine making, and they had been joined by an increasing number of small-scale wineries dedicated to making wines of the highest quality. Martin Ray's winery in Saratoga was the first of these; after that came such names as Mayacamas, Souverain, and Stony Hill in Napa County, Hallcrest in Santa Cruz County, and Ficklin, making sweet wines from Portuguese varieties, in Madera County.

While new, small wineries began to pop up in isolated fashion in California, the number of older wineries was steadily declining as they went out of business or were bought out by competitors who grew bigger and bigger. There were 414 licensed wineries in California in 1945; twenty years later the figure was 226. At the time, in the middle 1960s, the small wineries were so small as to be almost invisible, and it was supposed that the process of consolidation would go on till only a few giant combinations remained to make wine as an industrial product. In 1966, the year that Robert Mondavi built his new winery in the Napa Valley, 70 percent of California's wine storage capacity (the usual measure of a winery's size) was in the hands of only twenty wineries. But the weather was changing even then, though the fact was not yet clear.

It is often said that the Mondavi Winery was the first new one to be built in the Napa Valley after repeal. That is not exactly true—the Louis Martini Winery was being built as Prohibition came to an end, and the several small wineries in the Valley—Souverain and the rest—were all established in the 1940s. But the Mondavi Winery was certainly a new thing, ambitiously conceived and strikingly different from anything else on the scene. In retrospect, it may be seen as a symbol of the great change that was overtaking the fortunes of wine in America.

For whatever reasons—there is no doubt that they are many—by the decade of the 1960s Americans had begun to drink more table wine, to appreciate quality in wine, and to be prepared to pay for it, all things that had not been true in the generation since repeal. The year in which Mondavi built his new winery, 1966, was the last year in which fortified wines outsold table wines in the United States—a highly significant indicator of change. California made 86 million gallons of fortified wine in that year and 55 million gallons of table wine. Ten years later it made nearly 300 million gallons of table wine and only 13 million gallons of fortified wines. Production of fortified wines has continued to sink dramatically and is now a very minor part of the business. Accompanying this revolutionary change were the related changes that went with a new condition of things: outsiders flocked to the wine business, many of them with the high ambition of making fine wine; the number of wineries in California, after a long decline, suddenly shot up, from 231 in 1966 to 345 in 1976.[25] Wine clubs and wine societies began to blossom all over the country; colleges began to offer courses in wine appreciation; magazines and books began to appear to take advantage of a new and growing audience for information about wine—its history, its kinds, its appreciation. In short, there was a wine boom, a surge.

Mondavi rode that surge, to some extent passively, since it had to do with social forces that no one understood, but also helping to direct it by making wines to a high standard and so showing what could be done. In the early going, when he needed wine to sell, he had made wine from a number of varieties, but in a few years he had discarded Chenin blanc, Zinfandel, and Gamay in order to focus on Chardonnay and Sauvignon blanc among the whites and Cabernet Sauvignon among the reds. The Mondavi wines may be said to have arrived when, in 1972, a group of highly distinguished tasters— they included André Tchelistcheff, Louis Martini, Joseph Heitz, and other luminaries from the Napa Valley—sat down to evaluate thirty California Cabernets. The winner, in their experienced and severely critical judgment, was Mondavi's 1969 Cabernet Sauvignon, a wine that Charles Sullivan has described as "rich, elegant, and powerful, emphasizing varietal character," a wine "definitely meant for the cellar."[26]

People have sometimes wondered that Mondavi wines did not figure in the celebrated "Judgment of Paris," the competitive tasting of California versus French wines held in Paris on the occasion of the American bicentennial in 1976. The simple fact is that the sponsor of the competition, Steven Spurrier, took what he could get on a limited budget for purchasing California wines, then unobtainable in France: it was not a systematic selection. The outcome, as everyone knows, was that two wines from California were judged by a panel of Frenchmen to be "better" than any of the French wines: specifically, a Stag's Leap Cabernet was judged to be better than its nearest competitor, a Château Mouton-Rothschild among the reds, and a Château Montelena Chardonnay to be better than its nearest competitor, a Domaine Roulot Meursault-Charmes, among the whites. It was no doubt some consolation to Mondavi that the first of these winning wines was made by Warren Winiarski, who had been the original winemaker at the Robert Mondavi Winery; the second was made by Mike Grgich, who had succeeded Winiarski. And in any case, Mondavi, together with every other winemaker in the Napa Valley, participated in the prestige that this contest brought to Napa Valley wines.

Mondavi's wines, all highly regarded and commanding correspondingly high prices, were the fruit of unremitting effort in the pursuit of excellence. One of Mondavi's most cherished convictions was of the importance of comparative tastings. He constantly measured his own wines against the best that California and the rest of the world produced. Finding wines in some way better than his, so that he could work on improvements, was more important than merely confirming an established superiority.

We have a tasting once a week on Mondays at eleven o'clock. We compare our wines with finest imports, the finest California wines. And we bring in the top people of our organization here. We have about fifteen, twenty people that are sampling these wines. We have our key sales staff, we have our key administrative staff, key people in the vineyards.

We want everyone to know what part they play in wine, and to know the difference between wines, and why we can ask more money for our wines, and how our wines rank with the finest wines in the world.... We have our growers come in from time to time to taste what their wines are like and how they compare with all the rest.[27]

An in-house joke was that the Mondavi Winery, in order to support these tastings, was the largest importer of French *grand cru* wine in the state.[28]

Another article of faith was the importance of research. In Mondavi's words, "There's no one in the world that does more research work for fine wines than we ourselves."[29] "The test-tube winery," people called it, and Mondavi was proud of the name: "What we were doing was generating enormous excitement inside the winery, and it was creating quite a stir in the valley and throughout the wine business."[30] What research could mean, in a particular case, is well illustrated in an account of the winery's experiment with barrels from different sources written by Robert's younger son, Tim, who had become the company's winemaker. In order to discover what sort of barrel, or barrels, best suited them, the Mondavi Winery had studied the oak species used, the regional variations, the proportion of springwood to summerwood, the qualities of slow-grown wood versus fast-grown wood, the differing tannin contents and aromatic compounds of different oaks, and the special suitability, if any, of different woods for different varieties of grape. That covered the material in question, but there was also the matter of treatment in the cooperage: Was the wood sawn or split into staves? Air-dried or kiln-dried? How many years did drying last? In shaping the wood was steam used as well as fire, or fire only? What level of toasting was best? How thick should the staves be? And so on.[31] If, as time went on, fresh questions should arise, as they always do, then fresh experiments would be carried out. Mondavi was prepared to engage in an endless process. Meantime, as the current outcome of his inquiries, he preferred oak from the forest of Nevers.

Zelma Long, who began to work for Mondavi in 1970, and who succeeded Grgich as winemaker, remembered the constant experiment going on in the winery—"Let's ask a lot of questions about the process, and let's try lots of things" summed up the spirit of the place in her recollection. There was also "a tendency to try everything new that they came across. It seemed like every year we had a new press, a new centrifuge, some new piece of equipment."[32]

Fine wine, it is conventionally said, is made in the vineyard, and here, too, Mondavi sought the best. In the beginning he was of course dependent upon local growers for his grapes. In 1968 the Rainier Brewing Company in Seattle, looking for diversification, bought out Mondavi's original investors. Rainier left Mondavi in control of the winery and provided him with money for expansion, so that, in the next year he was able to buy 230 acres more of the To Kalon Vineyard, a property adjacent to his new winery building. The To Kalon (in Greek, "the beautiful") was originally the work of one Hamilton Crabb, who established it in 1872. Crabb's wines from To Kalon grapes were always regarded as among California's finest. The vineyard fell on evil days during and after Prohibition, but began to be restored by Martin Stelling in the 1940s. After Stelling's death in 1950 it was taken over by Ivan Schoch, one of Robert Mondavi's original investors. Schoch in turn sold a part of the property in 1962 to the Mondavis at Charles Krug, and in 1969 another large part to Robert Mondavi. The To Kalon vineyard was preeminently Cabernet Sauvignon territory, and Mondavi's possession of a substantial part of it was almost a guarantee that he could produce admirable Cabernets. By 1984 the Robert Mondavi Winery owned some fifteen hundred acres of Napa Valley land, eleven hundred acres of it in vineyard, including seven hundred acres adjoining the winery.[33]

The winery building itself was an important contributor to Mondavi's success. The lessons he had learned about public relations at Charles Krug were applied and developed at the new place. At the outset, he had told Cliff May, the man who designed the building, that he wanted "a winery where we could have cultural events, like plays or symphonies and things such as that, and I'd like to have an accommodation for at least five hundred to a thousand people. Then I told him that I would like to have tours through the winery. But I want something that has aesthetic value."[34] May came up with a simple but powerful design to meet these requirements: a big, wide archway opening onto a prospect of vineyards and mountains, and a bell tower joining two wings, one to house the tasting rooms and other public spaces, the other wing to house the winery itself. So from the very beginning the public was spatially as important as the wine making.

When people came, as they soon did in large numbers, they could be taught to understand wine as Robert Mondavi understood it. One premise was that wine was civilization, that its history was bound up with the achieve-

FIGURE 34. The Robert Mondavi winery building in the late 1960s, shortly after its opening; later plantings and ornaments have greatly enriched the view. Courtesy Special Collections, California State Polytechnic University, Pomona.

ments of the most interesting and splendid societies, from the Egyptian and Babylonian down to the present. He hired a researcher, Nina Wemyss, whose charge was to document and illustrate this history for public presentation in a variety of forms.[35] Wine was also an art form, and so arrangements for gallery displays and musical performances were part of the building. Another premise was that wine was inseparable from food, so the public spaces of the new winery made elaborate provision, in kitchens and dining rooms, for food service of all kinds, from light snacks to splendid dinners, for groups large and small.

After Robert Mondavi had been ousted from the Charles Krug Winery, his mother, Rosa, and his brother, Peter, devised, with legal advice, a scheme by which Robert, who still held his 20 percent interest in C. Mondavi and Sons, would be denied his proper share of the company's profits.[36] This was in 1972. Robert sued, and the suit, not determined until 1976, was decided in his favor. In settlement of the judgment, Robert Mondavi received enough money to buy out the Rainier Brewery's share of the company's stock for nearly $20 million.[37] Mondavi also acquired most of the rest of the To Kalon vineyard property, and the inventory of the large (6 million gallons) bulk wine producer in Lodi called the Woodbridge Winery, a winery that he later bought to produce a popular line of red and white table wines—known as "Bob Red" and "Bob White" to the winery workers who made them.

The decade following Mondavi's achievement of independence was one of confident expansion and growing prominence. In 1985 Mondavi bought the small Oakville winery called Vichon and then the Byron Winery in Santa Barbara County, which became the growing point from which Mondavi expanded operations to two thousand acres in Santa Barbara and San Luis Obispo counties, along the Central Coast of California. By far the most prestigious and impressive move was a joint venture with the Baron Philippe de Rothschild, the flamboyant owner of Chateau Mouton-Rothschild in the Médoc, to create a winery that should be devoted wholly to the production of a Cabernet meant to stand with the first growths of France. The enterprise was begun in 1978 at the suggestion of the baron himself, dramatic evidence of the high standing to which Mondavi had raised the wines of the Napa Valley. The first wines of the joint venture were made at the Mondavi Winery while a new, very expensive, winery was being built on property across Highway 29 from the Mondavi Winery in Oakville and christened "Opus One."[38] When the first wines were released in 1983, the label, to show the close association of the two strong men who had made Opus One, featured a Janus-faced silhouette combining the profiles of Mondavi and Rothschild.[39]

Before these heady days of wine-making celebrity, Robert Mondavi had had a prominent place among the winemakers of California but was unknown beyond that small circle. He had always been a leader in the affairs of the Napa Valley winemakers, tireless in both his suggestions and his activities designed to promote the wines of the region. He was also prominent among the winemakers of all of California: he was chairman of the trade organization, the Wine Institute, from 1962 to 1964; and he was also a board member of the promotional agency of the trade, the Wine Advisory Board. His standing was now enlarged well beyond the narrow limits of the California trade: Mondavi was the best-known wine man not only in the Napa Valley but also in the country, excepting of course those considerable parts of the country that still did not know or care anything about wine. His strong features made him easily recognizable: not a tall man, he stood erect, his face distinguished by a Roman nose and a firm jaw. And one saw him everywhere. No wine country event was complete without him: a wine auction, a wine tasting, a wine banquet needed Robert Mondavi. Professional meetings required his presence if they were to be effective. If the trade needed a spokesman, Mondavi was the first choice. Wine books, so the publishers thought, were necessarily prefaced by a few words from Robert Mondavi (one doubts that he read very many of them). Wine magazines, when they needed an authoritative opinion, sought out Robert Mondavi. In short, anything that wanted to attract attention or promote a cause in the world of wine wanted Robert Mondavi.

Mondavi himself appears to have reveled in this glare of publicity. He was not a good speaker; he had only a few leading ideas, but he was tireless in their repetition, and his evident intensity and enthusiasm carried conviction. He soon began to attract honors and awards in wholesale quantity. He was named "Man of the Year" by the American Wine Society in 1982, by *Wines and Vines,* the trade journal, in 1986; by *Decanter,* the English consumers' magazine, in 1988. The American Society for Enology and Viticulture gave him its Merit Award in 1990; the Institute of Masters of Wine, the very select company of wine professionals in England, made him an honorary Master of Wine in 1993. The academic people weighed in with their awards too: the Cornell School of Hospitality made him a member of the Cornell Society of Hotelmen; Johnson and Wales University, the school devoted to education in the culinary arts and the hospitality trade, made him a Doctor of Oenology, *honoris causa;* the California College of Arts and Crafts bestowed the Degree of Fine Arts. Foreign governments did not neglect him: the French made him a member of the Legion of Honor; the Italians, a member of the Order of Merit of the Republic. And all this is a mere selection.

As he was richly awarded, so he richly gave. Mondavi stepped down from his formal position as head of the Robert Mondavi Winery in 1990, leaving the direction of things to his sons Michael and Tim, though keeping an important unofficial presence. With the encouragement of his second wife, Margrit Biever Mondavi, Robert Mondavi now took up certain public and philanthropic purposes.

The first of these was a favorite cause, the harmony of food and wine. It is perhaps not fully recognized how active Mondavi was in the promotion of the proper enjoyment of food as well as of wine. With Richard Graff and Julia Child he was a cofounder of the American Institute of Wine and Food in 1981. In later years, food and philanthropy went together. In 1996 Mondavi bought land in downtown Napa, on the banks of the Napa River, and donated it to the American Center for Wine, Food and the Arts. The lavish building that went up, on elaborate grounds, to celebrate the terms of its name—wine, food, and the arts—was called "Copia." It opened to the public in 2001 but for various reasons never found its way and was closed in

November 2008—not, however, before the Mondavis had put millions of dollars into its struggle to survive.[40]

The trinity of wine, food, and the arts (the last term owing more to Mrs. Mondavi's interests than to her husband's) received even more splendid treatment at the University of California, Davis. A $10-million "Robert and Margrit Mondavi Center for the Performing Arts" opened in 2002, and some $35 million went into the building of the Robert Mondavi Institute for Wine and Food Science, for which ground was broken in 2005. The Institute is the material embodiment of Mondavi's belief in the inseparability of food and wine, though it may be doubted that the Department of Food Science and Technology and the Department of Viticulture and Enology are entirely happy with such a forced marriage.[41] There is no question, however, that Mondavi's gift has provided both departments with every material advantage and has enabled them to work in new directions.

These philanthropic activities no doubt gave Mondavi deep satisfaction, but they ran in tandem with serious, ultimately disastrous, troubles for the Robert Mondavi Winery. A crucial change had been made in 1993 when the Robert Mondavi Winery, till then a closely held family operation, decided to go public. The immediate cause was the episode of serious damage to Napa Valley vineyards by phylloxera, the root louse fatal to vines without resistant roots. Most of the valley's vineyards had been planted on a rootstock called AxR#1 that the French had long since discarded as inadequately resistant to phylloxera attack but that the University of California had recommended just at the time when California was planting a vast new acreage of wine grapes. Mondavi's vines were on AxR#1.

Phylloxera damage began to show up in Napa vineyards in 1980, and—after nearly a decade of denials, alternative explanations, and other confusions—there was at last general agreement that AxR#1 rootstock did not resist phylloxera attack and that wholesale replanting would be necessary. By the early 1990s it was estimated that 750 of the Mondavi Winery's 937 total acres of vineyard were infested.[42] Replanting would be an expensive business; there was no precise way to calculate the cost, but it would run into the millions, requiring first pulling the infected vines, then replanting with new stock, and finally waiting several years for the new vines to come into production. This work by itself would put a serious financial burden on the winery. At the same time, Mondavi's expansions in the 1980s had left the winery with heavy debt. And, to add to its woes, the winery was feeling the effects of a national recession and of increasing competition for its popularly priced wines from Australian and Chilean imports.[43] Perhaps even more troubling, critics were beginning to complain that Mondavi's premium wines were losing their edge—they were, it was said, "light, indifferent, innocuous"; or they were "dull and sparsely fruited"—ominous remarks about wines that had been accustomed to occupying the very top rank.[44] Just when the winery needed money, its sales and profits were in steep decline. To help meet these converging problems it was decided to go public.

The plan was to create two classes of stock. One class, to be owned entirely by family members, would have ten times the voting rights of the other class, to be offered to the public. By this means, it was supposed, control of the winery would remain private even as the winery went public.[45] The initial sale in June 1993 of 3.7 million shares, raised $37 million. But the plan to perpetuate family control, as it happened, did not work out. Family dissensions and severe financial pressures on the company led to the family members surrendering their privileged stock in return for a premium price; with the sale of the stock went control of the company.[46] Thus, a little more than a decade after going public, Mondavi and his family, though greatly enriched by the sale of their stock, were no longer part of the Robert Mondavi Winery. Even the family name was no longer theirs, at least for commercial purposes.

There was some talk of the family's buying back the premium part of the Robert Mondavi Company's operations, but that came to nothing. Instead, the company was bought outright by Constellation Brands, a company with headquarters in the New York Finger Lakes region that had for some years been aggressively acquiring wine-making properties in California and around the world.[47] By 2003 it could claim to be the world's biggest producer of wine, from properties on the east and west coasts of the United States, in Australia, New Zealand, South Africa, and Chile. The purchase of the Mondavi Winery crowned the series of purchases that Constellation had been making of increasingly distinguished wineries.

One sometimes gets the impression from writers and others that no one made good wine in California before Robert Mondavi appeared on the scene. That is historically ignorant and quite wrong. From the testimony of competent judges it is clear that excellent wines were made in nineteenth-century California—from Mondavi's To Kalon vineyards, for example, as they were developed by Hamilton Crabb; and from Emmet Rixford's La Questa vineyard in San Mateo County, to name only two instances from a list that might easily be extended to great length. In Mondavi's own day, the Cabernets from Inglenook and from Beaulieu had the highest reputation, and deservedly.

But no one had brought such glamour to California wine before, an achievement that partly rested on changing times but only partly. The main reason was Robert Mondavi's belief in California's ability to match the world's finest wines; to put it simply, he aimed to make the best, and he showed how to do it.

THIRTEEN

Cathy Corison

WOMEN BECOME WINEMAKERS

WOMEN AND WINE

At first glance, it would appear that the wine trade is open without restriction to women: there are women cellar rats, women sales reps, women vineyard managers, women lab technicians, women winemakers, women CEOs, women proprietors, and women anything else you can think of in the business of wine. But as long as we continue to note that such and such a person is a *woman* CEO or a *woman* winemaker, there is still an unwelcome hint of surprise in the observation: should a *woman* be in those positions? Perhaps the day will come when we no longer specify the female identity in talking about a winemaker or a grape grower, but, as the title of this chapter shows, that day is not yet. As Meredith Edwards put it, with some exasperation, after thirty years of wine making she was still being interviewed, not as a winemaker, but as a "*woman* winemaker."[1]

Women have, of course, had a presence in wine making in the past, the best known perhaps being the "Champagne widows" in France: la Veuve Clicquot and Mme. Elizabeth Bollinger are celebrated instances. But these were women who had wine making thrust upon them rather than having sought it, and in any case, widowhood is a poor way to get into a business. There were such women in California in the early days: Kate Warfield took over the Ten Oaks Vineyard winery in Glen Ellen after her husband's death in 1877 and ran it with great success; her widowed neighbor, Ellen Stuart, ran the winery at the Glen Ellen Ranch. Ellen Hood was notable for taking an active role in her husband's winery at the Los Guilicos Ranch in the Sonoma Valley *before* she was widowed in 1893.[2] But it would be easy to exaggerate the importance of these instances. Practically, the wine business was a man's business, closed to women or, perhaps, simply not thought of as an option for women.

From the end of the nineteenth century until the early years of the wine boom in America, women, so far as I know, were not heard of in the wine business.[3] The first indication of a change is taken to be 1965, when Mary Ann Graf got a bachelor's degree in fermentation science—that is, wine making—from the Department of Viticulture and Enology at the University of California, Davis. Not only did she graduate, she also got a job as winemaker at the old Simi Winery in Sonoma County. Hers was the first such degree awarded to a woman. She was followed in 1970 by Zelma Long, who first worked at the Robert Mondavi Winery under Mike Grgich, becoming winemaker there before migrating to Simi, which may thus claim to have pioneered women winemakers in this country. A third woman to graduate from Davis (1973) was Meredith Edwards, who, after making wine and consulting for a number of wineries, is now the owner and winemaker of the highly regarded Meredith Vineyard Estate in the Russian River Valley of Sonoma County.

After that slow start along the professional path that leads through Davis, the number of women making commercial wine has greatly increased. Some were trained at Davis, others at Fresno, and yet others, no doubt, at schools in Washington, Oregon, New York, and Virginia, to name no other places. The *New York Times,* in 1985, twenty years after Mary Ann Graf took her degree, reported that there were then perhaps three dozen women working as winemakers at wineries in different states: Ann Raffetto at Wagner Vineyards in the Finger Lakes region of New York; Cheryl Barber at Ste. Michelle in Washington State; and in California, there were women winemakers at such prominent wineries as Firestone (Alison Green), Buena Vista (Jill Davis), and Domaine Chandon (Dawnine Dyer).[4]

How did this change come about? It would not have happened, obviously, had there not been behind it the gradually increasing weight of the feminist movement, a movement with so many contributing forces that no one determining cause can be named. But it is safe to say that Mary Ann Graf would never have thought of studying wine making at Davis had not the idea of women's possibilities been in a long process of change. The goal of the movement is simple enough—equality in all social relations. No one, I suppose, thinks that that goal has been reached, but significant change has certainly occurred, and had already occurred by the early 1960s, when Mary Ann Graf entered the wine-making program at Davis.

Her future in the business, and that of the other women who soon joined her, was greatly assisted by the big change overtaking the wine business itself almost at the moment that Graf took her degree in 1965. From that point on, the American wine industry was transformed by a boom or surge, already noticed in the preceding chapter. The new wineries that appeared in the dozens and scores needed help, and because they were new they were not burdened with the prejudices of the established wineries. Women, therefore, found an opening that had not existed before, and they seized the opportunity. Expansion opened the doors.

It was not only in wine making that women began to appear in positions of authority. Ann Noble, the first woman in the Department of Viticulture and Enology at Davis was hired in 1974 to replace the distinguished Maynard Amerine, a striking development in what had been an all-male preserve. She has been followed by several more women appointed to positions in the department: Carole Meredith, Linda Bisson, Hildegarde Heymann. In the unofficial role of wine writers, women have been prominent, most notably the English Jancis Robinson and Serena Sutcliffe, as well as Americans such as Eunice Fried, Barbara Ensrud, and Dorothy Gaiter.

One can say, then, that progress has been made in opening the wine business to women, but no doubt every woman who has made it there has some story to tell about prejudice, misunderstanding, and unfair treatment. Ten years after she had graduated from Davis, Meredith Edwards was asked to teach a weekend course "on how a woman could gain entry into the wine business." "Now" she added, "that's damn pathetic, excuse me for saying *damn*. But, you know."[5]

GETTING INTO WINE

No one woman can be singled out as having made the decisive change in the possibilities open to women. Mary Ann Graf was an important sign of the changing times, but after her appearance there was still much more to be done—and there remains much to be done—in such fields as viticulture, sales, and management. It is possible, however, to find many women whose careers illustrate the newly emerging order. One such is Cathy Corison, proprietor of and winemaker at Corison Winery, south of St. Helena, near Rutherford, in the heart of the Napa Valley. She illustrates, among other things, the entry of young newcomers into the established wine business, newcomers with-

FIGURE 35. Cathy Corison. Courtesy Corison Winery.

out a background in the trade who bring with them new ideas and, most important, new ambitions; she illustrates, in the wines that she makes, the high prestige now associated with Cabernet from this stretch of the valley, a prestige that owes much to Robert Mondavi's achievement; she illustrates the prominence of women in what is called the high-end section of the wine business, rather than in the section where ordinary wine is made in industrial volume; she illustrates the determination to make wines of supple delicacy at a time when big, high-alcohol fruit bombs are more and more the public preference; and, willy-nilly, she illustrates the subject of women in wine.

Corison grew up in Riverside, out in the semiarid lands of Riverside County in Southern California. This was once a great region for citrus (the state's citrus experiment station is there) but not for wine. Nor was home a place for wine. Her father, a lawyer, was satisfied with Gallo's Hearty Burgundy. She got a glass of it with Thanksgiving and Christmas dinners, but did not find it attractive and did not ask for more. She entered Pomona College, some thirty miles from Riverside on the eastern edge of Los Angeles County, in 1971. By that point the turbulent times of the late 1960s in America's colleges had begun to quiet down, but there was still some simmering restlessness among the undergraduates. One form that this took was a scheme then in operation at Pomona to offer classes in nonacademic subjects—anything at all—by students and faculty alike. Since they were nonacademic, they did not carry graduation credit, but they offered fresh possibilities. In her sophomore year Corison decided to offer a course in trampoline technique, a thing she could do because she was an accomplished gymnast and diver (there was no women's diving team at the time at Pomona, so she earned a letter for her diving with the men's team). On the appointed day, she set up a table in the college ballroom to receive enrollments. Next to hers was a table where a young faculty member, John Winthrop Haeger, professor of Chinese language, was enrolling students in his course in wine appreciation. On an impulse, Corison, who knew only Hearty Burgundy and not much about that, put down her name on Haeger's list, and the die was cast. Presumably she went ahead with the course in trampoline, but her heart henceforth belonged to wine. One speaks of "impulse," but such conversions must come from a deep-laid, unrecognized disposition.

John Haeger, though trained in Chinese, was then a pure Francophile in wine, and so the instruction that Corison got from Haeger in that long-ago noncredit course was mostly in French wines. Haeger has since become a champion of American wine, particularly of Pinot noir, and has published two authoritative books: *North American Pinot Noir* and *Pacific Pinot Noir*.[6] To Corison, the fact that she was tasting French wines hardly mattered; whatever its national identity, the wine was marvelous, and this time she wanted more. She was a biology major; her main professor was a marine biologist, and she had had some idea of becoming one herself. Not now. On graduation, she says, she "made a beeline" for the Napa Valley.[7]

The beeline to the valley was easy enough to make, but what was the next step? Her father, on her leaving the Riverside house for her new life up north, had tucked two hundred dollars in her pocket. That was her capital. Yet she was determined, somehow, one day to have a small winery in which to make wines of distinction. That was one of the advantages of coming to the wine business as an outsider. If you knew anything about it, such an ambition would seem absurd and would never come to anything. But if you didn't know anything, you could give it a try.

Meantime, you have to start somewhere. Corison got a job at a wineshop in St. Helena that closed soon after she joined it. Not, however, before she had begun to learn more about wines at the weekly tastings held there. These were not such superficial tastings as one takes for granted today. The Napa Valley, whose prestige and prosperity were fast rising in 1974, was still relatively simple. The winemakers themselves came to these tastings of the wines that they had made, and there was much to be learned from the comparison of judgments and the exchange of information. And it was a good place to meet people in the wine business.

After this exemplary shop closed, Corison took a step nearer to wine making by working in the tasting room of the Sterling Winery in Calistoga, then only recently opened. The necessary next step was a degree from the winemaking program at the University of California, Davis. She began shuttling back and forth between the Napa Valley and Davis, studying half-time and working half-time. She had had a good deal of chemistry in school already, but the Davis people made her take a summer course at Berkeley in order to complete the prerequisites for an master's in food science. Surrounded there by premed students and somewhat intimidated, she got an A+ in the Berkeley course. After that, there were no further hitches in her progress to a degree. Her master's thesis, written simply in order to get the degree and not because she had any particular interest in the subject, was, she says, short and simple: "the shortest on record."

The degree was the lever she could use to pry open a door to wine making. But her major professor, Cornelius Ough, told her bluntly that there was no chance she would be hired in the Napa Valley. The department had something lined up for her in the Central Valley. She balked at this: no way was she going in that direction: that was not what she wanted. Instead, she took an internship at Freemark Abbey, under its winemaker Larry Langbehn and the highly regarded R. Bradford Webb. Webb was a partner and consultant in the winery at this point, but in the 1950s he had been the winemaker at the groundbreaking Hanzell Winery in Sonoma County. There, in that Petit Trianon of a winery ("a millionaire's plaything," Leon Adams had called it),[8] Webb, using stainless steel equipment, temperature-controlled fermentation, and small oak cooperage from France, produced, first, Chardonnays, and then Pinot noirs, that astonished and delighted the connoisseurs. The Hanzell wines, made only in small quantities, and only for a short time before the owner's death put an end to Webb's work there, nevertheless marked one of the decisive moments in the movement of California toward making wines of the highest quality.

Freemark Abbey, just north of St. Helena, revived an operation that had closed down in 1959 but had later reopened and was now, since 1967, making Chardonnays, Cabernets, and Rieslings of high repute. Corison spent eight months there in 1978–79. It was usual for Davis students to spend only a summer of internship, between the first and second years of their program. But Corison was out of school now and so had time to extend her stay. She underwent some hazing. One man would tighten the valves on tanks or the other sorts of closures on equipment so that she could not open them with her bare hands. So she carried a crescent wrench and got the work done. When her internship came to an end, the cellar men gave her as a parting gift a big pink crescent wrench with some black lace attached! The business of tightening the valves was, she thinks, merely testing her at first and, after that, just playing games. It was also, however, indisputable evidence that she was regarded as "other." At any rate, she had turned the boys in the cellar in the right direction with that crescent wrench.

Another episode was perhaps more typical of the prevailing mind-set. When Langbehn wanted to hire her at Freemark Abbey, the managers said no—not, Corison thinks, from hostility but out of sheer surprise. No women were working then in a wine cellar—only in the laboratory or in the bottling room. Langbehn himself had had doubts about her fitness for the work, so he had her perform a mock racking, a routine piece of cellar work that involves lugging heavy hoses around and moving ponderous barrels and monster pumps. She weighed about ninety pounds then, and she came out fine. Meredith Edwards had a comparable experience when she applied for a job at Almadén: "'She's just this girl.' They said to me, 'Well, there's no way that you could even pull a hose or do anything.' And I said, 'You know what, a lot of times there are ways to do things where you use your head, and you don't have to do it with brute strength.'"[9] When Maynard Amerine, Edwards's teacher and sponsor, heard of this episode, he called up the Almadén people and read them the riot act. They then fell over themselves in their haste to offer Meredith Edwards a job after all. She turned them down, not wanting, she said, to "work for them under those circumstances." But such circumstances must have been the rule.

MAKING WINE FOR OTHERS

Corison thinks that despite such obstacles as were put before her, she was "lucky" to have entered the field at a time of explosive growth in California wine. The trade desperately needed winemakers, even if the available wine-makers included women. Through her boss, Brad Webb, Corison got a job at the Yverdon Winery in January, 1979. Webb had been one of the Freemark Abbey executives who had opposed having her work in the winery, but he had now learned to think differently.

Yverdon was a curious place, two thousand feet up on the slopes of Spring Mountain, on the west side of the Napa Valley, home to such distinguished properties as Chateau Chevalier, York Creek, and Stony Hill. Yverdon was the property of a man named Fred Aves, an inventor and manufacturer of auto parts working in Los Angeles, now retired, who had founded his small winery in 1970. It was named for the Swiss town on the shores of the Lake of Neuchâtel where the owner's grandparents had lived and made wine, and construction of the place, unhurried and deliberate, was a labor of love on the part of Aves and his son. The square, solid structure of reinforced concrete was faced with native stone dressed by Aves himself. Massive double doors of native oak, cut, carved, and assembled on the spot, opened into the cellar. Small ornamental windows let into the fortresslike walls were filled with figures and symbols from the lore of wines and vines, done in stained glass made by the owner. There were comparable touches of personal craftsmanship and richness of detail throughout—altogether a remarkable construction. When she first saw it Corison thought: "If this place ever slides down the hill, it will go in one piece."

Here was a small, hands-on winery such as she had imagined owning, and if she did not in fact own it, it was entirely hers to operate. She was secretary, compliance expert, lab technician, cellar staff, forklift operator, shipping clerk, winemaker—in short, *everything*. If the phone rang, she was the one to answer it; if visitors came, they were hers to entertain. As she told an interviewer at the time, "I have lots to learn. And I am learning quickly. The lab work is second nature to me, but the machinery has to be learned by experience. Luckily machinery is very logical, so I can work it out. And having to learn everything about the entire operation of wine making is really exciting. I have a whole winery to run here; maybe I don't do it very well yet, but in a year I will."[10]

That confident remark about the logic of machinery, she said years later, was something she had learned from Aves himself, who taught her that when things went wrong with a machine, the cause was usually something simple, not complicated and difficult. She made only two Yverdon vintages, of about three thousand cases each, of Chenin blanc, Riesling, and Cabernet from vineyards at Calistoga. Then Aves closed the winery, though he kept his bond. That would allow him to reopen the place should he choose to do so.[11] He was a very private man, and in order to protect his privacy had, it is said, put up signs around his vineyards boldly proclaiming that "Trespassers will be shot." Corison says she never saw any such signs but can believe that they might have existed. He was a good man to work for, though—eccentric, but with much to teach her about the mechanics of wine making. Nor did working with a woman give him any difficulty.

Corison then migrated across the valley to the Chappellet Vineyard on Pritchard Hill. Donn Chappellet, like Corison a graduate of Pomona College, had opened his winery in 1967—it was the second substantial new winery to go up in the valley after Robert Mondavi's. First with Philip Togni as winemaker, then Joe Cafaro, and then with Tony Soter (another Pomona graduate), Chappellet had quietly established a reputation for excellent wines, particularly Chenin blanc and Cabernet Sauvignon. Corison succeeded these distinguished predecessors; she remained through the next ten vintages, through the decade of the 1980s. Chappellet, though not a large winery by California standards, was a much bigger operation than the one-woman show at Yverdon had been, producing about thirty thousand cases annually. Corison now had an assistant and a cellar crew. She also received a new education from the experience of making wine from the same vineyards over a long period: "You don't," she says, "just take a snapshot of a vineyard and know what it is about." After ten vintages she had, not a snapshot, but a studio portrait.

MAKING WINE OF ONE'S OWN

Learning to know the Chappellet vineyard in detail was one kind of instruction, but by 1987 Corison felt that it was time for a change: she wanted to get to know the range and variety of many different vineyards. Even before she left Chappellet she had begun making wine on her own account with grapes that she bought from different growers in different locations. When she cut loose from her secure base at Chappellet, it was to make wine in gypsy fashion, a feat made possible by the institution of "custom crushing." A person not in possession of what is called a bricks-and-mortar winery nor of a vineyard, can still make wine by buying grapes and making them into wine in rented space with rented machines in another person's winery. You need a license to do this, and you need money with which to buy the grapes and pay the rent, but that is all. You don't even need to know how to make wine, for you can hire a winemaker to do that. But that last was an expense that Corison did not need to meet. The system is now familiar, with a number of experienced, specialized firms devoted to providing the necessary facilities. Indeed, some of the Napa Valley's most expensive and sought-after wines, those cult wines that Jancis Robinson has said are "made by the teaspoonful and available only to those that have made their money by the tankful," are more often than not made by the custom crush method.

That was not the case when Corison began making her own wine. However, it was a time when many new wineries were going up in the valley and had production capacity beyond what they were using. So they had room for her—Robert Sinskey Vineyards on the Silverado Trail, Rombauer Vineyards north of St. Helena, Tony Soter's Étude Winery, and Ted Hall's Long Meadow Ranch were among the places where Corison made her own wine. Sometimes what she made at one place had to be moved and stored at another. And how was that done? You called up the trucking firm and they sent over a nice, bright, stainless steel tanker. When it came time to bottle the wine, the Sequoia Grove Winery, which had bought an expensive new bottling line, was glad to make some money toward its cost by letting others pay for the use of it.

Even if you have no capital costs for bricks and mortar and machines, you still need money to buy good grapes and expensive new barrels—essential if you are going to make good red wine. Corison had some breaks here. At Chappellet she had the winemaker's house to live in rent free, and this arrangement gave her the means to buy a small house in St. Helena that she could rent out. Her salary and a small rental income were important, but the main thing required of her was a disciplined concentration on what she required for making wine. Her indulgences were "grapes and barrels instead of cars and clothes and travel." And by this strict rule she was able to operate debt-free.

She started at eighteen hundred cases—enough for more than merely local sales. Her experience was invaluable: she had not only seen how wine was made but also knew how it was sold, a know-how that is often fatally lacking in ambitious new winemakers. Because she knew her way around, Corison was able to acquire distributors in important places, such as New York City, who were prepared to take small shipments—economically feasible only if the wine is expensive—and to do the work of selling. But in California she was her own salesperson. Her clients—local shops and restaurants—were mostly in the region from Napa to San Francisco and south to Palo Alto. To serve them she depended on an all-wheel drive Subaru: "You could get a barrel in it. And live out of it." It was also capable of taking twenty-five cases of wine to be delivered, a highly useful capacity, although over the legal load limit. The wines that she made, quickly acquired a good reputation, so her business matured even though it had no home. Charles Sullivan's account of Corison Wines (*Wines* because there was no winery) in his *Companion to California Wines* (1998) is brief but eloquent: "She buys grapes, rents winery space, and produces about 3,000 cases a year of highly praised Napa Valley Cabernet Sauvignon."

This all sounds desperately hand-to-mouth, improvised and anxious-making, not the sort of thing your ordinary bourgeois would imagine doing. But Corison was making wine, which was what she wanted to do. And she was asked to take on many jobs in consulting and in making wine for other people. From the beginning of the 1990s and for the next ten years, she made wine for Fritz Maytag, whom she remembers as great fun to work for. Maytag owned vineyards on Spring Mountain but did not yet own a winery. Instead, he set up his own equipment in other people's wineries to produce three wines: a Cabernet blend, a Pinot blanc, and a port-style wine, with Cathy Corison as winemaker. Looking back at those beginnings, Maytag later wrote: "We were blessed in these early vintages with the efforts and careful attention of a famous young winemaker here in St. Helena, Cathy Corison. With Cathy's help we learned a lot about our grape varieties and I am extremely proud of those early wines, especially the Cabernets."[12] She wasn't famous then, of course, but such language is the privilege of hindsight.

The port-style wine was Maytag's idea, not Corison's: he had some Portuguese vines, and he loved port, so experiments in that line were inevitable. Since the quantities were small, they crushed the grapes through old hop-jacks (containers for hops from Maytag's Anchor Steam Beer brewery in San Francisco);[13] then they heated the must and did the punching down while closely watching the fermentation. It had to be stopped on a dime when the moment came for fortification. And for that they used brandy made by Maytag's own still at the San Francisco brewery. "You stayed up late to make that wine," Corison remembers.

Another ten-year stint, beginning in 1993, was at Ted Hall's Long Meadow Ranch on the slopes of the Mayacamas Mountains, the western wall of the Napa Valley. Here she designed the new winery for the ranch as well as mak-

FIGURE 36. Corison and her Subaru: "You could get a barrel in it." Author's collection.

ing its wines. Another client was the Staglin Family Vineyard in Rutherford. She designed a winery for the Staglins too, but owing to a failure to obtain the necessary permit the winery was not built.

The wineries on this impressive roster—Yverdon, Chappellet, Spring Mountain, Long Meadow, Staglin Family—have several important things in common. All were new enterprises; all aimed at making wines of the highest quality; and all were individually owned or family owned rather than parts of a large corporate enterprise. There are exceptions, but it is still the general rule that women have flourished best in just such conditions and so have become identified with relatively small wineries dedicated not to quantity but quality.

Indeed, the number of women who are associated with wineries of the highest prestige, either as consultants or winemakers or proprietors, is impressive: Heidi Peterson Barrett, Merry Edwards, Mia Klein, Helen Turley, Su Hua Newton, and Delia Viader are among the stars of the profession. But what does it mean to say that the most prominent women in the trade are all relatively small-scale producers of fine wines? That they know how to make good wine, certainly. Does it also mean that they have little chance to succeed in the management of bigger enterprises? That women are safely sealed off in a special niche, where they will not trouble the masculine mainstream?

There are those who think so. In her survey of the careers of women in the wine trade, in both the new and old worlds, Ann Matasar has many stories of the varied achievements and increasing influence of women. But again and again she is forced to observe that her chosen examples do best as proprietors of small properties, or as members of wine-making families, or as entrepreneurs in individually owned wineries, not as managers or directors in the large corporations that seem increasingly to dominate the world drinks trade. One gets the notion from Matasar's account that the relation between women and the corporate world is rather like that of Beauty and the Beast, an opposition of the helpless against the merciless; and in this case Beauty does not seem to count for much. Corporations, in her account, are bastions of the cigar-chewing, locker-room-frequenting male, whose all-men's clubs and closed old-boy networks are impenetrable.[14] Perhaps so, but since so much change in favor of women's claims to equality has already come about, why think that the next step may not be made? At the moment, however, the note of pessimism is strong:

> Consolidation of the wine industry is clearly the wave of the future.... By absorbing the small family-owned wineries in which women have achieved their greatest success, the move toward consolidation, particularly given the accelerated domination of the alcoholic beverage giants, generates some uncertainty about women's future influence. Few women are found in senior management within these companies, and there is no reason to believe that this will change measurably in the foreseeable future.[15]

A WINERY OF ONE'S OWN

Following this dash of cold water, we may resume the Corison story. After eleven years of custom-crush wine-making and varied consulting, with a reputation established but no home for her wines, Corison got a near-miraculous break. It came about in this way. In 1992 she married William Martin, a designer by training, a resident of Boston but a man keen on wine and willing to move back with her to the Napa Valley. The idea of finding a wine-making property of their own was of course always in their minds. But the booming condition of the valley made the chance of such a thing seem remote indeed. Between 1966, when the boom was first fully established, and, say, 1990, when Cathy Corison was making wine in rented facilities, the acreage of grapes in the valley zoomed from 11,738 to 32,715. What had been in the early sixties still a mixed agricultural economy had become practically a monoculture. Looking at such changes, people saw that soon there would be no vineyard land left to plant, and so, in the scramble to get hold of what remained, the price of agricultural land simply took off. There was a matching growth in the number of wineries in operation: between 1966 and 1990 some 160 new wineries had been built in the valley, and this explosive surge showed no signs of slowing.[16]

One obvious result of such growth was a horrendous traffic jam along Highway 29, the main north-south artery of the valley. There were also environmental concerns: reckless development on the hillsides brought erosion and other problems; winery wastes created pollution, and so did the incessant automobile traffic. The ever-growing tourist hordes tempted the wineries to cater to them in ways that had nothing to do with wine making. Wineries became souvenir shops, restaurants, picnic grounds. Some made little or no wine at all. The authorities, finally, grew reluctant to grant licenses to new wineries unless they were well planned and were in fact wineries rather than some form of tourist attraction.

Conditions, then, were not favorable, yet one did not have to give up the idea of finding a place to buy. William Martin, armed with a huge folding map put out by the University of California showing all the varied soil regions of the Napa Valley, tramped the length and breadth of the valley on foot and, after a time, reported that a ten-acre plot for sale on Highway 29, south of St. Helena, lay smack in the middle of a patch of Bale gravelly loam, the ne plus ultra of soils for prime Cabernet Sauvignon vines.[17] The ten acres were planted to Cabernet Sauvignon, and there was also a house, in derelict condition, near the highway. The property at the time was owned by a nonresident Frenchman, who had wanted to build a tasting room along the highway as a tourist attraction but had been turned down by the county authorities, who had had enough of tourist attractions.

The owner then simply neglected the property, which was not regarded as particularly desirable. The house, as has been said, was derelict; in its dilapidated condition it had been taken off the tax rolls. The vines, it was supposed, were planted on AxR#1 rootstock and must, accordingly, be doomed to a quick and certain death by phylloxera. When Corison's interest in the place was known, one of the neighbors came to her with the news that the vines were in fact planted on resistant rupestris St. George stock and would continue to flourish. He knew this because he had planted them himself in the early 1970s. The Frenchman had never inquired into the matter and, as he was not popular locally, had never been told about the vines. The upshot was that Corison was able to buy the property at a price well below its potential market value, thanks in part to a Frenchman's frustrations. She never met the man but is inclined to think well of him.

Now all one had to do was build a new winery from scratch in order to transform into wine the yield from old Cabernet vines rooted deep in Bale gravelly loam. The escrow on the vineyard closed in 1995. William Martin designed a winery building barnlike in essence but gracefully proportioned, sporting a couple of cupolas on the ridge of the roof. He gave special attention to the big double doors that open fore and aft of the winery; they are made of mahogany and are furnished with Cremorne locks, elaborate devices of rods, sockets and plungers. No doubt there are simpler and more efficient locks, but William liked the idea.

Construction of this attractive but highly functional building did not begin until 1999, though Corison of course was already making wine, on the custom-crush plan, of the grapes from her own vineyard. The vintage of 1999 was the first to be made in the new winery building, even though it was then far from completed. It was still roofless when the vintage began; worse, there was no electric power, and no water supply. For water they ran a hose from the old house, where there was a well, to the winery; for power (not house current but an industrial 450 volts) they rented a diesel-powered generator. Working with these desperately improvised means was bad enough, but then it began to rain and the fermenting vats had somehow to be protected against that. The wine got made despite everything, but when the time came for the malolactic fermentation, the roofless winery was too cold to allow it to develop; the fermentation, critical for achieving the flavor and complexity of a fine red wine, was arrested. So they brought in propane heaters to warm up the barrels. And what was the result of all the struggle and improvisation? The '99 vintage was "fabulous." But, Corison adds, she thinks that she and her husband have not yet fully recovered from the stresses of that year.

The construction of the winery building proceeded by fits and starts: strictly speaking, even now it is not entirely finished, but it has been serving for twelve vintages. Having her own place means that Corison can concentrate on the main job—making the best wine possible. "This is heaven," she says, compared to those long years of peripatetic wine making. She has named the home vineyard, the ten acres of Cabernet surrounding the winery building, the Kronos Vineyard, partly for the sake of the alliteration with *Corison* and partly because the Titan Kronos, like wine itself, sprang from the union of earth and sky. The yield of the vines, now around forty years old, is dramatically low—less than a ton and a half per acre ("not a way to make money," she notes). It is farmed organically; after every harvest Corison plants a complex mix of legumes and other annuals as a cover crop—vetch, fava beans, peas, rye, and so on—which grows through the winter and is then spaded in (by a machine) in the spring to contribute its virtues to the soil.

Besides the Cabernet from the Kronos Vineyard, Corison makes another Cabernet from a blend of grapes all grown between Rutherford and St. Helena on Bale gravelly loam, and all from the same three vineyards that supplied her from the very first year that she made wine on her own account. The owners do business with her on the basis of a handshake. Making a wine of grapes from different sources is, Corison says, "conceptually different" from making wine out of a single vineyard. This may seem strange to the uninitiated, since the vineyards in question are all on the same soil type, all planted to Cabernet Sauvignon, and all within a short distance of one another, but to the experienced winemaker the vines all speak in different voices and have different things to say.

Corison also makes small quantities of other sorts of wine, depending upon the accidents of supply. In recent years she has made some Cabernet Franc and some Gewürztraminer—"just for fun." These wines are sold only at the winery.

There is currently much talk about "styles" of wine, particularly about what is taken to be the California style of big, fruity, high-alcohol table wines, both white and red. Will such wines be the standard at which everyone aims? Will such wines gather all the honors and awards? Will they define "wine" for the public at large? However these questions may be answered makes no difference to Cathy Corison, who does not chase after any fashion but is faithful to her own idea of excellence. As she says, "I make wine for myself." The idea is to combine power with elegance—"power" because there must be a substantial presence; "elegance" implying complexity and refinement. The winemaker in the Corison ideal is one who can keep these contrasting things in balance.

Like her wines, she personally avoids the exaggerated style. She is not to be found among the celebrity winemakers who are constantly on the road, starring at wine festivals, wine competitions, and wine conferences, who reveal their secrets in magazine interviews and whose opinions are taken as gospel. She makes four or five appearances a year at tastings and dinners in cities where her wines are sold. When I first called on her, she was just back from a dinner hosted by her distributor in Denver. New York City and Washington, D.C., might also figure in her travel plans. She enjoys putting on vertical tastings of her wines, an exercise whose pleasure is perhaps as much intellectual as it is sensual.

These appearances are of course a way of helping to sell her wines, and are as well a way of keeping up good relations with her distributors. But the wine trade, especially for a small producer such as Corison, is rapidly changing. More and more of her sales are now made at the tasting room or over the Internet or through a mailing list.

WHAT OF THE FUTURE?

Corison is approached from time to time by people interested in buying her enterprise. To them the answer is a simple and distinct No.

There are many suggestions that she make the winery bigger. The idea is not attractive. As it stands now, she runs the winery herself on a day-to-day basis. She has cellar help, of course, and vineyard help, and the essential help of her husband, who keeps the books and takes care of the computers. But running the place, with all the many demands expected and unexpected that that implies, is her work. She makes the wine. She helps to sell the wine. And in addition to this, she somehow manages to care for two teenage daughters. "So I should expand?" she asks. "Getting smaller would make more sense." In a way, this response may confirm Ann Matasar's observation that women do best in small enterprises, since many of them, if not most, must add, to all the responsibilities and risks in growing grapes and making wine, the care and feeding of children and husband.

Looking back over her thirty years of experience in making wine in California, or, more precisely, making Cabernet Sauvignon in the Napa Valley, Corison can see that a genuine social change has taken place in the course of her career. She never had any trouble in finding work, nor did she suffer any real injustice, but she was always conscious that she was looked on as "other." If, in her early days in the trade, she had been told that women would in no very long time be recognized as among the country's finest winemakers, and that women would hold every sort of position in the industry without exception, she would not have believed it. Of course, traces of the old unspoken assumption about the strangeness of women making wine surely still survive. Corison remembers being called "un petit oiseau" by one of the men at Château Ausone in St. Émilion—much depends on just how that was said, but she found it a bit condescending. At a Christmas dinner in Williamsburg, Virginia, where the wine being served was not very good, she and her husband brought some Corison wine to the table; a gentleman there, looking at the bottle with its high professional finish and attractive label, turned to her and asked, "Do you make wine as a vocation or an avocation?"

As to the indifference or hostility of the big corporations toward women, she has no experience of that, since she never looked in that direction. She would, however, certainly assent to the proposition that, in order to be considered equal with the men of the wine world, women must be better at their jobs than men are.[18] Unfair, certainly, but a guarantee that the women in that wine world will have earned their places and more.

NOTES

INTRODUCTION

1. John James Dufour, *The American Vine-Dresser's Guide* (Cincinnati: S. J. Browne, 1826), p. 11.

2. There are now wineries in each of the fifty states, though some are perhaps curiosities rather than economically feasible operations.

1. JOHN JAMES DUFOUR, OR THE USES OF FAILURE

1. Dufour says only that he was "maimed in my left arm" (John James Dufour, *American Vine-Dresser's Guide* [Cincinnati: S. J. Browne, 1826], p. 8; hereafter cited as "J. J. Dufour"). Perret Dufour says that the right arm was missing below the elbow (Perret Dufour, *The Swiss Settlement of Switzerland Country, Indiana*, ed. Harlow Lindley [Indianapolis: Indiana Historical Commission, 1925], p. 8).

2. J. J. Dufour, p. 7.

3. Ibid.

4. Ibid.

5. Ibid., p. 8.

6. James L. Butler and John J. Butler, *Indiana Wine* (Bloomington: Indiana University Press, 2001), p. 13.

7. J. J. Dufour, p. 18.

8. Ibid., p. 19.

9. Dufour's nephew says that, at one point, the barge carrying Dufour's lead sank, but Dufour himself makes no mention of such an event (Butler and Butler, *Indiana Wine*, p. 14).

10. The contract between Dufour and the Vineyard Society is given in Michael L. Cook and Bettie A. Cook, *Kentucky Court of Appeals Deed Books, A–G*, vol. 1 (Evansville, IN: Cook Publications, 1985), p. 220.

11. Butler and Butler, *Indiana Wine,* pp. 9–10. The exact site of First Vineyard is not marked by any monument today, but it has recently been determined by Thomas Beall, who is now re-creating Dufour's vineyard on the banks of the Kentucky River in Jessamine County.

12. Ibid.

13. Ibid., p. 30.

14. *Statutes at Large of the United States of America, 1789–1873,* 6 (Washington, DC, 1846): 126 (August 2, 1813).

15. P. Dufour, *Swiss Settlement,* p. 25.

16. Ibid., pp. 22, 24.

17. Perret Dufour, "Early History of Switzerland County," n.d., p. 25, manuscript, Indiana State Library.

18. François André Michaux, *Travels to the Westward of the Allegany Mountains* (London: B. Crosby, 1805), pp. 166–67.

19. A. J. Winkler, *General Viticulture* (Berkeley: University of California Press, 1962), p. 382.

20. It was perhaps the grape also known as Bland's Madeira, a grape of very minor importance compared to the Cape, or Alexander, grape. The grapes actually used in Madeira are (or were) mainly the Sercial, Verdelho, Bual, and Malmsey varieties. Genuine Constantia was produced from the Muscadelle de Bordelais, a white wine grape.

21. In 2007, with forty cuttings supplied from two vines in the collections of the USDA identified as the Alexander grape, Thomas Beall set out a vineyard on the site of Dufour's First Vineyard and has since increased it with cuttings from the vines first planted. He plans a commemorative first bottling of Alexander wine in 2011.

22. J. J. Dufour, p. 9.

23. Butler and Butler, *Indiana Wine,* p. 41.

24. Ibid., p. 54.

25. P. Dufour, *Swiss Settlement,* pp. 151–52.

26. Thomas Pinney, *A History of Wine in America* (Berkeley: University of California Press, 1989), p. 122.

27. Dufour is remembered locally in the Kentucky Wine and Vine Fest in Nicholasville, a few miles from First Vineyard.

28. P. Dufour, "Early History of Switzerland County," p. 35.

29. P. Dufour, *Swiss Settlement,* p. 70.

30. Liberty Hyde Bailey, *Sketch of the Evolution of Our Native Fruits* (New York: Macmillan, 1898), p. 44; J. J. Dufour, p. 25. Jancis Robinson (*Vines, Grapes, and Wines* [London: Mitchell Beazley, 1986], p. 224) says that wine from the native American grape called Isabella as grown today in Russia produces a wine that tastes like "an artificial strawberry drink," another way of saying that it is foxy.

31. Butler and Butler, *Indiana Wine,* pp. 52–53.

32. Ibid., p. 70.

33. Pinney, *History,* p. 123.

34. Auguste Levasseur, *Lafayette in America in 1824 and 1825,* trans. John D. Godman (Philadelphia: Carey and Lea, 1829), 2:176.

35. Nicholas Longworth, *A Letter from N. Longworth to the Members of the Cincinnati Horticultural Society on the Cultivation of the Grape, and Manufacture of Wine* (Cincinnati, 1846). By "sangaree" (from *sangria*), Longworth probably meant a red wine diluted with water or fruit juice and flavored with nutmeg.

36. P. Dufour, *Swiss Settlement,* p. 371.

37. It did not become "New" Harmony until the town was sold to Robert Owen and his associates.

38. In its heyday, Harmony under Rapp attracted attention as far away as England, where Lord Byron worked it into a late canto of *Don Juan:*

> When Rapp the Harmonist embargoed marriage
> In his harmonious settlement—(which flourishes
> Strangely enough as yet without miscarriage,
> Because it breeds no more mouths than it nourishes,
> Without those sad expenses which disparage
> What Nature naturally most encourages)—
> Why call'd he "Harmony" a state sans wedlock?
> Now here I have got the preacher at a dead lock.

(canto 15, stanza 35)

39. Karl Postel, quoted in Harlow Lindley, ed., *Indiana as Seen by Early Travellers* (Indianapolis: Indiana Historical Commission, 1916), p. 522.

40. Bailey, *Sketch,* p. 41.

41. Francis was then the Vevay postmaster, so he was in a privileged position to receive mail. The circular is reproduced in Butler and Butler, *Indiana Wine,* p. 86.

42. J. J. Dufour, e.g., p. 76.

43. It is much more in demand now for its historical interest than it was in its own day. It has been several times reprinted in recent years: in a facsimile edition by the Vevay Historical Society; in facsimile by Éditions La Valsainte, Vevey, Switzerland; and in an illustrated edition by Éditions La Valsainte and the Purdue University Press, Vevey and West Lafayette, Indiana, respectively, 2003. The last-named edition has been "Rewritten in modern english (american) *[sic]* by Carol Louise Hartman."

44. Butler and Butler, *Indiana Wine,* pp. 96, 150.

45. The town of Vevay has held, since 1968, an annual Swiss Wine Festival, which includes a judging of Indiana wines—none of them from Vevay.

2. NICHOLAS LONGWORTH

1. The story has many variants; in one, Longworth puts the property at fourteen and a half acres (Louis Leonard Tucker, "'Old Nick' Longworth," *Bulletin of the Cincinnati Historical Society* 25 [1967]: 248).

2. Charles Cist, *Sketches and Statistics of Cincinnati in 1851* (Cincinnati: Wm. H. Moore and Co., 1851), p. 334.

3. Ibid., p. 338.

4. *A Wine-Grower's Guide* (New York: Knopf, 1965), p. 206.

5. Nicholas Longworth, "On the Cultivation of the Grape, and Manufacture of Wine," in *Report of the Commissioner of Patents* (Washington, DC: Government Printing Office, 1847), p. 462.

6. Nicholas Longworth, "The Grape and Manufacture of Wine," *Western Agriculturist and Practical Farmer's Guide* (Cincinnati: Robinson and Fairbank, 1830), p. 307.

7. See Longworth's letter in Robert Buchanan, *The Culture of the Grape, and Wine-Making* (Cincinnati: Moore and Anderson, 1852), p. 26.

8. "Mr. Longworth is of opinion that upwards of five thousand varieties of the grape grow wild in Ohio, Kentucky, Indiana, Missouri, North and South Carolina, California, and other central and eastern States of the Union" (Charles Mackay, "The Queen City of the West," *Illustrated London News,* March 20, 1858, 297).

9. Longworth, "Grape and Manufacture of Wine," p. 302.

10. Cist, *Sketches,* p. 47.

11. Longworth, "Grape and Manufacture of Wine," p. 305. Adulteration with cheap whiskey was a very common practice, and one not necessarily regarded as adulteration: some might think it an improvement.

12. Buchanan, *Culture of the Grape,* p. 58.

13. W. J. Flagg, "Wine in America and American Wine," *Harper's New Monthly Magazine* 41 (June 1870): 112. Flagg was Longworth's son-in-law and had been manager of his wineries.

14. United States Department of Agriculture, *Annual Report, 1868* (Washington, DC: Government Printing Office, 1869), p. 575.

15. Nicholas Longworth, "The Process of Wine-Making on the Ohio," *Horticulturist* 4 (1850): 397.

16. John F. Von Daacke, "'Sparkling Catawba': Grape Growing and Wine Making in Cincinnati, 1800–1870" (Master's thesis, University of Cincinnati, 1964), p. 39.

17. Some of the loss was redeemed by distilling the spilled wine into Catawba brandy! (*Longworth's Wine House* [Cincinnati: Longworth, n.d. (c. 1864)].)

18. Nicholas Longworth, letter to the editor, *American Agriculturist* 9 (1850): 119.

19. Great Exhibition, London, *Official Descriptive and Illustrated Catalogue of the Great Exhibition* (London: Spicer Brothers, 1851), 3:1433.

20. *Domestic Manners of the Americans,* 5th ed. (1832; reprint, New York: Dodd, Mead, 1927), p. 6n.

21. Isabella Trotter, *First Impressions of the New World on Two Travellers from the Old* (London: Longman, 1859), pp. 204, 207. A cobbler is defined in the *Oxford English Dictionary* as a drink of American origin made of wine, sugar, lemon, and crushed ice; the earliest reference is from 1809.

22. Mackay, "Queen City of the West," 297.

23. Our standard American term *winery* is a novelty that did not exist in Longworth's day. The earliest instance in the *Oxford English Dictionary* is from 1882.

24. In 1857 the three leading wine houses were Longworth and Zimmerman, Zimmerman and Brothers, and G. and P. Bogen.

25. Von Daacke, "Sparkling Catawba," p. 61.

26. Cist, *Sketches,* p. 267.

27. It was, however, suggested to them in 1858, by a Frenchman who knew of its use in Europe against oidium (Von Daacke, "Sparkling Catawba," p. 69).

28. Letter to the editor (dated February 5, 1851), *Western Horticultural Review,* 1 (March 1851): 300.

29. Longworth letter, n.d., read to the meeting of the association on October 29, 1858, Robert Buchanan scrapbook, p. 95, Cincinnati Historical Society Library.

30. Minutes of the Cincinnati Horticultural Society, July 4, 1857, Cincinnati Historical Society Library.

31. Ibid., December 5, 1857.

32. Flagg, "Wine in America," p. 112.

3. GEORGE HUSMANN

1. Duden's book, a report on the years 1824–27, which he spent in what is now Warren County, Missouri, appeared in 1829 as *Bericht über eine Reise nach den westlichen Staaten Nordamerika's und einen mehrjährigen Aufenthalt am Missouri (in den Jahren 1824, '25, '26, und 1827)* (Elberfeld, Germany: Gedruckt bei S. Lucas, 1829). Published in translation as: *Report on a Journey to the Western States of America and a Stay of Several Years along the Missouri (during the Years 1824, '25, '26, and 1827)* (Columbia: State Historical Society of Missouri, 1980).

2. Friedrich Muench, *School for American Grape Culture* (Saint Louis, MO: Conrad Witter, 1865), p. 11.

3. "The Husmann Family," transcript, n.d., Gail Unzelman Collection, Santa Rosa, CA.

4. *Grape Culture and Wine-Making in California* (San Francisco: Payot, Upham and Co., 1888), pp. 371, 374.

5. Linda Walker Stevens reports that the original settlers at Hermann brought vinifera vines with them; when these failed, the scheme of wine growing was temporarily abandoned ("The Story of Wine at Hermann," *Missouri Folklore Society Journal* 21 [1999]: 25).

6. Husmann says that the first vine in Hermann was an Isabella, but other sources say it was a Catawba (see ibid., p. 26).

7. Siegfried Muehl, "Winegrowing in the Hermann Area," *Missouri Historical Review* 87 (1993): 247–48. The transport between Hermann and Cincinnati must have been very fast if fresh juice were to make the trip without beginning to turn.

8. See the thorough account of the Norton's origins by Rebecca R. K. Ambers and Clifford P. Ambers, "Dr. Daniel Norborne Norton and the Origin of the Norton Grape," *American Wine Society Journal* 36 (Fall 2004): 77–87. The Norton is

also known under the name of "Cynthiana," though there are those who stoutly deny the identity of Norton/Cynthiana.

9. "I do not admire the flavor of [Norton] wine. Writers tell us to the contrary, but grapes may be too ripe to make good wine; and I incline to the opinion that this was the case with my Norton's seedling" (*A Letter from N. Longworth to the Members of the Cincinnati Horticultural Society on the Cultivation of the Grape, and the Manufacture of Wine* [Cincinnati: L'Hommedieu and Co., 1846]).

10. Muehl, "Winegrowing in the Hermann Area," p. 244.

11. *The Cultivation of the Native Grape and the Manufacture of American Wines* (New York: George E. and F. W. Woodward, 1866), p. 20.

12. Ibid., p. 21.

13. Thomas Pinney, *A History of Wine in America* (Berkeley: University of California Press, 1989), p. 178.

14. "Autobiography of George Husmann," quoted in Linda Walker Stevens, "The Making of a Superior Immigrant: George Husmann, 1837–1854," *Missouri Historical Review* 89 (January 1995): 135.

15. One authority says that Husmann made his return in a Conestoga wagon with "an assortment of grape cuttings" (Dr. Axel Arneson, in an undated speech to the American Wine Society on the web site of Peaceful Bend Vineyard, May 25, 2005). How do such stories get started? In fact Husmann returned by sea and the isthmus of Panama (Linda Walker Stevens, *What Wondrous Life* [Hermann, MO: Hermann University Press, 2002], p. 6).

16. His writing career began even earlier at the level of the local newspaper, for which he wrote from 1853 on: his first contribution to the *Hermanner Wochenblatt* was November 18, 1853, and the subject was vine pruning (Linda Walker Stevens, "In Vinous Vein: George Husmann in Print," *Wayward Tendrils Quarterly* 8 [July 1998]: 2).

17. Husmann, *Cultivation of the Native Grape*, p. 11.

18. Ibid., p. 166.

19. Husmann, "First Annual Report," in *Missouri State Board of Agriculture, Second Annual Report, 1866* (Jefferson City, MO: Emory Foster, 1867), p. 26.

20. George Husmann, autobiography, transcript, n.d., p. 6, Gail Unzelman Collection, Santa Rosa, CA.

21. His own liability was twenty-seven thousand dollars, leaving him only four thousand dollars with which to begin anew (ibid.).

22. The *Union List of Serials* lists only seven libraries with files of the magazine; only those at the New York Agricultural Experiment Station and the Massachusetts Horticultural Society are complete.

23. Husmann, autobiography, p. 6.

24. Husmann said the varieties he sent to France included Concord, Clinton, Ives, Norton, Martha, North Carolina, Telegraph, Wilder, Taylor, Herbemont, Hermann, Rulander, Cynthiana, and Cunningham. (Husmann to H. W. Crabb, *St. Helena Star,* April 1, 1876). Evidently they were still fumbling about in the search for a standard rootstock.

25. Husmann, *American Grape Growing and Wine Making* (New York: Orange Judd, 1880), pp. v, vi, 79.

26. Ibid., p. 231.

27. Ibid., p. 213.

28. George Husmann, "Wine Making in Napa Valley," in *Transactions of the California State Agricultural Society* (Sacramento: State Printer, 1883), p. 154. Husmann's first vintage at Talcoa, of twenty-five thousand gallons, was sold to J. Gundlach and Company (W. J. Laferriere, "George Husmann," *Pacific Wine and Spirit Review* 45 [November 30, 1902]: 15).

29. Sullivan, *Napa Wine,* 2nd ed. (San Francisco: Wine Appreciation Guild, 2008), p. 116.

30. Not, however, before he had insisted upon the virtues of the Lenoir, a southern grape of the Bourquiniana species, and so did "much to muddy the waters" in the search for a resistant rootstock (Charles Sullivan, "U.C. Grapes and Wine," pt. 3, *Wayward Tendrils Quarterly* 19 [April 2009]: 22–23).

31. It is curious to see how much our ideas about desirable varieties have changed since Husmann's time. In 1898, toward the end of his active career, he recommended the following varieties for California: for white wine, Semillon, White Burgundy [Pinot blanc?], Red Veltliner, Sylvaner, Thompson Seedless, Sauvignon vert, Traminer, and Riesling. For red wine, Petite Sirah, Butan [?], Val de Penas, Carignane, Petit Bouschet, Alicante Bouschet, Spanna, and Tannat ("The Present Condition of Grape Culture in California," in *Yearbook of the Department of Agriculture, 1898,* by United States Department of Agriculture [Washington, DC: Government Printing Office, 1899], p. 559).

32. Husmann, *American Grape Growing,* p. 235.

33. Letter to the editor, *Napa Register,* October 25, 1889, quoted in William Heintz, *California's Napa Valley* (San Francisco: Scottwall Associates, 1999), p. 147.

34. *San Francisco Merchant,* February 1, 1884.

35. "The Wine Industry—the Situation as It Appears to Me," *Pacific Wine and Spirit Review* 42 (September 30, 1899, p. 17; 43 (January 31, 1901).

36. *Grape Culture and Wine-Making in California,* p. 26.

4. CHARLES KOHLER

1. See Roy Brady, "Alta California's First Vintage," in *The University of California/ Sotheby Book of California Wine,* ed. Doris Muscatine, Maynard Amerine, and Bob Thompson (Berkeley: University of California Press, 1984), pp. 10–15.

2. Charles Sullivan thinks that Kohler probably played the trumpet (personal communication, June 2008).

3. *Music of the Gold Rush Era,* vol. 1 of *History of Music in San Francisco,* ed. Cornell Adam Lengyel (San Francisco, Works Progress Administration, Northern California, 1939), p. 189. I am indebted to the authors of this work and the article

on San Francisco in *Grove's Dictionary of Music* for my account of Kohler's musical career in San Francisco.

4. This would have been the second Vigilance Committee, formed in 1856, the first (formed in 1851) having been disbanded before Kohler arrived in the city.

5. "Charles Kohler," manuscript, n.d., Bancroft Library, MSS C-D264, pp. 12–13, University of California, Berkeley. This story exists in several variant forms.

6. "The Methods of Making California Wines," *Alta California,* November 8, 1857. But the practices of the better-established winemakers, such as Vignes and Wolfskill, would have been a great deal more technically sophisticated than this.

7. "Charles Kohler," p. 15. The deed for this purchase was not recorded until April 1855, nearly a year after Fröhling's trip. Perhaps final payment was not made until then, but one may guess that the firm of Kohler and Frohling was given the use of the property in the interval. In the purchase of the vineyard, Kohler and Fröhling were joined by John Scholler, whose name appears on the deed and who may have put up the purchase price. Scholler withdrew from the partnership in 1856. See Leo J. Friis, *John Fröhling* (Anaheim, CA: Mother Colony Household, 1976), pp. 10, 14.

8. George Husmann, visiting the property in 1883, described the winery as a "shed" (*San Francisco Bulletin,* October 10, 1883). He may have had the original building in mind, rather than later developments.

9. Friis, *John Fröhling,* p. 8.

10. Ibid., p. 36.

11. In the name of the firm, I spell the name *Frohling* without the umlaut, as was the firm's own practice. Otherwise, it is *Fröhling.*

12. *Vitis vinifera,* as it was named by Linnaeus, means "the wine-bearing vine."

13. Alejandra Milla Tapia et al., "Determining the Spanish Origin of Representative Ancient American Grapevine Varieties," *American Journal of Enology and Viticulture* 58, no. 2 (2007): 242–51.

14. The name *Angelica* is said to have come from "Los Angeles," and is (or was) pronounced "an-hel-i-ca" (*Alta California,* November 8, 1857). There were (and are) various ways of making it, but the *mistelle* method is authentic.

15. This claim has been made by several sources, including Irving McKee, "Historic Winegrowers of Southern California, 1850–1890" (manuscript, n.d. [c. 1950?], Wine Institute, San Francisco). McKee writes that, after buying their Los Angeles vineyard, Kohler and Frohling "immediately improved" it "with cuttings imported directly from Europe." Like all such statements, it is not accompanied by anything like evidence.

16. *Los Angeles Star,* October 24, 1859.

17. Vincent Carosso, *The California Wine Industry, 1830–1895* (Berkeley: University of California Press, 1951), p. 32; *Alta California,* November 8, 1857; October 13, 1862.

18. Fröhling bought finished wine from, for example, B. D. Wilson in 1857 (Benjamin D. Wilson Papers, March 10, 1857, Huntington Library, San Marino, CA).

19. *Transactions of the California State Agricultural Society, 1859* (Sacramento:

State Printer, 1860), p. 108. This must mean they had some facility for making wine in or near San Francisco as early as 1859, but I have found no information about that.

20. *Alta California*, October 12, 1856; October 5, 1857; September 1, 1858.

21. Friis, *John Fröhling*, p. 9.

22. Ibid., p. 12.

23. Ernest Peninou and Gail Unzelman, *The California Wine Association and Its Member Wineries, 1894–1920* (Santa Rosa: Nomis Press, 2000), p. 56. The name *Kohler and Frohling* was subject to some variation. In 1855 John Scholler became a partner, and the firm was known as Frohling, Scholler and Kohler until 1856, when Scholler withdrew. In 1858 it became Kohler, Frohling and Bauck, but John Bauck left the partnership in 1860. For a time in the early days the firm was known as John Frohling and Company in Los Angeles and Charles Kohler and Company in San Francisco; thereafter it was Kohler and Frohling (Friis, *John Fröhling*, pp. 10, 14).

24. *Alta California*, October 6, 1858.

25. Carosso, *California Wine Industry*, p. 33.

26. *Alta California*, September 1, 1858.

27. *Alta California*, October 3, 1856. The theme of "purity" is a major emphasis at this time in all discussions of native wines, whether from California or elsewhere. Imported wines, it was widely held, were always adulterated either before shipment or after their reception in the United States. Domestic producers could take advantage of this belief by proclaiming that their wines were Pure, and this they noisily did. What truth the idea that foreign wines were always adulterated might have had, it is now impossible to say. Native wines too, it should be noted, were often said to be adulterated by unscrupulous merchants.

28. *California Farmer*, August 1, 1862.

29. At the time, the Anaheim settlement was in Los Angeles County; it is now in Orange County, which was separated from Los Angeles County in 1889.

30. Friis, *John Fröhling*, pp. 16, 17.

31. The German *Annaheim* was soon altered to the Spanish *Anaheim*. The name won out over the proposed *Annagau* (Hallock F. Raup, *The German Colonization of Anaheim, California* [Berkeley: University of California Press, 1932], p. 126).

32. Sonoma County was producing 250,000 gallons of wine by 1863.

33. Thomas Pinney, *A History of Wine in America* (Berkeley: University of California Press, 1989), p. 165. The figures are manifestly wrong: California was already making more wine than Ohio, but it is significant that the fact was not known at the time.

34. California had only 308,000 inhabitants in 1860 (James D. Hart, *A Companion to California*, new ed. (Berkeley: University of California Press, 1987), s.v. "Population."

35. *Alta California*, October 3, 1856.

36. According to Charles Sullivan, the collaboration between the Sainsevains and Kohler and Frohling was "short lived" (*A Companion to California Wine* [Berkeley: University of California Press, 1998], s.v. "Sainsevain"). Charles Stern, like Charles Kohler and John Fröhling, was a native German whose family had been in the wine

business. Richard Perkins, from Boston, migrated to San Francisco, where he took an interest in Kohler's enterprise and joined with Stern to form the New York agency expressly to market the wines of Kohler and Frohling (Charles Sullivan, "Los Angeles Wine, 1850–1870," *Wayward Tendrils Quarterly* 21 [October 2011]: 25–26).

37. *California Farmer,* November 16, 1860.

38. Charles Kohler to Benjamin D. Wilson, September 17, 1858 (Benjamin D. Wilson Papers, Huntington Library, San Marino, CA).

39. "City Items," *Alta California,* October 13, 1862.

40. Ibid.; July 16, 1867.

41. *Alta California,* October 13, 1862.

42. "An Account of the Wine Business in California, from materials furnished by Charles Kohler," manuscript, n.d. [c. 1877], Bancroft Library, MSS C-D 111, p. 10, University of California, Berkeley. The mixture of varietal and generic names in this list is good evidence of the uncertainty in naming its wines that then prevailed in California.

43. *Alta California,* October 13, 1862.

44. Friis, *John Fröhling,* p. 37.

45. *California Farmer,* December 12, 1862.

46. "Account of the Wine Business in California," p. 11

47. Why "Tokay" no one can now say: neither the grape from which Tokay is made nor any wine resembling Tokay is known in California. The name was much used after the repeal of Prohibition for a sweet fortified wine, but is not now, though it is still legally allowed as a generic name.

48. Peninou and Unzelman, *California Wine Association,* p. 147.

49. A sherry house is a building whose interior may be heated to a high temperature in order to "bake" the fortified wine that is to be called sherry. This method is borrowed from Madeira rather than from the Sherry region of Spain.

50. Ibid., p. 53.

51. "Charles Kohler," *San Francisco Merchant* 18 (April 29, 1887): 2.

52. "Grand Wine Vaults," *Pacific Wine and Spirit Review* 24 (May 13, 1890): 3

53. Pinney, *History,* 1989, pp. 335–56.

54. Peninou and Unzelman, *California Wine Association,* pp. 56, 148.

55. "Charles Kohler," p. 36.

5. ANDREA SBARBORO

1. Andrea Sbarboro, [Life of Andrea Sbarboro], n.d. [c. 1910–11], published as "Andrea Sbarboro: An Early American Success Story: The Memoir of an Italian-American Entrepreneur and Pioneer," ed. Heather Wheeler, *The Argonaut: Journal of the San Francisco Historical Society* 7 (Winter 1996–97): 7. This is Sbarboro's memoir, written in 1910–11, published from a manuscript now in the Bancroft Library, University of California, Berkeley.

2. I follow Sbarboro himself as to the year of his birth (ibid., p. 17). Others give 1840.

3. Ibid., p. 18.

4. Ibid., p. 21.

5. Her name was Maria Dondero. The marriage was childless, and she was an invalid long before her death in 1868.

6. Ibid., p. 31.

7. Their names were Alfredo, Romolo, Remo, Aida, and Romilda. *Aida* is accounted for by the fact that Sbarboro attended the first performance of the opera at La Scala in 1871: "I resolved then and there that, if I ever was blessed with a daughter, I would certainly name her Aida. And I did" (ibid., p. 42). Unluckily for this story, the first performance of *Aida* at La Scala was in 1872, not 1871.

8. Ibid., p. 43.

9. The five institutions were as follows: West Oakland Mutual Building and Loan Association, 1875; San Francisco Mutual Loan Association, 1882; Italian-Swiss Mutual Loan Association, 1887; San Francisco and Oakland Mutual Loan Association, 1889; and San Francisco Home Loan Association, 1890.

10. Ibid., pp. 42–43.

11. Ibid., p. 47. Others had a similar idea. Sbarboro's friend the Frenchman Justinian Caire, as the owner of Santa Cruz Island off the coast at Ventura, began to develop vineyards there around 1884. To carry out the work, he relied on Italian workmen, whom he recruited straight off the docks of San Francisco.

12. The capitalization was three hundred thousand dollars, figured at five thousand shares.

13. Charles Sullivan, "Italian Swiss Colony: The First Half Century, 1881–1883," typescript, 1980, p. 3, Charles Sullivan, Los Gatos, CA.

14. The "Chianti" stop on the same railroad, not far from Asti, also became a center of wine production.

15. Wheeler, "Andrea Sbarboro," p. 48. The benefits of share ownership would be long-deferred and uncertain, so that this adaptation of the building and loan society plan was in fact very different from its model. People who were saving to buy a house had a tangible goal and were in a position to afford the savings. Sbarboro's Italians were in a very different situation and can hardly be blamed for what Sbarboro himself called their "error in judgment."

16. Sullivan, "Italian Swiss Colony," p. 3.

17. Italian Swiss Colony managed to register the name as a trademark, despite the fact that it is certainly a generic term. I suppose the fact that it was an Italian rather than an English word was decisive.

18. Ibid., p. 19.

19. Wheeler, "Andrea Sbarboro," p. 49.

20. The extent of the increase in planting may be measured by the fact that California produced 10 million gallons of wine in 1880 and 18 million gallons in 1886 (Thomas Pinney, *A History of Wine in America* [Berkeley: University of California Press, 1989], p. 355).

21. Wheeler, "Andrea Sbarboro," pp. 49–50.

22. Ibid., p. 50.

23. Ibid.

24. The Madera facility is now the property of Constellation Brands and pumps out vast quantities of wine labelled Almadén, Paul Masson, Inglenook, and Taylor, among others.

25. Sullivan, "Italian Swiss Colony," p. 18.

26. Wheeler, "Andrea Sbarboro," p. 55.

27. This building and its contents survived the San Francisco fire of 1906. During the construction of the building, a spring had begun to flow in the excavation, and a well had been dug to preserve it for the sake of cheap water. When the fire threatened the building, the Italian Swiss Colony people, led by Sbarboro, had a source of water with which to flood the roof and save the building.

28. Sullivan, "Italian Swiss Colony," p. 26.

29. This development is reported in the *Pacific Wine and Spirit Review,* 55 (March 13, 1913).

30. Norman H. Clark, *Deliver Us from Evil* (New York: W. W. Norton, 1976), p. 107.

31. The official was the Methodist Bishop James Cannon, the "Dry Messiah" (Pinney, *History of Wine in America,* p. 433).

32. Wheeler, "Andrea Sbarboro," p. 72.

33. I may claim to have a privileged knowledge of this mentality, for I grew up in the constitutionally dry state of Kansas, and all my family, on both sides, were teetotalers from the cradle onward.

34. As Wayne Wheeler of the Anti-Saloon League put it, liquor was "poison" (Virginius Dabney, *Dry Messiah* [New York: Knopf, 1949], p. 12).

35. Wheeler, "Andrea Sbarboro," p. 74.

36. Sullivan, "Italian Swiss Colony," p. 43.

37. *Pacific Wine and Spirit Review* 50 (October 31, 1908): 40.

38. Wheeler, "Andrea Sbarboro," p. 85.

6. PERCY T. MORGAN AND THE CWA

1. The Kohler of Kohler and Van Bergen was Henry Kohler, no relation to Charles but at one time his partner and later his brother-in-law. S. Lachman was Samuel; the Lachman of Lachman and Jacobi was Samuel's half brother, Abraham.

2. All of these ideas were aired in a meeting of winemen in San Francisco called by the Board of State Viticultural Commissioners in June 1894 ("Meeting of Wine Makers," *Pacific Wine and Spirit Review* 32 [June 6, 1894]: 12).

3. Ibid.

4. One may wonder whether he even cared much to drink it. He told a reporter that Americans had not yet learned how to drink wine. They thought it should be

drunk "as is," but instead what they should do was to "fill one-third of the glass with wine and the fill up the remainder of the glass with water. . . . Wine drunk in that way is absolutely harmless and is conducive to temperance" (*Pacific Wine and Spirit Review* 46 [June 30, 1904]: 17).

5. "Percy T. Morgan to Retire from Wine Association," *Pacific Wine and Spirit Review* 53 (January 31, 1911): 14.

6. He had also before him the example of the big industrial consolidations being formed at this time, such as the sugar trust of 1891.

7. Sullivan, *Napa Wine,* 2nd ed. (San Francisco: Wine Appreciation Guild, 2008), p. 113.

8. California Wine Association, *Compliments of California Wine Association* (San Francisco: California Wine Association, January 1896), illustrated brochure, Gail Unzelman Collection, Santa Rosa, CA.

9. CWA minutes, quoted in Ernest Peninou and Gail Unzelman, *The California Wine Association and Its Member Wineries, 1894–1920* (Santa Rosa, CA: Nomis Press, 2000), p. 92.

10. "The Winemakers Combine," *Pacific Wine and Spirit Review* (November 6, 1894): 22.

11. Ibid. The design inspired one of the CWA's directors, Henry Epstein, to explanatory verse:

> *Allegory*
>
> Young Bacchus hails across the sea,
> "Come all the world, come drink with me.
> There's Wine Fruit at the masthead trim,
> And puncheons fill the hold within.
> We're laden deep with joyous freight;
> 'Tis vintage of the Golden State."
> The Bear he leans on, standing near,
> Is emblem grim of the Pioneer.
> The barge glides out the Golden Gate.
> Its pilot mark, the seal of state.
> If winds refuse to lend their aid
> The sturdy oarsmen ply the blade
> To spread abroad through every nation
> The Trade Mark of the Association.

12. Peninou and Unzelman, *California Wine Association,* pp. 43–71. Haraszthy soon withdrew from the association, but his participation was not much missed.

13. Unidentified clipping dated August 1894 in Percy Morgan scrapbook, Gail Unzelman collection, Santa Rosa, CA.

14. The Sherman Anti-trust Act, the first such legislation in this country, had been passed in 1890. It was not often applied until the administration of Theodore Roosevelt.

15. Daniel Titus to the Board of Directors of the CWA, October 5, 1894, Min-

utes of the Board of Directors, 1:147, California Wine Association Papers, California Historical Society Library, San Francisco (hereafter "CWA Papers").

16. "The Big Wine Deal," *Pacific Wine and Spirit Review* (March 7, 1895): 25.

17. Ibid.

18. The frost, in mid-April, reduced the crop by half (*Pacific Wine and Spirit Review* [April 23, 1896]).

19. "Wine War On," *Pacific Wine and Spirit Review* 38 (February 22, 1897): 10.

20. "The Association and the Corporation," *Pacific Wine and Spirit Review* (June 22, 1896).

21. Minutes of the Board of Directors of the CWA, 1:175–77, CWA Papers.

22. "Wine War On," p. 10.

23. *Pacific Wine and Spirit Review* (June 24, 1897): 12.

24. "Grape Growing and California Wine Industry," speech to the Annual Convention of Fruit Growers, San Francisco, *Pacific Wine and Spirit Review* 45 (December 31, 1902): 14.

25. "A Settlement of the Wine War," *Pacific Wine and Spirit Review* 41 (December 31, 1898): 7–8.

26. Unidentified clipping [San Francisco? c. 1900?], Percy Morgan scrapbook, Gail Unzelman Collection, Santa Rosa, CA.

27. Annual Report of the CWA, 1890, CWA Papers.

28. "Morgan Sees Assured Prosperity," *Pacific Wine and Spirit Review* 45 (August 31, 1902): 11.

29. "Grape Growing and California Wine Industry," p. 14.

30. Peninou and Unzelman, *California Wine Association,* p. 125.

31. Ibid., p. 94.

32. The major scare was a threatened tax of twenty-five cents a gallon on the brandy used to fortify wines. Morgan went to Washington in December 1905 and remained there for several months, successfully lobbying against the measure; instead of twenty-five cents, the tax was set at three cents, just sufficient to pay the expenses of government supervision of the fortifying process.

33. Annual Report of the CWA, 1902, CWA Papers. The CWA crushed 225,000 tons that year, enough to yield 30 million gallons (Peninou and Unzelman, *California Wine Association,* p. 134).

34. Annual Report of the CWA, 1906, CWA Papers.

35. The roster runs thus: Sonoma County, 16 wineries; Napa County, 18; Contra Costa, 3; Solano, 1; Alameda, 2; Santa Clara, 5; Santa Cruz, 1; Los Angeles, 2; San Bernardino, 2; Orange, 1; Sacramento, 3; Yolo, 2; Tehama, 1; San Joaquin, 6; Madera, 2; Fresno, 13; Kings, 2, Tulare, 1.

36. Annual Report of the CWA, 1901, CWA Papers.

37. It is said that the ideal of the "community of interests" is borrowed from another Morgan, namely, J.P. (Peninou and Unzelman, *California Wine Association,* p. 94).

38. Charles Sullivan, "The Great Wine Quake," *Wayward Tendrils Quarterly* 16 (April 2006): 2–3.

39. For this reason Morgan and the California wine trade generally supported the movement that culminated in the passage of the Pure Food and Drug Act of 1906, which required truth in labeling. As Morgan put it, a law was wanted "to enforce the labeling of an article, whether it be in barrels or in bottles, for what it actually is, and not for what the distributor chooses to say it is" ("Purity and Adulteration in Native Wines," address to the International Pure Food Congress, Saint Louis, September 1904, copy in Percy Morgan scrapbook, Gail Unzelman Collection, Santa Rosa, CA).

40. "Native Wines and Their Future," *Pacific Wine and Spirit Review* 47 (December 31, 1904): 15.

41. "How to Market California Wines," *Pacific Wine and Spirit Review* (August 31, 1905).

42. The California State Legislature had passed a bill in 1907 providing that "pure wines may be identified by the prefix 'Cal' or 'Cala' to the name of each wine"; fraudulent use of these terms was punishable by fine or imprisonment (Percy Morgan, "American Wines and the Pure Food Law," *Pacific Wine and Spirit Review* [July 31, 1907]: 16). I know of no instance of the use of this style apart from that of the CWA. The act was repealed in 1935 (Thomas Pinney, *A History of Wine in America* [Berkeley: University of California Press, 1989], p. 121).

43. "Circular: California Wine Association," *Pacific Wine and Spirit Review* (April–May 1906): 13.

44. Ibid., p. 19.

45. See the list in Pinney, *History of Wine,* 1989, p. 361.

46. *Pacific Wine and Spirit Review,* undated cutting [April or May 1906]: 26, Gail Unzelman Collection, Santa Rosa, CA.

47. "Wine That Went Up in Smoke," *Pacific Wine and Spirit Review,* undated cutting [April or May 1906]: 21, Gail Unzelman Collection, Santa Rosa, CA.

48. "California Wine Association," *Richmond Independent,* undated cutting [c. 1910], Gail Unzelman Collection, Santa Rosa, CA.

49. Minutes of the Executive Committee of the CWA, November 26, 1909, CWA Papers.

50. "Percy T. Morgan to Retire from Wine Association," *Pacific Wine and Spirit Review* (January 31, 1911): 14.

51. Annual Report of the CWA, 1917, CWA Papers.

52. "S.F. Capitalist Ends His Life with Shotgun," *San Francisco Examiner,* April 17, 1920.

53. Peninou and Unzelman, *California Wine Association,* p. 114.

54. Frank T. Swett, "Interesting Facts from Contra Costa," *Pacific Wine and Spirit Review* 49 (August 31, 1907): 16.

7. PAUL GARRETT

1. "Co-operation with Eastern Growers—Speech by Percy T. Morgan," *Pacific Wine and Spirit Review* 46 (August 31, 1904): 11.

2. "Fizz Water," *Time* 12 (August 6, 1928): 35.

3. *Fortune* (February 1934): 44.

4. "Classing of Wines as Food Is Urged," *New York Times,* November 4, 1935.

5. The property is now part of the Medoc Mountain State Park.

6. Col. Wharton Green, of Fayetteville, North Carolina, called his wine-making property the Tokay Vineyard, though any resemblance to Tokay was wholly imaginary: such hopeful names were commonplace in the nineteenth century.

7. Paul Garrett, untitled memoir dictated by the author, 1938, p. 7, John Barden Collection, Rochester, NY (hereafter "memoir"). Typescript copy courtesy of John Barden, Garrett's great-grandson and, with his wife, Polly, the assiduous guardians of Garrett's memory and achievement.

8. C. O. Cathey, "Sidney Weller: Ante-Bellum Promoter of Agricultural Reform," *North Carolina Historical Review* 31 (January 1954): 11.

9. The wine-making activity of the Garretts in North Carolina has a confusing number of addresses: Brinkleyville, Ringwood, Littleton, Weldon, Aberdeen, Chockayotte: all but Aberdeen are in the same region of northeastern North Carolina, mostly in Halifax County, not far south of the North Carolina–Virginia border.

10. Garrett, memoir, p. 12.

11. Ibid., p. 13.

12. Ibid., p. 20.

13. Ibid., p. 26.

14. Ibid., p. 13.

15. Ibid., p. 27.

16. Ibid., p. 35.

17. Ibid., p. 39.

18. Ibid., p. 42.

19. Ibid., pp. 42–43.

20. Ibid., p. 44.

21. The C. W. Garrett winery, before this arrangement, appears to have reverted to its original name, becoming again the Medoc Vineyard Company.

22. Ibid., pp. 45, 47. Clarence Gohdes, *Scuppernong* (Durham, NC: Duke University Press, 1982), p. 42.

23. Garrett, memoir, p. 48.

24. Ibid., pp. 50–51.

25. "Wine Depot," *Roanoke News,* December 17, 1891.

26. Garrett was able to buy the original Weller-Garrett winery at Ringwood in 1902 and so to close the long quarrel with Spooner Harrison. But the winery burned in 1906 (John Barden, personal communication).

27. Undated advertisement in the John Barden Collection, Rochester, NY. Other lists from Garrett produced at various times include such items as strawberry and raspberry wine, Angelica, muscatel, Rhine, sauterne, and cognac. None of these things is likely to have come from Scuppernong grapes. According to Clarence Gohdes, Garrett's "claret" came from Norton and Ives grapes (Gohdes, *Scup-*

pernong, p. 49). These could have come only from eastern sources, perhaps Virginia for Norton and Ohio for Ives.

28. A boast that appears on many pieces of Garrett's promotional literature in the Norfolk years, 1903–17.

29. That was the text after the move to Norfolk was complete. A copy of the book in the Huntington Library has an earlier form: "Compliments of Garrett & Co. Weldon, Medoc, and Tokay Vineyards, N.C., Norfolk, VA., and St. Louis, MO." No reference to the "famous Virginia Dare brand of Scuppernong wine" is made.

30. Virginius Dabney, *Dry Messiah* (New York: Knopf, 1949), p. 81.

31. The move is described in Gohdes, *Scuppernong,* p. 58; the motorboat in "Fizz Water," p. 36. The boat, the second of two such, still survives; it is a thirty-three-foot "Baby Gar" with a five-hundred-horsepower engine! (John Barden, personal communication.)

32. Paul Garrett, "The Right to Make Fruit Juices," *California Grape Grower* 4 (July 1923): 2–3.

33. "Fizz Water," p. 35.

34. "Garrett!" *Wine Review* 8 (November 1940): 17.

35. The records of the Prohibition Administration (now in Special Collections, Shields Library, University of California, Davis) show that Garrett and Company in 1923 had permits for bonded wineries in Brooklyn; Penn Yan, New York; Canandaigua, New York; Hammondsport, New York; Sandusky, Ohio; Saint Louis; Wilmington, North Carolina; Enfield, Medoc, North Carolina; Aberdeen, North Carolina; and Cucamonga, California.

36. The million gallons of unsold Vine-Glo was converted into brandy, so that Fruit Industries was ultimately able to repay its loans from the Farm Board.

37. "American Wines," *Fortune* 9 (February 1934): 118.

38. Ibid., p. 44.

39. *New York Times,* November 4, 1935. See Garrett's testimony before the Senate Committee on Finance, in U.S. Congress, Senate, Committee on Finance, *Hearings on the Liquor Tax Administration Act, 13, 15, 16 January 1936* (Washington, DC: Government Printing Office, 1936), p. 134.

40. Thomas Pinney, *A History of Wine in America* (Berkeley: University of California Press, 2005), p. 39.

41. Gohdes, *Scuppernong,* p. 78.

42. "Garrett!" p. 19.

8. ERNEST AND JULIO GALLO

1. Julio Gallo (1910–93) remained in partnership with his brother to the end of his life; as the company grew, Julio's role became that of viticulturist and winemaker, Ernest's that of the salesman and developer. In this chapter the name *Gallo,* when it does not simply mean the company, refers to Ernest. It should be kept in mind that

Julio was an inseparable part of the story, and so his name stands in tandem with that of Ernest at the head of this chapter, as it does on the bottles of Gallo wine.

2. The Gallo parents had died in a mysterious murder-suicide in June 1933, just a couple of months before the brothers applied for a wine-making license. The more than four hundred acres of vineyard belonging to the parents' estate was the brothers' most important asset at the beginning of their business.

3. Ernest Gallo, *The E. & J. Gallo Winery,* interview by Ruth Teiser (Berkeley: Regional Oral History Office, Bancroft Library, University of California, 1995), p. 132. Interview originally conducted in 1969; cited hereafter as "Gallo, *E. & J. Gallo.*"

4. Especially from North Coast wineries, which did not have Ernest Gallo's genius for sales. Such wines were blended with the wines that the Gallos made from their Central Valley grapes, and certainly helped to improve them. See Ernest Gallo and Julio Gallo, with Bruce B. Henderson, *Ernest and Julio* (New York: Times Books, 1994), p. 75.

5. Another reason for the overwhelming preference for fortified wines is that, on account of their high alcohol content, they were not as likely to spoil as unfortified table wines. In the first years after repeal, spoiled wines were common.

6. Gallo, *E. & J. Gallo,* p. 22; Gallo and Gallo, *Our Story,* pp. 82–83.

7. Gallo and Gallo, *Our Story,* p. 111.

8. Ibid.; Thomas Pinney, *A History of Wine in America* (Berkeley: University of California Press, 2005), p. 134.

9. Charles M. Crawford, *Recollections of a Career with the Gallo Winery and the Development of the California Wine Industry, 1942–1989,* interview by Ruth Teiser (Berkeley: Regional Oral History Office, Bancroft Library, University of California, 1990), p. 53.

10. There were, however, large quantities of wine imported from neutral Spain and Portugal, as well as smaller quantities from South America.

11. Gallo and Gallo, *Our Story,* pp. 138–40; Pinney, *History,* pp. 156–57.

12. The figures are taken from Gallo and Gallo, *Our Story;* Ellen Hawkes, *Blood and Wine* (New York: Simon and Schuster, 1993); Gallo, *E. & J. Gallo.*

13. Gallo, *E. & J. Gallo,* pp. 9–10.

14. Gallo and Gallo, *Our Story,* pp. 27–28.

15. The records of the Prohibition Administration now in the Department of Special Collections, Shields Library, University of California, Davis, show that the Gallos then had about 240 acres of vines at the home ranch in Modesto and another 200 in Fresno (inspector's report, August 22, 1933).

16. See, for example, Gallo, *E. & J. Gallo,* pp. 18–19.

17. Charles Crawford, "Vinicultural Research and the E. & J. Gallo Winery," copy of a speech to the Society of Wine Educators, typescript, January 1982, n.p., Wine Institute, San Francisco.

18. Gallo and Gallo, *Our Story,* p. 112.

19. R. Bradford Webb, who worked for Gallo in 1951, recalled that "Gallo was offering technologists the freedom of making better wine[,] and it was a rare opportunity" (R. Bradford Webb, *Brad Webb,* interview by William Heintz [Healdsburg,

CA: Sonoma County Wine Library Oral History, 1991], p. 32). The interview was conducted in 1988.

20. Heitz, *Creating a Winery in the Napa Valley,* interview by Ruth Teiser (Berkeley: Regional Oral History Office, Bancroft Library, University of California, 1986), p. 8.

21. Grape-growing California is divided into five climate regions, from region I, the coolest, to region V, the hottest. Most of the Gallo grapes would have come from region IV.

22. See the summary in Crawford, "Vinicultural Research," n.p.

23. California made vast quantities of "port," but, practically speaking, none of the varieties used in the production of Port grew in the state. Palomino, the traditional grape of Sherry, did grow in California, but California "sherry" was mostly made from neutral grapes such as the Thompson Seedless. The grapes for genuine Tokay and Madeira were unknown in the state.

24. Gallo and Gallo, *Our Story,* p. 220. In 1962 Gallo hired the distinguished winemaker Philip Togni to conduct its varietal studies.

25. Growers complained, however, that Gallo, by its very size, could dictate the market price and of course did so in its favor. But just the opposite claim has been made—that by keeping prices high, Gallo forced its competitors, who could less well afford it, to pay comparable prices ("Their Cup Runneth Over," *Forbes Magazine* [October 1, 1975]: 25).

26. Pinney, *History,* pp. 233–34.

27. The factory was capable originally of producing a half million bottles daily of a proprietary green glass called "Flavor-Guard." By this time Ernest Gallo had evidently had second thoughts about the virtues of clear glass in displaying wine. Because the Flavor-Guard bottle preserved "the rich, more delicious flavor of wine just as it comes from the winery," Ernest Gallo said, it "will be key to a vast untapped demand for wines in the United States" (*San Francisco Examiner,* October 31, 1958). The production of the factory was increased to a daily 1.5 million bottles in 1972 (*Modesto Bee,* July 13, 1972).

28. The materials required included "silica sand from Calaveras County, Calif., soda ash from the Green River Country of Wyoming, limestone from the Mother Lode region of California, and other ingredients from as far away as Mexico and Chile" (*Modern Packaging* [March 1959]: 94).

29. Anitra S. Brown, "The Genius of Gallo," *Market Watch* (May 1988): 13.

30. These and other antics are described in Hawkes, *Blood and Wine,* pp. 181–82.

31. Legh Knowles, *Beaulieu Vineyards from Family to Corporate Ownership,* interview by Lisa Jacobson (Berkeley: Regional Oral History Office, Bancroft Library, University of California, 1990), pp. 25–26.

32. Gallo, *E. & J. Gallo,* p. 56.

33. Ibid., p. 36.

34. Pinney, *History,* p. 447n49.

35. Unidentified clipping in Gallo file, Wine Institute, San Francisco.

36. Gallo and Gallo, *Our Story,* pp. 168–71. The bottlers were struggling against

the competition of Italian Swiss Colony; by joining Gallo and abandoning their own brands, they were quickly able to outsell Italian Swiss (see "Their Cup Runneth Over," p. 30).

37. Knowles, "Beaulieu Vineyards," p. 25. Knowles was later a prominent figure in the California industry as head of Beaulieu Vineyards.

38. Hawkes, *Blood and Wine,* p. 277; Pinney, *History,* p. 199.

39. Gallo and Gallo, *Our Story,* p. 271.

40. Ibid. The order was lifted in May 1983.

41. In 1964 Ernest Gallo said that European wine consumption averaged "twenty gallons per capita, while ours is less than one gallon" ("30 Years Back Was Repeal; 30 Years Ahead . . . ," speech to the American Society of Enologists, *Wines and Vines* 45 [August 1964]: 118).

42. Gallo, *E. & J. Gallo,* p. 55.

43. Other traditional wines, such as Retsina and May wine, were also allowed, but they had only a tiny market.

44. Hawkes, *Blood and Wine,* p. 192.

45. Gallo and Gallo, *Our Story,* pp. 232–33.

46. Ibid.

47. See "Address by Ernest Gallo . . . to the 25th Annual Membership Meeting of the Wine Institute, . . . May 26, 1959," in which he argues that wine ought to be perceived as the drink of prestige, but that Americans had not yet grasped the idea: "The prestige appeal of wine is not getting over to most people in this country. That is one of our industry's problems" (Gallo, *E. & J. Gallo,* appendix 2, p. 101).

48. "Their Cup Runneth Over," p. 25.

49. Brown, "Genius of Gallo," p. 13.

50. Hawkes's book *Blood and Wine* (1993) is mainly devoted to the suits and countersuits between Ernest and Julio Gallo on the one side, and their younger brother, Joe, on the other, over the commercial use of the Gallo name and the proprietary interest of Joe in the winery; Joe lost on both issues and was permanently estranged from his brothers. The book contains much detail, not wholly reliable, about the history and activity of the Gallo family through three generations.

51. Gallo, *E. & J. Gallo,* p. 66.

52. Gallo and Gallo, *Our Story,* p. 128.

53. Gallo, *E. & J. Gallo,* appendix 2, pp. 85, 88–89.

9. FRANK SCHOONMAKER

1. Information from Amanda Hawk, Princeton University Archives. Schoonmaker's career at Princeton has been the subject of several conflicting statements; one commentator says that he left after his sophomore year; another says that he graduated. Several sources say that he published his first book while still an undergraduate, but he was certainly not so precocious as that.

2. Quoted in Craig Claiborne, "The Wine Connoisseur from Spearfish, S.D.," *New York Times,* March 17, 1966.

3. This first trip to Europe is the subject of the usual misstatements: Hugh Johnson, for example, says that Schoonmaker, "a boy of seventeen . . . landed in Spain" (foreword to the English edition of *Frank Schoonmaker's Encyclopedia of Wine* [London: Nelson, 1967]).

4. Ibid.

5. Roy Brady manuscripts, January 20, 1992, and September 11, 1981, Roy Brady Papers, Special Collections, Shields Library, University of California, Davis.

6. Schoonmaker said that, when he began to write for the *New Yorker* (date not given), Harold Ross, the editor, heard him talk about wine and said that Schoonmaker "seemed to be the only S.O.B. in the office that knew anything about wine. . . . So he thought that I ought to go over to Europe and write some wine articles" (Michael Kolbenschlag, "Wineman Frank Schoonmaker," *Wine World* [January–February 1976]: 22). The index to the *New Yorker* shows nothing by Schoonmaker before the wine series beginning in November 1933.

7. Edouard Kressman, *The Wonder of Wine* (New York: Hastings House, 1968), pp. 123–24.

8. Frank E. Johnson, "Frank Schoonmaker, Visionary Wine Man," winemouse .com/features/visionary man.html (accessed February 14, 2005).

9. *Saturday Review* 11 (November 3, 1934): 253, 260–61.

10. Marvel (1901–70) is the subject of some confusion. Was he a reporter for the *San Francisco Chronicle,* or a New York newspaperman, or a copyeditor on the Paris edition of the *Herald Tribune,* or all of these things? Schoonmaker calls him "the Paris correspondent for the *Herald Tribune.*" According to his obituary in the *New York Times,* he was "for many years" on the city desk of the Paris edition of the *New York Herald Tribune;* he was a former food and wine editor of *Gourmet* magazine, and was eastern sales manager for the Taylor Wine Company at the time of his death. It seems likely that Schoonmaker met him in Paris. With Schoonmaker, he shares the title pages for *The Complete Wine Book* (1934) and *American Wines* (1941). He also collaborated with Schoonmaker under their pseudonym of "Frank Thomas" on *Wines, Cocktails and Other Drinks* (1936) and is listed as editor of *Frank Schoonmaker's Dictionary of Wines* (1951). No one, so far as I know, has been able to assess the extent of Marvel's contributions to Schoonmaker's work. He joined Schoonmaker's importing firm in 1937 and seems to have remained with it at least through the 1940s. I suspect that Schoonmaker signed Marvel's name to some letters and articles when he thought another voice should appear to be joined to the arguments he was making.

11. Johnson, "Frank Schoonmaker," p. 4.

12. Kolbenschlag, "Wineman Frank Schoonmaker," p. 23. The authors acknowledge "Professor Frederic T. Bioletti, head of the Division of viticulture of the University of California, who was kind enough to supply much of the information and many of the statistics incorporated in Chapter III [the American chapter]" (*Complete Wine Book,* p. 9).

13. Schoonmaker and Marvel, *Complete Wine Book,* p. 9.

14. Joseph Wechsberg, "A Dreamer of Wine," *New Yorker* 33 (May 17, 1958): 58.

15. W. N. McDonald, "California Wine on Eastern Seaboard Merchandising Front," *Wine Review* 8 (June 1940): 11.

16. Ibid.

17. Johnson, "Frank Schoonmaker," p. 4.

18. See, for example, "Belittling California Wines," *Wines and Vines* 16 (January 1935): 20.

19. "Importer now Sells California Wines," *Wines and Vines* 19 (December 1939): 8. As James Lapsley points out, Beaulieu was already represented by Park and Tilford, and Louis Martini had not yet released his Napa wines: Schoonmaker had scooped up the best of what was then available (*Bottled Poetry* [Berkeley: University of California Press, 1996], p. 244n).

20. Wente Sauvignon blanc had won one of the two grand prix awarded at the San Francisco world's fair in 1939. This was the first of Schoonmaker's varietal wines. One may note that the Larkmead Winery, after long eclipse, has been revived and is the source of excellent wines.

21. If Schoonmaker did not invent this word he certainly gave it currency. The first reference to the word as applied to wine in the *Oxford English Dictionary* is Schoonmaker and Marvel's *American Wines* (1941). According to Frank Johnson, when Lichine and Schoonmaker needed a name for their new wines, they "decided to call them 'varietals'—although it is not clear which of the two actually thought up the term" ("Frank Schoonmaker," p. 5). The word is now so well established that it has become a noun as well as an adjective and, as a noun, has driven out the word *variety:* wines are now made, in the current argot of the trade, not of choice varieties but of choice varietals.

22. "The Case Is Presented for Varietal Names," *Wines and Vines* 21 (November 1940): 8–9.

23. Ibid., p. 8.

24. Thomas Pinney, *A History of Wine in America* (Berkeley: University of California Press, 2005), p. 119 and n. 9.

25. To overcome this weakness, the scheme of "Meritage" wines was invented. These are Bordeaux blends under proprietary names.

26. McDonald, "California Wine on Eastern Seaboard," p. 12.

27. *Wines and Vines* 22 (November 1941): 33.

28. "California Wine Made to Order," *Wine Review* 8 (September 1940): 34.

29. *Fruit Products Journal* (May 1942): 282.

30. H. L. Mencken, *The New Mencken Letters,* ed. Carl Bode (New York: Dial Press, 1977), p. 484.

31. Brady manuscript, January 20, 1992, p. 11, Roy Brady Papers, Special Collections, Shields Library, University of California, Davis.

32. It is difficult now to grasp just how tiny was the acreage devoted to fine varieties in California in the 1930s. Schoonmaker estimated that there were then only 150 acres of Pinot noir, 350 of Cabernet Sauvignon, and fewer than 50 of Chardon-

nay in the entire state ("California vs. Imported," *Wines and Vines* 37 [December 1956]: 24).

33. Frank Schoonmaker and Tom Marvel, *American Wines* (New York: Duell, Sloan and Pearce, 1941), p. 99.

34. Ibid., pp. 80, 91.

35. Barbara Marinacci, "Julian Street and Martin Ray, 1939–1947, Part II," *Wayward Tendrils Quarterly* 14 (April 2004): S1–S2.

36. See ibid. for the fullest account of this episode.

37. Maynard Amerine, *Wine Bibliographies and Taste Perception Studies,* interview by Ruth Teiser (Berkeley: Regional Oral History Office, Bancroft Library, University of California, 1988), p. 41.

38. Dun and Bradstreet report, File D 1950–51, Box 14, Widmer Papers, Cornell University.

39. Louis M. Martini, *Wine Making in the Napa Valley,* interview by Ruth Teiser (Berkeley: Regional Oral History Office, Bancroft Library, University of California, 1973), p. 37.

40. Memoir by Peter Sichel in Patrick Matthews, *Real Wine* (London: Mitchell Beazley, 2000), p. 275.

41. Kolbenschlag, "Wineman Frank Schoonmaker," p. 36.

42. "Schoonmaker Tours Vineyards," *Wine Review* 10 (June 1942): 31; "'21' Brands, Inc., to Distribute Schoonmaker Wines," *Wine Review* 10 (September 1942): 21.

43. Kolbenschlag, "Wineman Frank Schoonmaker," p. 36.

44. Ibid.

45. Ibid.

46. Frank Schoonmaker, *Frank Schoonmaker's Encyclopedia of Wine,* 2nd ed. (New York: Hastings House, 1964).

47. Kolbenschlag, "Wineman Frank Schoonmaker," p. 36.

48. Street to Stanley Greene (of Bellows and Co., wine importers), March 22, 1943, Julian Street Papers, Box 17, Princeton University. The trade in wine with Spain during the war years was substantial. Most of it was Sherry.

49. "The Future of Quality Wine," *Wines and Vines* 26 (December 1945): 21, 37.

50. "Growers Retain Schoonmaker," *Wines and Vines* 27 (February 1946): 48.

51. Schoonmaker called his position at Almadén "General Director of Sales" (Kolbenschlag, "Wineman Frank Schoonmaker," p. 36).

52. The California adaptation of the Spanish process for Sherry had been worked out by William Vere Cruess at the University of California.

53. Johnson, "Frank Schoonmaker," p. 9.

54. At the wine judgings of the California State Fair in 1948, Almadén's Schoonmaker wines won fourteen medals. They were identified as cocktail sherry, sweet Vermouth, brut champagne, Vin Rosé, and the following varietals: White Riesling, dry Semillon, Sylvaner, Traminer, and Cabernet. A Gamay from J. E. Digardi, "another Schoonmaker discovery," won a gold medal (*Wine Review* 16 [October 1948]: 22).

55. The name was later changed to "News from the Vineyards."

56. Gabler, *Wine into Words,* 2nd ed. (Baltimore: Bacchus Press, 2004), p. 324. *The Wines of Germany* had a second edition in 1966 and was completely revised by Peter Sichel in 1980.

57. Roy Brady, *The Brady Book* (Santa Rosa, CA: Nomis Press, 2003), p. xxvi.

58. *Wines and Vines* 63 (January 1982): 46.

59. William Dieppe, *Almadén Is My Life,* interview by Ruth Teiser (Berkeley: Regional Oral History Office, Bancroft Library, University of California, 1985), p. 36.

60. Johnson, foreword to *Frank Schoonmaker's Encyclopedia of Wine.*

10. MAYNARD AMERINE

Epigraph. Amerine, *Wine Bibliographies and Taste Perception Studies,* interview by Ruth Teiser (Berkeley: Regional Oral History Office, Bancroft Library, University of California, 1988), p. 22. In fairness to Amerine, it must be pointed out that he was talking about wine-making professionals, not garden-variety wine drinkers.

1. University of California, College of Agriculture, *Report of the Viticultural Work during the Seasons 1887–93* (Sacramento: A. J. Johnston, 1896), p. 3.

2. Maynard Amerine, "Grapes and Wines in a Sunny Land," p. 9, manuscript, n.d., Amerine Papers, Special Collections, Shields Library, University of California, Davis (hereafter "Amerine Papers").

3. Ibid., p. 13.

4. There are many who think that the traditional answers should not be unchanging. The fairly recent success of the Italians with grape varieties traditionally used in Bordeaux suggests other possibilities for other places.

5. The emphasis on temperature in defining a site has since been widely criticized, though without much justification. Winkler and Amerine of course knew that many other conditions entered into the question. What they were doing was making a start, and no one, so far as I know, has ever doubted that temperature is important. In recent years the notion of "terroir" has been widely promoted instead of temperature, but no one has yet established an accepted definition of it, much less a means to measure it.

6. Such statements are never absolute. The Alicante Bouschet is currently being used for interesting wines in the Alentejo region of Portugal and perhaps in other places as well.

7. "The Golden Ages of Wine: Address to the Institute of Masters of Wine," July 30, 1969, p. 5, Box 42, Amerine Papers. The speech was published by the institute but in such a small edition that it is practically unobtainable.

8. H. P. Olmo, *Plant Genetics and New Grape Varieties,* interview by Ruth Teiser (Berkeley: Regional Oral History Office, Bancroft Library, University of California, 1992), p. 15.

9. Lynn Alley, Deborah Golino, and Andrew Walker, "Retrospective on California Grapevine Materials, Part I," *Wines and Vines* 81 (November 2000): 151.

10. This is according to a story about Amerine in the *New Zealand Herald,* October 13, 1977, Box 40, Folder 3, Amerine Papers). He is said to have kept the certificate framed on a wall of his home.

11. Maynard Joslyn, *A Technologist Views the California Wine Industry,* interview by Ruth Teiser (Berkeley: Regional Oral History Office, Bancroft Library, University of California, 1974), pp. 22, 44.

12. "Edmund Henri Twight—1874–1957," *Wines and Vines* 38 (May 1957): 31.

13. A. J. Winkler, *Viticultural Research at University of California, Davis, 1921–1971,* interview by Ruth Teiser (Berkeley: Regional Oral History Office, Bancroft Library, University of California, 1973), p. 13.

14. This was built on a then-remote section of the campus so as not to offend the townspeople who might disapprove (as many did) of wine entirely; and it was called the enology building in the confident belief that people would not know what the word meant.

15. Amerine, *The University of California and the State's Wine Industry,* interview by Ruth Teiser (Berkeley: Regional Oral History Office, Bancroft Library, University of California, 1972), p. 12.

16. The figure of 556 is from Amerine's remarks at the "Dedication of Maynard A. Amerine Professional Tasting Room, Sebastiani Winery, Sonoma, Calif., January 25 1984," Box 40, Amerine Papers.

17. Amerine, *Wine Bibliographies and Taste Perception Studies,* p. 27.

18. Amerine, *University of California and the State's Wine Industry,* p. 5.

19. Amerine and Winkler, "Composition and Quality of Musts and Wines of California Grapes," *Hilgardia* 15 (February 1944): 493–573.

20. All the members of the department participated in the tastings, as did other members of the Davis faculty and visiting wine men (Amerine, "Dedication of Maynard A. Amerine Professional Tasting Room").

21. Amerine and Winkler, "Composition and Quality of Musts and Wines of California Grapes," pp. 625, 553, 626, 520.

22. Amerine, *Wine Bibliographies and Taste Perception Studies,* p. 26.

23. Mancini impressed others too: a highly regarded music teacher and bandmaster, he founded the symphony orchestra in Modesto; and a park there, his gift to the city, is named for him.

24. To Martin Ray, August 12, 1954, Box 6, Ray Papers, Special Collections. Shields Library, University of California, Davis (hereafter, "Ray Papers).

25. "The library is the scientist's best friend—if he knows how to use it" (Amerine, "The Educated Enologist," *Proceedings of the American Society of Enologists* [1951]: 4).

26. Vernon Singleton recalls how Amerine, "by seemingly effortless panache," prepared, on time, "a fine dinner for eight" ("Maynard Andrew Amerine: Recollections about an Extraordinary Man," *Wayward Tendrils Quarterly* 8 [July 1998]: 10). In a letter to Martin Ray, May 18, 1953, Amerine notes that "I have had a busy week-end with dinner for 12 on Friday night, 8 on Saturday night and luncheon and dinner on Sunday" (Box 6, Ray Papers). A more simple note is struck in a letter

to Martin Ray, November 1, 1953: "Have a big pot of large lima beans going—with salt pork and onions. Will get a 1942 red from the Univ. Cellar for dinner" (Box 6, Ray Papers). It is good to know that at least some of the experimental wine made at Davis was put to its proper use. There are a few other references to make it clear that the good wines produced by experiment were recognized and properly exploited.

27. Amerine, *University of California and the State's Wine Industry*, pp. 38, 79. One of the two top wines distinguished at this judging was a Beaulieu "burgundy"— in fact a Cabernet Sauvignon, but that name was then practically unknown and unused.

28. Hutchison was a staunch supporter of the viticultural and enological work at Davis. "We're the only university that's going to have a department like this," Amerine recalls Hutchison saying. "We'd better have a good one" (*University of California and the State's Wine Industry*, p. 45). Hutchison's support is all the more notable given the fact that he was a Mormon.

29. Journal, July 10, 1937, Box 66, Folder 3, Amerine Papers.

30. André Simon lecture, London, March 29 1982, Box 66, Amerine Papers.

31. Briefly, Winkler at Davis objected to articles by Cruess at Berkeley describing a process by which wines high in volatile acid could by "recovered" by inoculating them with Jerez yeast; Winkler also objected to an article in which Cruess described a process of syruped fermentation to achieve high levels of alcohol without fortification (Department Correspondence, Viticulture and Enology Archive, Box 6, Folder 48, Special Collections, Shields Library, University of California, Davis).

32. Amerine and Joslyn, *Commercial Production of Table Wines,* Bulletin no. 639 (Berkeley: University of California, College of Agriculture, Agricultural Experiment Station, 1940); Joslyn and Amerine, *Commercial Production of Dessert Wines,* Bulletin no. 651 (Berkeley: University of California, College of Agriculture, Agricultural Experiment Station, 1941); Joslyn and Amerine, *Commercial Production of Brandies,* Bulletin no. 652 (Berkeley: University of California, College of Agriculture, Agricultural Experiment Station, 1941). Two of these, in different form, had a considerable life beyond their original publication. The bulletin on table wine was the basis of Amerine and Joslyn, *Table Wines* (Berkeley: University of California Press, 1951), the second edition of which was published in 1970. The bulletin on dessert wine was the basis of Joslyn and Amerine, *Dessert, Appetizer, and Related Flavored Wines* (Berkeley: University of California Press, 1974). The bulletin on brandy has had no further life.

33. Amerine, *Wine Bibliographies and Taste Perception Studies,* p. 35.

34. Beginning with "Claret," *Wines and Vines* (January 1938), and ending with "Champagne," *Wines and Vines* 19 (December 1938).

35. Maynard Amerine and A.J. Winkler, "Maturity Studies with California Grapes. 1. The Balling-Acid Ratio of Wine Grapes," *Proceedings of the American Society of Horticultural Science* 38 (1940): 379–87; "Maturity Studies with California Grapes. II. The Titratable Acidity, pH, and Organic Acid Content," *Proceedings of the American Society of Horticultural Science* 40 (1942): 313–24.

36. Amerine, *University of California and the State's Wine Industry,* p. 26.

37. Amerine to Winkler, June 20–July 3, [1943], Department Correspondence, Box 8, Folder A, Viticulture and Enology Archive, Special Collections, Shields Library, University of California, Davis.

38. Amerine to Winkler, November 15, 1943, Department Correspondence, Box 8, Folder A, Viticulture and Enology Archive, Special Collections, Shields Library, University of California, Davis.

39. Ron Iscoff, "Malibu's Wine Making M.D.'s," *Medical Sporting News* (November–December 1971): 41–43. A copy of this article is among Amerine's papers, accompanied by a copy of the note that Amerine wrote in reply to the man who sent it to him. "I may have been late for work a few mornings, but never for a week" is Amerine's comment (Box 14, Folder A, Amerine Papers). He does not deny the statement that he published "a definitive treatise on Asian wines" on his return, but no such item appears in the bibliography of his work that he himself drew up in Amerine and Herman J. Phaff, *A Bibliography of Publications by the Faculty, Staff and Students of the University of California 1876–1980, on Grapes, Wine, and Related Subjects* (Berkeley: University of California Press, 1986). Is any such work known?

40. Amerine, *University of California and the State's Wine Industry,* p. 57.

41. February 12, 1953, Box 6, Ray Papers.

42. The word *tasting* was avoided because, as Amerine used to say, "taste was only one of the senses involved."

43. *Wine Review* 7 (July 1939): 6, 20.

44. *Wine Review* 16 (May 1948): 10–12.

45. *Proceedings of the Wine Technical Conference* (Davis: University of California, Division of Viticulture, 1949), pp. 21–24.

46. *Wines and Vines* 18 (September 1950): 35–36.

47. *Proceedings of the American Society of Enologists* (1952): 97–115. The publication is now known as the *American Journal of Enology and Viticulture.*

48. Maynard Amerine and Edward B. Roessler, *Wines* (San Francisco: W.H. Freeman, 1976); the second edition, revised and enlarged, was published in 1983.

49. Amerine, *Wine Bibliographies and Taste Perception Studies,* p. 4. Amerine's skepticism about the results of most judgings is well expressed in his comment on the celebrated "Judgment of Paris" in 1976, the comparative tasting of French and California wines that was won by the Americans, to the great excitement of the press. After studying the actual scores awarded by the judges, Amerine concluded: "It seems obvious that because the judges used the score card in different ways and/or viewed the relation of scores to quality in differing ways that the results have no meaning" ("Sensory Evaluation of Wine—What Do the Results Mean?" speech to the Australian Institute of Food Science and Technology, September 27, 1976, Box 40, folder 2, Amerine Papers).

50. *Journal of Food Research* 13 (March 1948); *Food Technology* 4 (May 1950) and 5 (January 1951); *Scientific Monthly* (May 1953).

51. "An Historical Note on Grape Prices," *Wines and Vines* 14 (October 1946): 28–29; "Some Early Books about the California Wine Industry," *Book Club of Cal-*

ifornia Quarterly News Letter 16 (March 1951): 51–56; "Bordeaux and Burgundy," *Wine and Food,* no. 67 (1950): 166–68.

52. These include Amerine, "A Short Checklist of Books on Grapes and Wine of Interest to Enologists," which is an appendix to "The Educated Enologist," pp. 10–30; *A Short Check List of Books and Pamphlets in English on Grapes, Wines, and Related Subjects, 1949–1959* (1959); *A Check List of Books and Pamphlets in English on Grapes and Wines, and Related Subjects, 1960–68, with a Supplement for 1949–1959* (1969); *Vermouth* (1974); Amerine and Singleton, *A List of Bibliographies and a Selected List of Publications That Contain Bibliographies on Grapes, Wines, and Related Subjects* (1971); Amerine and Phaff, *A Bibliography of Publications by the Faculty, Staff, and Students of the University of California, 1876–1980, on Grapes, Wine, and Related Subjects* (1986); Amerine and Borg, *A Bibliography on Grapes, Wines, and Other Alcoholic Beverages, and Temperance* (1996).

53. Amerine, "The Educated Enologist."

54. Clare Bailey, interview by author, September 3, 2007.

55. Ray to John Melville, March 17, 1956, Box 6, Ray Papers. Ray was then involved in a fight with all the rest of the state's winemakers over the question of standards; in the course of this he had insulted and traduced nearly everyone, and had claimed Amerine as one of his collaborators. Amerine, who had repeatedly told Ray that he, Amerine, entirely disapproved of Ray's methods, very properly resented that claim; relations between the two men were permanently strained.

56. Clare Bailey, interview.

57. *Wine Spectator* 10 (June 1–15, 1985).

58. Amerine, *Wine Bibliographies and Taste Perception Studies,* p. 26.

59. Philip Hiaring, "One of the World's Great Wine Scholars Retires June 30th," *Wines and Vines* 55 (April 1974): 26.

60. Amerine, "The Golden Ages of Wine: Address to Institute of Masters of Wine."

11. KONSTANTIN FRANK

1. William Clifford, "New York Wine Comes of Age," *Holiday* (May 1968).

2. Hudson Cattell, "Dr. Konstantin Frank Dies at Age 86," *Wine East* 13 (November–December 1985): 6.

3. Quoted in Ed Van Dyne, "Dr. Konstantin Frank: A Retrospective," *American Wine Society Journal* 24 (Fall 1992): 79 (originally published in 1985).

4. Different sources give different dates for this move, but Hudson Cattell informs me that he got the date of 1941 from Frank himself.

5. Cattell, "Dr. Konstantin Frank," p. 21. The story is from Frank's son, Willibald.

6. Frank Prial, "They Labor Well in New York's Vineyards," *New York Times,* April 18, 1973, 49. A third version—certainly mistaken—is given by Leon Adams, who states that Frank remained in Russia and became director of the "local agricul-

tural institute," and that he did not leave Russia until after the war (*The Wines of America,* 2nd ed. [New York: McGraw-Hill, 1978], p. 103).

7. Russian, German, and French for sure: what the other two were is not said. Ukrainian? Moldovan?

8. Cattell, "Dr. Konstantin Frank," p. [1].

9. J. R. Magness and I. W. Dix, *Vinifera Grapes in the East,* USDA Bureau of Plant Industry (Washington, DC: Government Printing Office, March 1934), mimeographed report.

10. R. D. Anthony, *Vinifera Grapes in New York,* Bulletin no. 432 (Geneva: New York Agricultural Experiment Station, April 1917).

11. Ibid., p. 91.

12. Keith H. Kimball, "Another Look at Vinifera in the East," *Wines and Vines* 42 (April 1961): 63.

13. Ibid.

14. Charles Fournier, "Birth of a New York State Pinot Chardonnay," *Wines and Vines* 42 (January 1961): 32.

15. Ibid.

16. The 1954 date is from Hudson Cattell (personal communication, January 28, 2010); Fournier himself wrote that work with vinifera was carried on at Gold Seal under Frank's direction from 1953 ("A Scientific Look at Vinifera in the East." *Wines and Vines* 42 [August 1961]: 27).

17. Prial, "They Labor Well," p. 49.

18. Beginning with *American Wines and How to Make Them* (New York: Knopf, 1933), and including *A Wine-Grower's Guide* (New York: Knopf, 1945), and *American Wines and Wine Making* (New York: Knopf, 1956).

19. Quoted in Van Dyne, "Dr. Konstantin Frank," p. 78.

20. The thesis has been seen in this country, but the location of no copy is currently known (Hudson Cattell, personal communication, January 28, 2010).

21. Fournier explains in more detail that the main subjects of Frank's investigations were these: "(1) the adaptability of the rootstock to different soils and the resistance of its roots to low temperatures; (2) clone selection; (3) affinity between rootstock and scion; (4) influence of rootstock on earliness of scion; (5) cultural methods: soil management, trimming [pruning] type and timing, fertilizer; and (6) weather conditions" ("Scientific Look," p. 27).

22. Ibid.

23. Ibid.

24. Fournier, "Birth," p. 32.

25. Ibid.

26. Quoted in Van Dyne, "Dr. Konstantin Frank," p. 79.

27. Sheldon and Pauline Wasserman say that Frank left Gold Seal because "they persisted in blending the wine from the vinifera varieties with the inferior wine made from native varieties" ("Can't Be Done, but Dr. Frank Does," *Wine Spectator* [November 1–15, 1978]: 12).

28. Jim Gordon, Linda Jones McKee, Hudson Cattell, "Wines That Changed the Industry," *Wines and Vines* 90 (January 2009): 40. Another authority says that Bright's had a vinifera vineyard in 1946 (Kimball, "Another Look," p. 63). Kimball also notes that the winters at St. Catharine's, on the Niagara peninsula, where Bright's had its vineyards, are milder than in the Finger Lakes.

29. Paul Lukacs, *The Great Wines of America* (New York: Norton, 2005), p. 136.

30. Frank made a few bottles of *trockenbeerenauslese* in the first crush of vinifera grapes at Gold Seal in 1957, but outside of commerce (Wasserman and Wasserman, "Can't Be Done," p. 12).

31. Ibid.

32. *Winemaster* (Amsterdam, NY: Noteworthy Co., 1983), p. 18.

33. Leon Adams, *The Wines of America* (Boston: Houghton, Mifflin, 1973), p. 104.

34. Wasserman and Wasserman, "Can't Be Done," p. 12.

35. George C. Husmann, Elmer Snyder, and Frederick L. Husmann, *Testing Vinifera Grape Varieties Grafted on Phylloxera-Resistant Rootstocks in California*, USDA Technical Bulletin no. 697 (Washington, DC: Government Printing Office, 1939).

36. Nelson Shaulis, John Einset, and A. Boyd Pack. *Growing Cold-Tender Grape Varieties in New York,* Bulletin no. 821 (Geneva: New York State Agricultural Experiment Station, 1968), p. 10.

37. Prial, "They Labor Well," [n.p. in my copy].

38. Adams, *The Wines of America,* 2nd ed., p. 98.

39. Frank's article "The Phylloxera Menace in Vineyards" (*American Fruit Grower* [May 1954]): 36–37, is an indirect approach to his main object: in this, he recommends that eastern vines should not be planted on their own roots but grafted to phylloxera-resistant rootstocks. As the article develops, the emphasis shifts from phylloxera resistance to cold-resistance and to early maturity: "We need in eastern United States a rootstock which is not only phylloxera resistant, but is also resistant to cold, is adapted to our soil conditions, and is early maturing." Riparia was the obvious choice, and not the riparia of Geneva but that of Quebec (p. 37). It would appear that Frank had already found his Canadian rootstock by the time this article was published.

40. "An Update on Virginia Viticulture," *Wines and Vines* 62 (October 1981): 47.

41. Van Dyne, "Dr. Konstantin Frank," p. 80.

42. Louisa Thomas Hargrave, *The Vineyard* (New York: Viking, 2003), pp. 37–38.

43. Van Dyne, "Dr. Konstantin Frank," p. 77.

44. Ibid.

45. See G. S. Stoewsand and W. B. Robinson, "Review of Grape and Wine Toxicity Research," *Food Sciences* 6 (January 1971).

46. These statistics are approximate and always changing.

47. Cattell, "Dr. Konstantin Frank," p. 21.

48. Van Dyne, "Dr. Konstantin Frank," p. 80.

1. Rosa Mondavi came to the United States as a bride in 1908 and, for the next fourteen years, to the care of four children, added the unceasing work of providing for fifteen boarders—cooking, washing, cleaning the house—without hired help, "In fourteen years she had never once had more than six hours' sleep a night" (Angelo Pellegrini, *Americans by Choice* [New York: Macmillan, 1956], p. 145).

2. Wine making in Virginia continued long after repeal. When I was there in the 1960s, a local Italian store still sold (illegally) wine of its own making to customers. There was no sense of the illicit in this. It was simply that, if you wanted to buy wine, they had wine for sale. As I remember, it was pretty poor stuff, but that is not the point.

3. Mondavi, *Creativity in the California Wine Industry,* interview by Ruth Teiser (Berkeley: Regional Oral History Office, Bancroft Library, University of California, 1985), p. 10. The interview was conducted in 1984.

4. Ibid.

5. Ibid. Mondavi's admiration for John Daniel was widely shared. André Tchelistcheff, whose good opinion was not easily gained, was lavish in his praise for Daniel's high standards, calling them "exquisite" and "unbelievable" (Charles Sullivan, *Napa Wine,* 2nd ed. [San Francisco: Wine Appreciation Guild, 2008], p. 258).

6. The seventy-five thousand dollars in 1943 would be about seven hundred thousand dollars in 2010 dollars—still a sensational bargain price.

7. Peter Mondavi, *Advances in Technology and Production at Charles Krug,* interview by Ruth Teiser (Berkeley: Regional Oral History Office, Bancroft Library, University of California, 1990), p. 17.

8. Robert Mondavi, *Creativity,* p. 15.

9. Ibid., p. 18.

10. Peter Mondavi, *Advances,* p. 17.

11. Sullivan, *Napa Wine,* p. 240. This was the origin of what became, in 1983, the formal trade organization called the Napa Valley Vintners Association.

12. Robert Mondavi, *Creativity,* p. 28.

13. Sullivan, *Napa Wine,* p. 252.

14. Ibid., p. 251. The list of varietal wines shows that the nomenclature was still not straightened out (*Grey Riesling* is no longer allowed, *Traminer* is *Gewürztraminer*); more important, it shows that the idea of what varieties best suited the Napa Valley was still in flux.

15. "People say, 'Gee, who does all your public relations?' I didn't know what they were talking about. I said, 'Well, I'm only being honest. I speak to people about what I do, how I do it. And that's all I do'" (Robert Mondavi, *Creativity,* p. 25).

16. The idea of giving concerts at a winery was originated by Alfred Fromm at the Paul Masson Winery, where a summer series, "Music at the Vineyards," was offered from 1958.

17. Robert Mondavi, *Creativity,* p. 22.

18. James Lapsley, *Bottled Poetry* (Berkeley: University of California Press, 1996), p. 188.

19. Julia Flynn Siler, *The House of Mondavi* (New York: Gotham Books, 2007), p. 38.

20. Robert Mondavi, *Creativity,* p. 23.

21. Robert Mondavi and Paul Chutkow, *Harvests of Joy* (New York: Harcourt, Brace and Co., 1998), p. 7.

22. Ibid., ch. 3. The Oakville region is officially, since 1993, an American viticultural area of about four thousand acres.

23. "That little gamay got us off to a fine start, at $1.79 a bottle!" (Robert Mondavi, *Harvests of* Joy, p. 75.) What Californians called Gamay (or more commonly Napa Gamay) in the 1960s is now identified as the minor French variety Valdigué and must be so labeled.

24. Robert Mondavi, *Creativity,* p. 54.

25. According to the latest estimates (the number is almost impossible to fix precisely) there are currently seven thousand wineries in the United States, an astronomical increase since 1966 (*Wines and Vines* 91 (May 2010): 8).

26. Sullivan, *Napa Wine,* p. 283.

27. Robert Mondavi, *Creativity,* p. 56.

28. Siler, *House of Mondavi,* p. 82.

29. Robert Mondavi, *Creativity,* p. 47.

30. Robert Mondavi, *Harvests of Joy,* p. 106.

31. See Timothy J. Mondavi, "Barrels in Modern Winemaking," in *The University of California / Sotheby Book of California Wine,* ed. Doris Muscatine, Maynard Amerine, and Bob Thompson (Berkeley: University of California Press, 1984), pp. 198–202. A series of appendices in Cyril Ray's *Robert Mondavi of the Napa Valley* (London: Heinemann/Peter Davies, 1984), gives some idea of the Mondavi winery's innovative and experimental style, under the headings "The Oakville Laboratories," "Equipment at the Winery," "Selection and Propagation of Yeast Strains," "Malolactic Fermentation," and "Barrel-Ageing."

32. Long, *The Past Is the Beginning of the Future: Simi Winery in Its Second Century,* interview by Carole Hicke (Berkeley: Regional Oral History Office, Bancroft Library, University of California, 1992), pp. 8, 9.

33. Robert Mondavi, *Creativity,* p. 47. He had a large property on the Silverado Trail, along the eastern edge of the Napa Valley, as well as the Oakville property.

34. Ibid., p. 66.

35. As well as assisting the public relations of the winery, the research into wine history was also meant as a riposte to the so-called neoprohibitionism of the 1980s: wine was a contributor to health.

36. For an account of the plan and of the suit that followed, see Siler, *House of Mondavi,* pp. 97–124.

37. Sullivan, *Napa Wine,* p. 284.

38. The winery building, designed by William Pereira and associates, was not fin-

ished until 1991. "It had the distinction of being Napa Valley's most expensive new winery," costing about $26 million (Siler, *House of Mondavi*, p. 211). Mondavi himself says that it cost "about $29 million" (Robert Mondavi, *Harvests of Joy*, p. 225).

39. Further joint ventures made by the Mondavi Winery were with the Frescobaldi family in Italy in 1995 and with the Viña Errazuriz Corporation in Chile in 1996.

40. Sullivan, *Napa Wine*, p. 409.

41. Mondavi had first proposed the joining of Viticulture and Enology with Food Science and Technology in a Regent's Lecture at Davis in 1988.

42. Siler, *House of Mondavi*, p. 214.

43. See the concise summary of the situation in Sullivan, *Napa Wine*, p. 411.

44. Ibid., p. 412.

45. Siler, *House of Mondavi*, p. 216.

46. Ibid., pp. 338–39.

47. The California properties or brand names that Constellation owned by the time it bought the Mondavi Winery included Bisceglia, Guild, Almaden, Inglenook, Paul Masson, Taylor California Cellars, Cribari, Cook's Champagne, Deer Valley, Dunnewood, Franciscan, Mount Veeder, Simi, Estancia, and Ravenswood.

13. CATHY CORISON

1. Merry Edwards, *Meredith Vineyard Estate,* interviews by Victor Geraci (Berkeley: Regional Oral History Office, Bancroft Library, University of California, 2008), p. 32. The Edwards interviews were conducted in 2006.

2. Charles Sullivan, "More Women Making Wine Scene" (*Wine Spectator* [April 1–30, 1980]), is a good summary.

3. One should, however, credit such women as Mary Taylor, at Mayacamas, and Eleanor McCrea, at Stony Hill, who were full partners with their husbands in the building of their small but important wineries in the 1940s and 1950s.

4. Howard Goldberg, "Wine Making No Longer Male Domain," *New York Times,* July 10, 1985.

5. Edwards, *Meredith Vineyard Estate,* p. 27.

6. Both were published by the University of California Press (2004 and 2008, respectively). Haeger and Cathy Corison have stayed in touch and manage to dine together every year.

7. Unless otherwise indicated, all quotations attributed to Cathy Corison are from my notes of interviews.

8. Leon Adams, *The Wines of America* (Boston: Houghton, Mifflin, 1973). Roy Brady was even more outspoken: "One had a feeling that if a leaf were found on the drive when guests arrived there would be floggings in the slave quarters" (quoted in Thomas Pinney, *A History of Wine in America* [Berkeley: University of California Press, 2005], p. 214).

9. Edwards, *Meredith Vineyard Estate*, p. 22.

10. Thomas Pinney, "Pomona among the Vines," *Pomona Today* (Autumn 1979): 4.

11. The property was bought by Angus Wurtele in 1999 and is now operated as the Terra Valentine winery.

12. "A Grower's Winery," n.d., York Creek Vineyards web site, www.yorkcreek.com/winery/, accessed January 7, 2010.

13. The *Oxford English Dictionary*, 2nd ed., says that *hop-jack* is a variant of *hop-back*, and that a hop-back is a "vessel with a perforated bottom for straining off the hops from the liquor in the manufacture of beer."

14. See, for example, Ann B. Matasar, *Women of Wine* (Berkeley: University of California Press, 2006), pp. 88, 92, 98, 119, 165.

15. Ibid., p. 165.

16. Figures taken from Charles Sullivan, *Napa Wine*, 2nd ed. (San Francisco: Wine Appreciation Guild, 2008), 446–53.

17. This soil is alluvial, formed of rhyolitic rock of volcanic origin washed down from the mountains and gradually disintegrated. It is deep and moderately well-drained, but not rich. The famous Oakville and Rutherford Cabernet vineyards are on Bale gravelly loam.

18. "The vast majority of women interviewed for this book [there were sixty-eight of them] acknowledge that women must be better at their jobs than men in order to be deemed equal" (Matasar, *Women of Wine*, p. 13).

SOURCES AND WORKS CITED

MANUSCRIPTS

John Barden Collection, Rochester, NY
    Paul Garrett, untitled memoir, 1938
California Historical Society Library, San Francisco
    California Wine Association Papers
Cincinnati Historical Society Library
    Cincinnati Horticultural Society minutes
    Robert Buchanan scrapbook
Cornell University
    Widmer Papers
Huntington Library, San Marino, CA
    Benjamin D. Wilson Papers
Indiana State Library
    Perret Dufour, "Early History of Switzerland County," n.d.
Princeton University
    Julian Street Papers
Charles Sullivan Collection, Los Gatos, CA
    "Italian Swiss Colony: The First Half Century, 1881–1883," 1980
University of California, Berkeley, Bancroft Library
    "An Account of the Wine Business in California, from materials furnished by
    Charles Kohler," n.d., MSS C-D 111
    "Charles Kohler," n.d., MSS C-D 264
University of California, Davis, Special Collections, Shields Library
    Martin Ray Papers
    Maynard Amerine Papers
    Records of the Prohibition Administration
    Roy Brady Papers
    Viticulture and Enology Archive
Gail Unzelman Collection, Santa Rosa, CA

George Husmann autobiography, transcript, n.d.
"The Husmann Family," transcript, n.d.
Percy Morgan scrapbook
Wine Institute, San Francisco
Charles Crawford, "Vinicultural Research and the E. & J. Gallo Winery," n.p.
Irving McKee, "Historic Winegrowers of Southern California, 1850–1890," n.d.
[c. 1950?]

NEWSPAPERS AND SPECIALIZED PERIODICALS

Agricultural History
Alta California, San Francisco
American Fruit Grower
American Journal of Enology and Viticulture
American Wine Society Journal
California Farmer
Food Sciences
Food Technology
Fruit Products Journal
Grape Culturist
Journal of Food Research
Los Angeles Star
Market Watch
Modern Packaging
Pacific Wine and Spirit Review
San Francisco Bulletin
St. Helena Star
Vinifera Wine Growers Journal
Western Horticultural Review
Wayward Tendrils Quarterly
Wine and Food
Wine East
Wine Review
Wines and Vines

ORAL HISTORIES

Amerine, Maynard. *The University of California and the State's Wine Industry.* Interview by Ruth Teiser. Berkeley: Regional Oral History Office, Bancroft Library, University of California, 1972.

————. *Wine Bibliographies and Taste Perception Studies.* Interview by Ruth Teiser. Berkeley: Regional Oral History Office, Bancroft Library, University of California, 1988.

Crawford, Charles M. *Recollections of a Career with the Gallo Winery and the Development of the California Wine Industry, 1942–1989.* Interview by Ruth Teiser. Berkeley: Regional Oral History Office, Bancroft Library, University of California, 1990.

Dieppe, William. *Almadén Is My Life.* Interview by Ruth Teiser. Berkeley: Regional Oral History Office, Bancroft Library, University of California, 1985.

Edwards, Merry. *Meredith Vineyard Estate.* Interviews by Victor Geraci. Berkeley: Regional Oral History Office, Bancroft Library, University of California, 2008.

Gallo, Ernest. *The E. & J. Gallo Winery.* Interview by Ruth Teiser. Berkeley: Regional Oral History Office, Bancroft Library, University of California, 1995.

Heitz, Joseph. *Creating a Winery in the Napa Valley.* Interview by Ruth Teiser. Berkeley: Regional Oral History Office, Bancroft Library, University of California, 1986.

Joslyn, Maynard. *A Technologist Views the California Wine Industry.* Interview by Ruth Teiser. Berkeley: Regional Oral History Office, Bancroft Library, University of California, 1974.

Knowles, Legh F. *Beaulieu Vineyards from Family to Corporate Ownership.* Interview by Lisa Jacobson. Berkeley: Regional Oral History Office, Bancroft Library, University of California, 1990.

Long, Zelma. *The Past Is the Beginning of the Future: Simi Winery in Its Second Century.* Interview by Carol Hicke. Berkeley: Regional Oral History Office, Bancroft Library, University of California, 1992.

Martini, Louis M. *Wine Making in the Napa Valley.* Interview by Ruth Teiser. Berkeley: Regional Oral History Office, Bancroft Library, University of California, 1973.

Mondavi, Peter. *Advances in Technology and Production at Charles Krug, 1946–1988.* Interview by Ruth Teiser. Berkeley: Regional Oral History Office, Bancroft Library, University of California, 1990.

Mondavi, Robert. *Creativity in the California Wine Industry.* Interview by Ruth Teiser. Berkeley: Regional Oral History Office, Bancroft Library, University of California, 1985.

Olmo, H.P. *Plant Genetics and New Grape Varieties.* Interview by Ruth Teiser. Berkeley: Regional Oral History Office, Bancroft Library, University of California, 1992.

Webb, R. Bradford. *Brad Webb: Innovator.* Interview by William Heintz. Healdsburg, CA: Sonoma County Wine Library Oral History, 1991.

Winkler, A.J. *Viticultural Research at University of California, Davis, 1921–1971.* Interview by Ruth Teiser. Berkeley: Regional Oral History Office, Bancroft Library, University of California, 1973.

Adams, Leon. *The Wines of America.* Boston: Houghton, Mifflin, 1973, 2nd ed.; New York: McGraw-Hill, 1978.

Alley, Lynn, Deborah Golino, and Andrew Walker. "Retrospective on California Grapevine Materials, Part I." *Wines and Vines* 81 (November 2000): 148–52.

Ambers, Rebecca R. K., and Clifford P. Ambers. "Dr. Daniel Norborne Norton and the Origin of the Norton Grape." *American Wine Society Journal* (Fall 2004): 77–87.

Amerine, Maynard. "The Acids of California Grapes and Wines. I. Lactic Acid." *Food Technology* 4 (May 1950): 177–81.

———. "The Acids of California Grapes and Wines. II. Malic Acid." *Food Technology* 5 (January 1951): 13–16.

———. "An Application of 'Triangular' Taste Testing to Wines." *Wine Review* 16 (May 1948): 10–12.

———. "Bordeaux and Burgundy." *Wine and Food,* no. 67 (1950): 166–68.

———. *A Check List of Books and Pamphlets in English on Grapes and Wines, and Related Subjects, 1960–68, with a Supplement for 1949–1959.* Davis: University of California, 1969.

———. "The Composition of Wines." *Scientific Monthly* 77 (May 1953): 250–54.

———. "Edmund Henri Twight—1874–1957." *Wines and Vines* 38 (May 1957): 31.

———. "The Educated Enologist." *Proceedings of the American Society of Enologists* (1951): 1–30.

———. "An Historical Note on Grape Prices." *Wines and Vines* 27 (October 1946): 28–29.

———. "Hydroxymethylfurfural in California Wines." *Journal of Food Research* 13 (March 1948): 264–69.

———. "The Influence of the Constituents of Wines on Taste and Application to the Judging of Commercial Wines." In *Proceedings of the Wine Technical Conference,* pp. 21–24. Davis: University of California, Division of Viticulture, 1949.

———. "A Matter of Taste." *Wines and Vines* 31 (September 1950): 35–36.

———. *A Short Check List of Books and Pamphlets in English on Grapes, Wines, and Related Subjects, 1949–1959.* Davis: University of California, 1959.

———. "Some Early Books about the California Wine Industry." *Book Club of California Quarterly News Letter* 16 (March 1951): 51–56.

———. *Vermouth: An Annotated Bibliography.* Publication 4055. Richmond, CA: Division of Agricultural Sciences, University of California, 1974.

———. "Wine Judging Methods." *Wine Review* 7 (October 1939): 6, 20.

Amerine, Maynard, and Axel Borg. *A Bibliography on Grapes, Wines, and Other Alcoholic Beverages, and Temperance: Works Published in the United States before 1901.* Berkeley: University of California Press, 1996.

Amerine, Maynard, and Maynard Joslyn. *Commercial Production of Table Wines.* Bulletin no. 639. Berkeley: University of California, College of Agriculture, Agricultural Experiment Station, 1940.

———. *Dessert, Appetizer, and Related Flavored Wines: The Technology of Their Production.* Berkeley: University of California, Division of Agricultural Sciences, 1964.

———. *Table Wines: The Technology of Their Production in California.* Berkeley: University of California Press, 1951.

Amerine, Maynard, and Herman J. Phaff. *A Bibliography of Publications by the Faculty, Staff, and Students of the University of California, 1876–1980, on Grapes, Wine, and Related Subjects.* Berkeley: University of California Press, 1986.

Amerine, Maynard, and Edward B. Roessler. "Techniques and Problems in the Organoleptic Examination of Wines." *Proceedings of the American Society of Enologists* (1952): 97–115.

———. *Wines: Their Sensory Evaluation.* San Francisco: W. H. Freeman, 1976.

Amerine, Maynard, and Vernon L. Singleton. *A List of Bibliographies and a Selected List of Publications That Contain Bibliographies on Grapes, Wines, and Related Subjects.* Berkeley: Agricultural Publications, University of California, 1971.

———. *Wine: An Introduction for Americans.* Berkeley: University of California Press, 1965.

Amerine, Maynard, and Louise Wheeler. *A Check List of Books and Pamphlets on Grapes and Wine and Related Subjects, 1938–1948.* Berkeley: University of California Press, 1951.

Amerine, Maynard, and A. J. Winkler. "Composition and Quality of Musts and Wines of California Grapes." *Hilgardia* 15 (February 1944): 493–573.

———. "Maturity Studies with California Grapes. 1. The Balling-Acid Ratio of Wine Grapes." *Proceedings of the American Society of Horticultural Science* 38 (1940): 379–87.

———. "Maturity Studies with California Grapes. II. The Titratable Acidity, pH, and Organic Acid Content." *Proceedings of the American Society of Horticultural Science* 40 (1942): 313–24.

Anthony, R. D. *Vinifera Grapes in New York.* Bulletin no. 432. Geneva: New York Agricultural Experiment Station, 1917.

Bailey, Liberty Hyde. *Sketch of the Evolution of Our Native Fruits.* New York: Macmillan, 1898.

Brady, Roy. "Alta California's First Vintage." In *The University of California/Sotheby Book of California Wine,* edited by Doris Muscatine, Maynard Amerine, and Bob Thompson, pp. 10–15. Berkeley: University of California Press, 1984.

———. *The Brady Book: Selections from Roy Brady's Unpublished Writings on Wine.* Santa Rosa, CA: Nomis Press, 2003.

Brown, Anitra S. "The Genius of Gallo." *Market Watch* (May 1988).

Buchanan, Robert. *The Culture of the Grape, and Wine-Making.* Cincinnati: Moore and Anderson, 1852.

Butler, James L., and John J. Butler. *Indiana Wine.* Bloomington: Indiana University Press, 2001.

California State Agricultural Society Transactions, 1859. Sacramento: State Printer, 1860.

California Wine Association. *Compliments of California Wine Association.* San Francisco: California Wine Association, January 1896.

Carosso, Vincent. *The California Wine Industry, 1830–1895.* Berkeley: University of California Press, 1951.

Cathey, C.O. "Sidney Weller: Ante-Bellum Promoter of Agricultural Reform." *North Carolina Historical Review* 31 (January 1954): 1–17.

Cattell, Hudson. "Dr. Konstantin Frank Dies at Age 86." *Wine East* (November–December 1985): 4–5, 21.

Cist, Charles. *Sketches and Statistics of Cincinnati in 1851.* Cincinnati: Wm. H. Moore and Co., 1851.

Claiborne, Craig. "The Wine Connoisseur from Spearfish, S.D." *New York Times,* March 17, 1966.

Clark, Norman H. *Deliver Us from Evil: An Interpretation of American Prohibition.* New York: W. W. Norton, 1976.

Clifford, William. "New York Wine Comes of Age." *Holiday* (May 1968).

Cook, Michael L., and Bettie A. Cook. *Kentucky Court of Appeals Deed Books, A–G.* Vol. 1. Evansville, IN: Cook Publications, 1985.

Dabney, Virginius. *Dry Messiah.* New York: Knopf, 1949.

Duden, Gottfried. *Report on a Journey to the Western States of America and a Stay of Several Years along the Missouri (during the Years 1824, '25, '26, and 1827).* Columbia: State Historical Society of Missouri, 1980.

Dufour, John James. *The American Vine-Dresser's Guide, Being a Treatise on the Cultivation of the Vine, and the Process of Wine Making, Adapted to the Soil and Climate of the United States.* Cincinnati: S.J. Browne, 1826.

Dufour, Perret. *The Swiss Settlement of Switzerland County, Indiana.* Edited by Harlow Lindley. Indianapolis: Indiana Historical Commission, 1925.

Gabler, James M. *Wine into Words: A History and Bibliography of Wine Books in the English Language.* 2nd ed. Baltimore: Bacchus Press, 2004.

Gohdes, Clarence. *Scuppernong: North Carolina's Grape and Its Wines.* Durham, NC: Duke University Press, 1982.

Flagg, William J. "Wine in America and American Wine." *Harper's New Monthly Magazine* 41 (June 1870): 106–14.

Florence, Jack W. *Legacy of a Village: Italian Swiss Colony Winery and the People of Asti, California.* Phoenix, AZ: Raymond Court Press, 1999.

Fournier, Charles. "Birth of a New York State Pinot Chardonnay." *Wines and Vines* 42 (January 1961): 32.

———. "A Scientific Look at Vinifera in the East." *Wines and Vines* 42 (August 1961): 27–29.

Frank, Konstantin. "The Phylloxera Menace in Vineyards." *American Fruit Grower* (May 1954): 36–37.

Friis, Leo J. *John Fröhling: Vintner and City Founder.* Anaheim, CA: Mother Colony Household, 1976.

Gallo, Ernest, and Julio Gallo, with Bruce B. Henderson. *Ernest and Julio: Our Story.* New York: Times Books, 1994.

Garrett, Paul. "The Right to Make Fruit Juices." *California Grape Grower* 4 (July 1923): 2–3.

Gordon, Jim, Linda Jones McKee, and Hudson Cattell. "Wines That Changed the Industry." *Wines and Vines* 90 (January 2009): 39–44.

Great Exhibition, London. *Official Descriptive and Illustrated Catalogue of the Great Exhibition.* 3 vols. London: Spicer Brothers, 1851.

Haeger, John. *North American Pinot Noir.* Berkeley: University of California Press, 2004.

———. *Pacific Pinot Noir.* Berkeley: University of California Press, 2008.

Hargrave, Louisa Thomas. *The Vineyard: The Pleasures and Perils of Creating an American Family Winery.* New York: Viking, 2003.

Hart, James D. *A Companion to California.* New ed. Berkeley: University of California Press, 1987.

Hawkes, Ellen. *Blood and Wine: The Unauthorized Story of the Gallo Wine Empire.* New York: Simon and Schuster, 1993.

Heintz, William. *California's Napa Valley.* San Francisco: Scottwall Associates, 1999.

Husmann, George. *American Grape Growing and Wine Making.* New York: Orange Judd, 1880.

———. *The Cultivation of the Native Grape and the Manufacture of American Wines.* New York: George E. and F. W. Woodward, 1866.

———. "First Annual Report." In *Missouri State Board of Agriculture, Second Annual Report, 1866.* Jefferson City, MO: Emory Foster, 1867.

———. *Grape Culture and Wine-Making in California.* San Francisco: Payot, Upham and Co., 1888.

———. "The Present Condition of Grape Culture in California." In *Yearbook of the Department of Agriculture, 1898.* Washington, DC: Government Printing Office, 1899.

———. "Wine Making in Napa Valley." In *Transactions of the California State Agricultural Society,* pp. 154–57. Sacramento: State Printer, 1883.

Husmann, George C., Elmer Snyder, and Frederick L. Husmann. *Testing Vinifera Grape Varieties Grafted on Phylloxera-Resistant Rootstocks in California.* USDA Technical Bulletin no. 697. Washington, DC: Government Printing Office, 1939.

Hutchison, John. "Maynard Amerine: Wine Man of the Year." *Wines and Vines* 70 (March 1989): 18–19, 20–21.

Iscoff, Ron. "Malibu's Wine Making M.D.'s." *Medical Sporting News* (November–December 1971): 41–43.

Johnson, Hugh. Foreword to *Frank Schoonmaker's Encyclopedia of Wine,* by Frank Schoonmaker. London: Nelson, 1967.

Joslyn, Maynard, and Maynard Amerine. *Commercial Production of Brandies.* Bulletin no. 652. Berkeley: University of California, College of Agriculture, Agricultural Experiment Station, 1941.

———. *Commercial Production of Dessert Wines.* Bulletin no. 651. Berkeley: University of California, College of Agriculture, Agricultural Experiment Station, 1941.

Kimball, Keith H. "Another Look at Vinifera in the East." *Wines and Vines* 42 (April 1961): 63–64, 67.

Kolbenschlag, Michael. "Wineman Frank Schoonmaker." *Wine World* (January–February 1976): 20–23, 36.

Kressman, Edouard. *The Wonder of Wine.* New York: Hastings House, 1968.

Lapsley, James. *Bottled Poetry: Napa Winemaking from Prohibition to the Modern Era.* Berkeley: University of California Press, 1996.

Levasseur, Auguste. *Lafayette in America in 1824 and 1825.* Translated by John D. Godman. Philadelphia: Carey and Lea, 1829.

Lindley, Harlow, ed. *Indiana as Seen by Early Travellers.* Indianapolis: Indiana Historical Commission, 1916.

Longworth, Nicholas. "The Grape and Manufacture of Wine." In *Western Agriculturist and Practical Farmer's Guide.* Cincinnati: Robinson and Fairbank, 1830.

———. Letter to the editor. *American Agriculturist* 9 (1850).

———. *A Letter from N. Longworth to the Members of the Cincinnati Horticultural Society on the Cultivation of the Grape, and the Manufacture of Wine.* Cincinnati: L'Hommedieu and Co., 1846.

———. "On the Cultivation of the Grape, and Manufacture of Wine." In *Report of the Commissioner of Patents.* Washington, DC: Government Printing Office, 1847.

———. "The Process of Wine-Making on the Ohio." *Horticulturist* 4 (1850).

Longworth's Wine House. Cincinnati: Longworth, n.d. [c. 1864].

Lukacs, Paul. *The Great Wines of America: The Top Forty Vintners, Vineyards, and Vintages.* New York: Norton, 2005.

Mackay, Charles. "The Queen City of the West." *Illustrated London News,* March 20, 1858, 295–97.

Magness, J. R., and J. W. Dix. *Vinifera Grapes in the East.* USDA, Bureau of Plant Industry. Washington, DC: Government Printing Office, March 1934. Mimeographed report.

Marinacci, Barbara. "Julian Street and Martin Ray, 1939–1947, Part II." *Wayward Tendrils Quarterly* 14 (April 2004): S1–S15.

Matasar, Ann B. *Women of Wine: The Rise of Women in the Global Wine Industry.* Berkeley: University of California Press, 2006.

Matthews, Patrick. *Real Wine: The Rediscovery of Natural Winemaking.* London: Mitchell Beazley, 2000.

McKee, Irving. "Jean Paul [sic] Vignes, California's First Professional Winegrower." *Agricultural History* 22 (July 1948): 176–80.

Mechanics' Institute. *Report of the 11th Industrial Exhibition.* San Francisco, n.p., 1876.

Mencken, H. L. *The New Mencken Letter.* Edited by Carl Bode. New York: Dial Press, 1977.

Michaux, François André. *Travels to the Westward of the Allegany Mountains.* London: B. Crosby, 1805.

Mondavi, Robert, and Paul Chutkow. *Harvests of Joy: My Passion for Excellence.* New York: Harcourt, Brace and Co., 1998.

Morton, Lucie. "An Update on Virginia Viticulture." *Wines and Vines* 62 (October 1981): 47–50.

Muehl, Siegfried. "Winegrowing in the Hermann Area." *Missouri Historical Review* 87 (1993): 233–52.

Muench, Friedrich. *School for American Grape Culture.* Saint Louis, MO: Conrad Witter, 1865.

Muscatine, Doris, Maynard Amerine, and Bob Thompson, eds. *The University of California / Sotheby Book of California Wine.* Berkeley: University of California Press, 1984.

Music of the Gold Rush Era, vol. 1 of *History of Music in San Francisco,* ed. Cornell Adam Lengyel. San Francisco: Works Progress Administration, Northern California, 1939.

Newmark, Harris. *Sixty Years in Southern California, 1853–1913.* Los Angeles: Zeitlin and Verbrugge, 1970.

Pellegrini, Angelo. *Americans by Choice.* New York: Macmillan, 1956.

Peninou, Ernest, and Gail Unzelman. *The California Wine Association and Its Member Wineries, 1894–1920.* Santa Rosa: Nomis Press, 2000.

Pinney, Thomas. *A History of Wine in America: From the Beginnings to Prohibition.* Berkeley: University of California Press, 1989.

———. *A History of Wine in America: From Prohibition to the Present.* Berkeley: University of California Press, 2005.

———. "Pomona among the Vines." *Pomona Today* (Autumn 1979): 2–7, 30–34.

Prial, Frank. "They Labor Well in New York's Vineyards." *New York Times,* April 18, 1973.

Raup, Hallock F. *The German Colonization of Anaheim, California.* Berkeley: University of California Press, 1932.

Ray, Cyril. *Robert Mondavi of the Napa Valley.* London: Heinemann/Peter Davies, 1984.

Robinson, Jancis. *Vines, Grapes, and Wines: The Wine Drinker's Guide to Grape Varieties.* London: Mitchell Beazley, 1986.

Sbarboro, Andrea. *The Fight for True Temperance.* San Francisco: n.p., 1908.

———. [Life of Andrea Sbarboro]. N.d. [c. 1910–11]. Published as "Andrea Sbarboro: An Early American Success Story: The Memoir of an Italian-American Entrepreneur and Pioneer," ed. Heather Wheeler. *The Argonaut: Journal of the San Francisco Historical Society* 7 (Winter 1996–97): [1]–96.

———. *Temperance versus Prohibition.* San Francisco: H.S. Crocker, 1909.

———. *Wine as a Remedy for the Evil of Intemperance.* Hanford, CA: n.p., 1906.

Schoonmaker, Frank. "California vs. Imported." *Wines and Vines* 37 (December 1956): 24.

———. *Frank Schoonmaker's Encyclopedia of Wine.* New York: Hastings House, 1964.

———. "The Future of Quality Wine." *Wines and Vines* 26 (December 1945): 21, 37.

———."New Decalogues of Drinking." *Saturday Review* 11 (November 3, 1934): 253, 260–61.

———. *The Wines of Germany.* New York: Hastings House, 1956.

Schoonmaker, Frank, and Tom Marvel. *American Wines.* New York: Duell, Sloan and Pearce, 1941.

———. *The Complete Wine Book.* New York: Simon and Schuster, 1934.

Shaulis, Nelson, John Einset, and A. Boyd Pack. *Growing Cold-Tender Grape Varieties in New York.* Bulletin no. 821. Geneva, NY: New York State Agricultural Experiment Station, 1968.

Siler, Julia Flynn. *The House of Mondavi.* New York: Gotham Books, 2007.

Singleton, Vernon. "Maynard Andrew Amerine: Recollections about an Extraordinary Man." *Wayward Tendrils Quarterly* 8 (July 1998): 10–11.

Statutes at Large of the United States of America, 1789–1873. 17 vols. Washington, DC, 1850–73.

Stevens, Linda Walker. "In Vinous Vein: George Husmann in Print." *Wayward Tendrils Quarterly* 8 (July 1998): 1–5.

———. "The Making of a Superior Immigrant: George Husmann, 1837–1854." *Missouri Historical Review* 89 (January 1995): 119–38.

———. "The Story of Wine at Hermann." *Missouri Folklore Society Journal* 21 (1999): 25–42.

———. *What Wondrous Life: The World of George Husmann.* Hermann, MO: Hermann University Press, 2002.

Stoewsand, G. S., and W. B. Robinson. "Review of Grape and Wine Toxicity Research." *Food Sciences* 6 (January 1971).

Sullivan, Charles. *A Companion to California Wine.* Berkeley: University of California Press, 1998.

———. "The Great Wine Quake." *Wayward Tendrils Quarterly* 16 (January–July 2006): January, pp. 1–6; April, pp. 1–10; July, pp. 16–19.

———. "Los Angeles Wine, 1850–1870." *Wayward Tendrils Quarterly* 21 (October 2011): 25–26.

———. "More Women Making Wine Scene." *Wine Spectator* (April 1–30, 1980).

———. *Napa Wine: A History from Mission Days to the Present.* 2nd ed. San Francisco: Wine Appreciation Guild, 2008.

———. "U.C. Grapes and Wine," pt. 3. *Wayward Tendrils Quarterly* 19 (April 2009): 19–27.

Trollope, Frances. *Domestic Manners of the Americans.* 5th ed. 1832. Reprint, New York: Dodd, Mead, 1927.

Trotter, Isabella. *First Impressions of the New World on Two Travellers from the Old.* London: Longman, 1859.

Tucker, Louis Leonard. "'Old Nick' Longworth: The Paradoxical Maecenas of Cincinnati." *Bulletin of the Cincinnati Historical Society* 25 (1967): 246–59.

United States Congress. Senate. Committee on Finance. *Hearings on the Liquor Tax Administration Act, 13, 15, 16 January 1936.* Washington, DC: Government Printing Office, 1936.

United States Department of Agriculture. *Annual Report, 1868.* Washington, DC: Government Printing Office, 1869.

———. *Yearbook of the Department of Agriculture, 1898.* Washington, DC: Government Printing Office, 1889.

University of California, College of Agriculture. *Report of the Viticultural Work during the Seasons 1887–93.* Sacramento: A. J. Johnston, Superintendent of State Printing, 1896.

Von Daacke, John. "'Sparkling Catawba': Grape Growing and Wine Making in Cincinnati, 1800–1870." Master's thesis, University of Cincinnati, 1964.

Van Dyne, Ed. "Dr. Konstantin Frank: A Retrospective." *American Wine Society Journal* 24 (Fall 1992): 77–80.

Wagner, Philip. *American Wines and How to Make Them.* New York: Knopf, 1933.

———. *American Wines and Wine Making.* New York: Knopf, 1956.

———. *A Wine-Grower's Guide.* New York: Knopf, 1945.

Wasserman, Sheldon, and Pauline Wasserman. "Can't Be Done, but Dr. Frank Does." *Wine Spectator* (November 1–15, 1978): 12.

Wechsberg, Joseph. "A Dreamer of Wine." *New Yorker* 33 (May 17, 1958).

Winemaster: The Dr. Konstantin Frank Story. Amsterdam, NY: Noteworthy Co., 1983.

Winkler, A. J. *General Viticulture.* Berkeley: University of California Press, 1962.

INDEX

Acampo Winery, 217, 219, 220

Acero, Italy, 76

Adams, Leon, 207, 241

Adlum, John, 25, 26

Adulteration of wine, 28, 101, 120

Aestivalis, American native grape species, 51, 202

Agricultural Marketing Act, 122

Aguardiente, 153

Aguilar, Cristobal, 61

Ainsworth, Fanny, Mrs. Percy Morgan, 91

Alabama, xvii

Alexander I, of Russia, 195, 196

Alexander grape, 12, 13, 17, 18, 19, 21, 24, 26, 27, 43

Alexander, James, 13

Alexander Valley Winery, 98

Algeria, 184, 191

Algiers, 164

Alicante Bouschet grape, 134, 157, 176, 179

Allentown, PA, 45

All-Union Academy of Agricultural Sciences, 197

Almadén Vineyards, 160, 242; and Frank Schoonmaker, 162–163, 164, 165, 166, 167, 169

Alsace, 157

Alta California, San Francisco, 61, 65, 69, 70

Amateur Musical Club, San Francisco, 59, 65

American Center for Wine, Food and the Arts, 232

American Institute of Wine and Food, 232

American Society for Enology and Viticulture, 187, 191, 232

American Society of Enologists, 187

American Vineyard Foundation, 184

American Wine Company, 39

American Wine Growers Association, 35, 37

American Winegrowers' Association, 107

American Wine Press, 54

American Wine Society, 191–192, 210–211, 232

Amerine, Maynard, 163, 172, 175*fig.,* 179, 189, 238, 242; achievement, 192; army career, 183, 184–185; bibliographies, 187; *Check List of Books and Pamphlets in English on Grapes and Wines,* 187; "Composition and Quality of Musts and Wines of California Grapes," 178–180, 183; cook and host, 181, 279n26; criticizes California winemakers, 188–189; early years, 174; on Golden Age of wine, 192–193; learns about wine, 177; publications, 181, 185–187; receives honors, 191–192; research work, 183; as speaker, 191; *Table Wines,* 187, 188, 189; varietal project, 174–175, 176, 178–180; variety of interests, 180; visits France, 181–182; *Wine: An Introduction for Americans,* 191; wine judgings, 181, 281n49; wine tasting, 186; *Wines: Their Sensory Evaluation,* 186; writes official bulletins on winemaking, 182–183

Anaheim: 66–67; devastated by disease, 68

Anaheim disease. *See* Pierce's disease

Anaheim Wine Growers' Association, 67

Anchor Steam Beer brewery, 246

Angelica wine, 63, 65, 66, 70

Anti-Saloon League, 86–87, 88, 89, 120, 121

Anti-scientific reaction in wine making, 193–194

Antill, Edward, xviii

Antioch, CA, 133

Argentina, 148

Arkansas, xvii, prohibition in, 113, 116, 117, 120

Arlington Experiment Station, 199

Arminius, 40

Arnsberg, Westphalia, 62

Asheville, NC, 25

Asti, CA, 79, 80, 81, 85, community at, 84

Athens, 2

Atlanta, 125

Aurora grape, 213

Australia, xv, 69, 148, 192, 234

Austria, 148

Aves, Fred, 243, 244

AxR#1 rootstock, 233, 249

Bacchus, 17, 58, 93

Bacigalupi, H., 127

Baco grapes, 213

Baden, Germany, 60

Bailey, Clare, 189

Baldface Creek, 27

Bale gravelly loam, 249, 250, 251

Baltimore, 4, 8, 202

Baltimore, Lord, xvii

Bank of America, 78, 106, 127

Barber, Cheryl, 237

Barbera grape, 80, 137, 138

Barden, John, xi

Barden, Polly, xi

Barrel ageing, 146

Barrels, research on, 228

Barrett, Heidi Peterson, 247

Bates and Schoonmaker, firm, 154

Baudoin, Raymond, 152, 153, 155

Baum, Martin, 27

Bavaria, 198

Beaulieu Vineyard, 127, 218, 221, 223, 224, 225, 234

Beaune, 152

Beethoven, Ludwig van, 59

Belgium, 151

Bellini, Vicenzo, *La sonnambula,* 58

Benoist, Louis, 162, 163, 164, 165, 169

Beringer Brothers Winery, 218, 222

Berkley, VA, 116

Berlandieri, American native grape species, 202

Bespaloff, Alex, 168

Bettens family, 9, 10

Beutler, John, 60, 61

Bioletti, Frederic, 172, 199

Bisceglia Brothers, 75

Bisson, Linda, 238

Blackberry wine, 114, 115

Black rot (Guignardia bidwelli), xv, xvi, 36, 43, described, 12

Blauer Portugieser grape, 199

Blossom Prairie, TX, 112, 119

Bluffton, MO, 47

Bluffton Wine Company, 45, 47, 49, 55

Bohemian Club, 181, 191

Bolling, Robert, xviii

Bollinger, Mme. Elizabeth, 236

Bolsheviks, 196

Boone's Farm Apple Wine, 144

Boordy Vineyard, 202

Boralley family, 9

Bordeaux, 15, 152, 155, 157, 173, 182, 224

Bordeaux mixture, xvi, 12, 36

Borel, Antoine, 99

Borg, Axel, xi

Bottlers, wine, 119, 129–130, 219

Bottles and Bins, 222

Brady, Roy, 151, 160, 166–168

Brailow, Alexander, 205

Brand names, 80, 83–84, 102, 118

Brandy, 65; for fortification, 63, 129, 246

Brewers, Wine and Spirit Merchants of Virginia, 120

Bright's Winery, 205

Brinkleyville, NC, 108

Brooklyn, NYC, 120

Brooklyn Bridge, 198

Brun and Chaix Winery, 98

Buchanan, Robert, 35

Buen Retiro, 84, 86

Cork-finished wine, 146
Cornell School of Hospitality, 232
Cornell Society of Hotelmen, 232
Cornell University, 131
Cornishmen, 215
Corton, 161
Cotten, Sallie Southall, 118
Couderc, Georges, 202
Covington, KY, 219
Crabb, Hamilton W., 52, 73, 229, 234
Crawford, Charles, 131, 135, 136, 140
Cremorne locks, 250
Cresta Blanca Winery, 219
Cribari, Beniamino, 89, 127
Cribari Winery,132
Croatia, 148
Croatians, 215
Crosby, Everett, 213
Cruess, William Vere, 135, 173, 181, 221
Cucamonga, 158
Custom crushing, 244–245
Czechs, 215

D'Angerville, Jacques, Marquis, 154
Daniel, John, Jr., 218, 285n5
Davis, Jill, 237
Decanter magazine, 232
De Latour, Georges, 129
Delaware grape, xvi, 116, 159, 199, 201
Denver, 252
De Turk, Isaac, 73
Diamond grape, 159
Diana grape, 201
Dickens, Charles, *Great Expectations,* 65
Dinwiddie, Dr. E.C., 121, 123
Disneyland, 66
Dnieper River, 196
Domaine Chandon, 237
Domaine Roulot Meursault-Charmes, 227
Dowdell Winery, 73
Downy mildew (*Plasmopara viticola*), xv,
    xvi, described, 36
Dresel, Julius, 52
Dreyfus, Benjamin, 67
Dreyfus, Benjamin, and Co. 92
Dry Creek Valley, 146
Duden, Gottfried, 39
Dufour, Antoinette, 9, 10

Dufour, Daniel Vincent, 4, 15, 20
Dufour, Jean Jacques, the elder, 4, 8
Dufour, Jeanne Marie, 9
Dufour, John Daniel, 9
Dufour, John David, 9, 14, 15
Dufour, John Francis, 9, 14, 15, 20
Dufour, John James (Jean Jacques Dufour),
    xiii, xvii, xviii, 22, 24, 195; *American
    Vine Dresser's Guide,* 3, 21; and Alexan-
    der grape, 12–13; arrival in U.S., 1–6; and
    Kentucky Vineyard Society, 6–14; and
    New Switzerland, 9–11; returns to Swit-
    zerland, 14–15; returns to U.S., 19–20
Dufour, Mrs. John James, 4, 9, 15, 20
Dufour, Marguerite, 9
Dufour, Perret, 2
Dufour, Suzanne, 9
Dun and Bradstreet, 163
Durif (Petit Sirah) grape, 144
Dutchess grape, xvi, 204
Dyer, Dawnine, 237

Eagle Wine Vaults, San Francisco, 94
Economy, PA, 19
Edward Young, brig, 15
Edwards, Meredith, 236, 237, 238, 242, 247
Elk Grove Winery, 219
Elvira grape, 159, 201
"Empire of Bacchus, The," ode, 16
Engels and Krudwig Winery, 159
England, 69
Englemann, Dr. George, 39
Enologists, 131, 136, 187, 188, 192
Ensrud, Barbara, 238
Épernay, 30
Escalon, CA, 133
Escapernong wine, 115
Esterer, Arnulf, 209
Étude winery, 245
E. T. Willets, clipper ship, 69
Eureka College, 150

Fabrès, Oscar, 166
Fairbanks Trucking Company, 138
Farmer's Club, American Institute, 66
Fayetteville, NC, 117
Federal Farm Board, 122, 123
Federal Rehabilitation Agency, 125

Federal Trade Commission, 141, 142
Fête des Vignerons, 1, 2*fig.*
Ficklin Vineyards, 225
Finns, 215
Firestone Vineyard, 237
First Vineyard, 8, 10, 11, 15, 256n11; wine from,14; abandoned, 16
Flint, Timothy, 17
Florida, 211
Folle Blanche wine, 160
Foppiano, Louis, 75, 89
Fortune magazine, 108, 124
Fountain Grove Winery, 157, 160
Fournier, winemaker, 30
Fournier, Charles, 200, 201–202, 203, 204, 205
Fourth Regiment, Missouri Volunteers, 45
Foxy taste, 17, 25
France, 50, 69, 78, 132, 148, 153, 156, 191, 192 Amerine visits, 181–182; Schoonmaker in, 150–151
Franciscans, xvii
Franek and Co., 130
Frank, Frederick, 214
Frank, Konstantin, 197*fig.*, 210, 213; and American Wine Society, 210–211; designs vineyard plow, 197–198; establishes winery, 205–206; hired at N.Y. State Agricultural Experiment Station, 200; life in Russia, 195–198; "Protection of Grapes from Freezing Damage," 197, 203; rejects French hybrid grapes, 197, 203, 211; research at Gold Seal, 200–205
Frank, Willibald, 214
Frank Schoonmaker and Co., 154, 156, 160, 163, 164
Franklin, Benjamin, xvii
Freemark Abbey Winery, 241–242
Frei Brothers Winery, 127, 136, bought by Gallo, 146
French, in San Francisco, 64
French Colombard grape, 137
French *grand cru* wine, 228
French hybrid grapes, xvi, 197, 202, 203, 209, 210, 213, alleged to be toxic, 211
French hybrid wine, 203
French oak, 146
French Revolution, 4

Fresh grape market, 134–135
Fresno, CA, 83, 127, 136, 237
Fresno Vineyard Co., 98
Fried, Eunice, 238
Friends of the Los Angeles Junior Arts Society, 191
Fröhling, John, 60, 65; and Anaheim, 66; death, 67, 70; winemaker in Los Angeles, 61–64
Fruit Industries, 122, 124, 127
Fruit wines, 114
F.S. Importing Co., 165, 166
Fulton Winery, Italian Swiss Colony, 83, 85
Fumé Blanc (Sauvignon blanc) wine, 224
Furness, Elizabeth, 209

Gabler, James, 166
Gaiter, Dorothy, 238
Gall, Dr. Ludwig, 46, 51
Gallegos, Juan, 195
Gallizing, 46, 53
Gallo, Ernest, xiii, 75, 89, 169, 192, 225; achievement, 117, 148; builds glass factory, 138; character, 147; commitment to research, 136–137; controls distribution, 138–142; develops brand, 129–130; encourages planting of superior varieties, 138; enters wine business, 127–128, 135; expands markets, 142- 145; sales enterprise, 128, 129, 134, 135, 139–140; sells grapes in Chicago market, 134–135; varietal wines, 146
Gallo-ette, 143
Gallo Family Vineyards, 146
Gallo, Giuseppe (Joe), 133, 134, 135
Gallo, Julio, 127, 135, 136, 169, 174, conducts varietal studies, 136–137; on consistency, 140
Gallo wine, poor image of, 146; sales, 129, 132, 133, 139
Gallo Wineries, 118, 222; capacity, 132; Fresno, 132; Livingston, 132; Modesto, 128, 129, 132, 133, 138, 146, 147
Gamay grape, 220, 227
Gamay Beaujolais grape, 206
Gamay rosé wine, 224–225
Gamay wine, 221

Jaeger, Herman, 40, 50
Jamestown, VA, xv
Japan, 191
Jefferson, Thomas, xvii, 8, 14, 87
Jerez, 157
Jesuits, 5, 6, 39
Johnson and Wales University, 232
Johnson, Hugh, 168, 170
Johnson, William "Pussyfoot," xviii
Joslyn, Maynard, 177, 182, 183, 187
Judgment of Paris, 227
Jura, 26

Kansas, 49
Kansas City, 123
Kaskaskia, IL, 5, 6
Keller, Matthew, 195
Kentucky, 6, 21, 68
Kentucky Gazette, 6
Kentucky River, 8, 10
Kentucky Vineyard Society, 6–14, 21
Kesselstatt, Counts of, 167
Keuka Lake, 120, 125, 200, 203, 205
Kielmann, C.W., 45
Kielmann, Louisa, 45
Kingsburg, CA, Italian Swiss Colony winery at, 85
Klein, Mia
Knowland, Joseph, 57
Knowles, Leigh, 141
Kohler, Hans, 74
Kohler, Charles, xiii, 52, 90, 195; and Anaheim, 66–67; directs Kohler and Frohling, 63–74; early success, 64; high achievement, 73, 74; makes California wine available, 69–70; musical career, 58–59
Kohler, Charles, Jr., 74
Kohler and Frohling, firm, 52, 94–95; beginnings, 61–64; bottles for, 71; cellars, 94; contract for army and navy hospitals, 71; distribution of wines, 69–70, 71; foreign agencies of, 70; headquarters in San Francisco, 74; joins California Wine Association, 74, 92; moves to northern California, 71–72; new winery in Los Angeles, 73; plan for Anaheim, 66–67; promotion, 64–65; wine types, 65, 70

Kohler and Van Bergen, 90, 92, 94
Korbel Brothers, 160, 163, 165
Kosher wine, 199
Kressman, Edouard, 152
Kressman, firm, 182
Kronos Vineyard, 250–251
Krug, Charles, 58, 73, 219
Krug, Charles, Winery, 220, 225, 229, sold to Mondavis, 219; successful renewal, 220–223

Labels, wine: Dr.Frank's, 207; misleading, 83, 130, 153, 156, 188. *See also* Varietal wine labeling
Labrusca, American native grape species, 205
La Cantina, N.Y., 85
Lachman and Jacobi, firm, 90, 95, 98
Lachman, S., and Co., 90, 92, 94
La Côte, Switzerland, 1
Lake Erie vineyards, 37–38
Lake Geneva, 1
Landot, Pierre, 202
Landsberger, Isador, 58
Langbehn, Larry, 241, 242
Langendoerfer, August, 44
Lantarnam Hall, 105
Lanza, H.O., 127
Lapsley, James, 223
La Questa, 234
La Revue du Vin de France, 152, 153
Larkmead Winery, 127, 157, 218
Lawrence, Robert de Treville, 210
Lead, Dufour buys, 6
League of Women Voters, 150
Legaux, Pierre, 5, 195; and Alexander grape, 8, 12
Legion of Honor, 232
Le Havre, 1, 4
Lemoore, CA, Italian Swiss Colony winery at, 85
Lenoir grape, xvi, 25, 26, 43, 45
Lexington, KY, 6, 7
Lichine, Alexis, 154, 164
Linnaeus, Carolus, xiv
Lippincott, J.B., 118
Listán Prieto grape. *See* Mission grape
Little Rock, AK, 111, 112

TEXT
Adobe Garamond 11/14

DISPLAY
Adobe Garamond

COMPOSITOR
BookMatters, Berkeley

PRINTER & BINDER
Thomson-Shore